EUROPEAN
ENVIRONMENTAL
ALMANAC

Principal Editor
Jonathan Hewett

Institute for European
Environmental Policy
London

EARTHSCAN
Earthscan Publications Ltd, London

First published in the UK in 1995 by
Earthscan Publications Limited

in association with WWF-UK
registered charity number 201707

A catalogue record for this book is available from the British Library

ISBN: 1 85383 143 3

Cartography, typesetting and page design by PCS Mapping & DTP, Newcastle upon Tyne

Printed and bound by Biddles Ltd, Guildford and Kings Lynn

Cover design by Elaine Marriott

For a full list of publications please contact:
Earthscan Publications Limited
120 Pentonville Road
London N1 9JN
Tel. (0171) 278 0433
Fax: (0171) 278 1142

Earthscan is an editorially independent subsidiary of Kogan Page Limited and publishes in
association with WWF-UK and the International Institute for Environment and Development.

27/2/96

EUROPEAN

ENVIRONMENTAL

ALMANAC

The Institute for European Environmental Policy (IEEP), London is an independent institute for the analysis and advancement of environmental policies in Europe. It forms part of a network of partner Institutes with offices in several European countries. The Institute undertakes research on the European dimension of environmental protection and nature conservation. Major areas of interest are the development, implementation and evaluation of European Community environmental policy and the integration of environmental protection requirements into other Community policies.

Contents

Acronyms and Abbreviations

ADEME	Agency for the Environment and Energy Management (France)
ALTENER	EC programme for alternative energy
AMINAL	Administration for Environment, Nature and Rural Development (Belgium)
AONB	Area of Outstanding Natural Beauty (UK)
ARA	Altstoff Recycling Austria
BOD	biological oxygen demand
CAFE	corporate average fuel efficiency (US)
CAP	Common Agricultural Policy (EC)
CCR	Regional Coordination Commission (Portugal)
CEE	Central and Eastern Europe
CEPP	Committee for Environmental Preservation and Protection (Albania)
CFC	chloroflourocarbon
CGA	Air Management Commission (Portugal)
CHP	combined heat and power
CIEMAT	Centre for Energy, Environment and Technology Research (Spain)
CIS	Commonwealth of Independent States
CITES	Convention on International Trade in Endangered Species
CO	carbon monoxide
CO_2	carbon dioxide
CoE	Council of Europe
CSD	Commission on Sustainable Development
CSIC	Higher Council for Scientific Research (Spain)
CTP	Common Transport Policy (EC)
DG	directorate-general (European Commission)
DGPA	Directorate-General for Environment Policy (Spain)
DIREN	Regional Directorate for the Environment (France)
DRIRE	Regional Directorate for Industry, Research and the Environment (France)
DSD	Duales System Deutschland (Germany)
EBRD	European Bank for Reconstruction and Development
EC	European Community
ECE	Economic Commission for Europe (UN)
ECJ	European Court of Justice
ECMT	European Conference of Ministers of Transport
EEA	European Economic Area/European Environment Agency
EECONET	European Ecological Network
EFTA	European Free Trade Area
EIA	environmental impact assessment
EMGRISA	Spanish state company disposing of toxic waste
ESA	environmentally sensitive area
EU	European Union
FAO	Food and Agriculture Organisation
GATT	General Agreement on Tariffs and Trade
GDP	gross domestic product

GEF	Global Environment Facility
GNP	gross national product
H_2S	hydrogen peroxide
HCl	hydrogen chloride
HMIP	Her Majesty's Inspectorate of Pollution (UK)
IAEA	International Atomic Energy Agency
IBRD	International Bank for Reconstruction and Development (World Bank)
ICN	Nature Conservation Institute (Portugal)
ICONA	National Institute for Nature Conservation (Spain)
IEEP	Institute for European Environmental Policy
IFEN	Institute for the Environment (France)
ILO	International Labour Organisation
IMO	International Maritime Organisation
INAMB	National Environment Institute (Portugal)
IPCC	Intergovernmental Panel on Climate Change
IUCN	International Union for Conservation of Nature and Natural Resources/World Conservation Union
MAB	Man and the Biosphere (UN research programme)
MARN	Ministry of the Environment and Natural Resources (Portugal)
MEP	Member of the European Parliament
MOPTMA	Ministry of Public Works, Transport and the Environment (Spain)
MPAT	Ministry for Territorial Planning and Administration (Portugal)
MPC	maximum permissible concentration
mtoe	million tonnes of oil equivalent
NAFTA	North American free Trade Agreement
NEPP	National Environmental Policy Plan (Netherlands)
NGO	non-governmental organisation
NO	nitrogen oxide
NO_2	nitrogen dioxide
NO_x	nitrogen oxides (non-specific)
NRA	National Rivers Authority (UK)
OPET	Organisation for the Promotion of Energy Technology
PCB	polychlorinated biphenyl
PE	population equivalent
PEDAP	EC programme for the development of Portuguese agriculture
PHARE	EC aid programme for Central and Eastern Europe
ppb	parts per billion
Ramsar	Ramsar Convention on Wetlands of International Importance
RAN	National Agricultural Reserve (Portugal)
REN	National Ecological Reserve (Portugal)
RPB	River Purification Board (Scotland)
SAVE	EC programme on energy efficiency
SFT	State Pollution Control Agency (Norway)
SNV	National Environmental Protection Agency (Sweden)
SO_2	sulphur dioxide
SSSI	site of special scientific interest (UK)
SVM	Netherlands recycling organisation
TACIS	Technical Assistance to the CIS
TERN	Trans-European Roads Network (EC)
TGV	French high-speed train (train à grande vitesse)
THERMIE	EC programme on energy technologies

toe	tonnes of oil equivalent
UN	United Nations
UNCED	UN Conference on Environment and Development (Rio de Janeiro, June 1992)
UNDP	UN Development Programme
UNECE	UN Economic Commission for Europe
UNEP	UN Environment Programme
UNESCO	UN Educational, Scientific and Cultural Organisation
UNIDO	UN Industrial Development Organisation
VOC	volatile organic compound
VROM	Ministry of Housing, Physical Planning and Environment (Netherlands)
WHO	World Health Organization
WMO	World Meteorological Organization
WTO	World Tourism Organisation
WWF	World Wide Fund for Nature

Acknowledgements

This volume draws on the work of many people, including those in national environment ministries and agencies and in international organisations which undertake monitoring work. Readers who seek more detailed statistics are advised to consult the reports listed in the bibliography.

More personal thanks are given to the following: firstly, I am indebted to my colleagues at the Institute for European Environmental Policy. Nigel Haigh and David Baldock helped hatch the egg from which the Almanac emerged, and continued to give valuable support and advice. I am aware, too, of the insights gained from them during my time at the Institute. Duncan Smith patiently spent long hours digging up useful sources of information and making sense of them. Malcolm Fergusson made useful contributions, particularly on transport and energy, and Caroline Watson helped with the bibliography and maps. Kate Partridge provided much-needed administrative support and encouragement, and David Wilkinson and Alastair Baillie used their expertise to answer some of my obstinate questions. Guy Beaufoy drafted the chapters on Spain and Portugal with his customary efficiency. Sally Mullard eased the burden of other tasks, compiled the annex, and shared an office with me through times of stress. Within the wider IEEP Network, I thank R Andreas Kraemer, Jaörn Schnutenhaus, Rolf Huchthausen, Alexander Juras, Graham Bennett, Barbara Verhoeve, Mark Tuddenham and Arnaud Comolet. Matthew Leach wrote the chapter on energy, and Nigel Dudley the chapters on agriculture and forestry and nature conservation, with additional input from David Baldock. Jonathan Sinclair Wilson and Jo O'Driscoll at Earthscan persevered to bring the project to fruition, with support from Ivan Hattingh at WWF-UK. Gary Haley interpreted data of varying quality to produce the maps and figures.

Numerous individuals in ministries, national and international agencies, embassies and non-governmental organisations made the effort to respond to enquiries. I am particularly grateful to Jonathan Parker and David Stanners of the European Environment Agency (Task Force), Helmut Schreiber of the World Bank, Duncan Fisher of East-West Environment, Cynthia Whitehead of Environment Policy Europe, Gaynor Whyles and Sally Nicholson of WWF-UK, Andrew Dilworth of Friends of the Earth (England and Wales), the national European member organisations of WWF and FoE, and Mary Morrison of Greenpeace UK.

Finally, heartfelt thanks to friends and relations who sustained me while I was putting this volume together, particularly Clare and Nick; John, Sue, Beth, Andrew and Mitzy at 118; and Paulette, Sharon and other softballers in the park.

Jonathan Hewett

PART I

OVERVIEW

1

Introduction

Europe forms around 7 per cent of the land surface of the Earth. With a maximum length of some 3850 km and breadth of 5050 km it is the second smallest continent – less than a quarter of the size of Asia. Yet despite Europe's relatively small size, it is a land of stark contrasts, ranging from the icy tundra of the North to the Mediterranean and desert climates in the South. Between them lie four major morphological and three climatic zones. Massive mountain ranges, deep river valleys, stable rocky plateaux, active volcanoes and an intricate coastline all combine to give Europe its characteristically rich variety of landscapes.

Europe is two or three times more densely populated than the United States or Africa, and humans have had a striking impact on its landscape. There are practically no areas that can be considered as remaining in their 'natural' condition, and few which are uninhabited by humans. The last 200 years alone have seen massive changes in land use throughout the continent. Today, more than 42 per cent of the land is used for agriculture, whilst a growing number of people live in urban areas. Over 60 per cent of Europeans live in towns and cities covering just 1 per cent of Europe's total land area.

Politically, too, Europe accommodates great variety – and always has. It was the birthplace of the Greek and Roman classic civilisations and has accomodated powerful and shifting empires, from the Spanish, Hapsburg and Austro-Hungarian in the 16th century through to the British Empire and the birth of the Commonwealth. This century alone has seen two world wars, the rise and fall of authoritarian regimes in Central and Eastern Europe, and, more recently, civil war in the former Yugoslavia, and disputes in (for example) Northern Ireland and the Basque region.

Europe's cultural richness has always commanded worldwide influence and prestige. As the birthplace of the Industrial revolution, it has

A PEOPLED LANDSCAPE

Although Europe's citizens number only around a tenth of the world's population, population density is relatively high, averaging 67 people per km^2. This distribution is by no means uniform: it varies from 2.5 inhabitants per km^2 in Iceland to more than 400 inhabitants per km^2 in the built up areas of Germany and the UK. The majority of Europeans live in concentrated industrial and urban centres, served by complex transport systems, commercial networks and other infrastructure geared to supply them with goods and services. Not all these goods and services are essential, of course, and the infrastructure and centres necessary to support them consume a disproportionate share of the world's resources and produce an equally large amount of its pollution burden. At the end of the 1980s, Western Europe was emitting about 18 per cent of the world's atmospheric load of nitrogen oxides; around 35 per cent of its industrial waste; and at least 16 per cent of global greenhouse gas emissions. Europe consumed nearly 18 per cent of the world's commercial energy, while producing less than 10 per cent by its own means.

been a leader in world industry and commerce, and its financial institutions have led the way in shaping the modern global economy. Since 1945, Western Europe has experienced unprecedented levels of economic growth, although income and living standards in Europe vary as widely as the landscape.

Europe's environment, however, bears the scars of its rich history, and its impacts are many and varied. Some problems – such as river pollution, waste generation and its disposal, forest degradation, industrial accidents and coastal erosion – however serious, are relatively localised. Others have consequences which extend far beyond our geographical borders. Atmospheric and marine pollution, for example, do not respect political boundaries; the raw materials on which Europe's consumer society feeds are extracted from all over the world – often to the detriment of far-off environments; and the production of export crops and goods for the 'developed' world takes up valuable resources in the 'developing' world.

The increasing pressure from non-governmental organisations and environmental activists and a growing recognition by world leaders of the duty of care owed to the environment, together with political readjustments which have taken place over the last 10 years in Central and Eastern Europe, have seen a shift towards sustainable development thinking and practice.

The 1992 UN Conference on Environment and Development (or 'Earth Summit'), held in Rio de Janeiro, gave this ethos substance by adopting framework international conventions on climate change and the conservation of biodiversity, together with a comprehensive package of recommendations and targets for making progress towards sustainable development into the 21st century.

Europe, like the rest of the world, must now seek an enduring balance: between the production and consumption of commodities; the wealth of nations and the capacity of natural systems; the material aspirations of ordinary people and the limits of the planet. This search cannot proceed in isolation from like-minded efforts throughout the world. If Europe, despite its ample resources and highly skilled institutions, fails to

FROM ICE AGE TO SPACE AGE

Topographically Europe can be regarded as a peninsula of Asia, but it also forms a compact continent in its own right, bounded by the Atlantic and Arctic Oceans and the Mediterranean Sea. The Europe of today has been shaped by the gradually evolving physical conditions and by the changing uses to which our forebears put the available natural resources.

The Ice Ages covered Northern Europe and the Alps at least four times, retreating after the last glacial period some 12,000 years ago. In their wake, they left wide river valleys, fertile soils and wetlands. Fauna and flora soon colonised areas freed from the receding ice sheets, followed by migratory groups of early human hunters and gatherers. Later, agricultural practices spread from Asia to the Mediterranean and into the rest of Europe. With them, a pattern of settled communities based on farming and herding began to emerge. Animal power and wheeled transport brought this trend to ever-higher degrees of sophistication, and subsistence agriculture was replace by commerce, as farmers exchanged and bartered goods and services, and towns emerged as the centres of commercial activity. This led to increased wealth and power for some sections of society, and the second major stage in the evolution of modern life: the proliferation of predominantly urban civilisations, with growing industrial capacity, an abundant human labour pool and a corresponding hunger for material resources.

Agriculture and industry have had environmental consequences from the outset, although in the early years their relatively small scale, wide dispersal and minimal inputs helped limit their impacts. In the 19th century more far-reaching changes took place as agriculture and industry become more intensive and large-scale. The 20th century has seen this process accelerate, fuelled above all by machine technology and fossil-based energy as the mainstays of production, transport, military power, communications and everyday household life. The world wars which twice swept Europe this century speeded up the process of technological change, including the advance of nuclear power.

Space travel and exploration has enabled us, for the first time, to see the Earth as one integrated living system, vulnerable to human decisions and actions. In Europe, as in the rest of the world, links between the environment and human development have, in recent years, at last begun to move up to the top of the political agenda.

attain the goals agreed by Rio's cautious consensus seekers, the prospects for their successful implementation at global level will be badly damaged. By implementing changes towards sustainable development, however, Europe could lead the way to a better and safer future for all.

The Community must use more effectively its position of moral, economic and political authority to advance international efforts to solve global problems and to promote sustainable development and respect for the global commons.

Declaration of the European Council, Dublin, June 1990

2

International Cooperation and the Environment

As the gravity of environmental deterioration has become more evident and better understood, so, too, has the need for greater international cooperation, in order to develop and implement effective policies. Particularly during the past 20 years, many organisations, conventions and processes have been established to expand international work on environmental matters. In addition, the rapid political, economic and social changes in central and eastern Europe have altered the nature of its relationship with western Europe in recent years. The resulting array of legal and institutional arrangements which are now involved with international cooperation and the environment in Europe is too complex to describe fully here. However, some of the principal bodies and their activities are reviewed below.

THE EUROPEAN UNION

The European Union (EU), which evolved out of the European Economic Community in 1957, has, particularly in recent years, introduced hundreds of environmental measures which directly affect policy in its Member States. (See Chapter 3 for a more detailed discussion.) The Union also exerts a considerable influence over international affairs as a participant in global political discussions and through the leverage it deploys as one of the world's most powerful economic groupings. The EU is party to numerous international environmental law, conventions and 'soft law' pacts, which it is entitled to adopt and ratify alongside its Member States.

Some EU research programmes and bodies, such as the recently established European Environment Agency (see page 27) are open to countries beyond the EU, and other terms of association and financial assistance extended to non-member countries often include environmental components. Within the Union itself, the framework for environmental policy is set by a series of action plans; the Fifth Action Programme is currently underway.

THE COUNCIL OF EUROPE

The Council of Europe (CoE) was established in 1949 to foster unity and cooperation between the nations of Europe, emphasising human rights and pluralist democratic principles. The CoE has 32 member states.

The Council's achievements mostly take the form of cultural relations, raising awareness and advocacy. In addition, it services the Berne Convention on the Conservation of European Wildlife and Natural Habitats, which entered into force in 1982, and its convention on civil liability for damage resulting from activities dangerous to the environment was opened for signature by member states in June, 1993. The council is also currently preparing guidelines on the protection of the environment through criminal law.

The CoE regularly compiles inventories of the regions' important strongholds of biodiversity and has set up an award scheme for nature conservation management in Europe. CoE's Centre Naturopa publishes information on nature conservation and has run campaigns on soil and water conservation, farming and wildlife, wetlands and freshwater fish.

THE UNITED NATIONS

The United Nations was founded at the end of World War II as a democratic, multinational organisation whose aims were to:

save succeeding generations from the scourge of war... to reaffirm faith in fundamental human rights... to establish conditions under which ... justice can be maintained, and to promote social progress and better standards of life.

Charter of the United Nations

The UN system comprises the UN itself (including the development and environmental departments), and 15 further specialised agencies, as illustrated on page 9. Responsibility for environmental matters is devolved from the administrative core of the UN to various specialised and inter-agency bodies throughout the system.

The UN Environment Programme

The UN Environment Programme (UNEP) was founded in 1972 after the Stockholm Conference on the Human Environment. It coordinates environmentally relevant activities across the UN system by means of an inter-agency plan of action known as the System-Wide Medium-Term Environmental Plan.

UNEP also works to catalyse international response to environmental events and trends of world significance. It hosts a global environmental monitoring and assessment network (GEMS), promotes environmental awareness through information and education initiatives and sponsors preparatory steps towards new legal instruments for the protection and management of global commons such as the world's seas, forests and atmosphere.

Many key international environmental conventions have grown from UNEP's work, including the Convention for the Protection of the Ozone layer and the Convention on the Control of Transboundary Movements of Hazardous Wastes and their Disposal.

UNEP has helped devise a number of conventions dealing with the management of regional seas environments, beginning with the Barcelona Convention, a comprehensive agenda for the Mediterranean environment. UNEP's European regional office is based in Geneva.

The UN Development Programme

The UN Development Programme (UNDP) plays an interagency coordinating role similar to UNEP's: fair and just economic and social progress in developing countries and communities form the main goal of its work. Its activities are targeted mainly on poorer communities in the South, although it also backs several projects in Southern and Eastern Europe.

The UN Economic Commission for Europe

The UN Economic Commission for Europe (UNECE) is one of five regional UN commissions which form part of the UN Economic and Social Council. Established in 1947, UNECE provided an important pan-European forum during the Cold War years, when official contact between Western and Eastern Europe was otherwise strictly limited. In 1990, the Commission agreed two guiding tenets to be applied to all its activities: the assistance to countries of Central and Eastern Europe in their transition to market economies, and sustainable development.

UNECE has launched or negotiated a range of initiatives, including the 1984 Convention on Long-Range Transboundary Air Pollution. It services the implementation of a number of legal instruments, such as the 1991 Convention on the Environmental Impact Assessment in a Transboundary Context and the 1992 Conventions on Transboundary Effects of Industrial Accidents and on the Protection and Use of Transboundary Water Courses and International Lakes.

Other UN agencies or institutions whose work has environmental significance operate in the fields of trade, industry, commerce, investment and development funding, including the International Labour Organisation, which sponsors research into the effects of environmental change on employment, working conditions, health and safety.

THE WORLD BANK

Since its inception in Bretton Woods in 1944, the World Bank has grown to be one of the world's biggest sources of finance for international development, with 110 borrowing countries. About 20 per cent of Bank-funded projects have an environmental component. The Bank's chief function is to channel investment funding to developing countries and undertake policy and planning research work, including the negotiation of 'structural readjustment programmes' for national growth and debt relief in UN member countries, including several in Central and Eastern Europe.

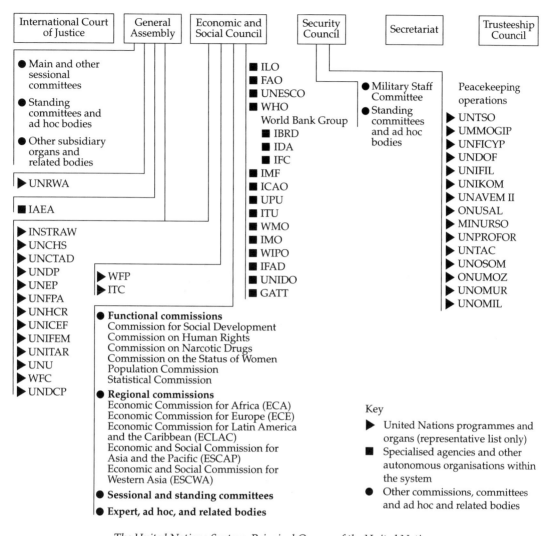

The United Nations System: Principal Organs of the United Nations

Following widespread criticism of the adverse environmental effects of some World Bank-funded programmes, an Environmental Department was created in 1985 to strengthen the impact assessment and auditing aspects of the Bank's work, and to factor environmental concerns into national economic planning. The Bank administers the Global Environmental Facility (GEF), a fund set up in 1990 to support environment-related projects in cooperation with UNEP and UNDP.

SPECIALISED UN BODIES

World Health Organisation (WHO)

WHO runs international monitoring, technical cooperation and information exchange programmes relating to environmental and personal health. It developed a European Charter on Environment and Health which was adopted in 1989 and all European countries subscribe to WHO's global Health for All strategy. Ongoing WHO research touches many sustainable development concerns, including drinking water quality. Founded in 1946, WHO membership is open to all UN member countries, and currently numbers 170.

UN Educational, Scientific, and Cultural Organisation (UNESCO)

UNESCO administers research, education and conservation programmes affecting the environment, including the Man and the Biosphere (MAB) programme and the International Hydrological Programme. UNESCO services the World Heritage Convention, which safeguards hundreds of sites of special cultural or natural significance around the world. It also works to incorporate environmental awareness into curriculum development at all levels of education and to promote better communications about environmental issues.

World Meteorological Organisation (WMO)

WMO undertakes and coordinates scientific and technical work on climate, weather, hydrology and the atmosphere. It advises governments on technical aspects of, for example, greenhouse gas emissions, pollution control and the potential impacts of climate change. It also applies meteorological research to aviation, shipping, water supplies and agriculture.

Food and Agriculture Organisation (FAO)

FAO works as a source of technical information on issues related to the production and consumption of natural resources, including fisheries, forestry and renewable sources of energy. The environmental and human consequences of poverty and underdevelopment are among its key concerns. Soil and water conservation, land tenure and use, nutrition, trade and genetic resources all feature in FAO's portfolio.

International Maritime Organisation (IMO)

IMO began life as an international watchdog organisation for improving safety at sea. It now supervises a wide range of international pacts and conventions on marine pollution and the general management of marine ecosystems and resources, including codes of practice to prevent dumping at sea and regulations to control oil or chemical spills.

UNCED AND WCED

The 1992 UN Conference on Environment and Development (the 'Earth Summit') was the largest international conference ever convened. In addition to government delegations from all UN member states, it drew almost a thousand non-governmental and voluntary organisations to Rio de Janeiro, to participate in a parallel Global Forum for independent interest groups.

The World Commission on Environment and Development monitored liaison between governmental and non-governmental representatives at Rio, and reported on follow-up activities after the event. WCED was originally founded under the auspices of Norway's prime minister Gro Harlem Brundtland. Its 1987 report, *Our Common Future* (also known as the Brundtland Report) has become a benchmark environmental report. It suggests basic definitions of sustainable development which were debated and applied to a range of global issues during the UNCED negotiations.

The outcomes of UNCED included the adoption of a Framework Convention on Climate Change, a Biodiversity Convention, a set of advisory Forestry Principles and a consensus document known as Agenda 21, setting common targets for progress towards sustainable development.

The Rio Declaration on Environment and Development

The United Nations Conference on Environment and Development,
Having met at Rio de Janeiro from 3 to 14 June 1992,
Reaffirming the Declaration of the United Nations Conference on the Human Environment, adopted at Stockholm on 16 June 1972, and seeking to build upon it,
With the goal of establishing a new and equitable global partnership through the creation of new levels of cooperation among States, key sectors of societies and people,
Working towards international agreements which respect the interests of all and protect the integrity of the global environmental and developmental system,
Recognizing the integral and interdependent nature of the Earth, our home,
Proclaims that:

1. Human beings are at the centre of concerns for sustainable development. They are entitled to a healthy and productive life in harmony with nature.
2. States have, in accordance with the Charter of the United Nations and the principles of international law, the sovereign right to exploit their own resources pursuant to their own environmental and developmental policies, and the responsibility to ensure that activities within their jurisdiction or control do not cause damage to the environment of other States or of areas beyond the limits of national jurisdiction.
3. The right to development must be fulfilled so as to equitably meet developmental and environmental needs of present and future generations.
4. In order to achieve sustainable development, environmental protection shall constitute an integral part of the development process...
5. All States and all people shall cooperate in the essential task of eradicating poverty as an indispensable requirement for sustainable development, in order to decrease the disparities in standards of living and better meet the needs of the majority of the people of the world.
6. The special situation and needs of developing countries, particularly the least

developed and those most environmentally vulnerable, shall be given special priority. International actions in the field of environment and development should also address the interests and needs of all countries.

7. States shall cooperate in a spirit of global partnership to conserve, protect and restore the health and integrity of the Earth's ecosystem... States have common but differentiated responsibilities. The developed countries acknowledge the responsibility that they bear in the international pursuit of sustainable development in view of the pressures their societies place on the global environment and of the technologies and financial resources they command.

8. To achieve sustainable development and a higher quality of life for all people, States should reduce and eliminate unsustainable patterns of production and consumption and promote appropriate demographic policies.

9. States should cooperate to strengthen endogenous capacity-building for sustainable development ...through exchanges of scientific and technological knowledge, and by enhancing the development, adaptation, diffusion and transfer of technologies.

10. Environmental issues are best handled with the participation of all concerned citizens, at the relevant level. At the national level, each individual shall have appropriate access to information concerning the environment that is held by public authorities... and the opportunity to participate in decision-making processes. States shall facilitate and encourage public awareness and participation by making information widely available. Effective access to judicial and administrative proceedings, including redress and remedy, shall be provided.

11. States shall enact effective environmental legislation. Environmental standards, management objectives and priorities should reflect the environmental and developmental context to which they apply. Standards applied by some countries may be inappropriate and of unwarranted economic and social cost to other countries, in particular developing countries.

12. States should cooperate to promote a supportive and open international economic system ... Trade policy measures for environmental purposes should not constitute a means of arbitrary or unjustifiable discrimination or a disguised restriction on international trade. Unilateral actions to deal with environmental challenges outside the jurisdiction of the importing country should be avoided. Environmental measures addressing transboundary or global environmental problems should, as far as possible, be based on an international consensus.

13. States shall develop national law regarding liability and compensation for the victims of pollution and other environmental damage. States shall also cooperate in an expeditious and more determined manner to develop further international law regarding liability and compensation for adverse effects of environmental damage caused by activities within their jurisdiction or control to areas beyond their jurisdiction.

14. States should effectively cooperate to discourage or prevent the relocation and transfer to other States of any activities and substances that cause severe environmental degradation or are found to be harmful to human health.

15. ...the precautionary approach shall be widely applied by States according to their capabilities. Where there are threats of serious or irreversible damage, lack of full scientific certainty shall not be used as a reason for postponing cost-effective measures to prevent environmental degradation.

16. National authorities should endeavour to promote the internalization of environmental costs and the use of economic instruments, taking into account the approach that the polluter should, in principle, bear the cost of pollution, with

due regard to the public interest and without distorting international trade and investment.

17. Environmental impact assessment, as a national instrument, shall be undertaken for proposed activities that are likely to have a significant adverse impact on the environment and are subject to a decision of a competent national authority.

18. States shall immediately notify other States of any natural disasters or other emergencies that are likely to produce sudden harmful effects on the environment of those States. Every effort shall be made by the international community to help States so afflicted.

19. States shall provide prior and timely notification and relevant information to potentially affected States on activities that may have a significant adverse trans-boundary environmental effect and shall consult with those States at an early stage and in good faith.

20. Women have a vital role in environmental management and development. Their full participation is therefore essential to achieve sustainable development.

21. The creativity, ideals and courage of the youth of the world should be mobilized to forge a global partnership in order to achieve sustainable development and ensure a better future for all.

22. Indigenous people and their communities, and other local communities, have a vital role in environmental management and development... States should recognize and duly support their identity, culture and interests and enable their effective participation.

23. The environment and natural resources of people under oppression, domination and occupation shall be protected.

24. Warfare is inherently destructive of sustainable development. States shall therefore respect international law providing protection for the environment in times of armed conflict and cooperate in its further development, as necessary.

25. Peace, development and environmental protection are interdependent and indivisible.

26. States shall resolve all their environmental disputes peacefully and by appropriate means in accordance with the Charter of the United Nations.

27. States and people shall cooperate in good faith and in a spirit of partnership in the fulfilment of the principles embodied in this Declaration and in the further development of international law in the field of sustainable development.

OTHER INTERNATIONAL BODIES

The Organisation for Economic Cooperation and Development

The Organisation for Economic Cooperation and Development (OECD) evolved out of the Marshall Plan for post-war reconstruction in Europe. It has 24 member countries, including most Western European states, Japan, Canada, Australia, New Zealand and the US. The European Commission also participates in the work of the OECD as a separate entity. Economic aspects of pollution control and other environmental issues fall within the OECD's policy research and development brief. Its work has strongly influenced legal developments in environmental management: for example, the OECD first formulated the 'polluter pays principle', which became a cornerstone of EC policy.

The World Conservation Union

The World Conservation Union (formerly the International Union for the Conservation of Nature, and still known as the IUCN) is an international organisation representing a combined state and non-governmental membership of 500 bodies. It has no legislative role beyond developing (and in some cases administering) protected areas and threatened species pacts such as the Ramsar Convention for the conservation of wetlands important as habitats for migratory birds. With UNEP and the World Wide Fund for Nature (WWF), IUCN has developed two versions of a World Conservation Strategy for sustainable development that have served as a blueprint for the development of National Conservation Strategies in many European countries.

The North Atlantic Treaty Organisation

The North Atlantic Treaty Organisation (NATO), although essentially a defence pact, has produced reports on coastal and inland water pollution, air pollution and other transboundary issues. With the end of the Cold War, its interest in environmental security is likely to grow.

REGIONAL BODIES

- The Nordic Council and the Nordic Council of Ministers initiates action plans and parliamentary conferences on regional environmental issues focussed, for example, on the North Sea and North East Atlantic. Membership includes Denmark, Sweden, Norway, Iceland, Finland and the autonomous territories of Greenland, the Faroes and Aaland Island.
- Regional European commissions established by environmental agreements include the Oslo Commission, which administers the Oslo Convention for the Prevention of Marine Pollution by Dumping from Ships and Aircraft, and the Paris Commission, the Secretariat for the Paris Convention for the Prevention for Land-Based Pollution.
- A Ministers' Conference meets periodically to agree joint action on issues affecting the North Sea and its feeder rivers. Similarly, a council representing Mediterranean states oversees the Mediterranean Action Plan and its matching legal formula, the Barcelona Convention.
- Institutions or rules that safeguard particular forms of wildlife in the seas of Europe and beyond include the International Whaling Commission, the North Atlantic Salmon Convention Organisation and the North East and North West Atlantic Seals Agreement.
- A system of legal provisions governing all aspects of protection and conservation of marine environments has been proposed in the form of UNCLOS III – the Third UN Conference on the Law of the Sea. But although most maritime European states except the UK and Germany have signed UNCLOS III, none has ratified it. Most have held back because of its proposed 'deep seabed' regime, which places limitations on undersea mining and prospecting. In the meantime, however, many countries have begun to absorb selected parts of UNCLOS III, such as the right to establish a 12-mile territorial sea limit, into national legal codes or constitutions.

MANY MAKING ONE

Faced with this apparent tangle of international players and rules, non-experts may feel confused over which of them is accountable for particular aspects of Europe's environment. Yet international cooperation is, by its very nature, a patchwork of consensus and compromise. It may seem to lack overall coherence, but such a multiplicity can often achieve swifter progress than a 'one-stop' grand design for environmental management. It is a task of organisations such as the European Environment Agency (see page 27) to marshall information from all these diverse sources, using databases and communications technology to assess and disseminate the facts.

THE ROLE OF NGOS

Although international relations are generally associated with governments and officialdom, non-governmental organisations, private voluntary organisations and pressure groups all play an important role.

The first generation of these organisations, represented by NGOs such as IUCN, WWF and the Sierra Club, set out to popularise a pro-nature case for preserving wildlife and wilderness. They later extended their scope into more science-based strategies for ecosystem conservation, species protection and sustainable development. Working in many cases with national governments and intergovernmental agencies, they established independent lobbying and project activities with highly respected scientific credentials.

A second wave of NGOs, typified by Friends of the Earth and Greenpeace, took to the international stage in the 1970s with issue-specific campaigns, most notably on pollution, animal welfare and marine issues. Often involving the skilful use of mass media influence, these campaigns appealed particularly to younger generations, for which issues of environmental security were high on the political agenda.

Many of the recommendations adopted at the 1972 Stockholm Conference were prompted by energetic lobbying from the non-governmental sector. The leverage this sector exerted on politicians and planners through its campaigns had an equally significant impact on events.

This influence was limited primarily to western European countries, where the support of voters could be lost or won by the decisions of governments in relation to environmental issues. But even in CEE countries and in the 'developing' world environmental NGOs and their influence grew. More than 2000 new 'grassroots' groups a year were formed worldwide during the 1980s.

RELEVANT TREATIES AND INTERNATIONAL ACTS

1940 Convention on Nature Protection and Wildlife Preservation in the Western Hemisphere, Washington DC, 12 October 1940, in force 1 May 1942: 222.

1945 Charter of the United Nations, San Francisco, 26 June 1945, in force 24 October 1945: 55–6, 58, 63–4, 67, 222.

1946 International Convention for the Regulation of Whaling, Washington DC, 2 December 1946, in force 10 November 1948: 123, 159–61, 163–76, 179–0, 220, 222, 235–7, 245.

1947 General Agreement on Tariffs and Trade, Geneva, 30 October 1947, not yet in force (in force provisionally since 1 January 1948 under the 1947 Protocol of Provisional Application): 23, 59, 62, 85, 9–106, 108–16, 118–21, 213, 219, 224, 227–9, 231, 245.

1949 FAO Agreement for the Establishment of a General Fisheries Council for the Mediterranean, Rome, 24 September 1949, in force 3 December 1963: 222.

1950 European Convention for the Protection of Human Rights and Fundamental Freedoms, Rome, 4 November 1950, in force 3 September 1953: 221–2.

1951 FAO International Plant Protection Convention, Rome, 6 December 1951, in force 3 April 1952: 222.

1952 International Convention for the High Seas Fisheries of the North Pacific Ocean, Tokyo, 9 May: 222.

1952 Agreement Relating to the Organisation of Permanent Commission of the Conference on Exploitation and Conservation of Marine Resources of the South Pacific, 18 August 1952: 237.

1958 Treaty Establishing the European Economic Community, Rome, 25 March 1957, in force 1 January 1958: 15, 55, 58, 85–90, 92–7, 99, 112, 151–7, 221, 223, 227, 230.

1958 Convention on Fishing and Conservation of the Living Resources of the High Seas, Geneva, 29 April 1958, in force 20 March 1966: 222.

1959 Antarctic Treaty, Washington, 1 December 1959, in force 23 June 1961:1 122–131, 133–9, 223, 231, 245.

1963 Convention on Civil Liability for Nuclear Damage, Vienna, 29 May 1963, in force 12 November 1977.

1963 Optional Protocol Concerning the Compulsory Settlement of Disputes, Vienna, 29 May 1963, not in force: 222.

1966 International Covenant on Civil and Political Rights, 16 December 1966, in force 23 March 1976, Optional Protocol to the 1966 ICCPR, 16 December 1966, in force 23 March 1976: 222.

1968 African Convention on the Conservation of Nature and Natural Resource, Algiers, 15 September 1968, in force 9 October 1969 (or June 1969): 222.

1969 American Convention on Human Rights, San Jose, 22 November 1969, in force 18 July 1978: 222.

1969 FAO Convention on the Conservation of the Living Resources of the South-East Atlantic, Rome, 23 October 1969, in force 24 October 1971: 220.

1971 Treaty on the Prohibition of the Emplacement of Nuclear Weapons and other Weapons of Mass Destruction on the Sea-Bed and the Ocean Floor and in the Sub Soil Thereof, 11 February 1971, in force 18 May 1972: 221.

1972 Convention for the Prevention of Marine Pollution by Dumping from Ships and Aircraft, Oslo, 15 February 1972, in force 7 April 1974:141, 150, 220, 233, 234.

1972 Convention for the Conservation of Antarctic Seals, London, 1 June 1972, in force 11 March 1978:123, 126–7, 137, 245.

1972 Convention on the Prohibition of the Development, Production and Stockpiling of Bacteriological (Biological) and Toxic Weapons, and on their Destruction, London, Washington, Moscow, 10 April 1972, in force 28 March 1975: 221.

1972 Convention on the Prevention of Marine Pollution by Dumping of Wastes and other Matter, London, Mexico City, Moscow, Washington DC, 29 December 1972, in force 30 August 1975: 39–40, 47, 140–50, 152–8, 216, 220–1, 232-3, 235, 246.

1973 Convention on International Trade in Endangered Species of Wild Fauna and Flora, Washington, 3 March 1973, in force 1 July 1975: 47, 62–3, 97, 99, 107–8, 111, 166, 168, 220–4, 228–9, 245.

1973 International Convention for the Prevention of Pollution by Ships, London, 2 November 1973, not in force (see 1978 Protocol): 220, 231.

1974 Nordic Convention on the Protection of the Environment, Stockholm, 19 February 1974, in force 5 October 1976: 225.

1974 Convention on the Protection of the Marine Environment of the Baltic Sea Area, Helsinki, 22 March 1974, in force 3 May 1980: 223.

1974 Convention for the Prevention of Marine Pollution from Land-Based Sources, Paris, 4 June 1974, in force 6 May 1978: 222, 233–4.

1974 Barcelona Convention for the Protection of the Mediterranean, Barcelona, 6 February 1976, in force 12 February 1978: 233.

1976 European Convention for the Protection of Animals Kept for Farming Purposes, Strasbourg, 10 March 1976, in force 10 September 1978: 222.

1978 Protocol Relating to the 1973 International Convention for the Prevention of Pollution from Ships, London, 17 February 1978, in force 2 October 1983: 231.

1979 Convention on the Conservation of Migratory Species of Wild Animals, Bonn, 23 June 1979, in force 1 November 1983: 167.

1979 Convention on the Conservation of European Wildlife and Natural Habitats, Berne, 19 September 1979, in force 1 June 1982: 167, 221.

1979 Convention on Long-Range Transboundary Air Pollution, Geneva, 13 November 1979, in force 16 March 1983: 222.

1980 Convention on the Conservation of Antarctic Marine Living Resources, Canberra, 20 May 1980, in force 7 April 1982:123, 12–32, 137–9, 167, 236, 245.

1981 African Charter on Human Rights and Peoples' Rights, Banjul, 27 June 1981, in force 21 October 1986: 222

1982 Regional Convention for the Conservation of the Red Sea and Gulf of Aden Environment, Jeddah, 14 February 1982, in force 20 August 1985: 222.

1982 United Nations Convention on the Law of the Sea, Montego Bay, 10 December 1982, not in force: 57, 59, 127, 131, 162, 167, 179, 222–3, 231, 236, 246.

1985 Convention for the Protection of the Ozone Layer, Vienna, 22 March 1985, in force 22 September 1988: 39, 222.

1985 Protocol on the Reduction of Sulphur Emissions or Their Transboundary' Fluxes by at Least 30 per cent, Helsinki, 8 July 1985, in force 2 September 1987: 22O.

1986 Single European Act, 17 February 1986, in force 1 July 1987:15, 94–6, 88.

1987 Protocol on Substances that Deplete the Ozone Layer, Montreal, 16 September 198 in force January 1989: 51, 60–1, 99, 110, 113, 139, 199–200, 220, 223–4, 229, 231, 239, 242.

1988 Protocol Concerning the Control of Emissions of Nitrogen Oxides or their Transboundary Fluxes, Sofia, 31 October 1988, in force 14 February 1991:220.

1989 Convention on the Control of Transboundary Movement of Hazardous Wastes and their Disposal, Basel, in force 24 May 1992:47, 99, 112, 133, 138, 220, 227–8, 229.

1989 African, Caribbean and Pacific States – European Economic Community: Fourth Lome Convention, 15 December 1989, in force 1991: 228.

1991 Convention on the Ban of Imports into Africa and the Control of Transboundary Movement and Management of Hazardous Wastes within Africa, Bamako, 29 January 1991, not in force: 112, 229, 233.

1991 Convention on Environmental Impact Assessment in a Transboundary, Context, Espoo, 25 February 1991, not in force: 222.

1991 Protocol on Environmental Protection to the Antarctic Treaty, Madrid; 4 October 1991, not in force: 123, 125, 128, 130, 135, 139.

1992 Treaty on European Union, Maastricht, 17 February 1992, not in force: 1–16, 946, 99, 115, 116, 117, 214, 221, 229, 230.

1992 Convention on the Protection and Use of Transboundary Watercourses and International Lakes, Helsinki, 17 March 1992, not in force: 230.

1992 Agreement on the Conservation of Small Cetaceans of the Baltic and North Seas, 17 March 1992:167.

1992 UNECE Convention on the Transboundary Effects of Industrial Accidents, Helsinki, 17 March 1992, not in force: 230.

1992 Convention on the Protection of the Marine Environment of the Baltic Sea Area, Helsinki, 9 April 1992, not in force: 154.

1992 United Nations Framework Convention on Climate Change, New York, 9 May 1992, not in force: 1, 6–7, 10, 28, 40, 50–1, 57, 61, 63, 67, 74, 81, 83–4, 119, 211, 214, 215–16, 218–22, 224, 230.

1992 Convention on Biological Diversity, Rio de Janeiro, 5 June 1992, not in force: 1, 7, 51, 57, 63, 74, 215, 219, 222, 226.

1992 Convention for the Protection of the Marine Environment of the North-East Atlantic, Paris, 22 September 1992 not in force: 55, 1–2, 154, 233, 234.

1992 North American Free Trade Agreement, Washington, Ottawa and Mexico City, 8, 11, 14, 17 December 1992, not in force: 101, 103, 231.

NON-BINDING INSTRUMENTS

Stockholm Declaration, Stockholm (1972): 1–13, 16, 18, 52–3, 58, 72,166, 210–11. World Charter for Nature, UNGA (1982): 1, 12–13, 16.

Agenda 21, Rio de Janeiro (1992): 1, 13, 19, 22, 50, 59, 63–4, 74–6, 79–84, 101–2, 116, 146, 147, 179, 217–18, 225, 237.

Rio Declaration on Environment and Development, Rio de Janeiro (1992): 1–2, 4–13, 16–19, 20–32, 59, 63, 74–8 ,102, 106, 146, 211–4, 218–19, 221, 224–5, 228, 230, 231.

Statement of Principles on Forests, Rio de Janeiro (1992): 1, 7–8, 10, 18, 219.

3

The European Union

The European Union has evolved over the past 38 years out of the European Economic Community, which was established in 1957 in order to improve the economic and social prospects of its members. Although the Community's founding document, the Treaty of Rome, mandated a Common Agricultural Policy and Common Fisheries Policy, it made no direct reference to environmental policy.

In 1972 the UN Conference on the Human Environment, held at Stockholm, encouraged governments to develop such an environmental framework as a matter of urgency. Later in the same year the EC's ultimate governing body, the European Council (see below), endorsed this call and called for the first of a series of Environmental Action Plans. This lent new authority to Community-wide regulations and financial instruments specifically geared to environmental protection (although measures requiring the control of hazardous chemicals and vehicle emissions were already in existence).

In 1987, the Single European Act provided the EC's first clear legal basis for environmental policy by calling for unified environmental standards and pollution prevention measures to be built into legislation then being developed for forming a single internal market by 1992.

The highest legal body in the EC, the European Court of Justice (ECJ), always had powers to annul environmental measures taken by Community institutions or Member States if they were judged incompatible with EC treaties: for example it could arbitrate on the interpretation of EC laws in relation to fisheries disputes. Yet the ministers of Member States who formed the European Council could still side-step or block virtually any measure that conflicted with their own government's policies. In 1990, the ECJ ruled that powers to apply economic measures such as fisheries regulations must be delegated at the administrative level of the European Commission.

Ratification of the Union Treaty signed at Maastricht in 1993 paved the way for the transformation of the European Community into the European Union.

Today, the EU has the firmest agenda yet for sustainable, non-inflationary economic growth to be achieved in ways that demonstrate respect for the environment.

The Union has responsibility for more than 300 measures affecting the state of the European environment which had become part of EC policy during the 1970s and 1980s. The EU has also emerged as an ambitious sponsor of environmental research and an important originator of overseas development projects and aid programmes.

In other major regions of the globe, a continental outlook on managing environment and development was for some time a more familiar mindset than in Europe. Now that situation has changed. If economic incentives had not already prompted moves towards a new Europe-wide political arena by the 1960s, environmental imperatives would soon have made it necessary to invent one.

European Environment Agency Handbook

AN EXPANDING MEMBERSHIP

The Community was established by six founding states:

- France
- Germany
- Italy
- Belgium
- The Netherlands
- Luxembourg

Today, it also includes

- Austria
- Denmark
- Finland
- Greece
- Ireland
- Portugal
- Spain
- Sweden
- the United Kingdom

The most recent countries to join, in 1995, were Austria, Finland and Sweden. Together with Iceland, Liechtenstein and Norway, they had already subscribed to a European Economic Area pact with the EU, under which member countries committed themselves to aligning their trade policies more closely with those of the Union.

Cyprus, Malta and Turkey have also recently applied for EU membership, followed by several countries in Central and Eastern Europe. The Czech Republic, Hungary and Poland appear likely to be the first CEE countries to open accession negotiations with the EU.

In some respects, the EU's expanding membership is likely to prove beneficial to the state of the European environment. The Scandinavian nations, for example, have long been recognised as leading exponents of environmental protection, and their influence may boost the momentum for new initiatives to improve standards Union-wide. (Norway, however, – with perhaps the highest environmental standards in Europe – voted against membership in a public referendum.)

Some of the other countries now contemplating membership have a poorer track-record in environmental protection. By working towards EU standards and regulations, they can expect to acquire a modern environmental policy framework at a stroke, though living up to it may prove no easy matter. However, they will also have to deal with the environmental impacts that will result from aligning their economies with the EU's Single Market.

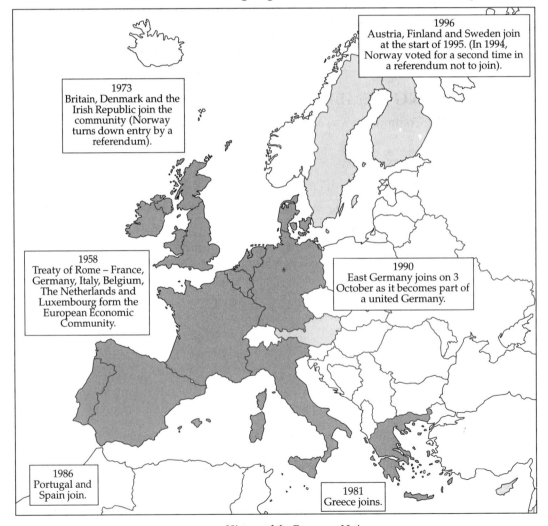

1996
Austria, Finland and Sweden join at the start of 1995. (In 1994, Norway voted for a second time in a referendum not to join).

1973
Britain, Denmark and the Irish Republic join the community (Norway turns down entry by a referendum).

1958
Treaty of Rome – France, Germany, Italy, Belgium, The Netherlands and Luxembourg form the European Economic Community.

1990
East Germany joins on 3 October as it becomes part of a united Germany.

1986
Portugal and Spain join.

1981
Greece joins.

History of the European Union

THE FIFTH ACTION PROGRAMME ON THE ENVIRONMENT

In 1972, following the Stockholm Declaration on the Environment, the European Council called for the first of a series of Action Programmes on the environment. The current Fifth Action Programme, entitled *Towards Sustainability: A European Community Programme of Policy and Action in relation to the Environment and Sustainable Development* was published in March 1992 and endorsed by the Council in February 1993.

It is intended to provide the framework for the EC's environmental policy for the period 1993–2000 and takes the pursuit of sustainable development as its principal theme. It builds on previous programmes but it is more strategic, setting out basic principles and medium-term targets that concur closely with the UNCED and other international agreements on the environment and sustainable development. The programme identifies three main groups of 'actors' who are expected to share responsibility for modifying their attitudes and activities along more sustainable lines:

- public authorities
- public and private enterprises and
- the general public.

In addition, five 'target sectors' are selected for special attention on account of their exceptional environmental impact and economic significance. These sectors are:

- industry
- energy
- transport
- agriculture and
- tourism.

An obligation to integrate environmental objectives into 'other' areas of policy was a feature of the Fourth Action Programme and a requirement introduced into the Treaty of Rome by the Single European Act. The Fifth Programme reinforces this obligation and goes on to deal with a range of more orthodox environmental themes, with an outline of objectives, targets and intended actions in each case.

The Programme recognises that it would be unrealistic to expect people, institutions and enterprises to conform obediently to a blanket requirement to 'act sustainably'. It proposes a broader mix of instruments that supplement regulation with market-based instruments and financial support mechanisms, backed up by research, information and education. It also provides for the establishment of three 'ad hoc dialogue groups' whose aim will be to improve policy coordination, implementation and management. Membership of these groups will be drawn respectively from the Commission, national government officials and independent environmental or other interest groups.

A strategy review, intended to indicate how much progress has been made, was published in 1995.

EU INSTITUTIONS

The Commission

The European Commission alone has the power to propose legislation and it oversees the operation of Community policies. Based in Brussels, the Commission is also the 'guardian' of the Treaty of Rome and may initiate action against Member States when it considers they are not acting in accordance with EC law.

There are 20 Commissioners, appointed by Member State governments, supported by the Commission Services (the Union's own 'civil service'), which is divided into 23 Directorates-General (DGs). DG XI is mainly responsible for handling environmental matters.

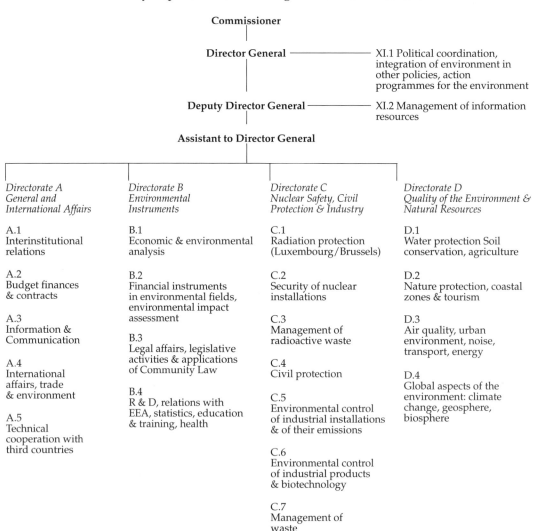

Organigram of DG XI – Environment, Nuclear Safety & Civil Protection

The Council

The Council meets in different formats according to theme (for example, environment, agriculture, economics and finance) and is attended by relevant ministers from national governments and their senior officials. The Commission is also represented.

The Council is chaired by the minister of the Member State which holds the Presidency of the EC, which rotates every six months. A Secretariat provides administrative support, and a Committee of Permanent Representatives (of Member States) undertakes much of the detailed negotiation.

The Council formally adopts EC legislation, although in some cases the Commission can adopt and amend measures itself, either after consulting national representatives, or by a qualified majority vote.

The European Parliament

The European Parliament consists of members (MEPs) directly elected every five years. Originally 518, its membership increased to 626 MEPs following the accession of Austria, Finland and Sweden in 1995. Plenary sessions are held generally for one week each month, with committee work undertaken during two other weeks. Proposals for legislation are usually referred to one of the Parliament's permanent committees (including an Environment Committee) to prepare a report and draft an opinion, which then go forward to the plenary session for a vote.

Although in some cases the Parliament may only put forward an opinion on proposals, changes to the Treaty in 1987 and 1993 extended the Parliament's powers to give it a second reading capability and a greater say in policy-making.

The European Court of Justice

The European Court of Justice is the final legal authority of the EU, ruling on issues of Community law. The ECJ judges cases where a member state has been referred to it by the Commission for failing to comply with Union legislation, and also rules on the legality of acts of the Community's institutions and on interpretations of EU law referred from national courts.

Other key institutions of the EU include the *Economic and Social Committee*, an advisory body whose membership is intended to reflect the interests of 'social partners', for example industry, trade unions and other interest groups. It examines and comments on Commission proposals. The *Court of Auditors* is an appointed body of independent financial experts examines and reports on the financial aspects of Community affairs.

EUROSTAT forms a separate unit within the Commission. It coordinates statistical information on behalf of all Union institutions.

The *Joint Research Centre* of the EU hosts comprehensive programmes of scientific research at its headquarters in Italy and in university departments and research institutes distributed throughout Europe. It investigates matters of general scientific concern and participates in several environmentally-relevant research programmes, such as the JOULE programme of research into non-nuclear energy sources.

LEGISLATION

The EU's legislative provisions and instruments take a number of different forms.

- *Directives* are most important, for example where the application of environmental standards, such as air or water quality standards, is concerned. They are binding on Member States in respect of the results to be achieved, but leave each country free to its own ways and means to achieve them, usually by a specified date.
- *Regulations* are directly applicable as law in Member States and are used mainly for precise measures.
- *Decisions* are also binding and are often used in environmental policy in relation to international conventions and procedural matters.
- *Recommendations* and *opinions* do not have legally binding force.

The form of the Directive has come to prominence because it provides the flexibility needed to cope with the different administrative, political and legal systems of individual Member States. This same flexibility means, however, that in practice the results of implementing a Directive can vary widely between countries. Implementation has become an important and controversial focus of policy debate.

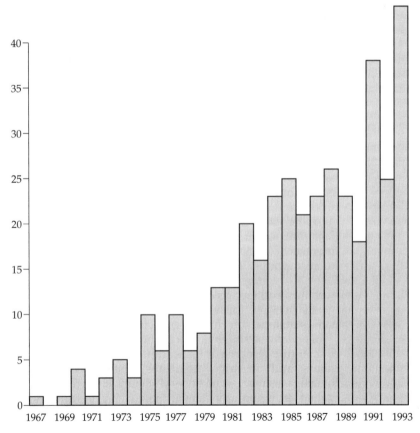

Number of items of environmental legislation adopted annually by EC since 1967

THE EUROPEAN ENVIRONMENT AGENCY (EEA)

The newest of all EU environmental institutions, the Copenhagen-based EEA began operations in October 1994 as a clearing house for environmental information systems throughout Europe. The need to integrate these systems, orchestrate and cross-check their findings and apply them to strategic effect for the common good was signalled by a series of ministerial conferences during the early 1990s. The Fifth Action Programme also reflects this concern, portraying the Agency's mission as 'crucial in relation to the evaluation and dissemination of information, distinction between real and perceived risks and provision of a scientific and rational basis for decisions affecting the environment and natural resources'.

The EEA works in harness with, not in place of, national and other authorities or independent organisations that have a similar mission to inform policy-makers and the public. It draws more than fifty national focal point institutions, reference centres and 'topic centres' together into an integrated network known as EIONET. The Agency does not have a policy enforcement role (like, for example, the Environmental Protection Agency in the USA) but sees reliable, objective information, openly shared, as a powerful policy lever in its own right. A special focus of the EEA's work is to develop practical yardsticks for applying a 'precautionary principle' of environmental risk management and for judging indicators of sustainable development that can provide solid bases for environmental decision making, in accordance with UNCED agreements and other global obligations.

KEY ENVIRONMENTAL MEASURES

Water

Existing EU Directives set quality standards for bathing and drinking water and for freshwater fish and shellfish waters. They set emission limits for releases of designated hazardous substances such as heavy metals, certain pesticides and most solvents. Other Directives seek to reduce or prevent water pollution by nitrates from the application or storage of fertiliser or manure on farmland, and define minimum standards for municipal wastewater; higher-quality treatment is required for sewage discharged to environmentally sensitive areas.

Waste

Directives require licensing systems for waste management and disposal operations, with waste management plans to ensure safe disposal. Stricter provisions apply to hazardous wastes and notification and consent procedures must be followed for movements of waste, with limited prohibitions. Other Directives deal with particular types of waste, including polychlorinated biphenyls (PCBs), waste oils, drink containers, batteries and sewage sludge.

Air

A 1984 Directive introduced the concept that industry should use the 'best available technology not entailing excessive costs' to ensure air quality and high emission control standards.

Directives set air quality standards for sulphur dioxide and smoke, nitrogen dioxide, lead and ozone. Emissions from large combustion plants (such as power stations) are limited in line with a Directive designed to respond to acid rain pollution. Other emissions limits apply to municipal waste incinerators and to motor vehicle exhausts.

Chemicals

A system of testing and prior notification applies to all new chemicals used in the EU, along with requirements on classification, packaging and labelling. A Regulation also covers the evaluation and control of chemicals in use since regulatory standards were introduced.

A series of Directives restricts the marketing and use of specified dangerous substances, including PCBs, asbestos and cadmium. Other measures govern pesticide authorisation and safety, the control of CFCs (chlorofluorocarbons), the use of genetically modified organisms and emergency procedures at industrial plants.

Fauna and Flora

Directives currently in force apply to the protection of wild birds and to conservation of wild plants and animals and their habitats. Other measures have been adopted to protect whales and seals, to regulate trade in endangered species and to provide for farming support schemes aimed at encouraging sound conservation practice in environmentally sensitive areas.

TOWARDS INTEGRATION

As EC policy in more 'traditional' environmental fields of pollution control and nature conservation came into effect, so it became clearer that progress on these fronts could be severely limited unless the damaging effects and potential contradictions of other policies were addressed. Early Action Programmes made some references to this theme, which was more firmly emphasised in the Fourth and Fifth Programmes. Amendments made to the Treaty of Rome have made integration of environmental protection requirements into other policies a legal obligation.

The Commission has produced policy documents addressing the need for such integration in the sectors of agriculture, industry and the internal market, transport, energy, liability, and overseas development. Integration has been the focus of discussions in Environment Council meetings and a number of joint Council meetings of environment and other ministers have been held on the subject. In 1993 the Commission also agreed new procedural rules intended to improve integration in its internal operations. Environmental integration requires policy-makers to tackle those areas where the effects of policies aimed largely at economic development appear to run counter to environmental protection. It thus goes to the heart of the objectives of EC (and most national) policies and poses a challenge to orthodox economic approaches. If real progress towards sustainable development is to be achieved, however, such tensions will have to be examined and resolved.

Other items of EU legislation affect the control of noise pollution, safe-guards over public access to information on the environment, environmental impact assessment requirements for development projects, an environmental management and audit scheme for industrial plants and a scheme to assess and award 'green labelling' endorsements on environmentally friendly products.

In recent years, a growing number of early Directives have been amended or replaced, as EC policy develops a 'second generation' of legislation. Other changes are also evident, such as increasing alignment with global conventions and the related emergence of newer areas of policy debate, not least over global warming.

FINANCIAL MECHANISMS AND INSTRUMENTS

In keeping with the 'stick-and-carrot' approach promoted by the Fifth Action Programme, a number of mechanisms and instruments have been formulated to provide financial incentives for sound environmental practice, and disincentives against unsustainable patterns of production and consumption. The most controversial proposal currently under discussion is a carbon tax that foresees the introduction of 'tax breaks' and penalties to discourage the use of fossil-based fuels.

The most specifically environmental mechanism is the LIFE instrument, which awards grants for projects and activities that further the aims of the Fifth Action Programme. The grants, which average half a million ECU, have supported the efforts of many local authorities, voluntary organisations and research institutions throughout Europe over the past few years, although the instrument is due to lapse in 1996.

Other forms of EU funding that can work to beneficial environmental effect include the Social Fund, which fosters community redevelopment and social initiatives in disadvantaged areas. Financial provisions built into the Common Agricultural Policy, such as 'set-aside' grant schemes, can, in principle, be used to similar effect. But because environmental protection is not a primary element in their design, they only rarely or coincidentally serve this aim in practice. It can be argued that such indirect measures further underline the need to integrate environmental aims into all aspects of Union policy and financing.

4

Central and Eastern Europe

The countries of Central and Eastern Europe (CEE) have undergone dramatic political changes since the late 1980s. National boundaries, economic systems and social structures differ strikingly from those of a decade ago. This chapter sketches some of the environmental implications of these changes.

RECENT HISTORY

Many CEE countries share a common recent history of economic reliance on relentless industrial development and state-controlled agricultural production systems. Centralised planning often meant that factories were concentrated in a few densely populated areas. Pollution controls over industry were rarely given serious attention, although the negative effects on public health were obvious in many parts of Eastern Europe and the Soviet Union.

In 1993, a study prepared by the World Bank and OECD identified and grouped areas in CEE which were associated with particular environmental health problems. These were locations where there were:

- over-exposure to lead
- acute respiratory diseases associated with air pollution
- chronic respiratory diseases assiciated with air pollution
- reasonably strong associations between mortality and air pollution
- associations between abnormal physiological development and air pollution
- high levels of nitrates in the drinking water
- problems with arsenic
- contaminated supplies of drinking water

Towns and districts included in these nine categories were estimated to cover between a fifth and a tenth of the region's population.

Local reserves of high-sulphur 'brown coal' and lignite were the principal industrial fuels, giving rise to high levels of sulphur dioxide emissions. Whether state policies were geared to self-sufficiency or to dependence on the Soviet Union, the emphasis lay on fulfilling production quotas and maintaining low, subsidised prices for goods, including energy supplies.

Acid rain and direct fallout from industrial emissions impacted heavily on the trees of Eastern Europe, and three quarters of Poland's forests suffered serious pollution damage and die-back. Acidification also began to afflict the vast, relatively intact boreal forests that fringe the Arctic Circle. It will be many years before the industries of CEE can be upgraded to match Western Europe's generally accepted standards of pollution control, and many years after that before the damage to the region's forests and soils can begin to be reversed.

Country	Dust	NOx (fixed source)	NOx (moving source)	Lead	CO_2 (million tonnes)	Hydro carbons	SO_2**
Bulgaria	808	336	52	0.2	na	164	1030
CSFR	1245	655	310	na	na	313	2800
E Germany	2200	408	300	na	360	500	5210
Hungary	na	124	120	0.5	88	na	1218
Poland	1615	1060	490	1.6	440	1000	3910
Romania	785	na	na	0.8	127	na	4800
for comparison							
Canada*	1710	na	na	na	471	2316	na
UK	533	1264	1378	3.1	585	2013	3552
USA	na	na	na	na	na	na	20700
W Germany	530	1000	1850	3.0	710	2650	1500

Notes * for 1985; ** 1989 figures

Emissions of various air pollutants, by country, 1988 (000 tonnes, except where stated)

Throughout Central and Eastern Europe, natural habitats have lost ground and with them many wildlife rarities which formerly lived in the region, notably the wolf, lynx and brown bear. These now-scarce wild carnivores used to be common all over Europe until forced out by settlement and agricultural and industrial development. As the pace of development quickens, particularly in the less intensive farming systems of rural Eastern Europe, they are under renewed threat of extermination.

Serious pollution in major rivers and lakes, continuing dependence on coal-fired power stations and antiquated nuclear reactors, disintegrating urban infrastructure and soils exhausted by 30–40 years of pollution, agro-chemicals and pesticides: these are just some of the problems affecting the region's environmental prospects.

Yet the outlook is not all bad. The region abounds in scientific and technical skills and its environmental heritage is in many ways less sullied by development than that of Western Europe. Put together, national

INDUSTRIAL POLLUTION AND THE CHERNOBYL DISASTER

Today, few parts of the former Soviet Union are free of health hazards left over from past mishandling of nuclear wastes and other toxic substances. Some 100,000 people still live in areas dangerously contaminated by untreated radioactive wastes, including dumped weaponry. An estimated 110 million acres of agricultural land have been poisoned by pesticide overdose, waste dumping and acid deposition.

The explosion of a faulty reactor at the Chernobyl nuclear power station in the Ukraine on 26 April 1986 served as a warning of the devastating consequences of nuclear accidents. Almost two million hectares of land around the site were contaminated; all inhabitants within a 30 km radius were evacuated; and 300,000 people remain under surveillance for symptoms of radiation-induced disease.

In areas of Byelorussia (Belarus) lying to the north of Chernobyl, cases of thyroid tumours in children have already increased twentyfold: evidence of the disaster's long-term legacy.

The accident highlighted the scant respect that pollution – in any form – pays to political boundaries. Data suggests that few countries in Europe escaped the effects of the accident: high levels of caesium-137 were recorded as far afield as Greece, and regulations regarding caesium levels in milk and food were adopted across Europe to limit the distribution of contaminated produce. The Chernobyl accident also brought home the consequences in terms of costs and disruption of economic activity that attend industrial disasters on such a scale.

parks and protected areas in CEE countries exceed the EU's in number and area. Though management standards are low in many cases, some of Europe's most important reserves of biodiversity (naturally occurring genes, species and ecosystems) lie within these areas in CEE countries.

Unsustainable patterns of production and consumption may have had serious environmental consequences in most CEE countries but the region has escaped other ills that have long prevailed in the West. There, 'consumer society' values and the primacy of market forces have spawned equally intractable problems of their own, from which the CEE region has been largely spared. Household waste, for example, has been generated at significantly lower levels in CEE than in Western Europe.

Lack of private wealth has also restricted the growth of car ownership, source of many of the West's chronic air pollution problems and much of its outsize contribution to greenhouse gas emissions to the atmosphere (see table on page 31). And though the effects of environmental pollution from CEE industries on Western Europe have been widely publicised, the export of airborne pollutants is not a one-way traffic.

Moreover, these are young countries. In most CEE countries, more than a quarter of the population is aged under 15 years, compared with less than a fifth in the northern countries of the EU. For these new generations, awareness of environmental issues has been raised the hard way, and it is to be hoped that they will learn from the lessons of both Western and Eastern Europe's past.

ENVIRONMENTAL AWARENESS

Well before the huge political upheavals of the 1980s, awareness of environmental damage in CEE was growing – and not only in the scientific community. Environmental pressure groups provided an important channel for political dissent in some CEE countries and gradually environmental concerns gained official recognition. International cooperation between researchers and officials from both sides of the Iron Curtain led to the formulation of joint environmental agreements negotiated in international forums.

Legislation and policy changes

Most CEE governments had adopted new environmental legislation by the mid-1980s and many had established institutions for pollution control and nature conservation, many of them based on the polluter pays principle. As in Western Europe, however, coordinating environmental protection with other policy objectives proved difficult, perhaps aggravated by the rigidity of central planning systems, general lack of capability to enforce pro-environment measures, and the limited potential for public protest and advocacy campaigns.

Many CEE countries began to restructure their economies in the late 1980s, in step with sweeping changes to institutional and legal codes that accompanied the political shift to 'democratisation'.

Levels of economic activity fell – in many cases drastically. As entire industrial sectors underwent restructuring, the closure of factories saw pollution from industrial sources decrease. Previously state-owned bodies were privatised and investment from overseas actively sought. On the land, collective and state farms were split up, sold or reallocated. Unemployment soared and export earnings plummeted as economies adjusted painfully to a free trade approach.

These changes, still underway throughout CEE, have since been paralleled by a bout of environmental legislation and institution-building, much of it based on lessons learned in Western Europe. The transformation is unlikely to take effect overnight or without hardship, but it does at least offer an opportunity to avoid some of the wrong turns made in the past by developers and planners in heavily industrialised countries such as Britain and Germany.

Environmental assistance

Various international agencies, bilateral aid programmes and international NGOs have offered assistance in the form of research partnerships, monitoring facilities and development expertise. The World Bank has been working with CEE governments to develop national environmental strategies. Outside environmental assistance to CEE between 1989 and 1993 amounted to some US$500 million: in 1989 the Polish government alone estimated that it needed US$260 billion to meet its medium-term environmental targets.

Following the political events of 1988 and 1989, the EC adopted the PHARE programme, intended originally to assist Poland and Hungary and subsequently extended to other CEE countries. Environmental protection is one of PHARE's seven priority sectors. The 'Group of 24' countries – members of the Organisation for Economic Cooperation and Development – have agreed to coordinate their assistance to CEE states through the EC and to liaise with other international investment fundholders, including the European Bank for Reconstruction and Development (EBRD).

The EBRD became operational in 1991 and now provides financial support through loans and investment in CEE countries to assist in the transition towards open market-oriented economies and to promote private and entrepreneurial initiative. It is directed by articles in its founding Agreement to: '...promote in the full range of its activities, environmentally sound and sustainable development.'

The EBRD has backed regional environmental programmes (such as schemes affecting the Baltic Sea and Danube Basin), public and private sector industrial restructuring projects, initiatives on environmental legislation and harmonisation, training schemes and methodologies for assessing liability. During 1991 and 1992, a total of just under 23 million ECU was approved for technical cooperation projects with significant environmental benefits to CEE states; all these projects are subject to rigorous environmental appraisal procedures.

Environment ministers from CEE states met counterparts from EU and EFTA countries at a summit in Dublin in 1990 to discuss ways to raise environmental quality standards throughout Europe, including the CEE region. This encounter was followed by a conference at Dobris Castle in Czechoslovakia in June 1991 that also involved the World Bank, UNECE, OECD and EBRD. As a result of these negotiations, an Environmental Action Programme for Central and Eastern Europe was developed and was launched at a follow-up ministerial conference in Lucerne, Switzerland, in April 1993. Some US$30 million of start-up funding was pledged by the US, the EU, Sweden, Canada and Japan. Progress is being reviewed at the next ministerial conference in Bulgaria in 1995.

	World Bank approved projects (7/89–6/92)	*Phare, EIB[1] and EBRD assistance[2] (1990–2)*	*Cumulative foreign direct investment (1991–2)*	*Totals*
Albania	41	275	20	336
Bulgaria	267	375	500	1142
former CSFR	696	1080	2200	3976
Hungary	1116	1625	4200	6941
Poland	2611	1290	1500	5401
Romania	830	850	500	2180
former Yugoslavia	992	na	na	992
Total	6553	5495	8920	20 968

Notes: 1 European Investment Bank; 2 excluding support for balance of payments

The inflow of public and private capital into Central and Eastern Europe, 1989–92 ($ million, approximate)

THE AMAZON OF THE NORTH

Russia's indecisive attitude to environmental protection still continues to set a bad example to CEE neighbours. Siberia, for example – a region bigger than the US and EU combined – used to be a relatively unspoilt wilderness. But since the 1970s millions of Russian settlers have flocked there, mainly to work in the booming oil and gas fields of the north-west. Gold and diamond discoveries have lured many more to Siberia's remote tundras in search of a 'northern Eldorado'. Destructive logging, poorly-monitored mining developments, oil spills and frontier settlements now scar the land, much of which is 'protected' within biosphere reserves.

Nature has not been the only victim. In 1968, one in four of Siberia's human inhabitants belonged to small-scale indigenous cultures, officially labelled 'Northern Minorities'. Now they poll fewer than one in fifty. These 'mini-nations' are being swamped by tides of big-business development. The attrition of the wild has led to many abandoning their traditional lifestyles as hunters, fishers and reindeer-herders. Others have retreated to the far backwoods, asking only to be left alone. Recalling the destructive impact of modern development on native Indian cultures in Latin America, the human rights pressure group Survival International has dubbed Siberia the 'Amazon of the North'.

5

Trade

As environmental policy becomes 'internationalised' and more countries pursue trade liberalisation and higher volumes of trade, so the need to understand and moderate interactions between trade and the environment becomes more pressing. The relationship betwen them is complex and involves many conflicts of principle. Some observers believe the two can only be reconciled by a moral change away from materialistic values. Yet no agenda for the environment that denies the determination of nations to pursue wealth through commerce is likely to succeed. World trade has increased eleven-fold since 1950: in 1990 the total value of world trade in good was $3485 billion, with an additional $810 billion in commercial services. This upward trend is continuing despite recent recessionary setbacks and trade and economic growth are phenomena that will not go away.

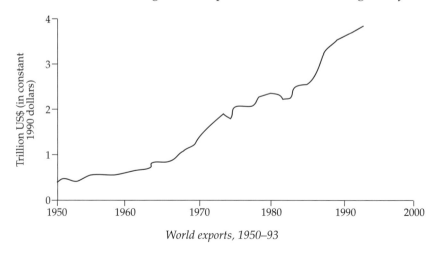

World exports, 1950–93

THE ENVIRONMENTAL IMPACTS OF TRADE

Most characteristics of trade have environmental implications. Trade in goods inevitably requires their transportation, which has implications on resource use and pollution, mainly by reason of its energy and infrastructure requirements. International trade is estimated to account for as much as one-eighth of global oil consumption and a similar fraction of development investment is spent on road construction and other transport infrastructure. In 1991, the 4 billion tons of freight transported by ship consumed as much energy as was used by Brazil and Turkey combined. The 17 million tons sent by air (the most energy-intensive mode of transport) used the equivalent of a year's energy consumption in the Philippines.

The nature of the goods traded is also pertinent, as the production of different goods has different environmental impacts. Primary products (minerals, unprocessed food and other raw materials) made up 21.6 per cent of world trade in goods and services in 1990, and their environmental impact is felt primarily at the point of production or extraction. Exporting countries can suffer environmental consequences ranging from the depletion of non-renewable resources to effects on climate change, air and water pollution and toxic chemical production and the problems of waste disposal. The best publicised example of this is the massive deforestation caused by the trade in tropical timber (see page 43). Manufactured products account for 57 per cent of world trade.

Not all of the effects of trade are adverse to the environment. Trade can help spread the use of technologies which are environmentally beneficial, such as pollution control, and renewable energies. Moreover trade can also encourage companies to emulate the innovations of their international competitors: US car manufacturers, for example, were forced to improve their fuel efficiency in order to compete with Japanese car imports.

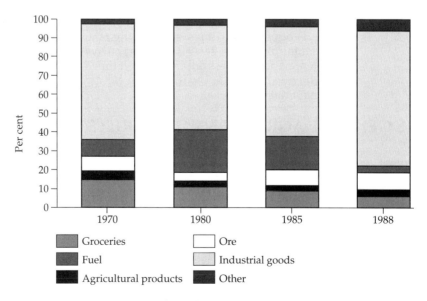

Composition of world trade (the world as an entirety)

POLICIES TOWARDS TRADE

Trade policies can affect environment impacts. Production and export subsidies can encourage higher levels of production of particular goods and thus of associated inputs and impacts. Subsidies or 'tax breaks' can be used to protect domestic industries which are inefficient or damaging; conversely, they can also be used to support industries that pursue higher than average environmental standards, or take proper care of resources at their source.

Tariff and non-tariff barriers also affect overall patterns of production. Troubles arise in many cases because the costs of production do not take account of its environmental impacts. This discrepancy can be passed on, and sometimes magnified, by free trade systems driven by market forces heedless of environmental costs of extraction, transport, manufacture and waste handling. Unless regulations or economic incentives are set in place to help ensure that the market prices of goods reflect these costs more fully, trade is almost bound to encourage environmentally damaging or unsustainable patterns of production and consumption. Existing trade policies and institutional arrangements do not provide much of a safeguard against this 'domino effect'.

Conflicts

Environmental policies can affect trade directly, while trade requirements, in their turn, can compromise policies for environmental protection. Many traders consider that legal and other instruments used to achieve environmental objectives are designed to run counter to the objectives of free trade.

For example, regulations which impose air or water quality standards, set stringent limits on potentially hazardous products or processes, or ban imports of products associated with particular environmental risks, may be seen by commercial interests to constitute unjustifiable barriers to trade. Economic instruments, including taxes or charges levied for environmental purposes, can affect competitiveness between producers in different nations, unless applied even-handedly. Such complexities underline the need to tackle conflicts between trade and environment at the international level.

THE GENERAL AGREEMENT ON TARIFFS AND TRADE

In essence, the provisions of the General Agreement on Tariffs and Trade (GATT) curtail the use of trade restrictions, such as tariffs, quotas and export subsidies, in the interests of free trade. The brainchild of the USA, GATT was formed under UN auspices in 1947, to help boost economic production after the Second World War by liberalising trade arrangements between signatory countries. Originally established with 23 signatory countries, GATT now has more than 100 contracting parties, which together account for 90 per cent of international trade. The World Bank estimates that between 1948 and 1993, official tariffs on manufactured goods have fallen from 40 to 5 per cent.

The provisions of GATT do not refer directly to environmental protection, although limited exceptions to its general free trade regulations are permitted for 'measures necessary to protect human, animal or plant life or health' and for 'measures relating to the conservation of exhaustible natural resources' (Articles XXb and XXg). The application of both these clauses is, however, conditional upon other requirements, such as measures not discriminating between domestically produced and imported goods and not forming disguised restrictions on international trade.

In practice, little use has been made of these provisions, and although hundreds of dispute panels have been appointed by GATT, only a small number have addressed Article XX. The most well-known dispute concerned with environmental protection has been the tuna–dolphin case, in which the US attempted – but failed – to insist on a ban of imports of Mexican yellow fin tuna on the grounds that they were fished using the purse-net seine method, which also kills large numbers of dolphins. Closer to home, in 1993, GATT's dispute panel considered a complaint from the European Community about Corporate Average Fuel Efficiency requirements in the USA, tax laws penalising manufacturers of vehicles with high fuel consumption. Although the regulations apply to all car makers, the measure hit German and other overseas manufacturers who only export large, 'gas-guzzling' cars.

The Uruguay Round

The most recent round of GATT negotiations was initiated in Uruguay in 1986, with the aim of cutting tariffs further and extending the types of goods and services to be covered. These negotiations proved complex and protracted, and the final agreement was not signed until April 1994 in Marrakesh.

Some environmental organisations and policy research institutes have argued for amendments to be made to GATT and the Uruguay Round measures, to take greater account of environmental and natural resource issues. Yet leaders of many 'developing' countries are suspicious of this lobby. They argue that the high environmental standards insisted upon in some Northern states are arbitrary, unscientific and unfair, and would prove inappropriate or prohibitively costly if applied to their own straitened circumstances. Such arguments paraphrase underlying suspicions in the South that high environmental standards are promoted by 'developed' countries as measures to protect domestic industries, rather than out of genuine concern for a healthy environment.

Mindful of these differences, the GATT Council decided in 1991 to form a Working Group on Environmental Measures and International Trade. The Group was mandated to examine the trade provisions of existing multilateral environmental agreements, in relation to the principles and provisions of GATT, the transparency of trade-related environmental measures at national level and the possible effects of packaging and labelling requirements. This initiative did not result in any significant changes to GATT; indeed, the environment was the most prominent among a set of contentious issues which were sidelined as the price of reaching final agreement on the Uruguay Round.

The World Trade Organisation

One outcome of the Uruguay agreement was the establishment of the World Trade Organisation (WTO), as a successor to the GATT secretariat and a permanent watchdog on global trade issues with effect from 1995.

NGOs and others have continued to demand that environmental objectives should merit priority in the terms of reference and work programme of the WTO. During the final Uruguay Round negotiations, broad agreement was reached that a permanent committee should meet in future to discuss trade and the environment, though there was some resistance to setting out a fixed agenda for it. Nonetheless, in December 1993 a statement from the negotiating teams outlined the general aims for the committee: to promote sustainable development, to preserve an open trading system, avoiding both protectionism and unilateral measures, and to ensure the responsiveness of free trade agreements to legitimate environmental objectives. As yet it is unclear when or whether the new committee will tackle more controversial areas of policy concern such as the 'dumping' of pesticides and other goods whose use is prohibited under national regulations on to importer countries where laxer standards apply.

Less contentious issues, such as the trade provisions of multilateral environmental agreements, the need for transparency in trade and environment policies, environmental controls on packaging and the knock-on effects on trade of ecolabelling criteria appear likely to receive early attention.

It is too early to tell how significant the environmental dimension of the Uruguay Round will prove, as the full implications of the changed tasks have yet to be resolved. It is, however, worth noting that the new treaty recognises the right of nation states to take measures to protect health and the environment, and for the first time allows discrimination between products on the basis of their processing and production methods. This could open the way for example for the US to insist on the same standards from importers as from domestic fishing fleets for 'dolphin-friendly' tuna.

THE EUROPEAN UNION

Within Europe, the largest trading bloc is formed by the 15 Member States which make up the European Union. The EU is roughly equal in size to the recently created North American Free Trade Agreement (NAFTA) area.

Trade is a policy area for which the Union, rather than the individual Member States, has clear legal competence and a mandate to act on its members' behalf. Indeed, with the creation of the common market and later of the single internal market, removing trade barriers and encouraging economic growth have ranked foremost among the Union's aims.

Certain aspects of EU trade policy, at least internally, resemble the free trade objectives of GATT (liberalisation aimed at the free movement of goods, persons and capital, harmonised standards, fair trade rules and the like.) Some policy areas are, however, less compatible with free trade, notably the EC's Common Agricultural Policy (see Chapter 9), which dispenses production and export subsidies, as well as setting tariff barriers in the path of food imports.

In addition, the Union Treaty provisions not only provide for an envi-

INTERNATIONAL ENVIRONMENTAL AGREEMENTS WITH TRADE PROVISIONS

Convention Relative to the Preservation of Fauna and Flora in their Natural State, 1933
The aim of this agreement is to preserve natural fauna and flora of the world, particularly of Africa, by means of national parks and reserves, and by regulation of hunting and collection of species. The agreement includes a prohibition against the import and export of trophies, unless the exporter is given a certificate permitting export.

International Convention for the Protection of Birds, 1950
The objective is to protect the populations of birds, and particularly migratory birds, from extinction. Ten West European states have signed the agreement. It includes a prohibition of the import, export, transport, offer of sales or sale of live or dead birds killed or captured during the protected season, or of eggs or their shells or their birds of young birds in the wild state during the breeding season.

International Plant Protection Agreement, 1951
The objective of the convention is to maintain and increase international cooperation in controlling pests and diseases of pests and plant products. The undersigned agree to strictly regulate the import and export of plants.

European Convention for the Protection of Animals during International Transport, 1968
The parties agree to fulfil the provisions of the convention governing the international transport of animals.

Convention on International Trade in Endangered Species of Wild Fauna and Flora (CITES), 1973
The trade of certain species is regulated in order to protect threatened animals from extinction. Certain species cannot be traded while the trade of other species is authorised by export and import permits. Endangered species are listed in three classes. Species threatened with extinction: appendix 1, species that may become endangered unless trade is strictly regulated: appendix 2, species that a party identifies as being subject to regulation within its own jurisdiction and as requiring international cooperation to control trade: appendix 3. The agreement is based on a long history of controlling trade in endangered species through the issue of export permits (species listed in appendices 1 and 2). It adds the twist of requiring an import permit for an export permit to be issued, in order to prevent circumvention to non-parties.

Montreal Protocol on Substances That Deplete the Ozone Layer, 1987
The Montreal Protocol is an application agreement to the Vienna Convention on substances which cause depletion of the ozone layer (1985).

The parties have agreed to reduce CFC production by 50 per cent by 1999. During negotiations in London in 1990, requirements were further restricted and completely new substances were included in the agreement. According to the latest decisions, CFC production will stop completely by 1996. The agreement will take effect three months after a sufficient number of countries have ratified it, in reality this takes approximately two years after an agreement is signed. In March 1993, 111 countries had agreed to the 87 year agreement. Among those who had not signed were South

Korea, Columbia and Vietnam. Brazil signed in 1990, as did Chile and Argentina.

In 1992, 21 more countries signed, including India, Indonesia and Israel. The amendments proposed in London 1990 were ratified by 51 countries, mostly the industrialized countries but also including Chile, China, India and Mexico. No country has yet ratified the changes made in Copenhagen in November 1992. The parties agree to, after a certain date, not export or import specific substances to non-parties and ban importation of CFC-containing products as of 1 January 1993.

Basel Convention on the Control of Transboundary Movements of Hazardous Wastes and their Disposal, 1989
Each party has the right to prohibit the import of hazardous wastes. Export should only be permitted when the importing country's government has given permission in writing. If there is reason to believe that the waste will not be disposed of in an 'environmentally sound manner', then it should not be exported. Trade with countries which have not signed the agreement is not allowed.

ronmental policy, but also require environmental protection requirements to be integrated into other policies (see Chapter 3). These arrangements are far more comprehensive than measures yet in place in the GATT and the WTO.

Many of the EU's environmental laws have been developed partly to facilitate the operation of the common or internal market. Those Directives which set standards for vehicle emissions and apply environmental rules to other products, are intended to avoid barriers to trade resulting from differing national standards. Similarly, common requirements in other areas of environmental protection, such as the control of water pollution from manufacturing industry, help to minimise distortions in competition which might otherwise arise.

Such provisions have not, however, prevented conflicts in the EC between free trade and environmental objectives. Some result from tensions between the Union's promotion of economic growth – the main aim of the internal market – and its environmental effects. A Task Force set up by the Environment Directorate in 1989 to consider impacts of the internal market warned of increases in freight traffic and vehicle emissions.

Other conflicts arise directly from EC trade or environment rules, not least in cases where a particular member state introduces environmental laws which are judged to clash with the objective of free trade within the EU (see box on page xx).

Free Trade vs Environment in the EU/EC

The best-known case of conflicting trade and environmental interests sprang from measures introduced by Denmark to restrict the use of non-returnable containers. A Danish law of 1981, amended in 1984, imposed stringent requirements on manufacturers and suppliers of beverages. All beer and soft drinks were to be marketed in returnable bottles only and bottle types had to be approved in advance. Metal cans were banned and other non-approved containers became subject to an annual quota of 300 000 litres per producer. The law also stipulated a compulsory deposit and return system.

Prompted by complaints from producers in other Member States, the European Commission took Denmark to the European Court of Justice (ECJ) for alleged breaches of EC law. In 1988 the Court ruled largely in favour of the Danish provisions, holding that only the quota for non-approved containers and the requirement for advance approval of bottle types were illegal. The judgement was hailed as a landmark in Community law for its apparent recognition that free trade could be restricted legitimately on environmental grounds.

Another case involving trade restrictions for environmental purposes arose from a decree on waste imports, made by the Regional Executive of Wallonia (Belgium) in 1987. It banned the storage, deposit or disposal of waste from outside Wallonia, which appeared to be receiving excessive quantities of waste from Germany and the Netherlands. The European Commission challenged the legality of Wallonian decree before the ECJ. The verdict of the Court in July 1992 upheld the 'proximity principle', that waste should be disposed of close to its source, but concluded that a blanket ban on imports of hazardous waste was incompatible with a 1984 Directive on transfrontier shipments of hazardous waste. The ECJ also highlighted the special nature of waste as a traded but unwanted 'good'.

EU TRADE IN TROPICAL HARDWOODS

As a partner in development projects, the EU has become involved in promoting the conservation of nature in developing countries. EUROSTAT recently compiled statistics on the import of tropical hardwoods by EU Member States, as part of a background study of the impact of EU trade on the state of natural resources in the tropics. The results show that in most Member States the amounts imported have remained steady or declined since 1976. A noteworthy exception is the UK, which in 1988 imported more than a quarter of the Community's entire stock by volume, mainly for the manufacture of furniture and DIY fittings such as door frames and toilet seats.

	1976	*1978*	*1980*	*1982*	*1984*	*1986*	*1988*
Denmark	66	35	40	41	59	36	35
Germany	1084	1009	1064	686	712	669	422
Greece				45	73	154	52
Spain					421	453	320
France	1754	1400	1665	1218	1112	1037	561
Ireland	38	39	43	44	44	45	46
Italy	1076	981	1197	855	807	670	499
The Netherlands	516	502	408	355	408	533	493
Portugal					293	362	239
United Kingdom	459	434	377	382	464	460	775

Tropical hardwoods – net imports (1000t)

6

Energy

Patterns of energy supply and demand in Europe are changing fast. In past decades of this century, fossil-based fuels – and grid electricity generated from them – supported heavyweight industrial development and spurred a rapid rise in domestic living standards across the continent. Now, however, the focus of economic activity in many EU countries has shifted from heavy to lighter industries and to the service sector. The CEE countries, as they make the transition from centrally planned to market-led economies, are likely to experience a similar economic shift.

Concern over the environmental effects of energy production and use has stimulated much recent international action in favour of low-impact

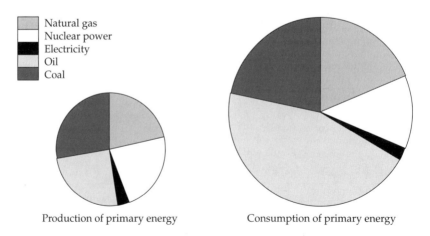

Natural gas
Nuclear power
Electricity
Oil
Coal

Production of primary energy   Consumption of primary energy

Energy production and consumption in the EU (%)

energy sources and pollution reduction. In the future, energy choices in all economic sectors will be increasingly influenced by legislative and financial measures aimed at reducing the adverse environmental effects of energy production and consumption, particularly on climate and air quality.

Total world energy consumption rose by a relatively modest 0.9 per cent between 1990 and 1991. Consumption in Western Europe grew much faster over the same period, at an average rate of 1.5 per cent in the countries of what is now the EU and at 3.5 per cent in nations aligned within the European Free Trade Association (EFTA).

Conversely, consumption fell within CEE countries and the European countries of the former Soviet Union, by 9.5 per cent and 2.4 per cent respectively. At the end of 1991, the percentage share of world energy consumption in the CEE region, the European CIS and Russia was 3.6, 4 and 10 per cent respectively, while the EU and EFTA nations consumed 15 and 1.9 per cent respectively, or roughly the same amount (put together) as the much larger continental areas to the East.

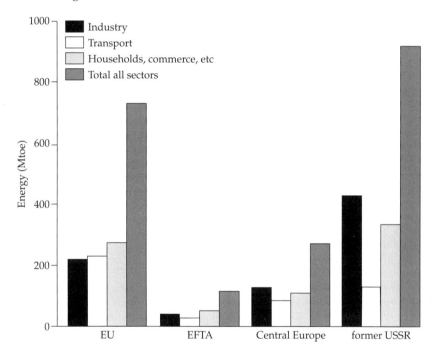

Energy consumption by sector and country group, 1990

DISTRIBUTION AND USE OF FOSSIL-BASED FUELS

European regions consume a mix of fossil fuels – oil, gas and solid fuels – in different proportions. Each of these different primary energy types have potential environmental impacts: impacts which are further influenced by the technologies used to produce them, the efficiency of those technologies; and the use of effective pollution controls. In the EU, oil is the primary fossil fuel consumed; in Central Europe it is solid fuels; and the countries of the former USSR rely primarily on gas and oil.

Solid fuels

Fossil-based solid fuels such as hard coals and lignite still provide a large proportion of world energy supplies, and European energy production and consumption reflects this global pattern. The distribution of solid fuel resources is, however, uneven. Proven reserves in the CEE region and Western Europe stand respectively at 6 and 7 per cent of the world total, while the countries of the CIS own some 22 per cent of world reserves, most of which (more than 17 per cent of the world total) are in Russia.

Consumption of solid fuels is generally linked to the availability of doorstep supplies; just 8–10 per cent of world production of solid fuels is exported. In Poland, coal supplied around 78 per cent of national energy needs in 1991, reflecting heavy dependence on domestically produced coal and lignite for industrial and household uses. This bias is characteristic of most CEE countries: coal and lignite provide on average 45 per cent of supplies of primary energy (as distinct from energy generated in coal-burning power stations) throughout the region, compared with an average of 25 per cent in Western Europe.

Power stations are the main customers for solid fuels. Some 67 per cent of gross consumption is set to power generation purposes in the EC and 46 per cent in CEE countries. Iceland and Norway do not use solid fuels for power generation, deriving most of their energy supplies from hydro power or geothermal sources. Other members of EFTA rely on solid fuels for between one-third and two-thirds of their power generation needs. Switzerland employs a combination of hydro power and nuclear sources.

During 1992 and 1993, economic recession reduced total primary energy consumption throughout Europe; the slump in demand for solid fuels was especially marked. In the next few years coal production in Europe will probably continue to decline on account of its environmental drawbacks and a general tendency for household and industrial consumers to switch to the cleaner, more convenient and cheaper alternative of natural gas.

In the longer term, cleaner coal-burning technologies are expected to herald renewed use of coal for power generation. It seems likely, however, that much of the consequent new demand will be met by coal imported from outside Europe, where lower labour and production costs make for cheaper prices.

Oil

Oil continues to dominate the world's energy mix, despite the uneven distribution of oil resources. Western Europe contains only 1–2 per cent of the world supply, CEE countries less than 1 per cent and the CIS around 6 per cent. Within these regional European groupings, oil reserves are distributed yet more unevenly: in Western Europe, the UK and Norway own the majority of oilfields, whilst within the CIS they are located mainly in Russia and the central European republics of Kazakstan and Turkmenia.

Norway was the largest European oil producer in 1991, extracting 96 million tonnes, of which 90 per cent was exported. The remaining 10 per cent met three-quarters of Norway's total national demand for primary energy. The UK produced a similar quantity, but consumed 92 per cent of it domestically. Excluding these major producers and exporters, the average level of oil production in 1991, measured in millions of tonnes (mt) was:

- 1.5 mt in Western Europe;
- 1.89 mt in CEE countries; and
- 2.1 mt in the CIS and the Baltic republics combined.

Oil is easily transported by tanker and pipeline and so lends itself to long-distance international trade. The main end-use for liquid fuels in Europe is for transport (see Chapter 7). Within the EU, of the 45 per cent of liquid fuels used for stationary purposes in 1991, one-quarter was used in industry, one-quarter was used for power generation and the remainder was used for other purposes such as space heating.

Within CEE countries and the CIS, the ownership of private motor vehicles is still much lower than in Western Europe despite an upsurge since 1989, and the demand for oil follows suit.

Gas

Gaseous fuels, particularly natural gas, form the liveliest growth area in the world energy mix. Gas reserves are distributed somewhat more evenly than oilfields, with 43 per cent in CEE countries and the CIS (mainly in Russia) and 6 per cent in Western Europe. The major reserves in Western Europe are found in the offshore waters of the UK, Norway and the Netherlands.

Global consumption of gaseous fuels represented 23.7 per cent of total energy consumption in 1991. Within Western Europe, the corresponding figure was 19.1 per cent, in CEE countries 22 per cent. This apparent consistency belies striking national differences in reliance upon gas. For example, Greece, Portugal and Iceland rely on gas (mainly in bottled form) for less than 1 per cent of primary energy consumption, whilst in the Netherlands the share is 51 per cent.

In many countries, gas is regarded as a premium fuel and is distributed widely to residential and commercial consumers for space heating, water heating and cooking. In the EU in 1991 these uses accounted for approximately 51 per cent of total gas consumption, while 33 per cent was used in industry and 15 per cent for power generation. In CEE countries, the CIS and the Baltic republics, distribution networks for gas are less developed, with fewer directly connected residential consumers.

Environmental impacts of fossil fuels

Environmental pressures exerted by the use of fossil fuels have attracted widespread attention from policy makers in recent years. Combustion of the fuels releases carbon dioxide, sulphur dioxide and nitrogen oxides into the atmosphere. The former is the main contributor to global warming; the other two cause acid rain; and nitrogen oxide also contributes to tropospheric ozone depletion. Metals and radionuclides are also released during the combustion process, and methane can be leaked both during combustion and transportation of gas.

Solid fuels contain high proportions of wastes and pollutants such as suphur, heavy metals, moisture and ash. The mining of solid fuels – particularly by the cheaper surface or open cast methods – has major local impacts on the landscape and on water quality. Accidents in extraction and transportation of oil can have severe environmental impacts. In 1988, for

---

ACID RAIN

The main vehicle of acidification or acid deposition pollution is rainwater tainted by sulphur dioxide emissions from factories or power stations where coal and other fossil fuels are burned. Reacting in the cloud layer to form dilute sulphuric acid, these exhausts poison forest and freshwater life distant from their source, transported there by wind and precipitation. By the time the problem was widely recognised and debated in the late 1970s, fish and other aquatic life had been severely affected in the lakes and rivers of southern Norway and western Sweden.

Around the same time, signs of acid overload began appearing on land, too. Millions of conifer trees began to wilt, turn brown and die in woods and forests all over northern and central Europe, especially in Germany where almost 70 per cent of forest production was affected. Soaring rates of respiratory illness in the 'Black Triangle' of industrial conurbations in Central Europe were also linked to the acid rain syndrome. Most industrial nations acknowledged the threat and agreed in 1983 to curb emissions from industrial sources by 30 per cent within a decade.

No sooner, however, was atmospheric sulphur on the retreat than another, more pervasive, acidification threat emerged – waste oxides of nitrogen (NOx) issuing from motor vehicle exhausts and from countless other domestic and industrial sources. Their impact on the landscape is much like that of sulphur-derived pollutants, although they act and spread more locally at first. Rising background levels of hydrated nitrogen (ammonia) and nitrates from farm wastes are also a factor, triggering the acid effect when they accumulate to saturation point in vulnerable soils and in lakes and other inland waters.

---

example, over 150 people died in the Piper Alpha platform explosion in the North Sea, and more recently, the 1993 Braer tanker spill contaminated the coastline and marine ecosystems of the Shetland Islands – it has been estimated that 2.5 million farmed salmon (worth some £35 million) were made unfit for consumption.

Environmental regulation of emissions from power stations is becoming stricter in Europe, and this is beginning to have an effect on fuel choice. Recent years have seen a shift away from solid fuels for energy generation, and an increased use of natural gas.. Many countries in the CEE region, for example, see gas as the most suitable choice in the short to medium term, since plants can be constructed quickly and cheaply, and combustion processes give rise to far less acid fallout than coal.

NUCLEAR POWER

Nuclear power accounted for around 5 per cent of world energy consumption in 1991. Within Western Europe, it provided 12 per cent of the region's needs, and in CEE countries and the CIS corresponding levels were 4 per cent and 3 per cent respectively. Disparities between different countries are, once again, important to note: of the 217 power reactors in the whole of Europe, 132 are in the EU, 68 in CEE countries, and just 17 in EFTA countries. Where there is a nuclear programme, the share of national electricity production contributed by nuclear plants is likely to be relatively high, but approximately half the countries of each regional grouping do not have nuclear power stations.

Concern over the safety of many of the Russian-designed reactors operating in CEE regions, the CIS and the Baltic Republics has prompted a series of international initiatives to provide finance and technical support for the improvement of nuclear safety in those countries. This process is hampered by the very great dependence of some countries in the region on nuclear power generation from just one or two reactors, as in Lithuania.

The future for national nuclear power programmes in Europe is mixed and uncertain: France remains committed to nuclear power but in the UK a far-reaching nuclear review is underway. Many countries of CEE, the CIS and the Baltics are opting to meet future requirements with multiple small non-nuclear units requiring relatively low capital investment, while the financial and political problems facing nuclear power are reconsidered.

RENEWABLE OR ALTERNATIVE ENERGY SOURCES

The productive potential of renewable and alternative sources of energy in Europe far exceeds their current levels of exploitation. Renewable energy technologies presently make a relatively insignificant contribution to energy supplies in most parts of Europe. The main exceptions include:

- large-scale hydroelectric power (HEP) generation in several countries where rivers and mountains abound;
- geothermal power plants in the few countries (mainly Iceland and Italy) where the right seismic conditions occur; and
- in countries with abundant forest resources, the use of forestry residues to fuel manufacturing processes within the industries themselves, or as a feedstock for small-scale electricity generation or combined heat and power systems (see box).

COMBINED HEAT AND POWER

In parts of Scandinavia and CEE countries, combined heat and power (CHP) systems are an established feature of energy production and use. CHP systems generate electricity while also using 'waste' energy to heat water, which is then piped to households for domestic space heating and to commercial and industrial buildings.

In Sweden, biomass (plant or animal material) suitable for processing and use as fuels provided 15 per cent of the country's primary energy consumption in 1991, much of it through district CHP systems burning wood, municipal waste or both. More than 8000 km of pipes were laid for heat distribution and 2.4 GW (24 billion watts) of CHP capacity installed. Sweden continues to invest heavily in methods to increase energy production from renewable sources, both through research into new wood energy conversion processes and through management research to optimise production of wood from fast-growing willow, poplar and other hardwood tree species in energy plantations.

In Austria, almost 100 district heating schemes are now in place, fuelled mainly by material from the country's plentiful conifer forests. They provide 1200 MW of total capacity, representing 10 per cent of the country's total energy consumption in 1991. District heating alone, as distinct from CHP, is still an economic practice where trees abound, such as in mountain areas of countries like Austria or Switzerland. In upland regions, forest areas have been protected and conserved under sustainable utilisation regimes for many years, partly because of their value as avalanche barriers.

Within the EU, renewable sources accounted for 9.8 per cent of total electricity supply in 1990. Some 89 per cent of this subtotal came from hydropower. Most of the major opportunities in Europe for hydropower have already been exploited and environmental objections are likely to prevent substantial expansion in the future. Of the remaining 11 per cent of electricity generated by renewables, industrial waste in Spain and geothermal generation in Italy made the greatest contributions. In Denmark, approximately 1.5 per cent of electricity demand is met by wind-powered turbines, many of them owned privately by consortia of local residents. The contribution made by renewables to heat production was smaller, around 3.5 per cent of total demand, of which forest residues supplied 80 per cent.

BIOFUELS

About 14 per cent of primary energy consumption worldwide is presently based on biomass – plant or animal materials that have not been fossilised. In theory, surplus biomass available now could supply the equivalent of about three times the world's entire current energy demand. Improved tree varieties selected for woodfuel production have been planted extensively in Sweden and Belgium. Fast-growing varieties of willow or poplar have formed the main stock of 'energy plantations', grown mainly on ill-drained lands unsuited to farming. Woodfuels supply almost 12 per cent of household energy supplies in the US and are popular in many parts of Europe, too. In France, the amount of wood used for heating was 22 million cubic metres in 1992 – 43 per cent of the country's entire wood harvest. In addition to household stoves or hearths, it was used to power industrial boilers and kilns, district heating plants and central heating in public buildings.

More than half the world's annual wood harvest is used as fuel and some 70 per cent of the world's people rely on wood or charcoal as their main or sole energy source, yet all forms of wood energy still account for just 6 per cent of world energy consumption, a frugal use compared with fuel oil or coal consumption. Many energy planners now look to sustainable 'energy plantations' and other biomass production systems to help mitigate global warming and climate change by reducing the use of fossil-based fuels and giving rein to the natural carbon absorption and carbon 'sequestration' functions of growing plants, especially trees.

In Germany and Austria, additional state subsidies are available to farmers who grow oilseed rape for 'biodiesel' production. Diesel fuel converted from vegetable oils can be used to power farm vehicles or electricity generators with only minor mechanical modifications. Fuel alcohol production from sugar-rich crops such as sweet sorghum is also under development in parts of Southern Europe. Growing field crops for energy use earns producers exemption from CAP quota restrictions on food production and land to be utilised that would otherwise be left idle under 'set aside' provisions.

In Britain the Non Fossil Fuel Obligation requires that 5 per cent of national electricity consumption should come from renewable energy sources by the year 2000. It is applied by levying a 10 per cent surcharge on all electricity bills and using the revenues to subsidise electricity suppliers that use no fossil fuels. The measure was introduced to bolster the profitability of the British nuclear industry, which remains its chief beneficiary. But it has also given farmers and landowners a degree of incentive to expand forestry activities, as wood can be gasified to power electricity generators. Some environmental groups have, however, criticised energy plantations for their monoculture and their tendency to drain riverbank and wetland habitats dry.

In CEE countries, the total contribution to electricity generation made by renewables was 7.3 per cent in 1990, virtually all of it from hydropower. The contribution made by renewables to heat supply was 3.1 per cent, with 88 per cent of the region's demand supplied by forest products or residues.

The use of renewables in the Nordic and Alpine nations is significantly higher than elsewhere in the EU or in the CEE region. Norway and Iceland generate almost all their electricity from hydropower, which also makes a large contribution in Finland, Sweden, Austria and Switzerland.

A renewable future?

Despite the currently stable price of oil on the world market and apparently plentiful reserves, developing renewable sources of energy is sure to gain priority for Europe. This is, in part, a reflection of changes in the world economy: growth in developing economies such as China, Brazil and parts of South-East Asia is bound to lead to increasing energy demands. According to World Bank projections, electricity demand in the developing world is likely to grow at 7 per cent a year over the next 20 years, compared with a growth of just 2–3 per cent in industrialised countries.

Developing power generation systems based on renewable sources of energy (RSE) will help counter this increased demand on existing sources. Moreover, renewable energy development does not require such high investment costs and long lead-times as projects for energy generation using oil, coal or hydro-power. Renewable energy systems can be decentralised and scaled to meet users' needs and can be expanded in step with rising demand, often creating new local jobs and livelihoods in the process. They also avoid a number of the environmental drawbacks that are associated with orthodox energy production systems.

ELECTRICITY GENERATION

Electricity is the ultimate 'convenience' fuel, instantly amenable to virtually any use. Loose though these terms may be, ready public availability of grid electricity has come to form a key distinction between 'developed' and less developed or under-developed economies.

Throughout Europe, electricity provides for about one-fifth of final energy consumption, although Western Europe's share of electricity for stationary energy use (ie not related to transport) is significantly higher than that of CEE countries. Particular countries pose striking variations: in Luxembourg, for instance, imported oil supplies an unusually large fraction of national energy demand while grid electricity accounts for just 9.9 per cent of the whole. By contrast, Norway relies heavily on electricity, generated mostly by hydropower.

Primary inputs used to generate electricity also vary enormously. In the EU, conventional thermal power stations supplied 56 per cent of grid electricity in 1991, compared with 35 per cent from nuclear reactors and 9 per cent from hydro power sources. In EFTA countries, the equivalent figures were almost a reverse image: hydro power sources generated 60 per cent, nuclear energy sources produced 28 per cent and thermal plant fired by coal or oil yielded 12 per cent of the region's power supply.

In CEE countries, the Baltic Republics and the European CIS, nuclear and hydro power sources both produced some 10–20 per cent of grid power, the remainder coming from thermal power stations.

ENERGY INTENSITY

During the decade 1980–90, world energy intensity – that is, primary energy consumption per head of population – grew by an average of 0.5 per cent a year. In Western Europe, the change over this period was roughly in line with the world average, where energy intensity grew by just 0.7 per cent, but in the CIS and the Baltic Republics growth speeded up to 2.2 per cent. In CEE countries, energy intensity actually fell by up to 1.9 per cent a year. Although these overall figures for Europe are high compared to the world average, they are still well below North America.

Over the same decade, electricity consumption per person grew in all parts of Europe. But primary consumption of energy per unit of GDP showed a different trend, falling in Western Europe and CEE countries by 1.2 and 1.4 per cent respectively, whereas in the CIS and the Baltic Republics it grew by 0.6 per cent.

This difference arises largely from the shift, particularly in the case of Western Europe, away from heavy industry and towards the service and commercial sectors. In CEE counties, this shift has only just begun to take place, and the fall in energy intensity reflects not only industrial restructuring, but also net improvements in the efficiency of energy use.

DEPENDENCE ON ENERGY IMPORTS

Levels of dependence on energy imports across Europe vary greatly, much in line with the availability of indigenous fossil-based fuel resources. Within Western Europe, Norway achieved a 'dependence' of minus 490 per cent in 1991, exporting enormous quantities of oil while generating most of its own electricity needs. The UK achieved a dependence on imports of just 5 per cent, thanks to indigenous coal and North Sea oil and gas.

By contrast, Luxembourg relied on imports to meet over 98 per cent of national energy demand. Excluding Norway and the UK, average dependence in Western Europe was 61 per cent. This pattern is repeated in the European countries of the former USSR, where overall energy dependency is 62 per cent. Again, there are wide variations: whereas Latvia imports 100 per cent of its energy requirements, Azerbaijan produces substantial amounts of oil and gas and has a dependence on imports of only 7.9 per cent.

There are signs of renewed vigour in programmes to promote greater efficiency of energy use in Europe. This trend arises partly from the need to meet national commitments to lower greenhouse gas emissions in line with the UNCED agreements on climate change. In CEE countries, substantial energy price increases have also provided a stimulus for reducing consumption and intensity. The potential for improving efficiency in Europe is hard to assess but is undoubtedly large, particularly for countries in transition from centrally planned to market economies.

INITIATIVES TO COUNTER ENVIRONMENTAL IMPACTS

Concern about the environmental impacts of energy production and consumption in Europe has until quite recently focused on local or regional impacts, such as those caused by acid deposition. Efforts to reduce inter-country or transboundary pollution of this type have been conducted within the framework of the UNECE. A second Sulphur Protocol has now been agreed, which aims to negotiate individual national emission levels to meet Europe-wide targets for the reduction of damage by sulphur deposition. At national level, efforts to control emissions of acid-forming gases are concentrated on the fixing of emission limits and requiring authorisations for combustion plant, and to a lesser extent through air-quality standards.

CARBON OR ENERGY TAXES

Carbon taxes are surcharges levied on commercial fuels in proportion to the amount of carbon dioxide they emit in use, per standard unit of energy produced. In principle, carbon taxation should force up the price of oil, coal and other fossil-based fuels, and so making indigenous production of renewable energy – including biomass – more attractive. The cost of the tax to manufacturing industries should (in principle) be balanced by benefits to agricultural industry and lower fuel import bills, so that national economic growth need not suffer overall.

The Netherlands, Sweden and Finland already impose such taxes and controversial plans are being shaped to introduce a carbon tax throughout the EU. Some Member States, led by the UK, strongly oppose this move on the grounds that it might sap the competitiveness of their industries. They argue for modest carbon taxes whose revenues can be ploughed back into developing renewable energy technologies that will compete with fossil-based fuels on their own merits, without penalising industry or interfering with market forces.

If a carbon tax is introduced in the EU along with other measures, the contribution of renewables to primary energy production in the EU could rise from 4.3 per cent in 1990 to an estimated 9.2 per cent in 2010. This estimate reflects the large potential for increasing production from large biofuels and by solar, thermal and windpower.

The global climatic effects of energy use did not become a significant policy issue until the late 1980s and in 1988 the Intergovernmental Panel on Climate Change (IPCC) was established under the auspices of UNEP and the WMO. Most individual nations developed targets for emission reduction, and the EU had reached political agreement by the end of 1990 to return carbon dioxide emissions in the EU as a whole to 1990 levels by 2000.

Negotiations for an international convention on climate change proceeded until June 1992, when the Framework Convention on Climate Change was signed in Rio. The Convention does not contain binding policy commitments, but indicates that all industrialised countries should aim as a first step to reduce emissions of greenhouse gases to 1990 levels by 2000.

ENERGY TRANSITION IN THE EU

The establishment of an internal market for energy in the EU was seen as an important part of the development of the single market in 1992. The countries of EFTA have agreed to join the internal market (with the exception of Switzerland), and whilst the market is not yet fully complete, the issue of interconnecting national energy supply networks is receiving urgent attention.

Guidelines are being drawn up for measures to develop Trans-European Energy Networks, and to create the technical, administrative, legal and financial conditions favourable to energy exchange across national boundaries. Since 1991, the EU has also established a programme (known as SAVE) for energy efficiency measures, budgeted at 35 million ECU.

In the field of renewable energy, the European Commission has established a programme (ALTENER) intended to help increase the renewable fraction of the Union's overall energy supply from nearly 4 per cent to 8 per cent between 1991 and 2005.

A Union-wide research programme under the title JOULE has given rise to impressive advances in renewable energy technologies, including new techniques for generating power from photovoltaic (solar cell) arrays, often for decentralised use in areas remote from electricity grids, such as small offshore islands or high mountain regions.

ENERGY TRANSITION IN EASTERN EUROPE

The energy-intensive nature of manufacturing in CEE countries, the CIS and the Baltic Republics derives from the dominance of heavy industry. It has been compounded by low energy prices which blunt incentives for improving efficiency. This situation, combined with the use of relatively 'dirty' indigenous fuels and low levels of combustion clean-up, continues to damage plant, animal and human health in many areas.

Since 1989, much policy and planning attention has been focused on reducing energy intensity by rationalising energy prices; many international redevelopment loans have been conditional on energy price reform.

Institutional reform of energy supply structures has also been a key feature of the transition process, with most countries aiming at privatisation of some, if not all, energy utilities. The countries of the former USSR have inherited a common energy infrastructure that poses particular problems. Disagreements over rights and responsibilities are causing interstate tension, and imbalances between energy supply and demand are disrupting the stability of some newly independent states.

Among new planning objectives that have been identified are requirements to modernise whole sectors of industry and to empower residential and commercial energy users to respond to price signals, for example by installing heat meters and temperature controls. The scarcity of investment capital in the region has, however, slowed progress towards these goals to well beyond the deadlines originally set by planners.

The region has been in economic recession for most of the 1990s and the accompanying drop in industrial production has resulted in a sharp decrease in pollution emissions. In Hungary, for example, industrial output fell by around 35 per cent during 1990–92, shadowed by a comparable drop in energy consumption and associated emissions.

Cooperation and technical assistance

Several programmes with specific energy objectives already provide financial and technical assistance to CEE countries and other countries of Eastern Europe in the process of economic transition, most of which reflect environmental concerns.

Projects in the energy field are now receiving large allocations under the EU's PHARE programme, in areas ranging from policy development to information campaigns on domestic energy-saving. Poland is expected to receive the largest share of funds and substantial amounts have already been committed during the restructuring programme of the country's energy supply system.

THERMIE is another EU programme directly relevant to energy transition in the East. It ran from 1990 to 1994 with a budget of 700 million ECU and established an extensive network of 'Organisations for the Promotion of Energy Technology', with centres in several CEE countries, the Baltics and the CIS. The network spreads information on mature energy technologies to industry, financial institutions and government.

TACIS, the Technical Assistance to the CIS programme, aims to support energy sector transformation activities in the former USSR. The budget is approximately 50 million ECU per year.

More generally, the operation of the single market opens the way to develop trans-continental pipelines and power grids that connect with CEE countries as well as linking the energy systems of EU and EFTA countries.

The European Bank for Reconstruction and Development aims to close the East–West energy gap by promoting improvements in production and consumption efficiency as well as the commercial exploitation of renewable and non-conventional sources of energy. Energy-saving measures are accorded high priority, in line with the Bank's least-cost strategy, although the difficulty of lumping enough energy-saving projects together to fulfil the Bank's conditions on minimum loan size has meant that few active programmes have begun.

Bilateral East–West agreements have been established in the energy field by many Western European countries to support the reform process in the East. For example, Denmark launched a programme in 1990, consisting mainly of technical assistance projects, which has supported about 80 projects in 9 countries of the CEE region and the CIS.

Energy Efficiency 2000 is a technical assistance programme organised at UN level by the UNECE Committee on Energy and is shortly to be extended into a second three-year phase. Financed by a UN trust fund worth an estimated US$1.3 million, it aims to reduce the energy efficiency 'gap' between the best available technologies and those used in practice.

It also seeks to level the energy 'playing-field' between the formerly centrally planned and internalised market economies of CEEC and those of the rest of the world, by enhancing trade and information exchange in the field of energy efficient technologies.

THE EUROPEAN ENERGY CHARTER

The objective of the charter, developed by the European Commission and signed in outline form in December 1991, is to put investment funds, knowledge and skills from the EU to work in the enterprises of the East, using energy transition as a catalyst for a genuine recovery and to underpin political stability. At present there are 49 national signatories to the framework charter, as well as the EU itself.

National participants include:

- EU Member States;
- EFTA countries;
- CEE countries (excluding the former states of Yugoslavia, whose participation in international treaty negotiations is suspended in line with UN Security Council decisions);
- the three Baltic states;
- the countries of the former Soviet Union (excluding Turkmenistan);
- the US;
- Japan;
- Canada; and
- Australia.

Signatories have agreed in principle to cooperate in the energy field with a view to providing safeguards over the treatment of outside investors in Eastern markets, encouraging investment and promoting free trade. The Charter text also accords companies investing in the East rights to transfer energy products through intervening countries to Western markets.

Protocols (separately negotiated annexes) are being negotiated on nuclear safety and energy efficiency, while a specific article in the Charter itself deals with environmental aspects of energy transition. It lays down requirements to pursue sustainable development in ways that are economically efficient but also minimise harmful environmental impacts, and to take specific account of environmental considerations when formulating energy policies.

7

Transport

Europe's transport networks count among the densest and most crowded in the world, a reflection both of the region's inveterate trading habits and its high population density. These networks and the vehicles which use them have environmental impacts which, particularly in recent years, have become impossible to ignore. As transport volumes increase, so does the need to tackle the environmental consequences of this growth by integrating environmental management goals into transport policy. Fundamental conflicts between transport growth and environmental protection mean, however, that practical progress towards such integration has so far remained limited.

THE TRENDS

Demand for passenger and freight transport has increased dramatically in Western Europe during the past 20 years – the result of a variety of factors, including economic growth, an increase in the volume of international trade and the distances over whch goods travel, and socioeconomic changes such as the increase in use of the private car. Within the EU, annual growth rates in the period 1970–90 averaged 2.5 per cent for goods transport and 3.1 per cent for passenger transport, compared with 2.6 per cent for economic activities in general.

Road transport accounted for much of this growth and private car use has multiplied to such an extent that it now accounts for 70 per cent of all traffic movements. Forecasts suggest private car journeys in the EU will increase by 25 per cent and road freight movements by 40 per cent between 1990 and the year 2010, unless policies change. Passenger transport by air is also growing rapidly across Europe, with increasingly large-capacity aircraft being used.

Factors likely to increase transport demands still further in the future include growth in industrial and other economic activity, social changes in CEE countries (particularly the rapid rise in car ownership) and the inevitable multiplication of transport linkages across Western Europe with the continuing development of the EU's internal market and the expanded European Economic Area.

Trans-European Networks

In October 1993, the European Council adopted a Decision to create a system of trans-European transport networks, including the Trans-European Road Network (TERN). These followed on from the high-speed rail network plan, developed in 1990. Other plans for conventional rail, seaports and airports will follow.

The trans-European networks are the subject of a specific title in the Maastricht Treaty. Its requirements include the establishment of guidelines and master plans for the networks, measures to ensure they are compatible in different countries and financial support for transport projects of particular interest to the Community.

The rationale for establishing these networks is that, in the past, communications links were developed to cater mainly for national trade and travel. Cross-border links between European countries, however, are often weaker, and long-distance routes fragmented or lacking. These weaknesses, which the EU is looking to remedy, could impede the free movement of people and goods between Member States.

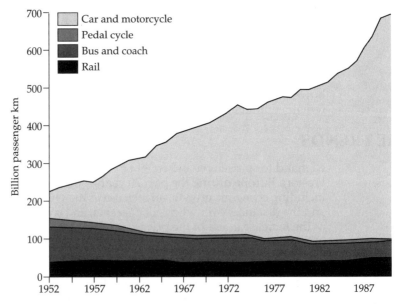

Note: The graph excludes 'walk' trips. The 1985 National Travel Survey shows that a person walks on average 8 km per week; this leads to a total annual national figure of around 23 billion km.

The growth in personal travel in Britain

The road network plans incorporate many schemes which environmental pressure groups feel could be particularly damaging to the environment. They argue that an increase in road networks across Europe will lead to greater traffic flows, and will exacerbate the environmental impacts of road travel, in addition to the immediate effects of construction. Some campaigners also question the necessity of spending large sums of public money on such projects.

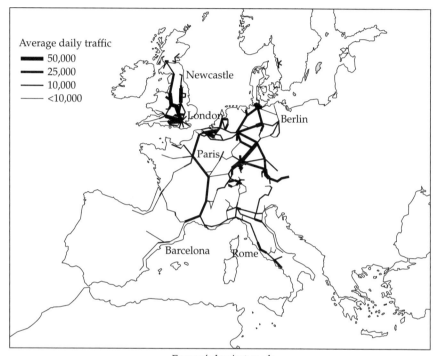

Europe's busiest roads

ENVIRONMENTAL IMPACTS OF TRANSPORT

The transport sector accounts for a high proportion of total annual emissions of major air pollutants. In the EU, transport characteristically emits some 50 per cent of the region's nitrogen oxide pollutants, up to 90 per cent of carbon monoxide and 20–30 per cent of its emissions of carbon dioxide (the main greenhouse gas). Transport methods also emit some 35 per cent of Europe's volatile organic compounds (VOCs), which contribute to the build-up of tropospheric photochemical oxidants.

Transport is a major consumer of energy resources, and accounts for nearly one-third of total energy consumption in many European cities. Despite recent improvements in vehicle engine efficiency, road transport accounts for over three quarters of the transport sector's oil consumption. Both increases in car ownership and the availability of larger and more powerful vehicles are likely to increase these consumption levels.

Transport infrastructure (roads, airports, railway lines, ports, canals etc) can have a major adverse impact on wildlife habitats, the countryside and residential areas, as well as drawing more traffic into circulation.

Mode	Occupancy rate			
	25%	*50%*	*75%*	*100%*
Petrol car (<1.4 litres)	2.61	1.31	0.87	0.62
Petrol car (>2 litres)	4.65	2.33	1.55	1.16
Diesel car (<1.4 litres)	2.26	1.13	0.75	0.57
Diesel car (>2 litres)	3.65	1.83	1.22	0.91
Rail (Intercity)	1.14	0.57	0.38	0.29
Rail (suburban electric)	1.05	0.59	0.35	0.26
Bus (double decker)	0.70	0.35	0.23	0.17
Minibus	1.42	0.71	0.47	0.35
Air (Boeing 727)	5.78	2.89	1.94	1.45
Cycling				0.06
Walking				0.16

Note: Units are in megajoules of primary energy / passenger kilometre

Energy consumption for different transport modes

Built-up urban areas bear the brunt of the environmental damage caused by transport, particularly in the form of pollutants from private motor vehicles. Yet it is in urban areas that alternatives to the use of private cars, such as public transport and cycle lanes can prove the most straight forward to provide. Improving public transport systems and encouraging walking and cycling can bring direct environmental and health benefits too. While some smaller countries, not least Denmark and the Netherlands, have pursued integrated transport policies that aim to optimise these benefits, most others lag far behind.

Some EU countries, such as Sweden, are leading innovators in environmentally sound transport policy making in Europe. They have concentrated on limiting air pollution and noise by setting emission control standards for new vehicles.

The recent introduction of catalytic converters for new cars by law in much of Europe, and the further tightening of standards for all classes of vehicle represent important steps forward. Total emissions from motor vehicles of nitrogen oxides and other regulated pollutants are expected to decline in most countries during the next 10 years, unless emissions reduction policies are outstripped by a growth in car ownership and use.

Other problems – notably carbon dioxide emissions, noise, landtake and the unregulated disposal of vehicles – are coming to the fore in the transport and environment debate. Yet, so far, policies have generally aimed to accommodate increases in motor transport demand and to mitigate damage, rather than develop alternative approaches which might encourage consumers to use more environmentally sound or less wasteful forms of transport.

SOME IMPACTS OF MOTOR VEHICLE TRANSPORT

- Raw materials and energy are consumed and pollution is emitted during vehicle manufacture.
- Environmental harm from the extraction, transport and refining of fuel oils can cause environmental damage (see Chapter 6).
- Motor transport is a major source of the greenhouse gas carbon dioxide in the atmosphere, leading to global warming.
- Use of motor vehicles releases many pollutants into the air, especially oxides of nitrogen, lead and carbon monoxide. The resultant health effects include respiratory and heart diseases, certain kinds of tumour and, in the case of lead, brain damage in small children.
- The action of sunlight on the acidified air that surrounds most highways and urban areas creates blankets of 'photochemical smog' laced with ozone.
- Traffic gridlock, noise and vibration cause congestion and stress and disrupt local communities, particularly in inner cities. Off-course vehicles destroy trees and property.
- Used parts, notably tyres and batteries, cause major waste disposal problems. Hazards also arise from operations to break up scrap vehicles.
- Road construction developments, including secondary development on new routes and intersections, lead to landtake which affects wildlife habitats, public amenity values and the integrity of protected areas.
- Extraction of stone and aggregates for road construction places extra demands on rural land and leads to additional noise, nuisance and traffic.
- Injuries and fatalities from motor vehicle accidents now exceed the tolls of both World Wars I and II.

LIMITING THE ENVIRONMENTAL IMPACTS

The EU Common Transport Policy

At the core of EU policy attitudes towards transport lies the Common Transport Policy (CTP), set in motion by the 1957 Treaty of Rome.

During the 1980s, the EC and other international bodies (notably the OECD and the European Conference of Ministers of Transport) showed growing awareness of the harm that mass transport (especially by road) can do to environmental and public health.

As a result, changes to the CTP have been proposed that will take greater account of environmental concerns, by reference to the Fifth Action Programme on the Environment and various new policy initiatives, discussion documents and legal instruments touching environmental care and sustainable development.

A Green Paper on the impact of transport on the environment, subtitled 'A Community strategy for sustainable mobility', was published by the European Commission in February 1992. This paper and the debate it prompted served to highlight the awkward dilemmas that the EU faces as it seeks ways of integrating environmental objectives into transport policy.

The transport White Paper which followed placed careful emphasis on the need for transport to pay its full costs – including environmental costs.

Yet it failed to produce any evidence that 'sustainable mobility' was a feasible objective. Forecast rates of growth, especially for road transport, still appear likely to prove unsustainable.

In addition, attempts to manage transport demand appear incompatible with the core EU policy of liberalising transport markets. The planned volume of investment in transport infrastructure to cater, for instance, for the EU's TERN programme also appears set to exacerbate environmental problems.

THE SWISS LORRY BAN

Traffic between Italy and other EU Member States passes mainly through the 'transit countries' of Austria and Switzerland. The European Commission plays an active role in negotiating transit agreements with these two countries. Arrangements have involved significant concessions from the EC, for example in imposing limits on both the total quantity of through traffic and its timing, and respecting the lower lorry weight limits in force on Swiss roads.

Nonetheless, some areas still suffer the effects of through traffic with relatively little benefit to their own economies and Switzerland is threatening a ban on road freight traffic within 10 years. This will mean the Swiss government is repudiating its agreements with the EU and it may have serious repercussions in the enlargement negotiations with Austria, which gained some concessions but agreed to open its roads to EU traffic after a transitional period.

Switzerland's stance seems likely to affect the volume of goods traded on some routes – and perhaps even the future balance between road and rail traffic in Europe.

Local developments

Many initiatives have been taken at local level in Europe to reduce the environmental impacts of transport. These include traffic calming measures such as park-and-ride schemes; traffic bans or limits, particularly in city centres; road pricing and tolls to reduce access and raise funds; and strict parking controls. Promoting public transport and encouraging cycling and walking – for example by developing pedestrian zones and improving cycling facilities – can also help limit the impact of urban traffic and boost the efficiency with which fuel resources are used.

Impact and assessment policies

Major transport infrastructure projects generally require an environmental impact assessment to judge their likely side-effects before the relevant authorities can give their consent to them.

The methodology used for assessments often differs greatly between countries and resulting decisions can be contentious. For instance, it is often argued that an assessment of a short section of road cannot reflect the true impact of the road as a whole, nor of the general impact of roadbuilding and traffic.

To counteract these uncertainties, there is much to be said for some form of strategic environmental assessment to reflect the full effects of transport plans and policies Union-wide. However, no such assessment has so far been undertaken by the Commission for the TERN master plans.

TRANSPORT AND THE SUSTAINABLE CITY

According to UN figures, three-quarters of the population of the developed world will live in large cities by the year 2000, many with populations of over 50 million. The world's existing mega-cities are already suffering overcrowding and pollution, and these symptoms of urban overload are not confined to developing regions such as Bombay or Manila. Transport, welfare services and public amenities in European cities such as Athens, Rome and London are falling well below optimum levels, and in many cases are continuing to decline.

Traffic-related pollution became so severe in central Athens in 1992 that more than 200 cases of ozone poisoning and asphyxia were admitted to hospitals daily during the hottest summer months of July and August. The city administration responded first by banning private cars from the central zone according to the alphabetical order of the initial letter of their licence plates; 'A-M' days alternated with 'N-Z' days. Even this desperate ruse failed; drivers simply acquired second cars to beat the ban. At the height of the heatwave, the city centre had to be closed completely to private cars and taxi traffic was reduced by half.

The environmental problems caused by urban transport flows are undeniable, yet it is in cities themselves that practical solutions are most likely to be found. One approach is being developed by the Climate Network, an alliance begun two years ago in Hanover and 19 other German cities and now including around 20 other municipalities in Austria, Switzerland and neighbouring states in Central Europe.

The administrations of these cities have set themselves a common target for reducing emissions of greenhouse gases to a level (at least 30 per cent by the year 2005) that significantly undercuts international limits proposed at Rio under the Framework Convention on Climate Change. They intend to achieve this by restricting private car traffic and upgrading public transport systems, as well as by retro-fitting public buildings to cut down on energy waste and by using local bylaws and commercial rate levies to encourage urban commerce and industry to convert to cleaner products and processes.

TRANSPORT TRENDS IN CEE COUNTRIES

The rapid changes that have overtaken CEE countries in the past few years hold profound implications for future transport habits, and for the state of the environment. The switch to a market economy has seen an influx of private vehicles and led to the privatisation of some mass-transit systems. The economic and political disruption of which these changes form a part has also had an adverse effect on the functioning of public transport.

Cars

Car ownership is increasing rapidly. At present demand is met largely by cars imported from Western Europe, but domestic production (often through joint ventures involving Western manufacturers) is on the increase. It is worth noting that this influx is not confined to new cars, but includes a significant proportion of imported secondhand cars from Western Europe, which command higher prices in the East as a result of the burgeoning demand.

Projections of car traffic growth in Poland foresee an almost three-fold increase in traffic over the period 1990–2010. Overall estimates for the CEE region suggest that car ownership will double by the year 2010, to around 250 cars per thousand people. This is still well below current ownership levels in Western Europe, which average 400–500 cars per thousand people.

Similarly, the average distance driven per car is projected at 11,000 kilometres per year in Poland by the year 2020 – still far less than the UK average of around 16,000 kilometres.

	1980	*1989*	*1990*
Ex-Czechoslovakia	149	199	na
Ex-East Germany	160	234	na
Hungary	94	164	184
Poland	67	127	138
West Germany	388	480	384*
Great Britain	277	366	383
Ex-Yugoslavia	108	140	147
USA	598	643	na

Note: * including former GDR

Car ownership per 1000 population in selected CEE countries

Roads

Until recently, road networks in CEE countries were generally well-maintained and not heavily used, although there were very few motorways, bypasses and ringroads. As in the West, there is a strong desire in some quarters to construct modern motorway systems as a means to foster economic development.

The World Bank and EBRD are already financing some major construction schemes, and joint ventures in transport infrastructure with western companies are being sought by CEE countries. It seems likely that toll-roads will increasingly be developed as a means of financing construction; but, particularly in these cases, it is likely that new roads will benefit international hauliers more than local people.

Public transport

Under their former governments, most of the states of the CEE region developed extensive public transport facilities, with integrated networks of rail, bus, underground and tram services. These systems were supported by generous state subsidies and were reliable and generally well supported by the travelling public. Drastic subsidy reductions and other financial pressures, however, have led to rapid fare increases, often accompanied by cuts in numbers and standards of services. There are already clear signs that public transport in CEE countries is entering a spiral of decline, which will add further impetus to the growth in private car use noted above.

Urban roads are generally not well-adapted to high levels of car use or parking. Increasing motorisation is thus likely to lead to the rapid spread of congestion, and further a decline in public transport, with a consequent deterioration in environmental quality. The gradual integration of CEE countries into the EU now appears likely, and plans for transport links between countries in the EU and their eastern neighbours are already under development. Hostilities in former Yugoslavia have already made it imperative to secure overland routes between Greece and the rest of the EC through other parts of the CEE region.

A SUSTAINABLE FUTURE?

The European Commission has adopted the expression 'sustainable mobility' in recent communications on transport and sustainable development. However, there appear to be few grounds for asserting that mobility based on present personal transport habits can ever be environmentally sustainable in a fully-fledged sense.

Many transport experts emphasise that what makes transport sustainable is access or choice, not mobility. People require goods, services, social contact and so on, and travelling is principally a means to achieve these rather than a virtue in itself. This argument is central, for example, to the concept of sustainable cities, or to the protection of rural areas from urban sprawl.

Despite claims by manufacturers of '[more] environmentally friendly' cars, no motorised form of transport is without environmental impacts. Walking and cycling remain the only commonly available means of personal transport which are 'green' in the sense that they generate virtually no noise or pollution – much less space and energy are required to keep pedestrians and cyclists on the move than to keep motor vehicles in service.

The production processes for bicycles (and even shoes) do, of course, consume resources, and country footpaths are vulnerable to erosion through overuse by hikers and mountain-bikers, for example. But the harm these forms of personal transport do is negligible compared to the negative impacts of motorised transport. Walking and cycling are also available to millions of citizens (including children and some older people) who are excluded from driving their own cars. They have significant health benefits and can prove quicker and more convenient than private cars for many journeys.

Many argue that, failing a miraculous mass conversion to unmotorised personal transport, the best and least-cost scenario for reducing transport's power to pollute is to upgrade public transport services so that many more travellers can be persuaded to forego private car journeys, thus drastically reducing per capita emission levels. Accompanying steps to curb pollution from public transport vehicles would further compound the environmental benefits of such a shift. Many European cities and countries are reviving electrified tram and trolleybus systems, restoring navigable urban waterways and introducing regulations or incentives to increase the use of lead-free fuels in mass transit vehicles.

PLANES, BOATS AND TRAINS

Aircraft movements over Europe, especially during summer holiday months, have increased more than eightfold since 1960, due largely to both increased business travel and the wide availability and cheap price of foreign holidays.

A 1991 report by the World Wide Fund for Nature (WWF) warned of a number of negative impacts that aircraft and air traffic movements can have on the state of the environment. Many European airports already impose heavy surcharges on landing fees to mitigate the noise pollution caused by aircraft. This measure has had a direct influence on moves by aircraft manufacturers to design planes with quieter engines, which attract lower landing fees. A further factor highlighted in the report was the effect that aircraft engine emissions can have on conditions in the atmosphere.

Assuming that promised cuts in pollution emissions from industrial installations on the ground are actually fulfilled, nitrogen oxides and greenhouse gas emissions from aircraft could, according to WWF, grow to contribute 28–37 per cent of the global warming effect within 20 years, up from their present 3–4 per cent.

Although the amounts of pollutants emitted by aircraft are small compared with industrial sources, they are released directly into the most vulnerable layers of the atmosphere and so have a disproportionately large effect. Airline operators mostly refuse to accept WWF's interpretation of the likely effects and believe that improvements in engine manufacture will curb emissions problems before they reach hazardous levels.

Flying is still thought by many to be the fastest and most convenient means of long-distance travel, but competition is coming from an unexpected source: the rail industry. High-speed mass terrestrial transport systems such as France's TGV train network are becoming the preferred carrier for many business and leisure travellers undertaking medium-haul inter-city journeys within Europe. The new Channel Tunnel rail link is likely to increase the popularity of continental rail travel to and from the UK.

8

Waste

The growing quantities of waste accumulating in Europe, as in the rest of the 'developed' world, can be seen as an indication of our failure to use materials and energy efficiently. Waste is often defined in legislation as material which is unwanted or unused. However, much waste can be a potential source of secondary raw materials or recycled goods, as well as a source of pollution.

SOURCES OF WASTE

Statistics on waste production and management should be interpreted with some caution, as definitions and methods of estimation vary between country and sector, and data is not always widely available. Recent estimates suggest, however, that nearly 10 billion tonnes of waste were produced in OECD countries in 1992, and waste volumes are growing at around 3 per cent per year. Of this total, 1.5 billion tonnes (including over 300 million tonnes of hazardous waste) came from industrial sources, and 420 million tonnes were municipal waste. Some 7 billion tonnes were from agriculture, energy, mining, demolition and sewage.

The importance of sources of waste in Europe varies between countries – in general, Western Europe produces more industrial and municipal waste, while in the CEE region waste from mining activities is comparatively important.

Industrial waste

Estimates for the late 1980s indicate that Europe produced some 38 per cent of the industrial wastes generated worldwide. In the countries of Central and Eastern Europe, where reliance on heavy industry and manufacturing is greater than in the West, the output of industrial waste was

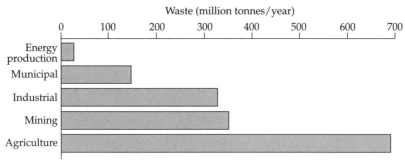

Waste production by sources in OECD Europe, 1990

particularly high, most notably in the former East Germany and Czechoslovakia. Around 16 per cent of industrial waste was considered hazardous in 1993.

Municipal waste

The average annual tonnage of municipal waste produced per capita in European OECD countries increased from 300 kg in 1975 to over 350 kilos in 1990. The levels of municipal waste generated in Western Europe is higher than in Eastern Europe, and tend to be linked to income levels – more products and activities lead to more waste.

Agricultural waste

Crop residues, slurry, animal carcasses, manure and other forms of agricultural waste account for over a quarter of all waste produced in Europe. Many agricultural residues are organic and biodegradable, and hence are relatively easy to dispose of – at least in theory – by composting and/or using as fertiliser. However, today's intensive farming methods are producing an increasing amount of waste, and the use of chemicals in agriculture further complicates waste management.

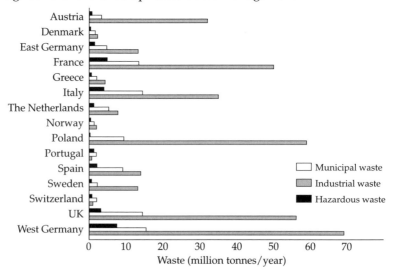

Agricultural waste production by sources

DISPOSAL METHODS AND ENVIRONMENTAL IMPACTS

Some difficulties of dealing with waste result simply from the vast and growing quantities involved. Other problems arise from the nature of the waste, particularly where it contains hazardous substances, and with the methods of disposal used to 'lose' wastes in the land, air or water.

As with sources of waste, disposal methods vary greatly between countries in Europe – in the UK for example, over three-quarters of municipal waste is buried in landfill sites, whereas landfill disposal accounts for less than 10 per cent of waste in Switzerland.

Landfill

Despite regional variations, landfill remains the favoured method of disposal for municipal waste in most European countries. Former quarries or specially excavated sites are used as waste tips, which are capped with clay or soil when full. Environmental problems arise when chemicals and metal salts leaching from the landfill site become dissolved in underground or surface water, or when leaks occur of the explosive methane. It is produced as organic wastes decompose and is also a potent greenhouse gas.

Methods of tackling such problems include lining landfill sites with an impermeable membrane to control leaching, and monitoring possible leaks. Finding sufficient space for landfill has become difficult in some countries, particularly around major conurbations. The publication of official lists of abandoned former landfill sites or industrial dump sites has raised public awareness of this potentially dangerous legacy, and accidents arising from leaching and contamination have also helped to raise the alarm. Some sites containing toxic chemical wastes or low-level radioactive wastes have caused grave concern, particularly where they are located near drinking-water sources or residential areas.

Incineration

Incineration is increasingly used across Europe as an alternative to landfill for disposing of municipal waste. Emissions to air form the principal environmental impact, along with furnace ash residues, which themselves require disposal. Incineration offers the possibility of recovering energy to power electricity generators and/or district heating systems. The relatively high proportion of organic matter in municipal waste also makes it suitable for composting, although this practice is common in only a few countries, such as Denmark, Spain and Switzerland.

Hazardous wastes

Hazardous wastes probably represent one of the most intractable environmental problems in waste disposal. Most hazardous wastes are by-products of industrial processes which employ toxic substances. Incineration and landfill form the principal disposal routes. Physical, chemical and biological methods of pre-treatment are sometimes used before disposal.

WASTE MANAGEMENT

National policy on waste management in Europe seeks generally to ensure that waste is collected and disposed of in a satisfactory manner. Regulations usually require activities involving the treatment, storage, transport or disposal of waste to be undertaken by licensed operators only, who must adhere to certain minimum standards.

More stringent requirements may be imposed for operations handling hazardous waste and further measures introduced for certain types of waste considered to merit special attention, such as polychlorinated biphenyls (PCBs), oils, solvents and radioactive substances.

Minimising the generation of wastes at source by designing them out of industrial products and processes not only helps to limit waste of resources; it also reduces the quantities of waste going to disposal and the associated environmental difficulties.

Such thinking lies behind the theoretical 'hierarchy' of strategic objectives for waste management, endorsed by the EU.

Objective	Method (in order of preference)
1. Prevention	'Cleaner' manufacturing methods and product design leading to 'cleaner' products and processes.
2. Recycling and reuse	Research and development; improved collection and sorting; financial/market incentives.
3. Safe disposal	Higher standards of disposal; limits on hazardous waste disposal; environmental monitoring.
4. Regulating transport	Licensing; notification/consent procedures for movements; minimum safety standards.
5. Remedial action	Identification and clean-up of contaminated sites; development of clean up techniques.

Hierarchy of strategic waste management objectives

Theory has progressed further than practice in most cases. Although recycling rates have increased in many countries, particularly for glass and paper or board, total volumes of waste continue to increase. Some attempts are being made to implement the idea of 'producer responsibility', by encouraging or requiring industrial and commercial interests to develop systems to take back and recycle waste.

Packaging waste

Packaging waste – discarded product wrappers, boxes and moulded containers, mostly of plastic – makes up 30–35 per cent, by mass, of municipal waste in European OECD countries. It forms the subject of an EC Directive, and the growing volumes of packaging waste have led a number of countries to introduce schemes intended to limit the quantities going for disposal.

In Germany, the Packaging Ordinance of 1991 placed responsibility on producers to take back packaging after use and to recycle or reuse it. For retail packaging, targets of recycling 72 per cent of glass and metals and 64 per cent of paper, plastics and laminate by 1995 were set. German industry responded by establishing a company, Duales System Deutschland (DSD) to run a collection and separation system for packaging waste.

Subscribing manufacturers pay a fee to DSD and can then mark their packaging with a green dot to indicate that it will be taken by DSD, which ensures that the waste is recycled. Neighbouring countries complained that German exports of material collected by DSD disrupted their own markets for recycled material.

In France, a Decree introduced a mandatory scheme for limiting packaging waste in household use, with effect from January 1993. Producers or importers are required to take back and recover packaging or belong to an approved body to undertake this function for them. The Eco-Emballages company was established to discharge this obligation, charging a fee to producers and importers in return. It has a target of recycling 75 per cent of packaging waste by 2003.

In Belgium, a voluntary agreement was signed in 1991 between the Flemish regional government and relevant trade associations, with targets for waste reduction and recovery. This was followed by a national scheme established by industry, FOST-PLUS and the imposition of tax penalties on excessive packaging.

Agreements have also been established (with varying terms and targets) in The Netherlands and Austria. In the UK, industry has been encouraged to develop voluntary initiatives and was requested in July 1993 to prepare a plan to recover 50–75 per cent of packaging waste by 2000.

International measures

International policy has concentrated on regulating transfrontier shipments of waste under measures introduced by the OECD, EU institutions and various regional treaties and agreements dealing with specific sea, river or land areas (see below).

In addition, the Basle Convention on the Transboundary Movements of Hazardous Wastes and their Disposal came into force in May 1992. It places some restrictions on international movements of certain potentially hazardous wastes by air or water. However, the high costs of disposal in industrialised countries encourages some producers to seek cheaper alternatives, for example in CEE or 'developing' countries.

SEAS AND INLAND WATERS

The dumping of wastes in Europe's seas and inland waters has turned reaches of major rivers and some offshore waters into pollution zones. The Baltic, the Mediterranean and the North Sea all suffer from chronic pollution problems as a result of waste dumping at sea, on land and in feeder rivers, while waterways such as the Rhine, the Scheldt and the Danube rank amongst the world's dirtiest rivers.

The eight countries bordering the North Sea are all set, by their own admission, to fail to meet the 50 per cent target for reducing (by 1995) inputs of surplus agrochemicals and farm wastes, and of more than 40 chemical substances listed as 'toxic, persistent or bioaccumulative' (tending to accumulate to lethal levels in animals), controls which they agreed to in the London Declaration issued at the North Sea Conference in 1987.

A further North Sea ministerial conference at The Hague in 1991 repeated these expressions of concern but added little of substance to the range of measures proposed to deal with the problem. Slack laws governing pollution releases into open waters have long encouraged industrial operators to regard the sea as an easy option for waste disposal. Some governments have declared a vested interest in allowing this form of disposal. The UK, for instance, continues to allow the dumping of more than a million tonnes a year of untreated sewage sludge off the Thames and Tyne estuaries.

Water quality in the Scheldt, a river shared between Belgium and The Netherlands, consistently falls below basic safe standards, as industrial pipelines dump an estimated 40 to 60 tonnes a year of halogenated hydrocarbons, the most toxic of industrial solvents, directly into the Scheldt and thence into the sea.

Some 400,000 tonnes of waste or spilled oil a year enters the Sea's waters every year, as a consequence of operating discharges from British and Norwegian drilling rigs, from procedures used to swill out empty tanker vessels and as run-off from land-based refineries and port facilities. Major tanker accidents have also added their share, the latest occurring in 1993 when the *MV Braer* foundered off Shetland.

During the 1980s the effects of pollution on the sea's wildlife triggered a growing concern from environmental pressure groups. Oil and tar slicks were seriously affecting marine and bird life, and in 1988 and 1989, two thirds of the entire population of Common Seals inhabiting the North Sea died as a result of an unidentified virus (that some marine biologists believed might be linked to high levels of PCBs, toxic residues left behind when certain plastic waste products break down in water). Dolphins and porpoises, once common throughout the North Sea, are now rarely sighted. Such disappearances may signal the inability of the sea's ecosystems to support these sensitive 'indicator species' of wild mammal.

Fish stocks have been seriously diminished by overfishing, and some of the remaining catch is unmarketable on account of tumours and sores thought to be caused by contact with toxic wastes. Conflicts continue to grow between the fishing industry and land-based manufacturing industries which the fishermen are convinced have spoiled their livelihood. The dumping of waste 'fly-ash' from power stations and waste incinerators has turned parts of the seabed off North-East England into a wasteland, bereft of marine life, and fishing fleets in these areas have shrunk accordingly.

The problems of the North Sea are echoed in some of Europe's other, more enclosed seas, such as the Baltic and the Mediterranean. The latter suffers further from the inability of coastal resorts to raise the performance of sewage treatment facilities to cope with the annual influx of up to 100 million tourists.

There are, however, signs that the situation is beginning to improve, albeit patchily, in many of Europe's most polluted rivers and bays. Quality standards are holding steady or gradually improving in bathing and fishing waters, in response to EU regulations and regional agreements such as the Mediterranean Action Plan. Water quality has improved in a number of UK rivers since the establishment of a National Rivers Authority to regulate industrial discharges from the late 1980s.

Recent years have seen the re-emergence of otters and salmon in the waters of the river Thames, from which they were virtually wiped out by pollution discharges in the 1950s. Water quality standards in the Rhine have risen perceptibly every year since 1987.

Many of the problems arising from waste disposed in Europe's waters, however, remain, and, moreover, a completely new crop of problems is only now beginning to emerge in the East as the countries of Central and Eastern Europe begin for the first time to tackle the state of their waters, and to bring them in line with EU requirements.

WASTE RECYCLING

Recycling both industrial and municipal waste has become an established industry in its own right and a popular form of public participation in environmental management in many European countries over the past 25 years. Recycled materials now constitute more than half the raw materials used in paper and board manufacture in the EU, substantially reducing forestry inputs for this purpose.

The amount of municipal solid wastes and household garbage recycled in Britain has doubled over the past four years, from 2.4 per cent in 1989 to over 6 per cent at the beginning of 1994. The number of bottle banks for recycling glass has risen over a similar period from fewer than 500 country-wide to more than 10,000 today. More than 20,000 voluntary groups around the country now collect aluminium cans for recycling – a source of fund raising income worth a potential £36 million (around $56m) a year.

Recycling plastic wastes remains a key requirement, as some of the most potentially hazardous substances that enter the waste stream arise from the breakdown of plastic (especially PVC) materials at raised temperatures in dumpsites, landfills or incinerator plants. These substances include dioxins and furans which, though produced only in minute trace amounts on any single site, are many times more toxic than most chemical wastes. (The accidental release of the dioxin TCDD from a factory in Seveso, Italy in 1976, afflicted hundreds of local residents with the painful and disfiguring skin disease chloracne for more than two years after the event.) Furans have potent and proven carcinogenic effects if inhaled or ingested by humans or other animals.

Safe methods of reprocessing plastics have been developed but have yet to be widely used. There is still little demand for recycled products, and the sorting of plastic wastes from other rubbish is extremely labour intensive. There are just three large-scale plastics recycling plants operational in the UK today.

Environmental pressure groups continue to insist that recycling methods and 'end-of-pipe' waste processing procedures used in industry are not, in the last analysis, the best way to deal with wastes. The onus, they assert, is on industrial designers and engineers to devise new products that give rise to fewer harmful by-products or residues in their production, use or disposal.

Although some dismiss such calls as too idealist, certain industries and corporations have already introduced pollution prevention programmes into production processes. In many cases, such schemes make financial sense, too, reducing raw material inputs and re-using by-products that formerly had to be disposed of at growing expense as more air and water quality regulations came into effect. Policy makers have encouraged such initiatives by refining and endorsing 'green labelling' schemes for 'environmentally friendly' products. An EU-wide scheme is already in place, even though reliable criteria that can be used to quantify descriptions as loose as 'environmentally friendly' have proved hard to establish in practice. Nonetheless, talk of industry's environmental 'burden' is gradually being supplemented by a new vocabulary of environmental challenge and opportunity among Europe's industrialists. Private 'green investment' schemes and trusts investing in non-polluting companies and corporations have lent financial weight to this trend.

EIAS AND ENVIRONMENTAL AUDITS

Over the past 25 years there has been a tenfold increase in the number of European organisations offering technical consultancy services to industry in such forms as environmental impact assessments (EIAs) or waste management audits. The techniques and standards applied in environmental auditing of existing industries are not universal and a key future policy need will be to set agreed parameters for these services, making it possible – in effect – to audit the auditors so that a measured degree of faith can be placed in the results of their scrutiny.

Environmental impact assessments are usually undertaken in order to judge the safety and acceptability of industrial and other development proposals before their outset. They can follow a set pattern of assessments of the proposed production process from the extraction of raw materials and the transport of inputs and finished goods to and from the factory gate, to the use of the end-product by the consumer, the disposal of by-products of manufacture and the final disposal or re-use of the product at the end of its lifespan. For each stage, investigators model or forecast the positive or negative impact these procedures are liable to have on the air, soil or water, on living ecosystems and the diversity of plant and animal life in habitats surrounding the production site and on the quality of human life in immediate or 'downstream' vicinities. The objectivity of EIAs remains a matter of some dispute; it is an unusual EIA that comes up with recommendations that can be endorsed by all who hold a stake in the fate of proposed developments, especially in the case of major public works like highway construction projects.

Environmental audits are applied to existing industrial operations. They can adopt a similar systems approach to chart the flow of production processes and collect data on the mass balance or budget of all materials introduced into and produced by the process under scrutiny, including waste by-products and processing inputs such as lubricants and solvents. Calculations can then be made of, among other things, waste emissions, and pilot tests may be run to bear out the results in a contained way. On the basis of this information, consultants can then offer recommendations on ways to substitute low-waste for high-waste solutions to manufacturing needs. In many cases, companies find that solutions lie not so much in 'technological fixes' as in changing attitudes among the plant management and workforce. Many companies that have undergone an audit find that it helps them achieve savings in running or capital costs, as low-waste processes often turn out to be energy-saving or labour-saving, too. They can also win the company extra goodwill in industrial relations and in the marketplace.

9

Agriculture and Forestry

Apart from some fragments of natural or near-natural habitat found, for example, in Scandinavia beyond the Arctic Circle and in parts of southeast Europe, the nature of Europe's landscape has been determined mostly by humans' habits of land-use, starting with a general wave of deforestation in the Neolithic period.

It is almost impossible to know the extent to which past land management has affected Europe's biodiversity (its complement of naturally occurring genes, species and ecosystems). Our knowledge of extinctions is generally limited to impacts on larger species, such as mammals like the sabre-toothed tiger. Although widespread deforestation and drainage are likely to have caused similar losses amongst smaller animals and in the plant kingdom, little information exists on them, and they will probably remain unquantified.

Several important 'natural habitats', with associated species and ecological processes, have evolved artificially – as a result of past human land management systems. For example, most of Europe's treeless moorlands, fens in the Netherlands, the chalk downs of southern England, many French forests and large areas of Mediterranean *maquis* (scrubland) owe their existence to ancient systems of livestock grazing or woodland management.

Today, Europe's seminatural habitats vary in provenance between those which are almost wholly artificial to others that have something approaching a natural ecological dynamic. Domestic mammals have frequently replaced wild herbivores in maintaining treeless areas, whilst artificial aquatic habitats, such as canals, drainage ditches, reservoirs and ponds have often taken the place of natural wetland areas.

HISTORICAL DEVELOPMENT

It is sometimes assumed that land-use methods developed only slowly for hundreds of years until modern farming and forestry technologies brought sweeping changes in the late twentieth century. But this is an oversimplification. Although there are examples of land management systems that can be traced back unchanged for centuries, such as transhumance and the Alpine farming systems that survive in parts of Central Europe, most areas have been in sometimes erratic, but more or less constant, flux for hundreds if not thousands of years.

Until fairly recently, the overall trend was for farmland to replace forest cover – once the dominant vegetation over most of Europe. However, for various reasons, this trend has gradually and partially been reversed in recent years, resulting in a marked increase in forest cover. Forest restoration in Austria and Switzerland, for example, is mainly in response to concerns about soil erosion, avalanches and flooding. Economic forces have led to the abandonment of slash-and-burn agriculture, a rapid increase in forest cover, and a booming forest industry in Sweden and Finland. More recently, forest expansion in Spain, Portugal, Hungary, Ireland and the UK has been the result of government policy, and is thus mainly state- rather than market-driven.

The density of forest cover as a percentage of land use varies throughout Europe, from 1 per cent in Iceland to 66 per cent in Finland. In general, agriculture still accounts for more land than forestry outside Scandinavia, and in the European Union as a whole, trees cover only 24 per cent of the land area.

AGRICULTURE

In some parts of Europe, agriculture is undergoing a formative process of intensification while elsewhere increasing amounts of land are being abandoned. Within EU member states, the shape of agricultural development is largely determined by the Common Agricultural Policy, or CAP.

The post-war period in Europe saw a rush for intensification, encouraged by planners intent on national self-sufficiency in food and other resources. Fertilisers and pesticides, new methods of livestock rearing and new crop varieties were brought into use. As a result, many long-established woods, scrubland and hedges of were cleared for cultivation, and pastures ploughed up to make way for arable production.

The Common Agricultural Policy

The Common Agricultural Policy was one of the linchpins on which the European Community was founded. Its objectives are strategic, agricultural and social: to ensure self-sufficiency for EC Member States (a particular concern in the post-war years); and to maintain the welfare of rural populations. The CAP relies on artificial pricing mechanisms to guarantee farmers adequate remuneration for their products and to protect domestic food production through a range of trade barriers to overseas competitors.

The CAP certainly benefits small farmers, particularly in countries in Southern Europe, such as Spain, where agriculture remains an important

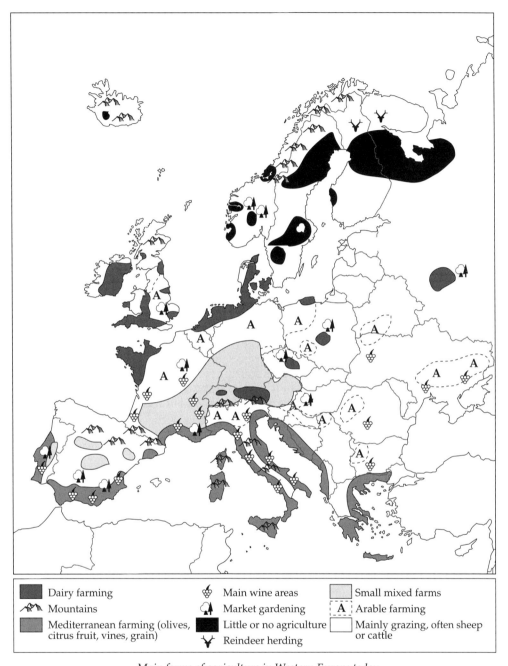

Main forms of agriculture in Western Europe today

source of income and employment compared to the UK, for example. However, critics argue that the negative effects of the policy far outweigh these advantages, and cite:

- the high levels of farm production encouraged by the CAP – levels far in excess of EU requirements;

- the intensification of production, and its resulting environmental and social impacts;
- the skewing of the benefits to rich, large-scale farmers, who are often better equipped to take advantages of EU subsidies than their smaller competitors;
- the intricate web of bureaucracy, rules and regulations governing the CAP, which render the system open to fraud; and
- the dumping of surpluses on the world market – often with disastrous economic consequences for farmers in 'developing' countries.

The sheer cost of the protectionist policies of the CAP became a matter of increasing concern to governments of Member States in the early 1990s. In 1993, for example, the CAP cost 35 billion ECU out of the total EU budget of 65.5 billion ECU. The CAP was thus a major sticking point in the Uruguay Round of the GATT, dragging negotiations on for over a year and, at one point, threatening the negotiations with complete collapse.

In the past few years, some controversial changes have been agreed, including provisions for opening up European markets; cutting cereal prices by about one-third (to bring them more in line with world levels); and encouraging set-aside schemes, whereby farmers agree not to use certain amounts of land for agricultural purposes.

Although these moves have created concern about reduced support for farmers, changes within the CAP are likely to affect the type rather than the existence of farm support, at least in the short term. In general, the emphasis within the CAP is shifting from price support to direct payments to farmers. This shift in itself has important implications for agriculture and the rural environment. More fundamental changes in support may be forced on the EU as membership is opened to CEE countries.

INTENSIFICATION

During the past 50 years, the rapid intensification of agriculture and forestry management has created profound environmental changes in rural Europe. Intensified farming or forestry depends on using heavy inputs of pesticides, fertilisers and other agrochemicals to boost yields per unit area, together with heavy machinery to reduce labour inputs. Intensification also involves the introduction of a small range of high-yielding crop varieties, and the expansion of field sizes to maximise the efficient use of farm machinery.

The unwanted effects of intensification, including persistent surpluses of some food products and increased susceptibility to pests and diseases in uniform 'monoculture' systems, have begun to prompt a reaction in favour of 'extensification'. This involves a return to more labour-intensive, value-added and 'organic' systems of production. Changes in technology, international trade and socio-economic conditions, are resulting in yet further modifications to regional trends in land use. In Central and Eastern Europe, widespread privatisation is bringing about changes that may have an equally profound impact on the future condition of the land.

Future trends

At the end of the 1980s, with the adoption of a series of extensification measures by the architects of the CAP, environmental groups were optimistic that 50 years of intensification might soon be reversed, heralding a return to more traditional farming methods.

Several years on, however, there has been only limited progress in this direction. In Western Europe, the following main trends are emerging:

- In many areas, particularly those with more fertile soils and good climatic conditions, most farming continues to be intensive, although larger farms are obliged to set aside some of their land under CAP rules introduced in 1992 to avert surplus food production. In these cases there has been a general fall in use of chemical fertilisers, achieved partly through more frugal and efficient application techniques.
- In some regions of marginal arable potential – especially where farms are small, incomes are low and there is a ageing and falling agricultural population – farming is being abandoned altogether in many instances. This trend may accelerate in the future.
- In other regions, including some of those areas of special need targeted by governments for special grant schemes, widespread extensification has occurred, often based on diversifying crop mixes and land uses to produce speciality products for niche markets. Yet intensification persists in many areas, often thanks to funding made available under the CAP. In southern Europe in particular, grants are still made available for intensifying land use, for example for draining wetlands in Greece, removing ancient olive groves in Portugal and irrigating pasture in Spain. Moreover, support for land consolidation is still intact in many northern countries.

Some changes in the CAP are likely to increase pressure on the environment, for example, the encouragement of the production of maize as a livestock feed and the reinforcement of incentives to overgraze upland areas with sheep in some countries. On the other hand, lower prices may lead some farmers to cut their use of inorganic fertilisers and pesticides.

Agriculture in Central Europe

In Central and Eastern Europe, political changes also have begun to impinge on agricultural policy. Privatisation and the potential for new markets in the West might be expected to result in the widespread intensification of farming. Yet current economic hardships are, if anything, having the opposite effect. Subsistence farming to meet family needs and bartering or exchange of goods outside formal markets have taken priority in the survival stratagems of many needy farming communities.

Marginalisation and Abandonment

As farming becomes less economically attractive, there is a growing tendency for people in many areas to leave the land. Often the result has simply been a continuing increase in average farm size, as surviving farms buy up their smaller neighbours. The concentration of holdings has been particularly marked in parts of the UK, France and Germany.

In other areas, including Sweden, Finland, central Spain and northern Greece, the widespread abandonment of farming has resulted. In Portugal, 245,000 hectares of agricultural land are classified as unused, including 36 per cent of Algarve farmland.

In Hungary, economic problems threaten to put an estimated 150,000 hectares out of production by the year 2000. In the Pyrenees, abandonment means that some mixed farming systems are reverting solely to pasturage.

In some cases, farm abandonment leads to the reversion of land to forest or scrub through natural succession. However, much marginal farmland is converted to forestry plantations or water reservoirs, or used for leisure purposes, such as hunting or golf. The environmental impacts of these uses can be damaging for nature conservation.

EXTENSIFICATION

Extensification, or the reduction in the intensity of land use, has followed an erratic course in modern Europe, and the land areas affected are smaller than might be expected. Sometimes extensification has been driven by changing attitudes, both in the farming community and amongst consumers seeking more 'natural' food products. In Germany, Scandinavia and elsewhere, organic farming has grown rapidly, carved out a small niche in European markets and attracted enough attention to require a new EU Directive controlling certification. However, it remains a minor segment of European production, with the area under organic production in European countries ranging from 1–3 per cent of total farmland.

Other forms of extensification have been stimulated directly by the policy and planning interventions of governments and the EU. These include the designation of Environmentally Sensitive Areas (ESAs) in some countries, where farmers may be paid by governments to practise less intensive methods, and Nitrate Vulnerable Areas where incentives for reducing fertiliser use and related measures are being brought in to reduce water pollution. However, some environmental grants, such as those awarded for hedge and woodland management and for the protection of wetlands, encourage, but do not require, steps towards less intensive agriculture.

The situation in CEE countries remains confused. Although the intensive and poorly controlled use of agrochemicals has been the norm over sizeable areas of Central Europe, economic pressures are resulting in a marked reduction in several countries. Within Poland, for instance, a halving of average farm income between 1989 and 1993 has led to the use of nitrate fertiliser being reduced to a third of its former level across most of the country's rural areas.

Environmental Impacts of Agriculture

Against this background of change, many adverse environmental impacts still arise from agriculture. As some problems recede, new ones emerge to take their place (see table opposite). In addition to the landscape changes evident over large areas of Europe, three major issues currently give cause for special concern: soil erosion, pollution and habitat loss.

Environmental issues	Associated agricultural issues
Human health consequences of residues in food, water and soil	Use of pesticides, fertilisers, hormones, vetinary products and feed supplements
Loss of fauna and flora	Abandonment of 'traditional agriculture', use of pesticides and fertilisers, drainage, habitat destruction
Surface and groundwater pollution, including marine	Excessive applications of fertilisers and livestock waste pollution leading to leaching to groundwater and run-off to surface waters. Poor management of farm wastes, such as manure and silage liquor
Air pollution	Ammonia and nitrous oxides derived from intensive livestock units, slurry spreading, burning of straw and wastes
Aquifer depletion, salinisation of soils and water supplies	Excessive or poorly managed irrigation
Soil compaction, erosion and pollution	Inappropriate farming methods, eg ploughing of vulnerable soils, use of heavy machinery, spreading of sewage sludge contaminated with heavy metals
Biotope loss	Drainage, land consolidation, land improvement, removal of hedges and ditches, abandonment of traditional systems
Landscape change	Increased field size, mechanisation, removal of traditional features, abandonment of farming, construction of new buildings, monoculture
Odours	Intensive livestock farms, spreading of wastes

Agriculture and the environment – key concerns

Soil erosion

Although the focus of much environmental concern during the 1930s after the dustbowl disasters in the US, the threat of soil erosion is now often underestimated. Soil erosion is caused by certain highly mechanised agricultural systems and techniques, the expansion of farmland onto vulnerable soils and steep slopes, the use of artificial fertilisers to the exclusion of organic nutrients, and by continual arable cropping without fallow rotations.

Almost 300,000 square kilometres of land in the European coastal zone of the Mediterranean have been classified as undergoing at least moderate desertification, affecting the livelihoods of about 16.5 million people. In Spain, 33 tonnes of soil per hectare per year are lost in many areas. More than half of Portugal's main grain-producing area is held by the National Soil Service to be too vulnerable to soil erosion to support continuous farm production.

In wetter areas of Europe, soil erosion has generally been dismissed as a minor problem, although losses substantially greater than soil renewal rates have been recorded in Germany, Belgium and the UK.

Pollution

A more widespread and visible form of damage is caused by pollutants that are accidentally or deliberately released into the environment. Whilst the most serious effects stem from a variety of water pollutants, in some areas air pollution from farming is also important. Freshwater and shallow coastal marine ecosystems are also suffering as a result of agricultural pollution.

Major pollutants include:

- chemical pesticides used against insects, molluscs, worms, fungi and weeds;
- soluble inorganic fertilisers, particularly nitrates and phosphates, which leach into groundwater systems or run off into ditches and streams; and
- solid or liquid animal wastes, which drain directly into watercourses or leak, or are illegally dumped, from slurry tanks and stores.

The total nutrient load in European waters has increased dramatically in the last few decades. In the EU, for example, the use of synthetic nitrogen fertiliser increased from 3 million tonnes a year in 1960 to 9 million tonnes in 1991.

In Denmark, it has been calculated that out of 805 000 tonnes of nitrogen fertiliser used every year, only 360,000 tonnes is absorbed by crops, with 445,000 tonnes released to the environment.

In Belgium, the Netherlands, Denmark, France, Germany, the UK and elsewhere, intensive livestock production has led to problems of manure disposal, with a doubling of average load over the same period. In the Netherlands the figures are much higher.

Excessive levels of nutrients affect groundwater and freshwaters, leading to eutrophication and fish kills; in the marine environment, eutrophication is most problematic in shallow seas such as the Baltic. Nitrate levels in drinking water exceed EU limits for 5–6 per cent of the population of Germany, and are expected to be exceeded for up to 25 per cent of people in the Netherlands within the next few years.

More than 300 million kg of pesticides are sold in the EU every year, and consumption levels in other parts of Europe are also high. The total quantities applied in agriculture have stabilised, or even decreased, in the last few years, principally because more potent pesticides have been introduced.

Growth has continued in some Mediterranean countries, with over 47,000 tonnes of active ingredients being applied in Spain in 1991 and over 97,000 tonnes in France. Recent attention has focused on the control of certain pesticides most frequently found in drinking water, including two commonly used herbicides, simazine and atrazine.

In some parts of the continent, atmospheric pollution from agriculture is also significant. Pollutants include the greenhouse gas methane, emitted from decaying animal wastes, nitrous oxide from soils fertilised with synthetic nitrogen fertilisers or animal manure, and acid rain from ammonia evaporating from manure and slurry. Up to 20 per cent of acid rain may be due to ammonia emissions from farming in areas like Flanders, The Netherlands, Denmark and northern Italy.

The spray drift of pesticides is also important from a human health and wildlife perspective. Studies in the UK show that the drift of pesticides into hedgerows can reduce by two-thirds the survival rate of partridge chicks by killing the insects available to them as food. Losses of other life forms, such as flowering plants, fungi, butterflies and other insects have also soared.

Wildlife and habitat loss

Perhaps the most profound impact of agricultural changes on the environment of Europe is the steady elimination in almost every country of semi-natural habitats that serve as important wildlife 'reservoirs'. Losses include:

- semi-natural and ancient forest remnants, and hedgerows;
- low-intensity pasture, particularly in upland districts;
- permanent pastures and ancient meadows;
- steppe pasture;
- lowland heath and some upland moors; and
- wetlands, coastal meadows, and marshes.

Habitat loss affects most European countries. Ireland has lost over 16 per cent of its hedgerows since 1936. Some 97 per cent of the UK's ancient meadows have been ploughed up in the last 50 years. Land reclamation threatens 80 per cent of coastal meadows in Portugal, and Spain has drained some 60 per cent of its wetlands in the past 25 years.

Since many species classified as being of European importance now rely on semi-natural habitats managed by farmers, the future use of less intensive agricultural systems is also important for the fate of nature conservation. The loss of long-established human traditions and livelihoods (such as woodland craftwork enterprises) is often tied in with habitat loss; such cultural impacts can also be hard to absorb.

The Outlook

With the recent GATT agreement and the 1992 reforms of the CAP now in place, new directions are being set for agricultural policy in Europe. Increasingly it is recognised that agricultural subsidies should be directed towards environmental and social goals.

In most European countries, a new generation of policies is being developed to provide payments to farmers who adopt more environmentally sensitive practices. However, these schemes still apply only to a small fraction of agricultural land. Intensive crop or animal husbandry, accompanied by set-aside, remains the dominant pattern on most farms.

The door is now open to more sustainable forms of agriculture and policies that place greater emphasis on good environmental management and less on maximising production. Nonetheless, many farmers will react cautiously to this changing climate of opportunity unless it is underpinned by solid economic incentives. They will need to be persuaded that it is a turning point for agriculture rather than a passing phase brought about by temporary food surpluses in Europe.

FORESTRY

Forestry in Europe is controlled largely by individual governments and, in some countries, by private landowners and companies. Although efforts are being made to set international environmental policies for forestry, these remain weak and have had minimal effect in practice. Unlike farming, forestry does not form the subject of a unified EU management strategy, although a number of grants available under the CAP are having an increasing influence on choices affecting forestry in Europe, particularly in the Mediterranean region.

Although widespread privatisation is introducing a more free-market approach to forestry in CEE countries and in certain Western European countries such as the UK or Finland, government influence on forest policy remains potent throughout Europe. In the past few years, there have been several attempts to introduce regional or international environmental policies for temperate forests. Significant in the European perspective was a Council of European Ministers on Forests, organised jointly by the governments of Finland and Portugal and held in Helsinki in June 1993. Countries participating in the meeting signed four resolutions, aimed, amongst other things, at promoting sustainability in forest management and offering support to forestry in CEE states. Environmental groups lobbied hard to tighten up environmental aspects of the resolutions, with limited success. The initiative has since developed into the Helsinki process, which is formulating a series of criteria for good forest management.

Environmental Impacts of Forestry

Environmental problems in Europe's forests tend to be matters of quality rather than quantity. Critical issues include the loss of old-growth forests, intensification of management in secondary forests and a decline in tree health due to several factors, including pollution.

INTERNATIONAL FOREST INITIATIVES

At a time of mounting concern about forests around the world, there have been several other international initiatives that could affect European forests.

A major international conference organised by the Conference on Security and Cooperation in Europe, and held in Montreal in 1993 has developed into the Montreal Process, looking at temperate forest management.

Tentative steps towards a Global Forest Convention were toned down by the UN Conference on Environment and Development (UNCED) in 1992 into a set of 'non-binding Forestry Principles' but they have since been brought up again in international forums by various governments.

In addition, the Commission on Sustainable Development (CSD), set up in the wake of UNCED, planned a major meeting on forests for April 1995.

The result of the Helsinki meeting, the CSD and other developments is likely to be an increased emphasis on multiple-use forestry. In Europe, where, with a few exceptions, native forest no longer exists, the main debate will be aimed at improving management in secondary and semi-natural forests to reflect wider environmental and social issues.

Until quite recently it had been assumed by many that Europe's forests were relatively free of environmental problems. The area under forest was increasing and foresters in many countries believed that they had achieved sustained yields of timber. But since the early 1980s, problems have mounted steadily. While forest cover continues to increase, an overall decline in quality has been flagged as a serious concern.

Many forests have undergone a loss of authenticity (see below), measured in terms of both their composition of species and of the natural ecological processes they harbour. Environmental benefits, including soil conservation and contribution to the stability of hydrological systems, have also declined.

Tree health and the health of other forest species has also degenerated in some areas, partly because of air pollution. Along with these ecological issues, the emphasis on timber production has meant that some forests have declined in social worth, for example, in their capacity for non-wood products and their recreational and aesthetic value.

TREE HEALTH

An apparently novel form of forest decline was noticed in Germany during the late 1970s and early 1980s. Similar damage was noticed in other countries, particularly in Central Europe, and latterly also in southern Scandinavia and most of Western Europe. Characteristically, the trees worst affected are of old growth or are isolated or exposed at the edges of stands. Most commonly, damage takes the form of a general decline in vitality and loss of health, and has several distinctive features depending on species, including discoloration of leaves, premature leaf and needle fall, erratic twig branching and loss of crown density. In many cases the syndrome is fatal.

Identifying the causes of the decline has been, and to some extent remain, a matter of controversy. The onset of damage was often associated with extremes of climate, including drought, but effects continued beyond the period usually associated with temporary water-stress. It is now generally agreed that such decline is caused by multiple stress, including the effects of air pollutants, combined with other factors such as drought, cold, pests and diseases, nutrient deficiencies, bad forest management and the impact of agrochemicals.

A variety of air pollutants is believed to play a part, although their relative importance differs between countries. For example, in Germany the main pollutant appears to be low-level ozone, while in the industrial regions of the Czech and Slovak Republics sulphur dioxide from coal is thought to be the main culprit.

Nitrogen oxides, abundant in traffic exhausts, also feature near highways and urban centres. Air pollution can affect many other forest species, including epiphytic lichens and mosses, vines, some flowering plants and sensitive invertebrates living on trees and on the forest floor.

According to measurements by national assessors working to guidelines laid down by the UNECE, in 1991 over 22 per cent of trees suffered from defoliation exceeding 25 per cent in Europe and the former USSR. Decline affected an estimated 6 billion cubic metres of timber. Damage on this scale could cause long-term changes in forest composition and reduce the average age of surviving trees.

Authenticity

From an ecological point of view, it is important that the landscape contains forests of widely differing ages. In most natural landscapes, the majority of the forest will be old, with trees hundreds of years in age being common. The presence of dead and dying trees is important to create habitats for certain dependent species plants and animals.

Yet today, under intensive forest management, these so-called old-growth forests are in danger of disappearing, taking with them those species that rely on old trees for their survival. Despite the large area of forest cover in Western Europe, only around 1 per cent of the whole is old-growth forest. Natural forests are arguably under greater threat here than almost anywhere else in the world, despite a growing stock of trees. For example, Finland has 60 per cent forest cover, making it proportionally one of the most heavily forested countries in the world. But only 1–2 per cent of this is old growth, and in the south of the country old forests have been reduced to fragments of a few hectares.

In some CEE countries, old-growth forests survive in greater areas but many are now coming under intense pressure from private forestry operations, often carried out by foreign timber companies. Old-growth or semi-natural forests are particularly at risk today in the Baltic states, notably Latvia with its biologically rich 'wet forests', Poland, Bulgaria and the former Yugoslavian states, where ancient eastern beech forests are being logged out.

Intensive Forestry vs Multiple-use

Many managed forests, including some traditional forestry systems such as coppice with standards, can still be important and varied habitats for wildlife. Yet over the last few decades forests have, like farmland, been managed with increasing intensity, and a comparable range of environmental problems has resulted.

Plantations and intensively managed forests are changing the nature of forests, narrowing the variety of the tree species mix and genetic variation within species. An expanding area of Europe is covered with conifer monoculture and in many countries, including the UK and Denmark, the majority of these plantation trees are of non-native species. Forest management can destroy wildlife habitats, increase soil erosion, cause damage to water systems, trap acid pollutants from the atmosphere, change the balance of fire in the system and increase pest and disease attack.

Forest fires are a major concern in many Mediterranean countries, particularly Spain, Italy, France and Greece. Although causes are complex, methods and species used for planting new woodland often increase susceptibility to fire.

The use of agrochemicals against tree pests is another concern in some areas, especially in the East; it undoubtedly plays a role in reducing biodiversity.

Finally, much modern forestry is also very unsightly, with dense and impenetrable tracts of conifer plantation that cover uplands and heath. Aesthetic and cultural objections to modern forestry are often the deciding factor when new planting schemes are barred from long-established open landscapes.

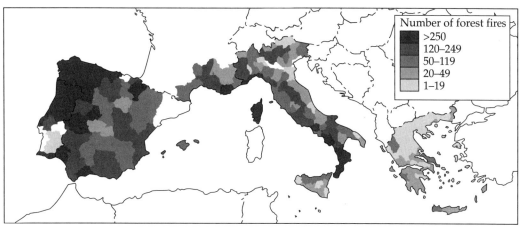

Average number of forest fires, 1989–91

The Outlook

There are now signs of growing public commitment to environmentally sensitive forestry in Europe. Increasing areas of forests in some countries, such as Finland and Sweden, are owned by people mainly as a recreational resource, and management is therefore less intensive. The wider benefits of forestry beyond timber production are being more generally recognised. The advisory Forestry Principles adopted at UNCED state (in Section 2b) that forests should be:

> **... sustainably managed to meet social, economic, ecological, cultural and spiritual needs [in such forms as] ...wood and wood products, water, food, fodder, medicine, fuel, shelter, employment, recreation, habitats for wildlife, landscape diversity, carbon sinks and reservoirs and ...other forest goods, products and services.**

Whether this good intention is translated into positive management improvements in Europe will depend on how successfully these issues are promoted in international policy forums, how seriously national governments respond to these developments, and the extent to which NGOs and other independent interest groups succeed in shifting opinions.

More environmentally responsible forestry will only be achieved if forest managers and local people are convinced of the case for change. In the short term, continued threats to Europe's remaining old growth forests, which constitute a vital reservoir of species and natural ecosystems, is probably the most critical issue confronting environmentalists and policy makers in the continent today.

10

Nature Conservation

RANGE OF HABITATS

Despite its relatively small area and long history of human occupation, Europe contains a wide range of natural habitats, including examples of most forms of temperate and boreal vegetation. Land cover varies from icecap and tundra in Greenland and Scandinavia, through to arid semi-desert in the Mediterranean and subtropical laurel forest on the Canary Islands and Madeira.

In between are forests, wetlands, bogs, plains, high mountain environments and a range of marine ecosystems. Thousands of different habitat types exist, many of which have still not been properly classified or studied.

Habitats in Europe can be divided into three main biogeographical zones: Mediterranean, Macronesian (chiefly south-west Spain and Portugal and islands off the coast of Africa) and Euro-Siberian, the latter being by far the largest. Within these regions, specialised Alpine environments are found wherever the land is high enough. Despite their smaller sizes, the Mediterranean and Macronesian zones are particularly diverse, and the latter has a high number of endemic species.

Europe is ecologically connected to other areas of the Earth, particularly the 'Old World'. Migratory birds provide links deep within Africa and Asia. Connections with the northern polar regions mean that Europe shares species and habitat types with Arctic North America, including some of its largest mammals such as the brown bear.

Perhaps more than anywhere else on Earth, the European landscape has been influenced by human occupation often over thousands of years. Despite a scarcity of completely or virtually natural areas, Europe still supports a wide variety of wildlife and natural ecological processes.

Some wild plant and animal species remain confined to scattered fragments of wilderness areas; others have adapted to highly modified environments, such as pastures; and a third group lives in habitats that would not exist without human intervention, but support wild species. Such habitats include canals, drainage ditches, reservoirs, tree plantations, railway embankments, harbour piles, old quarries, abandoned buildings, mines and industrial wasteland.

THREATS TO WILDLIFE HABITATS

Changes in agriculture, forestry and population distribution, coupled with mass tourism, urban sprawl, expanding transport systems and continuing industrialisation, are all having a major impact on the survival of wildlife. Species loss occurs mainly through loss of habitats, but other factors, including pollution, hunting and unsustainable resource use, also have significant effects. Within the EU, 95 per cent of flora and fauna species have been squeezed into less than a quarter of the land area.

	World		Europe	
	Total number	*Threatened (%)**	*Total number*	*Threatened (%)*
Mammals	4327	16	250	42
Birds	9672	11	520	15
Reptiles	6550*	3	199	45
Amphibians	4000	2	71	50
Fish (freshwater)	8400*	4	227	52
Invertebrates	>1 000 000	?	200 000*	?
Higher plants	250 000*	7	12 500*	21

* estimates

Relative number of threatened species (according to IUCN categories)

Agriculture

Agriculture has probably had the greatest impact on habitat loss over Europe as a whole. Semi-natural habitats, such as ancient water meadows and wetlands, have been drained, while irrigation systems have blocked or diverted natural watercourses. Pollution from animal wastes and surplus fertilisers has run off into surface waters, causing eutrophication in many lakes, ponds and rivers. Pesticide poisoning has directly killed off wildlife species or affected their ability to breed. Agrochemicals have also taken their toll, including pesticide spray drift. Although much of this damage is past history, it continues to spread, notably in southern EU member states and some CEE countries.

Specific impacts on wildlife have been recorded in many areas. The decline in snipe in Western Europe has been linked to the disappearance of rough grazing areas through drainage, forestry and improvement. Losses of the green frog and fire-bellied toad have been linked to agrochemicals, and fertiliser use on dry grasslands has threatened sensitive species such as wall and sand lizards in Southern Europe. The intensification of grassland management has been identified as an important cause of decline in almost half of Germany's butterfly species.

Forestry

Some 90 per cent of heaths in The Netherlands, Denmark and Wallonia (Belgium) have disappeared, and between 1915 and 1985, Spain's grassland contracted by 60 per cent. Forestry is the other major land-use in Europe. Damage to forest wildlife has occurred in many cases when natural and old-growth forest has been replaced by modern plantations or regrowth, and the intensive management of secondary forest. These processes can destroy important forest habitats such as peatlands, reduce important habitats such as dead wood and soil humus, and increase the risk of fire. Intensification of management, combined with air pollution, may have been a factor in the decline of tree cover (see Chapter 9). In Central European countries such as the Czech and Slovak Republics and parts of Poland, trees have succumbed in great numbers to the ill-effects of air pollution.

Some semi-natural habitats, particularly heaths and moors, have been seriously threatened by inappropriate afforestation programmes, which have caused decline, for example, in bird species such as hen harriers, merlins and golden plovers. Afforestation and fencing of plantations has also disrupted the migration patterns of red deer in Scotland. Some forest habitats in Europe are now seriously threatened, including forest edges, treeline forests in several mountainous countries, wetland forests and natural lowland conifer forests.

Tourism

Habitat loss and pollution from tourism and settlement are significant in many coastal regions and areas of natural beauty. Hotel and tourism facilities have destroyed large areas of natural coastland in the Mediterranean, especially the Adriatic and Aegean.

Species at risk include the Mediterranean monk seal, perhaps the most endangered seal species in the world, and several species of marine turtle. Increased pollution from tourism has affected fisheries and other marine life. Tourism has also increased the risk of forest fires, particularly in drier areas such as Portugal and Italy, so that in some places fires are now an important cause of habitat loss. Mountain regions have been affected by ski developments, causing land erosion and disturbance of animal populations. Lake and river habitats are being affected by leisure boat traffic.

Transport

Transport systems threaten wildlife by destroying habitats, and through pollution and direct road-kills. The rapidly expanding European road network affects many important wildlife sites, particularly as new highways are usually routed to avoid human settlements. All roads increase the fragmentation of habitats; many invertebrate species cannot easily cross roads, so local populations are isolated and their survival threatened. The essential movement of even amphibian and mammal species can be effectively blocked by a medium-sized road.

Road and other traffic also releases significant amounts of air pollution, and road vehicles are thought to be a major factor in the rise in (low-level) ozone pollution that has contributed to tree die-back in Germany and elsewhere. Cars kill thousands of mammals, birds and reptiles every year. They are, for example, believed to be responsible for around 50 per cent of barn owl deaths in the UK, and are a major cause of mammal death in Spain's Doñana national park.

Industry

Industrial development continues to make inroads into natural habitats through landtake and in the effects of air, water and soil pollution. Releases of acidifying air pollutants by industry, including sulphur and nitrogen oxides, have caused significant damage by acidifying freshwaters. This has led to a consequent loss of fish, amphibians and other aquatic life, particularly in Scandinavia. Acidification also damages soil life, tree-living lichens and mosses, and susceptible members of other plant and animal groups, including some flowering plants and invertebrates.

Recreation

Increasingly, recreation has an impact on wildlife. Hunting for sport is controlled in many countries, but can cause widespread damage, particularly when migratory animals are shot. The toll on migrating passerine birds in Spain, France, Italy and Malta and elsewhere has international significance, approaching 3 million deaths a year. Demand from domestic gardening has resulted in threats to wild bulbs in Turkey and parts of Greece. The trade in lowland peat, cut for potting compost, means that all but a few lowland peat bogs have been destroyed in the UK, but cutting continues.

MARINE WATERS

Marine ecosystems have suffered increasingly as a result of human activities, principally overfishing, and pollution.

Overexploitation of fish stocks has been a growing problem for some years. Cod and herring catches in the Northeast Atlantic are currently thought to amount to four times the sustainable take. This abuse unbalances marine ecosystems, putting other species at risk. Overfishing of the sand eel in northern Britain is responsible for a disastrous failure to breed among several auk species, including the guillemot and puffin, as the birds rely on the fish as a major food source. Some fishing nets also trap and kill seabirds in large numbers.

Attempts to remedy shortfalls in the fish harvest by investing in aquaculture (fish or shellfish farming) have created problems of their own, releasing additional pollution in the form of pesticides and waste products, for example. Boats also give rise to oil spills or leaks, chemical pollution and litter.

THE TOLL OF TOURISM

In 1952, the Spanish island of Majorca attracted 132,000 foreign visitors. It seemed like a large number then, but by 1982 the annual influx of tourists was four million and in 1990 it approached six million. Although the visitors have made tour, travel, hotel and property businesses wealthy, many ordinary residents of tourist destinations like Majorca often resent the disruption of lifestyles and the disfiguring 'visual pollution' that large-scale recreational tourism has brought. At local festivals around Spain effigies representing tourists and tourism have been ritually burned.

The nature of tourism in Europe is changing too. During the early 1990s, recession caused an almost 30 per cent decline in departures to Mediterranean destinations, mainly from other European countries. Resort areas like the Costa Brava were hit by unemployment and a general economic slump. Many local authorities took steps to boost the appeal of coastal environments and clean up bathing waters by improving wastewater treatment facilities, motivated as much by commercial necessity as by EU water quality Directives. 'Green' tourism holiday developments (often sited inland) became a market growth area in many countries, while efforts to promote internal tourism redoubled: state-subsidised seaside holidays were, for example, offered to Spain's senior citizens from 1991.

New environmental factors also entered the picture. In Britain alone, one thousand new cases of skin cancer, caused by exposure to the sun, are reported every year, many proving lethal. Depletion of the ozone layer in the stratosphere is expected to give rise to ever-higher incidences of skin cancer in future. This trend may slow the growth of beach tourism in Southern Europe and encourage rural leisure activities distributed more generally around the region, especially in uncrowded highland areas. While it may take some pressure off Europe's favourite playgrounds, it may simply shift it elsewhere.

According to the Countryside Commission, more than 18 million domestic visitors already flock to Britain's countryside for recreation on a typical summer Sunday. Total visitors to listed attractions, such as stately homes and gardens, sporting venues or country festivals, topped 1.6 billion in 1990. Many National Parks now report serious soil erosion problems caused by the sheer number of visitors.

Elsewhere, golf courses and other leisure developments have drained water tables and drastically altered the landscape. Conflicts between farmers and citizens over rights of regular access to ordinary farmland are also brewing in many parts of Europe. Travel and tourism constitute the world's largest industry, worth more than $3 trillion a year, and its biggest employer, too. But at what cost to nature?

NATURE CONSERVATION INITIATIVES

In recent decades, public concern over threats to wildlife has been reflected in a rapid increase in official and voluntary nature conservation initiatives throughout Europe. These initiatives range from protest and direct action against developments such as road expansion and mining, through the acquisition of land for conservation, to international treaties and agreements affecting species protection and management of land. Until recently, most action was taken by individual governments but efforts are now being made to coordinate action on a regional or global scale, particularly in respect of networks of conservation sites.

International Initiatives

Since the late 1980s, there has been a proliferation of conservation initiatives at regional and international level. In 1990, a European Ministerial Conference on the Environment adopted a European Conservation Strategy, which outlines broad conservation aims and is intended to provide a framework and stimulus for national policies.

Changes in CEE countries have opened the way for a range of new responses, including an Environmental Action Programme for Central and Eastern Europe, adopted at an intergovernmental meeting in Lucerne in April 1993. Nine countries are now party to a Danube River Basin Environment Programme and all the Black Sea states are cooperating on a Black Sea Environmental Programme. The World Conservation Union (IUCN) has also drawn up an East European Programme that creates a framework for several site-specific projects in the CEE region and IUCN's Commission on National Parks and Protected Areas is working on an Action Plan for Protected Areas in Europe.

Within the EU, the Fifth Action Programme on the Environment makes reference to the protection of nature and coastal zones, and most Member States are party to a range of global conservation treaties, including the Ramsar Treaty for the protection of wetlands important as waterfowl habitats; the EC Habitats Directive; the Convention on International Trade in Endangered Species (CITES); and the Convention on Biological Diversity. Several other international developments, including agreements about fishing and marine pollution, also have important implications for conservation.

National Government Responses

International conservation developments are influenced by national policies, and vice versa. Governments set policies, buy or set aside land for nature conservation and national parks, and help shape developments in land use, particularly in respect of agriculture and forestry. In some countries, local authorities also play an increasingly important role in land management.

Most European countries produced detailed statements of environmental policy for the UN Conference on Environment and Development in 1992, although the extent to which they reflect reality and action varies widely between states. In general, conservation policy is more fully developed in Western European than in CEE countries, although there are notable exceptions. Some countries, including Sweden, Finland and the UK, have carried out detailed surveys of threats to biodiversity and wild habitats; elsewhere, our knowledge of the status of wildlife and threats to it, remains fragmentary. Plans required under the Convention on Biological Diversity may help address such problems.

Non-Governmental Initiatives

The role of NGOs is increasing in importance at national and international levels alike. National conservation NGOs are already well established in most Western European countries, reflecting diverse interests and high levels of public support. For example, in The Netherlands, one of Europe's most conservation-conscious countries, roughly one person in ten is an active supporter of WWF, the World Wide Fund for Nature. However, NGO networks remain poorly developed in some Central and East European states.

Groups of NGOs have begun to collaborate on specific projects within and between countries. In the UK, for example, conservation NGOs meet regularly through the Wildlife Link and Scottish Wildlife Link organisations, and have already collaborated on a biodiversity action plan and a peat conservation campaign. In Sweden, since the early 1980s, four organisations have funded a Secretariat on Acid Rain.

Such umbrella groups are multiplying at an international level as well. Birdlife International is a consortium of bird conservation societies which cooperate closely in Europe. The European Environmental Bureau is an umbrella group for environmental NGOs with a particular interest in EU legislation and policies. WWF has national organisations in 13 European countries, coordinated through an international secretariat based in Switzerland; most other European states have WWF project offices or NGOs with particular affiliations to WWF.

Other NGOs with an international brief include the German Europäische Stiftung für Naturerbe, the Federation for National and Nature Parks of Europe and the European Union for Coastal Conservation.

Towards a European Ecological Network

Strategies for nature conservation can take a variety of forms. The traditional, and still most direct, response to a conservation problem is to set aside land specifically for the protection of species or habitats. Europe already has an extensive national park and nature reserve network, although the degree of protection varies between countries.

In the UK, 'national park' refers to an area with some special protection and tighter planning restrictions, but it is far from a strict nature reserve and most such areas are under farm and forestry management. In other countries, such as Switzerland, the same designation refers to strictly protected areas where public access can be limited.

More recently, the idea that nature conservation can take place effectively through the designation of a number of isolated sites has come under criticism. The first response to this has been the development of the principle of a European ecological network, EECONET, first proposed by the government of the Netherlands in 1991. The principles behind EECONET are that conservation policy should shift in emphasis from species to habitat protection, from a focus on sites to a focus on ecosystems and connections between them, and from national to international measures.

The EECONET proposal is that these aims would best be realised by developing a network of sites so that the full range of Europe's habitat types is represented and the most important areas of each are conserved. Linkages or corridors would be developed between sites to assist migration and dispersal, not only to prevent further damage, but to encourage positive management steps to further enhance ecosystem stability, particularly where ecosystems have been damaged.

To provide such a framework, special skills, facilities and knowledge will be required, among them a full understanding of natural systems, joint international arrangements for designating and protecting sites, and sound methodologies for identifying areas that merit conservation.

New thinking in conservation policy also recognises that protected sites cannot, on their own, provide sufficient protection for biodiversity. Sites have to be supported by changes in management policy over more extensive areas of land, including sizeable tracts of forestry and agricultural land. Changes in farming support within the EU's CAP might contribute to this goal. Indeed, in some countries the emphasis is now turning away from strictly protected areas to the management of land for dual or multiple roles, which include a conservation element. This can include initiatives, and important secondary responses such as planning and, for example, multi-purpose forestry, high nature-value farming, fisheries management, green tourism and pollution control.

At the moment, many of these wider concepts are still at a planning stage, or within the realms of theory. The extent to which they will be taken up in practice depends, to a large extent, on the success of Europe's environmental NGOs in keeping conservation on the public agenda. It will also depend on how far conservation organisations succeed in linking their aims with those of local people concerned to maintain livelihoods and a fulfilling range of economic activities, particularly in farming areas. Such a approach will only flourish if conservation is seen less as a specialised, separate activity and more as an integral part of other land management systems.

PART II

COUNTRY PROFILES

Albania

Area	28 748 km^2
Population	3.4m
Urban	34%
Rural	66%
Capital	Tirana (251 000)
City populations	6 > 50 000; 1 > 100 000
Economy	
GNP per capita	US$623 (1990)
GDP change	−40% (1989–92)
Climate (Tirana)	
Average daily max and min	31/17°C (July)/12/2°C (January)
Annual precipitation	1 353mm
Land-use cover	
Agriculture	42%
Forest	36%
Other	22%

Albania lies in southeastern Europe, bordering Montenegro, Serbia and Macedonia to the north and east, and Greece to the south-east. It has a coastline of 450km on the Adriatic and Ionian Seas. Much of the terrain is mountainous, with around half the country above 500m, rising to more than 2500m in the north and west. Around two-thirds of the population live on the coastal plain.

INSTITUTIONS AND POLICY

Albania is divided into 26 administrative districts *(rreth)* and under the new constitution adopted in April 1991 a National Assembly of 140 deputies is directly elected by popular vote.

Decree No 7451 of 1991 set up the Committee for Environmental Preservation and Protection (CEPP) as the primary national government body responsible for environmental matters. The CEPP is attached to the Ministry of Health and Environment Protection and is assisted by five advisory commissions. Under the same ministry, the Sanitary Inspectorate and the Institute of Hygiene and Epidemiology are responsible for waste disposal and air and water quality.

A new Law on Environmental Protection was adopted in January 1993 as the legal framework for environmental regulation. It bans hazardous waste imports and requires environmental impact assessments to be undertaken for development projects and plans. Detailed regulations on waste, air pollution, protected areas, coastal water, groundwater and pesticides are being drawn up.

AIR POLLUTION

Industrial sources have accounted for much of the country's air pollution, notably metalworks, thermal power stations, chemical and cement factories. Total annual SO_2 emissions have been estimated at 267 000t from industrial plants, including 150 000t from copper smelting at Kukës, Rubic and Lac. Other major sources of air pollution are the large metallurgical complex at Elbasan, power stations at Korçe and Tirana, petrochemical works at Fier and Ballsh, cement factories in Vlorë, Elbasan and Fushe-Kruje (100 000t of dust annually), and chemical plants in Durres, Tirana and Vlore.

Locally produced fuels tend to have a high sulphur content (3–6 per cent in lignite, 4–5 per cent in coal and as high as 7 per cent in bitumen), resulting in high emissions of SO_2 when burned in thermal power stations. Little pollution abatement equipment appears to be installed, and industrial technology is often old. Acute damage to vegetation has been recorded near some works. Air quality has been poor in and around the major industrial centres, although industrial plant built since 1988 should be located at least 4–5km from residential areas. The widespread use of wood or low-quality coal for domestic fuel adds to pollution, in urban areas in particular; air pollution from transport has not been a major problem because of the relatively few motor vehicles in use.

WATER RESOURCES AND POLLUTION

Albania has abundant water resources, with relatively high precipitation, and an annual river flow of around 37bn m³. There are more than 240 lakes, including large lakes on the country's northern and eastern borders. Virtually all drinking water comes from groundwater sources. However, supplies are often erratic and losses through the ageing distribution network have been estimated at 40 per cent. Tirana and Durres have the country's only drinking water treatment works. Over 70 per cent of water abstractions are used in agriculture, principally for irrigation.

Water pollution results primarily from industrial and sewerage discharges. Some factories have effluent treatment equipment, which is generally rudimentary and sometimes out of service. As there are no sewage treatment works in the country, river quality tends to be poor downstream of industrial and urban centres. The river Shkumbini has been amongst the worst affected, receiving around 35m m³ of waste water annually from the Elbasan complex, containing phenols (1.2t), ammonia (180t), sulphates (450t), copper (3t), cobalt (6t), magnesium (1.2t), zinc (1.5t) and cyanide (1.6t). The Gjanica, Lana, and Kiri are also severely affected. Discharges from oil wells are estimated at around 1.4m m³ per year. Effluent from mining activity and run-off from agricultural land adds to the pollution of surface waters, and in some cases groundwater, too.

SOLID WASTE

Domestic waste has not posed significant environmental problems in Albania, principally because of the low level of arisings, except in the larger cities. However, hazardous and other industrial waste is collected and landfilled alongside domestic waste, often in sites which are not regulated; leaching into groundwater and rivers is thus thought to be a hazard in some areas.

The mining and processing of minerals produce large volumes of hazardous waste, as do oil refineries and other industrial installations. Large and uncontrolled dumps have developed near some plants, liable to wind-blown pollution and posing a threat to groundwater.

NATURE CONSERVATION

Albania has a rich variety of flora and fauna, with a diverse range of habitats. Of an estimated 3100–3300 vascular plant species, 24 are found only in Albania. Coastal and wetland areas are of importance for birds, including the Dalmatian pelican. Otter appear abundant, and the brown bear population in the northern mountains has been estimated at 500–800. Loggerhead turtle are thought to lay their eggs on the Ionian coast.

Protected areas are established under the 1951 Law on Hunting (No 1351) and the 1963 Law on Forest Protection (No 3349). Seven national parks cover more than 23 000ha, although these appear to have suffered significant damage. Six forest national parks cover around 8000ha, and in addition 25 nature reserves (35 000ha) have protected status; some fishing and hunting is permitted in the less strictly protected reserves.

ENERGY

Albania has extensive reserves of oil, gas and coal, enabling a high degree of self-sufficiency in fuel supplies. Some high-quality coal is imported, as most indigenous production consists of lignite, of lower calorific and higher sulphur content, used in thermal power stations and domestic heating. Around 2mt of lignite were produced annually in the late 1980s, mostly from deposits in central Albania, falling to 1.1mt in 1991. Oil production declined from over 2mt of crude in the late 1970s to just under 1mt in 1992. Refining is centred on Ballsh and Fier. Annual production of natural gas is estimated at around 600m m^3; the gas is used to produce fertiliser and to generate electricity, as well as being piped for domestic use in some cities. Concessions for oil and gas exploration along the Adriatic coast were offered in 1993 to encourage foreign capital investment, and five international oil companies were due to begin offshore drilling. Tenders were also invited for a recovery enhancement programme in existing oilfields in the south of the country, to include $5m for clean-up work.

Hydroelectric stations provide around 80 per cent of the national electricity supply (4,100GWh in 1989), three plants on the river Drin alone having a combined generating capacity of 1.35MW. Some electricity is exported to the former Yugoslavia and Greece, although low river flows reduced output in 1990.

AGRICULTURE

Agriculture accounts for around 30 per cent of net material product and 50 per cent of employment in Albania. A privatisation programme, initiated in July 1991, is intended to distribute agricultural land to around 380 000 owners, with an average farm size of 1.5ha. Over half of the 700 000ha of arable land is irrigated, which spreads contamination where water is diverted from polluted rivers. The area of land used for agriculture has more than doubled since 1945, reflecting the increase in population; hillsides have been terraced, forests cleared and wetlands drained to provide more land for cultivation. Soil erosion has become a problem in upland areas, affecting around 10 per cent of arable land. Livestock numbers have been growing, putting pressure on grazing land in some areas. The increased and uncontrolled use of fertilisers and pesticides has led to the pollution of surface and groundwater, particularly in the plains. In recent years, shortages of agricultural inputs like seeds and fertiliser began to affect cereal output, which fell by almost 60 per cent in 1991–92; only half the country's arable land was sown in spring 1992.

FOREST RESOURCES

Around 36 per cent (1m ha) of the country's land area is forested, mostly in mountainous areas, where oak, beech and black pine predominate. The principal threat to forests is the increasing volumes of wood which have been extracted to supply the construction, mining and timber industries, as well as fuelwood for domestic use; over 90 per cent of households depend on wood for heating and recent shortages of other fuels (eg paraffin) have helped exacerbate treecutting around populated and accessible areas. Depite afforestation programmes, the total area of forest has fallen by around 20 per cent since 1950, and the annual level of wood extraction has been estimated at three times the sustainable yield. Acid rain is known to affect forest health close to major centres of pollution.

TRANSPORT

Albania's road network extends to around 21 000km, although some roads are of poor quality, particularly in the northern mountains. Motor vehicles have not been a major source of air pollution, since private ownership was illegal until 1991. Estimates of the total number of motor vehicles range from 10 000 (1987) to 14 500 (1970), although the number of cars in the principal cities has increased greatly since 1990. Bicycles and mules are in widespread use. The country has around 500km of railways, and the main shipping port is at Durres, with others at Vlorë, Sarandë and Shengjin. Rinas (near Tirana) is the main airport.

Austria

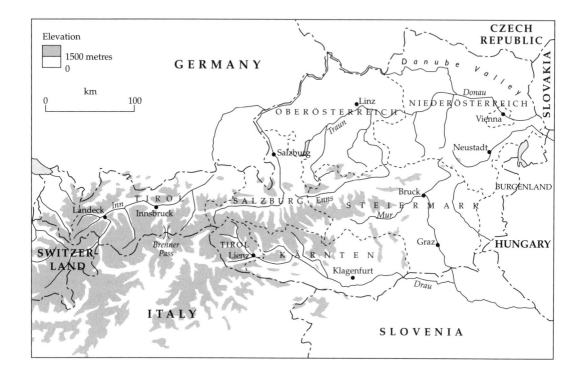

A ustria lies in southern central Europe, bordering eight other countries, and is amongst the most mountainous states of the continent. The Alps dominate the west of the country, rising to over 3700m; lower land is found in the north and east, along the Danube valley.

INSTITUTIONS AND POLICY

Austria is a federal republic and has a National Council of 183 directly elected members. The nine states *(Länder)* send representatives to the Federal Council. The states have extensive environmental competences and, in some cases, are responsible for the implementation and enforcement of federal legislation. The Federal Ministry for Health and Environmental Protection was established in 1972, and in 1984 an amendment to the federal constitution made explicit reference to environmental protection. The Federal Ministry for Environment, Youth and Family was created in 1977 and the Federal Environment Agency in 1985.

The Agency is responsible for scientific research and monitoring. An Ecofund was established in 1987 by merging the existing environment and

Area	83 855 km²
Population	7.82m
Urban	59%
Rural	31%
Capital	Vienna (1.53m)
City populations	8 > 50 000; 3 > 200 000
Economy	
GNP per capita	US$20 140 (1991)
Climate (Vienna)	
Average daily max and min	25/15°C (July)/1/–4°C (January)
Annual precipitation	660mm
Land-use cover	
Agriculture	41%
Forest	46%
Other	10%

water management funds; it provides grants and loans for environmental projects. Overall, environmental investments accounted for 2.7 per cent of GDP in 1991. New federal legislation on environmental information and on environmental impact assessment (EIA) should help to bring Austrian environmental legislation into line with that of the EC, which Austria joined on 1 January 1995.

AIR POLLUTION

Emissions of SO_2 and particulates were reduced sharply during the 1980s; total SO_2 emissions fell from 195 000t in 1980 to 49 000t in 1990, and emissions of particulates from 75 000t in 1980 to 39 000t in 1989. These reductions were achieved primarily in the energy and industry sectors, and reflect the introduction of limits on the sulphur content of fuels and regulations on emissions from combustion plant.

Emissions of NO_x fell much less rapidly, from 233 000t in 1980 to 209 000t in 1990, as traffic growth offset reduced emissions from other sectors; motor vehicles account for around 70 per cent of total NO_x emissions. Vehicles also contributed to an increase in volatile organic compound (VOC) emissions during the 1980s. Another factor in this increase was a greater domestic and industrial use of solvents, reaching 416 000t in 1988 (366 000t in 1980). CO_2 emissions reached 63.3mt in 1991.

Austria has an extensive air quality monitoring network, with 100–180 measuring points for different concentrations of pollutants. Ambient levels of SO_2 have generally declined since the 1970s, although concentrations remain high, exceeding $200\mu g/m^3$ (30-minute average) in some industrial and urban areas, particularly in the winter. The same limit value for NO_2 is also exceeded in some built-up areas, and levels have not changed much in recent years. Austria suffers from high concentrations of low-level ozone compared to other countries; recommended levels were exceeded at most monitoring points in 1990 and levels above $400\mu g/m^3$ (30-minute average) have been measured in the summer months, around Vienna.

The Clean Air Act for Boiler Plant (1988) came into force on 1 January 1989 to replace the Furnaces Emission Act; all boilers above 50kW thermal output require a permit. Under the Smog Alarm Act, which came into force on 1 June 1989, federal authorities may restrict polluting activities if specified air quality standards are breached. An amendment to the Motor Traffic Act introduced vehicle emissions limits which, in effect, required all new cars to be fitted with catalytic converters from 1 October 1987; almost 30 per cent of cars had catalytic converters by the end of 1991. Leaded regular petrol was prohibited in 1985 and leaded super petrol in November 1993. The sulphur content of fuels is also being reduced, and from October 1995 a limit of 0.05 per cent sulphur by weight will apply to diesel oil as well as to petrol. A national CO_2 Committee was established in 1990 to develop a strategy to achieve Austria's target of a 20 per cent reduction in CO_2 emissions from 1988 levels by 2005.

WATER RESOURCES AND POLLUTION

The country is rich in water resources and its rivers and streams total more than 100 000km in length. Around 2.6bn m^3 of water are abstracted annually, over 50 per cent for industrial use, 31 per cent for domestic use, and 11.5 per cent for agriculture. 53 per cent of total abstractions, and 98 per cent of drinking water supplies, come from groundwater sources. Increasing consumption of groundwater by industry and agriculture has resulted in a fall in the water table in some areas, particularly in eastern parts, which receive less rain. In Marchfeld, for example, a prime cereal-growing area, the water table fell by 1.5m between 1966 and 1984. Groundwater is also contaminated by pollution from waste, industrial sites and from agricultural run-off; the large aquifer south of Vienna is no longer suitable for supplying drinking water. Elevated nitrate levels are of concern in some areas, particularly in the eastern half of the country.

The total load of organic pollutants from industry, discharged into watercourses, has been reduced from 17m population equivalents (PE) in 1979 to 2.7m PE in 1989. Paper and pulp industries and food processing accounted for 80 per cent of this total. The proportion of sewage receiving biological treatment has increased from 5 per cent in 1971 to 70 per cent in 1991; the major conurbations have plants with biological treatment. Surveys indicated that 27 stretches of river improved in biological quality between 1979 and 1989; nine deteriorated over the same period. It was intended that the water quality of every river should be fit for bathing by 1995.

Water pollution control is based on the Water Rights Act, which was amended in 1990. The Act contains general obligations to avoid the pollution of water bodies and provisions requiring the authorisation of discharges to water, abstractions and operations involving the handling of substances likely to cause water pollution.

SOLID WASTE

Total waste arisings were estimated at 44.12mt in 1992, including 26mt of mineral origin; 620 000t was classified as hazardous waste. In 1990 2.5mt of household waste was produced, including 440 000t collected separately for reuse and recycling. Of household waste, 67 per cent was disposed to land-fill sites (160), the remainder handled by three incinerators and 19 composting plants. Estimates in 1987 put the number of disused landfills at 4100 and of unauthorised dumps at 533. One incinerator in Vienna takes 60 000t of hazardous waste annually, plus 54 000t of sewage sludge; in addi-tion, there are nine plants for the chemical and/or physical treatment of hazardous waste. In 1990, 22 300t of hazardous waste was exported (mostly to Germany). A system for the separate collection of hazardous waste was introduced in 1984.

An amendment to the constitution in 1988 made the Federal Ministry of the Environment responsible for hazardous waste, whereas most other aspects of waste management are the responsibility of state and local authorities. Amendments to the Hazardous Waste Act have required the Federal Ministry's approval for hazardous waste imports and exports since 1989. Under the new Waste Management Act, which came into force on 1 July 1990, a national waste management plan is produced every three years (from 1992); the Act also provides the basis for further waste avoid-ance and recycling measures and the licensing of all waste collectors and handlers. Since January 1991 local authorities have been required to make separate collections of hazardous waste from households; toxic substances may no longer be discarded with the normal household waste. The Waste Dump Clean-up Act is intended to contribute, through a levy, to the esti-mated 10bn Schilling required to fund remediation work at 3500–4000 old landfill sites. A Federal Waste Exchange was established in 1974 to foster contacts between producers and potential users of recyclable waste.

NATURE CONSERVATION

There is a wide variety of landscapes within the country, from low-lying plains to extensive Alpine regions. Large areas of semi-natural habitat have disappeared in recent decades, as a result of drainage, intensive agri-culture and forestry, and housing, transport and tourism developments. Between 1946 and 1986 185 000ha of wetlands were drained, and in 1991 the national register of dry meadows listed 159 out of 918 areas as facing destruction. Austria's Red Data Book lists 409 vertebrate animal species and 2873 fern and flowering plant species; 234 and 1081 species respec-tively are endangered.

Nature conservation is primarily the responsibility of the state authori-ties; each state has adopted nature protection acts with provisions on species and habitat conservation and protected areas. Nature protection areas, the most strictly protected category, covered more than 375 000ha in 1991. Along with 1.35m ha of landscape protection areas and 135 000ha other protected categories, a total of 1.86m ha (22 per cent of national terri-tory) is under some form of legal protection. In 1991 there were three national parks, with a further three planned, together covering 270,000ha.

ENERGY

Austria relies on imports for over 80 per cent of its coal, oil and gas supplies. Domestic production in 1991 included 1.28mt of oil, 2.08mt of lignite and 1.33m m³ of gas. An oil refinery at Schwechat, near Vienna, handles indigenous oil production and oil imported via a pipeline from the Adriatic port of Trieste. Gas is imported principally from eastern Europe. Electricity generation is dominated by hydroelectric stations (around 70 per cent of total electricity production); the largest, Altenwörth, produces 1.95bn kWh annually. A nuclear power station was built in the 1970s at Zwentendorf (Lower Austria), but was not commissioned as a result of a referendum in 1978; the Nuclear Prohibition Act (1978) prohibits the use of nuclear fission for electricity generation.

AGRICULTURE

Agricultural production is concentrated to the north of the Alps, along the Danube valley and in the plains in the east of the country. Arable land covers around 17 per cent of the territory, meadowland and pasture 24 per cent. The total area of farmland has decreased by 420 000ha since 1956, and more than 50 000ha of arable land has been consolidated; 116 000 hill farms have been abandoned in the last 40 years. However, most farms are still small-scale units; over half of the 260 000 farms in Austria were under 10ha in area in 1990/91. A tax on fertiliser was introduced in 1986 to discourage excessive use, and other schemes are intended to support more extensive forms of production. A set-aside programme began in 1987.

FOREST RESOURCES

Forests cover 3.86m ha, 46 per cent of the land area, an increase of 0.25m ha since 1961. Conifers, primarily Norway spruce, make up around 75 per cent of forest cover; beech and oak are the most widespread broadleaved species. Of the country's remaining ancient woodlands, around 50 areas covering 1700ha are being designated as natural forest reserves. One-third of the forest area is classified as protective forest, because of its importance in protecting against avalanches, erosion and flooding. More than 800 projects were underway in 1992 to rehabilitate 230 000ha of protective forest areas, 75 per cent of which are considered to require attention. In general, however, Austria's forests appear to be in fair health; only 7.5 per cent of trees surveyed in 1991 suffered defoliation of 25 per cent or above, and 55 per cent were not defoliated; broadleaved species showed higher levels of damage than conifers. Air pollution is thought to be a contributory factor to tree damage, along with damage by pests, game and domestic animals; around 10 per cent of forests are used for woodland grazing.

The Forestry Act of 1975 contains measures intended to safeguard the sustainable use of forests, including obligations for reafforestation. Clear-cutting areas greater than 2ha is prohibited and requires authorisation above 0.5ha, and other provisions introduced limit values for the deposition of air pollutants; 19 per cent of sampled areas exceeded the sulphur deposition values in 1989.

TRANSPORT

Austria has become an important route for European transport crossing the Alps, as well as between western and eastern Europe. The volume of road freight handled increased by 600 per cent from 3.2mt in 1970 to 22mt in 1991; by comparison the growth in rail freight over the same period was only 18 per cent. Around 80 per cent of road freight in transit through Austria travels through the Brenner Pass (over one million lorries annually); the level of air pollution has become a major concern along this and other principal transit routes such as the Inn valley. A night ban on all heavy goods vehicles except low-noise ones was introduced in 1989, and negotiations with the EC resulted in a system of 'ecopoints' to limit movements of transit road freight; emissions should be reduced by 60 per cent by 2003.

Combined road/rail freight transport is also being promoted, with investment of 10bn Schilling planned by 1996. In 1991 there were 27 terminals for combined transport, which carried 12.3mt of freight. Rail links east to Hungary, the Czech Republic and Slovakia are also being improved. With these and other measures intended to promote less environmentally damaging transport, it is hoped to reduce emissions to air from the transport sector to 50 per cent of 1985 levels by 2000.

Belgium

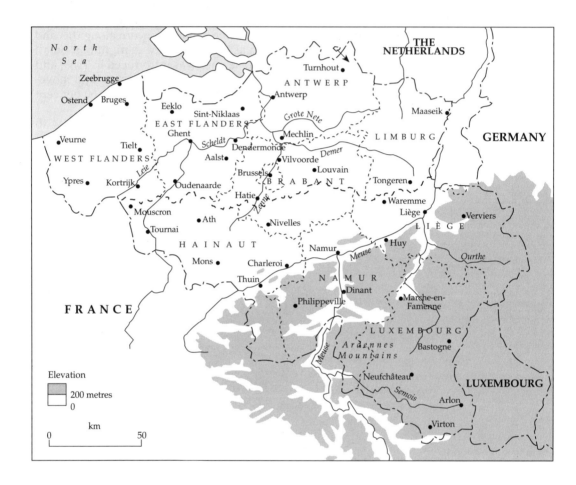

Belgium lies in northwestern Europe, with a short coastline on the North Sea, between France and the Netherlands. It borders Germany and Luxembourg to the south-east. The north of country is low-lying, dominated by the river Scheldt and its tributaries. The land rises to the south, reaching more than 600m in the Ardennes mountains.

INSTITUTIONS AND POLICY

Belgium is a constitutional monarchy, with an elected Senate and Chamber of Representatives (212 members). The three regions of Flanders, Brussels and Wallonia have a high degree of autonomy, includ-

Area	30 518 km²
Population	9.98m
Urban	97%
Rural	3%
Capital	Brussels (136 000; conurbation 0.95m)
City populations	7 > 100 000; 4 > 200 000
Economy	
GNP per capita	US$18 950 (1991)
Climate (Brussels)	
Average daily max and min	23/12°C (July)/4/−1°C (January)
Annual precipitation	855mm
Land-use cover	
Agriculture	46%
Forest	20%
Other	34%

ing legislative powers and responsibility for implementation with respect to environmental matters. The nine provinces and 589 communes have local competences where not otherwise regulated by regional or national legislation. In addition, there are three language communities (French, Flemish and German) with autonomy over cultural and 'personalisable' affairs.

The national Ministry for Public Health and the Environment takes responsibility for policy on environmental matters with a national dimension and in other fields not delegated to the regions (eg nuclear safety). The Institute of Hygiene and Epidemiology assists through scientific research and monitoring work. Each region has its own ministers, departments, agencies etc, with different arrangements in each region:

- In Flanders, the Administration for Environment, Nature and Rural Development (AMINAL) forms part of the Department of the Environment and Infrastructure, with four agencies covering different sectors.
- In Wallonia, the Directorate for Natural Resources and Environment is supported by an advisory council and consultative committees on waste and water
- The Brussels Institute for the Management of the Environment is the primary institution in the capital region.

The Interministerial Conference on the Environment was established in 1989 to improve coordination between national and regional ministries with environmental competences.

The regions of Wallonia and Flanders have both produced environment policy plans, and an integrated pollution permitting system came into force in Flanders in 1991; in Wallonia, separate permits apply for discharges to air, land and water. The environmental legislation of the European Community has influenced considerably the development of environmental policy in Belgium. Whilst EC and international relations are the responsibility of national government, the implementation of EC policy generally falls to the regions.

AIR POLLUTION

Annual emissions of SO_2 decreased from 840 000t in 1979 to 440 000t in 1987, as nuclear power stations replaced some fossil fuel ones, and low-sulphur oil was used more widely in place of coal. Emissions of NO_X fell less significantly during the early 1980s before increasing later, to 300 000t in 1990 (compared with 340 000t in 1979). The growth of road traffic made further improvements difficult. Average ambient concentrations of SO_2 fell significantly during the 1970s and 1980s, but air quality standards are sometimes exceeded in industrial centres, such as Ghent, Liège and Antwerp. Elevated levels of ozone have been recorded periodically, during the summer; hourly averages above $200\mu g/m^3$ were measured on 16 days during 1989. Emissions of CO_2 from power stations and industry fell during the 1980s, but were offset by increased emissions from mobile sources; CO_2 emissions totalled 133.4mt in 1990.

Air pollution control policy has evolved from the 1964 Air Pollution Act, which provided the basis for detailed measures to be introduced by decree. In practice, national and regional legislation has been shaped by EC legislation, including Directives on air quality and emissions from industrial plant.

WATER RESOURCES AND POLLUTION

Belgian territory drains into the North Sea, primarily via the rivers Meuse and Scheldt and their tributaries. Surface water supplies most of the country's water needs; water abstractions totalled 9.03bn m^3 in 1980, of which over 90 per cent came from surface water sources. Groundwater sources accounted for around two-thirds of drinking water in 1985, although the proportion supplied from groundwater was set to increase.

Surveys indicate that the biological quality of most rivers is poor, particularly in and around major cities and industrial areas in the northern half of the country, despite improvements in some parameters; chemical plants account for a considerable proportion of total emissions. Discharges of municipal wastewater form another important source of pollution; less than a quarter of the population was served by treatment plants in 1980. In the case of groundwater, aquifers relatively close to the surface are worst affected. Nutrient leaching from manure is a particular problem in Flanders, where 30 per cent of wells contained water with nitrate concentrations above 50mg/l; groundwater quality in Wallonia appears more satisfactory. In some areas groundwater is contaminated by heavy metals, such as cadmium and zinc from former industrial sites in northern Limburg. Sampling of bathing waters in 1992 showed 90 per cent of sea sites and 60 per cent of freshwater sites complied with the EC Directive's mandatory values for coliforms.

Nationally, the pollution of surface and groundwater is regulated through two Acts of 26 March 1971; key EC Directives were implemented by means of a further Act in 1983, and water quality objectives laid down in a Decree of 4 November 1987. Many matters are dealt with at regional level.

SOLID WASTE

Total waste arisings in 1990 were estimated at 34.3mt, over 75 per cent of which was generated by manufacturing industry. Annual arisings of municipal waste are thought to have increased by around 10 per cent during the 1980s, to 3.4mt in 1990. The majority of waste is disposed to landfill or incinerated; in Flanders, 55 per cent of household waste is incinerated and 8 per cent composted. Around 380 000t of toxic waste is generated annually in Flanders and Wallonia. Imports and exports of waste increased from 1.56mt to 1.97mt between 1988 and 1990. Belgian legislation on waste management is based largely on EC Directives. A range of ecotaxes was agreed in 1993, to be applied to disposable drinks containers, razors and cameras, paper, industrial packaging and batteries.

NATURE CONSERVATION

Belgium's fauna and flora include 65 mammal, 169 bird and 23 reptile and amphibian species, and 1415 species of vascular plant. A considerable proportion of species appear to be threatened or in decline, including 40 per cent of mammal and 50 per cent of bird and vascular plant species.

According to species distribution maps, the position of wildlife in Wallonia appears stronger than in Flanders, where industrial, urban and infrastructure developments have had a concentrated impact. The Condroz plateau and Fagne-Famenne lowlands south of the Sambre and Meuse probably constitute, with the Ardennes, the most important areas for nature conservation in Belgium.

The Nature Conservation Act of 12 July 1973 forms the basis of legislation at national level, with decrees on specific measures, including species protection. The act also establishes three categories of protected areas, nature reserves, forest reserves and nature parks, and provides for private nature reserves to gain official authorisation and thus become eligible for state subsidies. The Hautes Fagnes-Eifel nature park was established in 1978 and covers 67 850ha. By 1987 there were also 324 nature reserves (18 860ha) and plans for 16 more nature parks. Six Ramsar Convention wetland sites have been designated, covering 7945ha (1992).

ENERGY

The structure of Belgium's fuel supply has changed greatly during the past 40 years. In 1950 the country was heavily dependent on coal, its primary indigenous fuel, which accounted for 89 per cent of gross domestic energy consumption. However, coal production has fallen drastically in recent years, from 5.59mt in 1988 to 0.64mt in 1991, and the last mine closed in 1992. Imported oil, gas (mostly imported) and nuclear-generated electricity became more important energy sources. Primary energy supply increased from 40.3m toe in 1970 to 50.6mtoe in 1991, by which time solid fuels accounted for 20 per cent of the total, gas for 17 per cent, and oil for

41 per cent. Belgium's nuclear power programme expanded to seven reactors, which produce around 60 per cent of electricity generation. Plans for further nuclear power stations were suspended in 1988.

AGRICULTURE

Agriculture accounted for less than 2 per cent of GDP but around 9 per cent of export earnings in 1991. The total area of agricultural land fell by 270 000ha between 1960 and 1985; there were 1.35m ha of agricultural land in 1991, including 0.63m ha of permanent grassland.

Livestock accounts for two-thirds of agricultural production, principally pork, beef and dairying. Intensive pork and poultry farms are concentrated in Flanders, where the large quantities of livestock manure, particularly in the northwest, give rise to emissions of ammonia and the leaching of nutrients into surface and groundwater.

Cereals, potatoes and sugar beet are the main arable crops; vegetables and fruit are also important. The low plateaux both sides of the rivers Sambre and Meuse form the most naturally fertile areas, where large cereal farms are situated. The annual consumption of nitrogen fertiliser fell slightly during the late 1980s, to 186 000t in 1990, whilst pesticide consumption increased by 14 per cent between 1985 and 1989 (measured by weight of active ingredients). An ecotax on pesticides was agreed in 1993, applying at different rates to three categories in order to encourage the use of less hazardous formulations.

FOREST RESOURCES

Forest cover amounts to around 610 000ha, divided almost equally between coniferous and broadleaved species. Cover is highest in the south, around 80 per cent of the forest area being found south of the Sambre and Meuse; more than half of the province of Luxembourg is forested. The timber cut was estimated at 2.8m m³ in 1985, compared with annual forest growth of around 5m m³. The forest condition survey in 1992 indicated that 16.9 per cent of trees sampled suffered 25 per cent or more defoliation; conifers appeared worse affected than broadleaved species.

TRANSPORT

Belgium has one of the densest transport network in Europe, particularly for rail, motorways and inland waterways. The rail network extended to 3460km in 1991, having contracted from 4165km in 1988. The road network covered 142 000km, including 1670km of motorway. There are more than 1500km of navigable waterways, including 860km of canals; they carried 18 per cent of total goods tonnage in 1989.

Antwerp, on the Scheldt estuary, has become the second largest port in Europe, handling around 100mt of freight each year; Ghent and Zeebrugge are also major ports.

Road traffic volumes continue to increase; the number of passenger cars in use grew from 2.61m in 1975 to 3.97m in 1991.

Bulgaria

Bulgaria is situated in southeastern Europe and is bordered by Turkey, Serbia, Macedonia, Greece and, mostly along the Danube, by Romania, with an eastern coastline of 370km on the Black Sea. Of the land area, 28 per cent lies above 600m. The Balkan mountains, running east–west through the country, rise to over 2300m and divide the plains bordering the Danube from those in the south-east. The Rhodope mountains lie to the south-west and reach 2900m. The climate is continental, but influenced by the Mediterranean in the south and the Black Sea in the east.

INSTITUTIONS AND POLICY

A new constitution was adopted in July 1991 and includes two articles (15 and 55) that refer to environmental protection. The President and National Assembly of 240 members are directly elected by popular vote. The country is divided into nine administrative regions *(oblast)* and 274 local

Area	110 948 km^2
Population	8.96m
Urban	68%
Rural	32%
Capital	Sofia (1.14m)
City populations	10 > 100 000; 3 > 300 000
Economy	
GNP per capita	US$5130 (1992)
GDP change	6% (1992)
Climate (Sofia)	
Average daily max and min	27/16°C (July)/2/−4°C (January)
Annual precipitation	661mm
Land-use cover	
Agriculture	56%
Forest	35%

authorities *(obshtina)*; the latter have responsibilities for local services such as water supply, sewerage and solid waste disposal, and local environmental protection matters.

The Ministry of the Environment was established in 1990 to take over from the State Committee for Environmental Protection. The Ministry has six departments dealing with different media and policy, an Environmental Monitoring Centre, an Inspectorate for the Protection of Underground Resources, and 16 Regional Environment Inspectorates. The Ministry is assisted by two advisory councils, dealing with environmental accidents and strategic matters, and the Insitute of Ecology (part of the Bulgarian Academy of Sciences).

The Act on the Prevention of Air, Water and Soil Pollution (1963) and the Nature Protection Act (1967) constituted the framework for environmental protection until adoption of the Environmental Protection Act of 1991 (amended in 1992). In 35 articles it sets out a basic framework for environmental policy, with provisions covering:

- monitoring and information
- a system of charges for polluting emissions, to be paid into municipal and national environmental protection funds
- environmental impact assessment for projects and programmes
- the rights and duties of the Minister of the Environment and municipal authorities
- sanctions for environmental damage.

The Act is to be supplemented by more detailed legislation on the marine environment, protected areas, air and water pollution and waste disposal.

AIR POLLUTION

Air pollution is a particular problem in major industrial centres and urban areas; for example, in 1989 average annual concentrations were recorded of:

440µg/m³ of dust in Dimitrovgrad
281µg/m³ of SO_2 in Srednogorie
43µg/m³ of NO_2 in Sofia.

The principal sources of emissions consist of thermal power plants, chemical plants, metalworks, fertiliser and cement factories and oil refineries. Total emissions in 1989 were estimated at:

1.7mt of SO_2
0.3mt of NO_x
0.15mt of hydrocarbons
2mt of other pollutants.

In urban areas, domestic heating fuelled by coal or lignite contributes significantly to particulate and SO_2 levels, as do motor vehicles, which account for around half of all NO_x emissions. Although the fleet is not large (1.4m vehicles), the average age of vehicles is high, estimated in 1992 at 14 years for cars and 10 years for buses.

Thermal plants generate 60 per cent of Bulgaria's electricity, and these account for a high proportion of SO_2 emissions, which more than doubled during 1970–88 from 0.66mt to 1.53mt. The Maritza-Iztok complex, with an installed capacity of 2,500MW and fuelled by lignite, probably accounts for around half national SO_2 emissions; the plants had electrostatic filters for particulates but no desulphurisation equipment in 1991. Emissions to air of heavy metals from industry in 1985 were estimated at:

2,812t of lead
660t of zinc
560t of copper
77t of arsenic
30t of cadmium and other heavy metals.

Air quality standards are fixed by the Ministry of Health, and emission standards by the Ministry of the Environment, for the same 171 pollutants. Emissions standards are calculated for each source using a formula intended to allow air quality standards to be met. In practice, they have been exceeded in many urban and industrial areas.

WATER RESOURCES AND POLLUTION

Apart from the Danube, there are few major rivers in Bulgaria; the river length totals 19 761km, draining into the Black Sea and eventually the Aegean Sea. Annual flows are estimated at 20.7bn m³ for rivers and 4.5bn m³ groundwater; thermal and mineral water springs 0.93bn m³. A reservoir capacity of 6bn m³ is Abstractions for drinking in 1990 industry consumed 3.39bn m³. Domestic supplies are intermittent in some areas, because of shortages. Around 27 per cent of Bulgaria's arable land is irrigated (1.25m ha), primarily along the Danube and Maritza rivers, accounting for 3.3bn m³ of water consumption in 1990. Groundwater sources accounted for around 36 per cent of total abstractions in 1988.

Water quality is poor in the lower and middle reaches of many major rivers; 75 per cent of the total length monitored is thought to contain pollutants above permitted levels. The Danube, Maritza, Provadiiska, Iskar and Struma appear to be worst affected. Industrial sources, particularly chemical plants, metalworks and mineworkings, are one cause, although effluent from sewage works (55 per cent without treatment) and intensive livestock farms, and run-off from agrochemicals, also contribute to water pollution. These sources also contaminate groundwater, which provides over 60 per cent of domestic water supplies. Elevated levels of nitrates and sulphates are widespread in some areas (eg Turgoviste, Bourgas, Stara Zagora); lead, arsenic and manganese are present in groundwater in some areas.

The Water Law of 1969 regulates the use of water, along with ordinances laying down detailed measures. Drinking water standards, laid down in Standard 2823–83, are the responsibility of the Ministry of Health, which oversees monitoring by the Insitute of Hygiene and Epidemiology. Surface water standards are set for 87 parameters, according to three quality classes, and monitoring is undertaken by the Ministries of Environment and Health and the Insitute of Meteorology and Hydrology (over 200 sampling points). Emission limits are established on the basis that receiving waters should meet class II standards (considered acceptable for fish farming and recreational use), with separate standards for discharges to sewerage systems. The Ministry of the Environment monitors groundwater quality at 276 points and two-level protection zones limit agricultural activity around drinking water sources. A National Water Council issues permits for major water users.

SOLID WASTE

Domestic waste arisings in 1990 were estimated at 8.7mt, having increased by 40 per cent since 1980. Domestic waste is disposed to landfill, for which there are at least 1600 sites, although disposal and site maintenance is poorly regulated and some areas are running short of landfill capacity. Plans for incinerators in eight urban centres were put forward in the 1980s.

Industrial waste arisings in 1990 were estimated at 190mt, having almost doubled from 99mt in 1980; over 80 per cent consisted of spoil from mining activities. Slag and ash from chemical production and ore processing, along with fly ash from thermal power stations, accounted for much of the remainder. Hazardous waste is often disposed to landfill with domestic waste or held on site where generated; there are no specialised facilities to deal with hazardous waste, although some solvents are recovered and acid and alkali wastes neutralised.

Under the Environmental Protection Act of 1991, waste disposal and the management of dangerous substances, and the collection and disposal of domestic waste, are primarily the responsibility of local authorities. The

Ministry of Regional Development, Housing and Construction provides guidance on the siting and construction of landfills, as well as operating criteria, issued by means of an ordinance. An ordinance on waste disposal, including the movement and disposal of hazardous waste, has been drafted. Waste movements are the responsibility of the Ministry of Transport. Waste producers have been obliged to report since 1981 on the quantities of waste they generate and reuse, but not on waste treatment or disposal.

NATURE CONSERVATION

Bulgaria is a country of high biological diversity, the Balkans forming a crossroads between Asia and Europe. Of 3350 vascular plant species, 250 are endemic to Bulgaria and 300 to the Balkans. The number of strictly protected vascular plant species has been increased from 60 in 1975 to 330 in 1990; 763 are listed in the national Red Data Book of endangered species.

Vertebrate species number over 700, including 90 mammals, 360 birds, and 52 amphibians and reptiles. The Red Data Book lists 19 mammals,100 birds, and 15 amphibian and reptile species.

Bulgaria has many caves, which provide a habitat for 80 endemic troglodyte species. Mountainous and forest areas provide habitat for wolves, jackals, wildcat, birds of prey and bears (population estimated at 840). Wetlands near the Danube and Black Sea are valuable habitats for migratory birds. The Nature Protection Act of 1967 provides for the protection of wild fauna and flora by means of ordinances issued by the Minister of the Environment. Ordinances issued in 1986 extended protection to:

327 bird species
10 amphibian species
24 reptile species and
44 mammal species.

Bulgaria has 11 National Parks (113 600ha) and 99 reserves (61 000ha) amongst the areas protected under the Nature Protection Act. These areas increased from a total of 106 000ha in 1975 to 380 000ha in 1990 (3.5 per cent of national territory). As part of a protected areas programme, the Ministry of the Environment is intending to increase the areas given some legal protection to cover 7–7.5 per cent of the country by 1995/96. Bulgaria has four Ramsar wetland sites (2097ha), two World Heritage sites and 17 Biosphere Reserves.

ENERGY

Bulgaria is dependent on imports for most of its fossil fuel supplies, particularly oil and gas, although it has minor reserves of both. There are large deposits of lignite, however, from which around 30mt is produced annually for use in electricity generation and domestic heating. Crude oil is imported for refining at Burgas and Varna. Power cuts became widespread during winters in the 1980, but energy demand lessened in the late 1980s and early 1990s as heavy industry declined and energy prices were increased. Coal and oil imports from Ukraine and Russia became more expensive and international pressure grew for improvements in nuclear safety.

The Kozloduy nuclear power station near Vratsa began operation in 1974, providing 30–40 per cent of the country's electricity in recent years. The Russian-designed plant consists of four 440MW and two 1000MW pressurised water reactors. After a series of accidents and a highly critical report in 1991 by the International Atomic Energy Agency, two of the 440MW reactors were closed; the larger units are generally considered safer but have required frequent outage for maintenance. International aid was made available to undertake safety work. Plans for a second, larger nuclear power plant, at Belene, were shelved after public protests.

Uranium ore is produced at 33 mines and processed within Bulgaria, resulting in extensive radioactive pollution; however, the government has announced its intention to reduce mining. It appears unlikely that nuclear waste can be sent to Russia in future, and in 1991 the Academy of Sciences was asked to prepare a programme for land disposal.

Hydroelectric power stations generate 5–6 per cent of total electricity production from 87 plants; a further 10 plants were out of operation in 1992. Total installed capacity is 1970MW. The first 210MW unit of a pumped storage station at Chaira came into operation during 1993, and is due to be followed by three further units.

AGRICULTURE

Agriculture accounted for around 14 per cent of net material product in 1990, but production declined by around 20 per cent during 1989–92. Around 55 per cent of the total land area is farmed; around 1m ha are thought to suffer from medium or severe erosion. Around half the arable area is used for cereals; vines, tomatoes, cotton, sunflowers, sugar beet, potatoes and tobacco are other important crops.

Inorganic fertilisers and pesticides are applied at a relatively low rate, limited in recent years by the cost of imports. Shortages of seed have also limited production. Pasture is little fertilised and is thought capable of supporting livestock densities three or four times present levels.

The 1991 Ownership and Use of Farmland Act provided for the redistribution of land from state cooperatives, for which 1.7m claims were received. A maximum of 30ha per person can be restituted, although most claims are for much less. Slow progress in issuing titles to land, the small size of new farming units, and the difficulty for individuals of raising capital for machinery, seed or fertiliser have added to production problems. Confusion over ownership and the selling off of fodder from the former cooperatives before the return of animals encouraged the reported slaughter of 1.9m sheep, 235 000 cattle and 460 000 pigs in 1992 alone. The break up of cooperatives has increased the number of small farms being worked primarily for subsistence.

FOREST RESOURCES

Forests cover around 35 per cent (3.9m ha) of the land area of Bulgaria, mostly state owned and predominantly (69 per cent) in mountainous areas. Timber production fell from 8.6m m^3 in 1960, above annual growth rates, to 4.7m m^3 in 1990. Large-scale afforestation increased the proportion of conifers from 17 per cent to 34 per cent over the same period, whilst the proportion of native beech forests declined from 32 per cent to 20 per cent. Forestry is regulated by the 1958 Forest Act, under which 30 per cent of the forest area was classified as non-commercial in 1990.

The 1991 forest damage survey showed 21.8 per cent of trees suffering 25 per cent or more defoliation. Acid deposition, lower rainfall and higher temperatures than normal are believed to have played a part, along with pest attacks and elevated concentrations of heavy metals in forest soils. Silver fir and oak are the species worst affected by acid rain, with serious dieback thought to occur in 17 000ha and 20 000ha respectively.

TRANSPORT

Waterways play an important role in goods transport in Bulgaria, accounting for 70 per cent of total tonnage moved in 1990. Much of this is transported via the Danube, on which Ruse and Lom are the principal ports, and the Black Sea, served by Varna and Burgas.

Bulgaria's road network totalled 90 898km in 1991, including 276km of motorway. Around 1.3m cars, 25 000 buses and 126 500 lorries were in use. The rail network extends to 4300km and is being progressively electrified, reaching over 60 per cent of the total length by 1990. Sofia's underground railway is being extended to 112km.

Cyprus

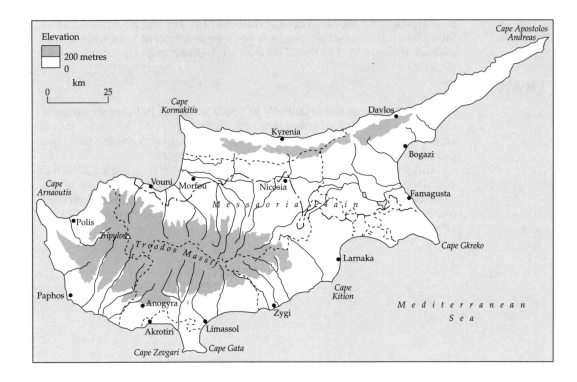

Cyprus is an island in the northeastern Mediterranean, 800km west of the Greek mainland and 75km south of Turkey. The south-west of the island is dominated by the mountainous Troodos massif, rising to nearly 2000m. To its north and west lie the Messaoria plain and another belt of hills.

INSTITUTIONS AND POLICY

Cyprus became an independent republic in 1960. Executive power lies with the directly elected President, and the Council of Ministers he or she appoints. A House of Representatives is elected as the legislature. The island has been divided since 1974, when the northern third was occupied by Turkish forces; a Turkish Republic of Northern Cyprus was declared but not recognised internationally. Most of the information in this section refers to the (predominantly Greek Cypriot) Republic which controls the rest of the island. In 1990 Cyprus applied to join the European Community.

The Environmental Conservation Service was established in 1981 as

Area	9251 km²
Population	710 000
Capital	Nicosia (166 500)
City populations	3 > 50 000
Economy	
GNP per capita	US$9790 (1990)
Climate (Nicosia)	
Average daily max and min	37/21°C (July)/15/5°C (January)
Annual precipitation	345mm
Land-use cover	
Agriculture	49%
Forest	19%
Other	32%

part of the Ministry of Agriculture and Natural Resources. The Minister chairs the Council for the Protection of the Environment, which advises the Council of Ministers. Environmental matters have been regulated largely through planning law and other general legislation, but a new framework environmental law is intended to provide the basis for more specific measures on pollution control and nature conservation. The Planning Bureau issued a policy directive in 1985 to require public bodies to undertake an environmental assessment of major development projects. An Environmental Action Plan was published in 1987.

AIR POLLUTION

The principal sources of air pollution are mines and quarries, vehicle emissions and industrial plant. The island's two major power stations are both oil-fired, and other industrial emitters include cement factories, foundries and an oil refinery. Total sulphur emissions from stationary sources were estimated at 20 000t in 1988. Extended periods of dry weather lead to dusty conditions in some areas.

WATER RESOURCES AND POLLUTION

Cyprus depends largely on groundwater sources for its water supplies; 90 per cent of annual precipitation falls in winter and much returns to the atmosphere through evapotranspiration because of the hot, dry climate. Many rivers run dry outside the winter months. A series of dams and reservoirs has been constructed to improve supplies and expand water storage capacity, which reached around 300m m³ in 1990. A number of large-scale projects have involved the damming and diversion of rivers to provide irrigation and meet domestic water demand, notably the Southern Conveyor Project which covers much of the southern part of the island. Total water abstraction in 1988 was estimated at 140m m³, of which 100m m³ was used in agriculture. Some groundwater aquifers near the coast are affected by the intrusion of seawater, as a result of overabstraction.

In 1991 Nicosia was the only town with a sewage system and treatment facilities, although plans were advancing to develop these in other towns and tourist centres. Some major hotels and residential developments on the coast have their own sewage treatment works. Nitrate pollution from pits used for sewage disposal has affected groundwater in some areas; industrial discharges have also caused isolated problems.

NATURE CONSERVATION

Although a relatively small island, Cyprus has a wide range of habitat types, including semi-Alpine, forest and freshwater ecosystems in the Troodos mountains, coastal wetlands, dunes and marine areas. There are around 1800 species of flowering plants, of which 123 are endemic; fauna species include 20 mammals, 357 birds and 27 reptiles. The largest wild mammal on the island, the Cyprus moufflon, recovered from near-extinction in the 1930s. Green and loggerhead turtles come ashore to lay their eggs on sandy beaches in the breeding season, particularly on the west coast. A conservation project was launched in 1978 to protect their declining populations.

As it is situated on important migration routes between Europe and Africa and Asia, Cyprus is visited by many bird species. The salt lakes and marshes of Larnaca and Akrotiki form particularly important habitats for migratory birds; mountain areas provide refuge for birds of prey, including the imperial eagle and Eleonora's falcon. Some bird species are widely hunted, despite limited bans. Coastal zones face particular development pressures from tourism on the south and west coast, and from industry and port infrastructure around Larnaca and Limassol. By 1991, one nature reserve (823ha) had been established, at Mount Tripylos, and a further 16 potential sites (4516ha) identified. In addition, 69 national forest parks, covering 20 375ha, were proposed for designation.

ENERGY

Cyprus depends on imports for virtually all its fuel requirements, primarily in the form of oil and coal. Total primary energy supply increased from 0.64mtoe in 1971 to 1.53mtoe in 1990. Crude oil is imported for refining on the island, and the two main power stations burn oil; electricity production in 1991 totalled 2077m kWh. Road and air transport accounted for 70 per cent of final energy consumption in 1990.

AGRICULTURE

The agricultural sector contributed 7.2 per cent of GDP in 1990 and is a key export producer, accounting for 35 per cent of export earnings (and 12 per cent of employment) that year. Around 430 000ha of land was in use for agriculture on the island as a whole; the 1985 agricultural census identified 179 000ha of agricultural holdings, of which 126 000ha was cultivated. Arable crops accounted for around 75 per cent of agricultural production in 1990. Wheat and barley are grown on the central plain, citrus fruits around the coast, and potatoes and other vegetables in most parts. Olives, carob, almonds, grapes and bananas are also grown. Around a quarter of the cultivated area is irrigated. The livestock sector produces sufficient pork, poultry and eggs to meet local demand. Irrigation, poor soil fertility and the increasing use of agrochemicals have led to pollution by nitrates and pesticides in some areas, and around 44 800ha of agricultural land is thought to suffer from soil erosion. The fisheries catch totalled 2737t in 1991; several marine fish farms were developed during the 1980s.

FOREST RESOURCES

Forests cover around 175 000ha and are found most densely on the Troodos mountains. Most forested land is state-owned, and initiatives by the Department of Forests, part of the Ministry of Agriculture and Natural Resources, led to the reafforestation of more than 14 000ha during 1977–90. Fires in the dry season represent one of the major threats to the country's forests, but the total area affected was reduced to an annual average of 0.17 per cent for 1975–90, as more effective prevention and fire-fighting methods were introduced. Timber production amounted to 40 700m^3 in 1991.

TRANSPORT

The road network has undergone considerable development since 1974 and in 1991 extended to 5400km of paved roads and 4700km of unpaved roads. Major infrastructure projects have improved the principal rural roads and expanded the main highways. Annual expenditure on road construction increased fourfold during the 1980s, reaching more than C£27.3m in 1989. The number of motor vehicles in use reached 377 000 in 1991. The international airports at Larnaca and Paphos handled more than 3.5m passengers in 1991, including many tourists (1.56m arrivals in 1990). The principal seaports of Limassol and Larnaca trebled in size between 1979 and 1986 and further development is planned; they take more than 65 per cent of the country's sea freight.

Czech Republic

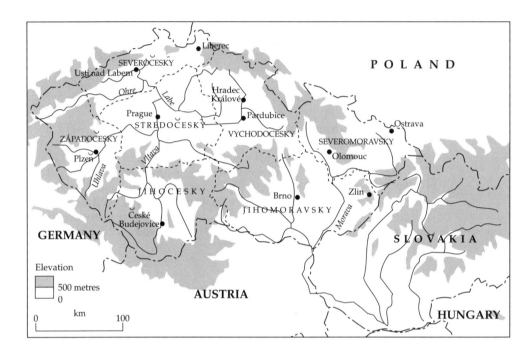

The Czech Republic is situated in central Europe and borders Germany to the west, Poland to the north, Austria to the south and Slovakia to the east. Bohemia, in the west of the country, is a predominantly upland area, with a plateau surrounded by mountains which rise to 1600m in the north-east. Moravia is generally lower lying, although mountains rise along the borders with Poland and Slovakia, and more fertile, particularly along the Morava and Dyje rivers which flow into the Danube.

INSTITUTIONS AND POLICY

The Czech Republic became a fully independent state on 1 January 1993. The National Council has 200 members elected by proportional representation. There are 75 district authorities, plus the Magistrate of Prague (the authority for the capital).

The Ministry of the Environment was established in January 1990 and includes an Environmental Protection Agency responsible for monitoring and inspection; the Agency has 30 Regional Inspectorates. The Ministry also oversees the State Environment Fund, established by Act 388/1991, which receives income from charges payable for air and water discharges, waste management activities, and groundwater abstraction, and fines imposed for environmental offences. This income is used to support

Area	78 864km^2
Population	10.3m
Urban	56%
Rural	44%
Capital	Prague (1.2m)
City populations	10 > 90 000; 4 > 150 000
Economy	
GNP per capita	US$7160 (1992)
GDP change	−7% (1992)
Climate (Prague)	
Average daily max and min	23/13°C (July)/0/−5°C (January)
Annual precipitation	411mm
Land-use cover	
Agriculture	55%
Forest	33%
Other	12%

investment, research and other environment-related activities.

As in Slovakia, a number of environmental laws of the former Czech and Slovak Federal Republic are still in force, including the Act on the Environment 17/1992. Its provisions on environmental impact assessment (EIA) were implemented nationally through the Act on EIA 244/1992, which lays down those activities which must be made subject to assessment and what information an assessment should include.

AIR POLLUTION

Air pollution is a severe problem particularly in Northern Bohemia, where much of the country's industry is located. The ready availability of lignite in this area has led to a concentration of industrial facilities, including thermal power stations, chemical and metalworks, papermills and glass and ceramics fac-tories. In 1990 total emissions were estimated at:

1.8mt for SO_2, down from over 2.1mt in the mid-1980s
742 000t for NO_x
631 000t for particulate emissions.

Eight out of the ten largest emitters of these pollutants were situated in Northern Bohemia, few of them with effective pollution abatement equipment installed. Very high concentrations were recorded in some areas in recent years, exceeding 100μg/m^3 annual and 24-hour averages of:

100μg/m^3 and 1000μg/m^3 for SO_2
600μg/m^3 for NO_x
120μg/m^3 and 600μg/m^3 for particulates.

Air quality can also be poor around other industrial and urban centres such as Prague, Ostrava, Plzen and Brno; pollution from industry is compounded by emissions from domestic heating systems and motor vehicles.

Air pollution control policy is based on the Clean Air Act 309/1991 and the Act on the State Administration of Air Protection 389/1991, which replaced legislation from 1967. Emission limits are based on lowest achievable emissions for existing plant; new plant is required to use best achievable means. Emission and air quality limits were drawn up by the former Federal Committee on the Environment. Larger polluters are required to pay a charge for emissions, and under Decree 41/1992 smog warnings must be given above certain concentrations.

WATER RESOURCES AND POLLUTION

The Czech Republic has 60 000km of rivers and is situated on the continental divide; its territory is drained via the Labe (Elbe) to the North Sea, the Danube, and in the north-east the Oder. There are five glacier lakes and 149 reservoirs with a capacity above 1m m^3. Water demand rose by 47 per cent during 1960-85 and supplies are short in some areas, particularly for drinking water. Annual demand in 1990 was 2.7bn m^3 from surface waters (69 per cent for industrial and energy use) and 0.7bn m^3 from groundwater (77 per cent for drinking water and 9 per cent for agriculture). The public water supply serves 84 per cent of the population and suffers from losses of around 30 per cent in the distribution system. Tests on the water supply showed that only 4.4 per cent of treated surface water and 7.3 per cent of groundwater met the most important hygiene standards. Nitrate and phosphorus levels have increased steadily over the past 25–30 years, largely as a result of agricultural fertiliser run-off.

In 1991 there were 5086 registered dischargers of effluent to watercourses, contributing a biochemical oxygen demand (BOD) of 248 816t. Industrial discharges (excluding power stations) amounted to:

557m m^3 to the Elbe catchment area
184.1m m^3 to that of the Oder
71m m^3 to that of the Morava.

During 1988, 457 water pollution accidents were reported, adding to the load from regular industrial, municipal and agricultural sources.

In 1988 only 41 per cent of wastewater discharges received treatment, and around one-third* of the major rivers were thought to be incapable of supporting fish life. Survey statistics from 1990 covering 11 water quality parameters indicate that only 4 of the 13 principal rivers included significant stretches where all samples fell into the top three (of five) water quality categories. The Jizera and Ohre appeared least severely affected by pollution. Although major cities such as Prague, Usti nad Labem and Hradec Kralove have inadequate sewage treatment plant, some improvements are being made; 29 new sewage works were brought into operation during 1991.

The Water Management Act 138/1973 is being revised and is likely to involve permits and higher water charges for users, the preparation of water management plans and the designation of water protection areas.

---

* Refers to former Czech and Slovak Federal Republic

The Act on the State Administration of Water Management 130/1974, amended 458/ 1992, sets out the responsibilities of district and community offices regarding drinking water, sewerage and abstractions.

SOLID WASTE

Information on waste generation and disposal in the Czech Republic is rather limited. However, a survey estimated total waste arisings at 630mt in 1987, of which over 80 per cent resulted from mining and related activities; the industry (7.5 per cent), energy (4 per cent) and construction (4 per cent) sectors accounted for most of the remainder. Municipal waste accounted for 2.6mt, and a total of 14.6mt was classified as hazardous.

The majority of waste is disposed to landfill; an industrial waste landfills survey recorded a total of 844 sites which received 602.6mt (464.4m m^3) of waste in 1987. Studies appear to indicate a lack of facilities with the necessary technical means to ensure environmentally safe disposal. Small quantities of waste are sent for incineration, eg in Prague and Brno.

Waste policy is based on the (Federal) Waste Management Act 238/1991, which includes provisions for the monitoring and safe disposal of waste, and Decree 69/1991 of the Federal Committee for the Environment, which laid down categories of waste types. All operators of waste disposal sites must pay an annual fee proportionate to the quantity of waste received, under Act 62/1992 on charges for the deposit of waste. Under Decrees 401/1991 and 521/1991, waste producers are required to maintain records of their waste and to draw up waste programmes for approval by the district authorities. The district offices are also to draw up waste management programmes.

NATURE CONSERVATION

Of around 1900 higher plant species in the Czech Republic, around 60 per cent are thought to be threatened or requiring attention; a comparable proportion (57 per cent) of 449 vertebrate animal species surveyed in 1988 were placed in the same classification, many of them birds. Another survey assessed 362 out of 550 plant communities as endangered.

A new Act on the Protection of Nature and the Landscape (114/1992) came into force in July 1992, replacing the previous Nature Conservation Act 40/1956. The Act sets out the responsibilities of the different authorities involved in nature conservation, provides for the protection of trees, plants, animals and minerals, and lays down provisions for six categories of protected areas.

In 1991 there were three national parks and 22 protected landscape areas; 1225 additional small-scale protected areas (less than 2000ha) had also been designated. The total area under protection of some kind totalled 12 199km^2, 15 per cent of the land area.

ENERGY

The Czech Republic is heavily dependent on brown coal and lignite, which account for 65 per cent of primary energy consumption. Domestic production of oil and gas is minimal, and most supplies are imported. Over 75 per cent of electricity is generated by thermal power stations, mostly burning brown coal; its sulphur content can be as high as 15 per cent and many plants have little or no satisfactory desulphurisation equipment, leading to high levels of acid emissions. Northern Bohemia alone has four large power stations above 1000MW capacity burning brown coal. Plans are under development to fit flue gas desulphurisation to 3600MW of plant, around one-third of the total coal-fired capacity.

There are four 440MW nuclear reactors at the Dukovany power station, near Trebic, which provided 21 per cent of electricity generated in 1992. A larger plant with two 1000MW reactors is under construction at Temelin, and will increase the country's nuclear-generated capacity when they begin operation, planned for 1996–97. A small proportion of electricity (3 per cent) is produced by hydroelectric stations.

AGRICULTURE

Around 55 per cent of the country consists of agricultural land, over three-quarters of which is arable. Although production fell by around 17 per cent* during 1990–92, domestic agriculture has provided most of the country's food requirements since 1945. The intensification of agriculture over the past 30 years has been accompanied by increased pollution from agricultural sources, such as fertilisers, pesticides and livestock wastes, and soil erosion and pressure on natural habitats. In addition to grain and livestock, vines, hops and fish represent important produce.

Under the Czech Republic's Agrarian Policy Programme of 1992, the area under cultivation should be reduced from 4.3m to 4.0m ha and the number of people employed in agriculture halved to around 200 000. A privatisation programme aims to increase the number of farms in private hands, and 24 per cent of the state budget for agriculture was intended to support environmental improvement work in 1993. Subsidies of CKr71.3m for alternative agriculture and CKr227.2m for water and landscape protection areas were made available in 1991.

FOREST RESOURCES

Forests cover around 33 per cent of the land area of the Czech Republic, and coniferous plantations have been replacing the ancient beech and oak forests. This results partly from efforts to increase timber production, which more than doubled between 1950 and 1980 to 13.9m m^3 annually. Oak and beech cover fell to around 11 per cent of the forest area by 1985. Many forest areas also suffer from air pollution, particularly in the mountains of Northern and Eastern Bohemia where rain deposits the high levels of pollutants from nearby industrial centres, resulting in some of the severest forest dieback in Europe; few trees remain alive in some areas. By 1986 around half the forested area (1.3m ha) was thought to be affected by air pollution.

TRANSPORT

The former Czechoslovakia had one of the highest levels of car ownership in CEE: 45 per cent* of households owned a car, of which there were 3.12m* in 1989. The road networks, which carried 80 per cent of freight (by weight), covered 73 640km*. Vehicle emissions contribute significantly to air pollution, particularly in Prague, where a ring-motorway to the south-east is planned to relieve traffic pressure in the city centre. The rail network covers 9400km; some lines were being closed in 1992 for financial reasons.

Denmark

Denmark consists of the Jutland peninsula, north of Germany, five larger islands and around 400 smaller islands at the entrance to the Baltic Sea. The North Sea lies to the west, while the Skagerrak and Kattegat straits separate Denmark from Norway and Sweden respectively. The terrain is low-lying, at an average elevation of only 30m above sea level. Greenland and the Faroe Islands are autonomous territories which form part of the Kingdom of Denmark; they are not covered here.

Area	43 093km²
Population	5.16m
Urban	87%
Rural	13%
Capital	Copenhagen (1.39m)
City populations	5 > 80 000; 2 > 250 000
Economy	
GNP per capita	US$23 700 (1991)
Climate (Copenhagen)	
Average daily max and min	22/14°C (July)/2/–2°C (January)
Annual precipitation	603mm
Land-use cover	
Agriculture	66%
Forest	12%
Other	22%

INSTITUTIONS AND POLICY

Denmark is a constitutional monarchy and has a parliament *(Folketing)* of 179 elected members. The 14 counties and 275 municipalities are overseen by elected councils and have extensive powers. At national level, the Ministry of Pollution Control was established in 1971, becoming the Ministry of the Environment in 1973. It is assisted by a number of agencies, including the Environmental Protection Agency, the National Forest and Nature Conservation Agency, and the National Environmental Research Institute.

The Environmental Protection Act, amended in 1991, provides the legal basis for much of Danish environment policy. It covers soil and groundwater protection, surface waters, licensing, waste management, and recycling, and allows for detailed regulations to be made by the Environment Minister. Implementation in many areas is delegated to the counties and municipalities, including the licensing of specified plants and activities, and planning. In some cases, appeals against the decisions of local authorities may be made to the national Environmental Appeals Board. Provisions on environmental impact assessment are contained in planning legislation, which was amended by in 1991 by a new Planning Act. A national Action Plan for Environment and Development was adopted in 1988, followed by sectoral plans for energy, transport and agriculture. Denmark acceded to the European Community in 1973.

AIR POLLUTION

In common with the other Scandinavian countries, Denmark's soil and water bodies suffer from acidification as a result of sulphur and nitrogen depositions. Around 25 per cent of the sulphur originates from Danish sources. From a peak of 464 000t in 1977, annual emissions of SO_2 fell by 60 per cent during the 1980s, to 181 000t in 1990. This decrease reflected the greater use of low-sulphur fuels, pollution control equipment, and improvements in energy efficiency. Emissions of NO_x increased to 307 000t in 1986 before declining to 269 000t in 1989.

Measurements of air quality show a generally improving trend for SO_2 since the early 1970s, although annual concentrations of soot in Copenhagen increased during the early 1980s. No breaches of the EC limit value for SO_2 have been recorded, but concentrations of NO_2 rose during the 1980s and annual values above $150\mu g/m^3$ were measured at several sites in Copenhagen in 1989, probably as a result of increased road traffic. Lead levels dropped sharply following the introduction of lower lead-content petrol.

Air pollution control is based on the 1991 Environmental Protection Act, which requires specified industrial plants to obtain a licence and operate within emission limits. Energy-related measures are expected to reduce SO_2 emissions by about 60 per cent and NO_x emissions by about 50 per cent by 2005, compared to 1988 levels.

WATER RESOURCES AND POLLUTION

All Denmark's borders are formed by water, except for Jutland's southern border with Germany; no part of the country lies more than about 50km from the coast, which extends to 7300km, and watercourses are therefore short in length. The country is heavily dependent on groundwater, which provides more than 95 per cent of supplies. Total abstractions increased significantly during the 1970s, from 720m m^3 in 1970 to 1205m m^3 in 1977, as a result of more widespread irrigation. Abstractions totalled 1305bn m^3 in 1988, 52 per cent feeding into the drinking water supply and 30 per cent being used for irrigation. Groundwater supplies are considered over-exploited in the major urban areas, and are threatened principally by pollution from agricultural sources (nitrate and pesticides) and contaminated industrial sites, including landfills. Elevated levels of nitrate are found throughout the country but most frequently in northern Jutland, where an increasing number of drinking water supplies were found during the 1980s to contain concentrations above 50mg/l.

Excessive nutrients have also affected surface and marine waters, which receive most of their phosphorus load from wastewater discharges and fish farms, in addition to nitrogen predominantly from agriculture. Annual discharges from municipal wastewater treatment plants in the mid-1980s reached 20 000t of nitrogen and 6000t of phosphorus, but were reduced by 1989 to 18 000t and 4000t respectively. In addition, wastewater from areas not served by sewerage works contributed around 2900t of nitrogen and 900t of phosphorus.

Surveys indicate no general improvement in river quality during the past decade; around one-third failed biological standards in 1989, and the quality of a further third was held to be critical.

The condition of lakes appears to have improved since the 1970s, particularly as a result of lower nutrient discharges. Measurements suggest that oxygen concentrations in the southwestern Kattegat have fallen steadily since the mid-1970s, which appears typical for seawaters around Denmark. Of sea bathing waters sampled in 1992, 95 per cent complied with the faecal coliform values under the EC bathing water Directive; bathing was banned at 27 points.

The Water Supply Act regulates water abstraction and supply, and makes local authorities responsible for monitoring water quality. Orders made under the Act set standards for water quality. The Environmental Protection Act includes provisions on the protection of groundwater and surface water, requiring licences to be obtained for disposal or discharges likely to pollute groundwater and for wastewater emissions to surface waters. Growing problems of eutrophication and incidences of algal blooms during the 1980s prompted the development of an Action Plan for the Aquatic Environment, approved by parliament in 1987. The Plan aims to prevent further deterioration of the aquatic environment and to reduce emissions of nitrogen by 50 per cent and phosphorus by 80 per cent. It includes measures to limit nutrient discharges from agricultural activities, industry and municipal sewage plants.

SOLID WASTE

Industrial production and consumption in Denmark more than doubled since the 1960s, leading to the generation of large quantities of waste. On the basis of surveys undertaken in 1985, annual waste arisings were estimated at 9.3mt, excluding agricultural and mining/quarrying waste. Household waste accounted for around 20 per cent of this total, and industrial waste for 25 per cent. In addition, 0.55mt of residue resulted from waste treatment.

Landfills and refuse dumps represent the principal disposal route, taking 57 per cent of total arisings in 1985; however, 75 per cent of household waste was incinerated, and 10 per cent went to composting centres. There were 38 waste incineration plants in operation in 1991, along with around 100 landfills and 100 refuse dumps, the latter receiving inert material. Recycling rates increased to 35 per cent for paper and cardboard and 60 per cent for glass in 1990; the government has a target of recycling 50 per cent of waste by 2000.

The Environmental Protection Act of 1991 replaced much of the previous legislation on waste management. Municipal councils are responsible for implementing most aspects of waste policy, including the household waste disposal plans drawn up by the counties. Following two Recycling Plans covering 1987–89 and 1990–92, a Waste and Recycling Action Plan for 1993–97 was published in 1992. It has the overall objective of reducing the volumes of waste produced and encouraging recycling, and foresees the increased use of incineration; the quantities of waste disposed to landfill should be reduced. Drink containers must be recyclable and cans are banned; 99 per cent of beer and soft drink bottles are returned. Charges are levied on packaging and disposable tableware, and on waste delivered to landfill sites and incinerators.

NATURE CONSERVATION

The decline in Denmark's original native flora and fauna has been partly offset by migrant and introduced species which have become established. However, intensive agriculture, and industrial and urban development have adversely affected many types of habitat; a review in 1991 indicated that woodland, grassland, coastal and wetland habitats contained the largest numbers of species in need of protection. Agriculture, changes in forestry and vegetation, and eutrophication constituted the principal threats. Of around 1200 vascular plant species and 50 mammal species, 261 and 19 respectively were considered in need of special protection.

Legal protection for species and habitats is based on the Nature Protection Act (1992), which partly replaced several earlier measures, including the Nature Management Act of 1989. It provides for regulations to be made on the protection and exploitation of wild animal and plant species and prohibits the alteration of specified types of habitat, including heath, wetlands and permanent wet grassland. County Nature Conservation Boards have the power to adopt conservation orders to protect areas for nature conservation; compensation is payable to the owners or users of property thus affected. By 1991, legal protection extended to around 380 000ha, in addition to 960 000ha under the EC birds Directive and the Ramsar wetlands convention.

ENERGY

Denmark's energy supply is based primarily on oil and coal, which together account for over 80 per cent of gross energy consumption. Around 40 per cent of energy requirements were met from indigenous sources in 1988, largely oil, which has been extracted offshore in the North Sea since 1972; 7.8mt was produced in 1992, sufficient to meet domestic demand. Gas is also extracted, some for export to Germany and Sweden; production totalled 3.7m m^3 in 1991. The proportion of energy consumption met by oil fell from 93 per cent to 47 per cent between 1972 and 1988, replaced largely by coal and gas. Final energy consumption varied between 12 and 15mtoe during the 1980s. Denmark has few energy-intensive industries, and space heating accounts for the largest share of energy consumption, falling from 39 per cent in 1972 to 29 per cent in 1988.

Production of energy from renewable sources has been encouraged. The number of wind turbines doubled between 1988 and 1992 to 3400 units with a capacity of 460MW; they provided 3 per cent of electricity consumption in 1992. More than 300 small-scale combined heat and power (CHP) plants, often fuelled by gas, were in operation, and 11 large, communal biogas plants had been established, using farm manure from local farms. An energy action plan entitled 'Energy 2000: A Plan of Action for Sustainable Development' was published in April 1990. It aims to improve energy efficiency and develop the use of renewable and low-emission energy sources. An energy/CO_2 tax was introduced in 1992.

AGRICULTURE

Agriculture is the dominant land use in Denmark, taking up more than 65 per cent of the surface area. Cereals covered more than half the cultivated area in 1990, grass and green fodder crops around 20 per cent.

Agriculture accounts for 4.5 per cent of employment (1991), around half the level of 1975; the number of farms has also decreased, from around 200 000 in 1950 to 82 000 in 1991. However, the total area under cultivation decreased by only 11 per cent over the same period, reflecting a general increase in farm size.

Agricultural products accounted for 25 per cent of total export earnings in 1989, largely from pork and dairying, which are the principal sectors.

Drainage for cultivation was undertaken on over 500 000ha between 1937 and 1966, encouraged by grants.

An Action Plan on Sustainable Development in Agriculture was published in 1991, outlining policies to reduce emissions of nutrients and pesticides from farming, which affect primarily the aquatic environment. Pesticide consumption fell by around 40 per cent between 1985 and 1991 (measured in tonnes of active ingredients).

FOREST RESOURCES

Forests cover almost 0.5m ha, tree cover having increased steadily since early last century. Conifer cover has expanded substantially and now composes two-thirds of the total; beech and oak are the most widespread deciduous species.

The annual volume of timber felled is about 2m m³, compared with 3m m³ annual growth, with consumption standing at 8–9m m³ annually, substantial volumes are imported.

Remaining areas of older deciduous forest form important habitats for fauna and flora, and fringe areas and oak scrub are protected. A support scheme was introduced in 1989 to encourage the planting of deciduous species. Forestry policy seeks to double the wooded area during the next 80–100 years, envisaging afforestation at an average of 5000ha annually.

The forest condition survey in 1992 found 25.9 per cent of trees sampled suffering from 25 per cent or more defoliation, compared with 29.9 per cent in 1991.

TRANSPORT

Transport volumes increased significantly during the 1980s, and by 1991 there were 1.61m cars in use and the road network extended to 71 000km, including 653km of motorway. A total of 73bn passenger-km was travelled in 1988, an increase of 40 per cent over 1970. Car travel accounted for 70 per cent of the total, and other forms of road transport for a further 20 per cent.

Freight transport volumes increased to almost 16bn t-km, 60 per cent in relation to international movements. Road haulage carried most of domestic freight (78 per cent in 1988), whereas international freight was carried largely by sea (88 per cent). The state rail network covered 2340km.

Transport volumes are projected to continue increasing, passenger transport by 40 per cent and domestic freight by 55 per cent between 1988 and 2010.

Construction began in 1988 of a road and rail link, by bridge and tunnel, across the 18km-wide Storebaelt between the two principal islands of Zeeland and Funen, and other major links are planned between Copenhagen and Malmo in Sweden, and Lolland to the German mainland.

A Transport Action Plan for Environment and Development was published in 1990, setting out objectives for reducing the energy consumption, emissions and environmental impact of transport in Denmark.

Estonia

Estonia is the northernmost of the three Baltic republics (the others being Latvia and Lithuania) and lies to the north-west of the Russian plain. It has a coastline on the Gulf of Finland to the north and the the Baltic Sea and Gulf of Riga to the west; land borders are shared with Russia and Latvia. Most of the land is low-lying, with only 10 per cent of the territory above 100m, rising in the south-east to 318m. There are over 1500 islands and 1400 lakes; rivers are generally short and flow into the surrounding seas or larger lakes in the east.

INSTITUTIONS AND POLICY

Estonia became a fully independent republic in 1991, and a new constitution was adopted in 1992; a 101-member national assembly *(Riigikogu)* is elected by proportional representation. Article 53 of the constitution refers

Area	45 215km²
Population	1.6m
Urban	71%
Rural	29%
Capital	Tallinn (0.5m)
City populations	5 > 50 000; 1 > 200 000
Economy	
GNP per capita	US$6320 (1991)
GDP change	–26% (1991)
Climate (Tallinn)	
Mean temperature	16.3°C (July)/–6°C (February)
Annual precipitation	687mm
Land-use cover	
Agriculture	32.5%
Forest	40%
Other	27.5%

to the environment. The Ministry of the Environment, which also oversees the Forest Department and Fisheries Departments, was established in 1991. Much of the inspection and licensing work is undertaken by the Ministry's 19 Local Environmental Protection Departments. The Nature Protection Law (23 February 1990) forms the framework for environmental legislation, although all former USSR environmental standards in force on 20 August 1991 have been declared to remain in force until repealed or replaced. An extensive system of charges was established by a regulation of 13 February 1990; charges and taxes for the use of resources and polluting emissions etc are paid into the Estonian Environment Fund, which received 6.29m crowns in 1992.

AIR POLLUTION

Much of the country's air pollution originates from the north-east of the country, in and around Kohtla-Järve and Narva, where energy and chemical industries are based on the extensive oil-shale deposits in the area. Emissions from stationary sources in 1990 totalled 207 818t of SO_2 and 302 062t of particulate matter; over half came from two large power stations near Narva which burn oil-shale. Other industrial sources, domestic heating and vehicle emissions contribute to air quality problems in Tallinn, Kohtla-Järve and Narva in particular. Indices of the principal pollutants show that national maximum permissible concentrations (MPCs) were exceeded regularly, although monitoring showed decreases in 1992, probably reflecting a lower level of industrial activity. Vehicle emissions in 1990 included 45 600t of NO_x, more than double the 21 686t NO_x from stationary sources.

A system of air pollution charges was es⸍
of 13 February 1990, and is based on:

- actual emission levels
- the charge per tonne and class (1-5) of t
  concerned, and
- factors such as land-use in the area (v⸍
  highly than industrial areas, for exam⸍

Emissions should not cause MPCs to be exceeu⸍⸍,
averages):

$50\mu g/m^3$ for SO_2
$40\mu g/m^3$ for NO_2
$150\mu g/m^3$ for particulates.

Permits for emissions to air are issued by the Ministry of the Environment
and/or its regional offices.

WATER RESOURCES AND POLLUTION

Estonia has over 1400 lakes, the largest of which is Lake Peipus ($3555km^2$),
on the Russian border. Most of the country's 420 rivers are short and only
three have an average run-off above $50m^3$: the Narva, Emajõgi and Pärnu.
All of Estonia lies within the catchment of the Baltic Sea.

Total water abstractions were 2.7bn m^3 in 1992, down from 3.3bn m^3 in
1990. Around 80 per cent of total supplies come from surface water, but
groundwater (0.4bn m^3 abstracted in 1990) accounts for two-thirds of
drinking water supplies. A total of 1.98bn m^3 was consumed in 1992 by
thermal power stations; other industry consumed 125m m^3, agriculture
30m m^3 and domestic supplies 104m m^3.

Wastewater discharges totalled 2.69bn m^3 in 1992; of the 0.45 bn m3
requiring treatment, almost half received mechanical treatment only, 5 per
cent went untreated and 37 per cent did not meet treatment standards.

Many towns lack sewage works, although work has been carried out in
recent years to improve sewage treatment facilities at Tallinn and Kohtla-
Järve. The total BOD of wastewater discharges almost halved in 1991–92,
because of falling industrial production.

Groundwater is heavily polluted by agricultural run-off and industrial pollution (for example oil, phenols, sulphates) in some areas. Nitrate
levels of 200mg/l have been recorded in some rural wells. Intensive
abstractions have lowered groundwater levels in a number of regions.
Drinking water supplies have generally worsened with regard to chemical
characteristics, but improved according to biological characteristics; 22
per cent and 12 per cent of water sources sampled in 1992 did not meet the
respective health standards. Water resource and wastewater charges were
introduced on 1 January 1991 to supplement permits required for abstractions and discharges.

STE

Annual waste arisings total around 15mt, of which 1mt is domestic and 12mt from industry; these add to an estimated 250mt accumulated over the years, over 90 per cent from oil-shale production. An inventory of hazardous wastes produced by industry in 1990 showed that 10.5mt of waste resulted from the extraction, processing and use of oil-shale and 0.46mt from phosphorus mining. Nearly all waste is dumped or landfilled; there are around 400 landfill sites, covering over 550ha, most of which do not meet environmental protection requirements.

Charges are imposed for the production and disposal of waste, according to its toxicity. A new waste law was adopted on 14 May 1992, with the intention of ensuring the safe disposal of hazardous waste through a licensing system; three licences were issued by the Ministry of Environment in 1992 for the treatment of batteries, mercury bulbs and toxic chemicals.

NATURE CONSERVATION

Most of Estonia's industrial development is concentrated in the north of the country. Over 40 per cent of the territory is forested, and bogs occupy around 20 per cent; meadows and grassland form other important habitat types. There are 1560 species of vascular plants and 473 vertebrates (including 316 bird and 66 mammal species); 155 and 104 species respectively are listed in the national Red Data Book. 189 plant species are protected and 12 animal species strictly protected. A series of fines applies to species which are harmed illegally. Game species hunted include brown bear, lynx, beaver, wolf, pine marten and polecat.

Protected areas include the West Estonian Archipelago Biosphere Reserve (1.56m ha), which includes the islands of Hiumaa and Saaremaa, five large state nature reserves, and more than 120 other reserves. The total area under protection was estimated at 12 per cent of national territory in 1992. Nature conservation policy is based on the Nature Protection Law of 1957; a new nature conservation act is expected to come into effect soon.

ENERGY

Around half of energy demand is met from domestic sources, notably oil-shale and peat; the rest comes from imports of oil and gas, formerly from Russia. Oil-shale production in 1992 was 18.8mt, compared with a peak of 31.3mt in 1980; 90 per cent is used for electricity generation, all but 4 per cent of which is based on oil-shale combustion. Oil-shale is relatively low in calorific content and has a high ash content; 6–6.5mt of alkaline ash is produced annually, in addition to that discharged to air. Oil-shale also contains sulphur, chlorine, nitrogen and heavy metals. 663 000t of peat were produced for fuel use in 1992.

AGRICULTURE

Agriculture accounted for 20 per cent of net material product in 1990 and, with forestry, for 13 per cent of employment. Only around 28 per cent of agricultural land is arable, and meat and dairying dominate agricultural production. Oats constitute the main cereal crop; potatoes, millet, fruit and vegetables are also grown.

Under Soviet rule, collective and state farms dominated, with an average farm size of over 3500ha. However, all but 50 large experimental farms are being privatised under a land reform programme which began in 1989; there were around 10 000 private farms by 1992.

Agricultural and food subsidies have been reduced since 1989, and domestic food prices have risen dramatically; in 1992 around 70 per cent of household income went on food. Domestic and export demand for livestock produce has collapsed, and grain production fell by 45 per cent in 1992, following severe drought and lower fertiliser and pesticide inputs.

The fisheries catch in the Baltic Sea amounted to 35 776t in 1992, down from 45 636t in 1991; herring accounted for more than 80 per cent of the total. Fisheries are also supported on Lake Vortsjärv and Lake Peipus.

FOREST RESOURCES

The total wooded area was estimated at 2.02m ha in 1993, a figure which includes woods previously counted as agricultural land, and an increase over earlier estimates (1.8m ha) of forest; pine, birch and spruce predominate. An area of 3837ha was afforested in 1991, and 2.15m m^3 of timber felled in 1992 (3.01m m^3 in 1991).

Forest fires damaged 1729ha during a drought in 1992. Forest survey results from 1992 indicated that 14 per cent of spruce and 37 per cent of pine trees sampled were moderately defoliated or worse; those in the north-east and north-west were worst affected, partly as a result of acid rain.

TRANSPORT

The road network extends to 30 200km and the railway to 1030km, including connections with Russia and Latvia. Tallinn is the principal port, handling 80 per cent of sea freight. The transport sector accounted for 4.8 per cent of fuel consumption in 1985. There were around 200 000 cars in 1990, concentrated in urban areas, where vehicle emissions make a major contribution to NO_x pollution. However, the limited availability and high price of fuel has restricted growth in road transport.

Finland

Area	338 145km^2
Population	5.03m
Urban	60%
Rural	40%
Capital	Helsinki (0.49m)
City populations	6 > 100 000; 3 > 170 000
Economy	
GNP per capita	US$23 980 (1991)
Climate (Helsinki)	
Average daily max and min	22/13°C (July)/–3/–9°C (January)
Annual precipitation	688mm
Land-use cover	
Agriculture	9%
Forest	77%
Other	14%

Finland lies between Sweden and Russia, with a coastline to the west and south on the Baltic Sea. Southern and central areas of the country are low lying, with many lakes. The land rises in the north to reach over 900m close to the border with Norway. One quarter of the territory lies within the Arctic Circle, and the majority of the population is concentrated in the south.

INSTITUTIONS AND POLICY

Finland is a republic with an elected parliament of 200 members. Local government plays an important part in public administration, principally at the level of 12 administrative counties, which are responsible for the supervision and enforcement of much environmental legislation. There are also 460 municipalities, most of which have an environment department. The Ministry of the Environment was established in 1983 and handles housing and physical planning as well as environmental protection matters. The National Board of Waters and Environment forms part of the Ministry and shares responsibility for aspects of water management with the Ministry of Agriculture and Forestry.

Environmental controls are based on a range of legislative measures, although a number of different requirements were brought together in 1992, when the Environmental Licence Procedure Act came into effect. One environmental licence, issued by the county or municipal authorities, replaced those previously granted separately under air pollution, waste management and public health legislation. Provisions on environmental impact assessment entered into force in 1993.

Finland joined the European Community on 1 January 1995.

AIR POLLUTION

The air in Finland is relatively clean in comparison with many European countries; it is considered a danger to human health only periodically in city centres and some industrial areas. Before district heating systems and centralised waste management became more widespread, most urban air pollution was attributable to small heating boilers and the burning of waste. Motor vehicles have become an increasingly significant source of emissions.

Annual emissions of SO_2 fell by 60 per cent during the 1980s, to 242 000t in 1989. This reduction reflects the increased use of nuclear power, of hard coal rather than heavy oil, and of less polluting processes and equipment in key industrial sectors, such as paper and pulp, chemicals and metals. Industry contributed 40 per cent of SO_2 emitted in 1990. Finland aims to achieve a reduction of 80 per cent in sulphur emissions between 1980 and 2000.

NO_x emissions increased from 252 000t in 1985 to 290 000t in 1990, largely as a result of growth in road traffic and the production of energy. These sectors accounted for more than 80 per cent of NO_x emissions in 1990. The government seeks to reduce NO_x emissions by 30 per cent by 1997 (from the 1980 level). The majority of acidic depositions in Finland originate from outside the country, including 75 per cent of sulphur and 90 per cent of nitrogen compounds; the south is worst affected.

Lead emissions have fallen by around 80 per cent since the early 1970s, following reductions in the lead content of petrol. Emissions of toxic metals come principally from industrial plants such as metalworks and oil refineries, including some on the Kola peninsula in Russia.

Average concentrations of SO_2 in urban areas have generally fallen since the early 1970s, as district heating networks replaced small heating boilers. Air quality trends for NO_2 and particulates appear less positive, largely as a result of increased emissions from road traffic. Sand and grit spread on the roads in winter also contribute to elevated levels of particulates, the limit values for which are breached regularly in the larger conurbations. Ozone concentrations above $65\mu g/m^3$ (24-hour average) are recorded in the summer months. Regional standards for SO_2 apply to large agricultural and forestry areas: annual average concentrations should not exceed $25\mu g/m^3$ and annual sulphur deposition $0.5g/m^2$.

The principal item of air pollution legislation is the Air Pollution Control Act of 1982, which requires an environment licence to be obtained from the provincial authorities for any activity which will adversely affect air quality. General recommendations and regulations, for example on air quality and emission standards, are issued by the Council of State. A CO_2/energy tax was introduced in 1990.

WATER RESOURCES AND POLLUTION

Inland waters cover $33\ 522km^2$ in Finland, around 10 per cent of the total area. Lakes tend to be small and shallow, with an average depth of 7m; many are interconnected. The total length of rivers exceeds 20 000km, but most are short in length, with low flow rates. There are five major drainage basins. As much as 30–40 per cent of the annual total of $3100m^3$ discharged into the sea takes place during the spring thaw. Surface waters provide more than 90 per cent of total abstractions, which were estimated at 3bn m^3 in 1989, but around half of drinking water supplies come from groundwater.

Coastal waters in eastern Finland suffer from an oxygen deficit of 30–60 per cent in summer as a result of wastewater discharges. Increased levels of nitrogen and other nutrients from agriculture, sewage, industrial sources and fish-farming resulted in widespread eutrophication and algal blooms during the 1980s, particularly in the Gulf of Finland.

The low flow of rivers, shallow depth of lakes, and extended period of ice cover tend to make water courses in Finland highly sensitive to pollution. Acidification from airborne pollution has become more evident, although not as severe as in Sweden or Norway. The results of a survey in the mid-1980s classified 31 per cent of river length as 'poor' and 'bad' (the lowest of 5 quality classes), and 45 per cent as 'good' or 'excellent'. The quality of lakes and coastal waters appeared generally superior, with only 4 per cent of their area in the poorest two classes. The worst affected lakes were close to centres of population and typically were eutrophic. The survey found most lakes on the periphery of water systems to be in a natural state, although not necessarily fit for human consumption because of high humus levels.

Discharges from the pulp and paper industry have accounted for a large proportion of BOD in Finnish waters, around 75 per cent of that in wastewater discharges in the late 1980s. However, discharges of phosphorus and chlorine are being reduced. Treatment of municipal wastewater increased to serve more than 75 per cent of the population by 1990; as a result, related discharges of BOD and phosphorus fell by 70 per cent between 1970 and 1986.

Groundwater reserves are threatened by rising nitrate levels from agriculture, notably in southeast Finland, but remain fairly low compared with other countries. Groundwater in some areas is also affected by:

- increased salinity from salt spread on roads in winter
- pesticide residues in areas around tree nurseries
- phenols and metals from wood-treatment plants
- leachate from landfill sites.

The Water Act (1961) regulates water use, and includes a system of discharge permits granted by Water Courts. The Public Health Act (1965) and its implementing regulations (1965) include requirements covering sewerage and domestic water use. The National Board of Waters and the Environment, responsible to the Ministry of Environment, promotes the utilisation and management of national water resources and undertakes research. A second national water protection programme sets out objectives for pollution reduction to 1995, including discharges from industrial and municipal sources, and the rehabilitation of watercourses.

SOLID WASTE

Annual waste arisings are estimated at around 80mt, 65 per cent of which originates from agriculture, forestry and extractive industries. Around 700t of the total is thought to be hazardous. Municipal waste accounts for 3.1mt, although two-thirds of this comes from non-residential sources.

Most waste is disposed to landfill, including more than 75 per cent of municipal waste. An inventory of 750 municipal landfill sites in 1983 suggested that 180 were on water-permeable locations and 30 above groundwater reserves. Virtually all dangerous waste is handled by a national treatment centre run by Ekokem Oy Ab; this has an incineration plant, a physicochemical plant and a specialised disposal site. It handled 86 000t in 1990, including some imports. Recycling rates increased to 41 per cent for paper and cardboard and 36 per cent for glass in 1990. A deposit-refund system operates for drink bottles and a tax is levied on non-returnable containers.

Waste management policy is based on the Waste Management Act, which was adopted in 1979 and amended in 1981 to cover hazardous wastes. Establishments producing other than household waste are required to draw up a waste management plan if they intend to handle disposal themselves. The plans are used to assist provincial and municipal authorities, which are responsible for the transport of municipal waste. The government aims to provide for 50 per cent of municipal waste to be recycled by 2000, enabling many landfill sites to be closed.

NATURE CONSERVATION

Although Finland is sparsely populated and many parts of the country are relatively untouched by human activities, few areas remain in their natural state. Commercial forestry operations, wetland drainage and other developments have affected the environment extensively.

Species of fauna found in Finland include 62 mammals and 235 birds; 16 per cent of vertebrate animal species are considered threatened. The comparable figure for the country's 1550 vascular plant species is just under 15 per cent. Surveys of threats to vulnerable species in the 1980s indicated that forestry, the intensification of agriculture (notably the loss of meadows), peatland drainage and construction were amongst the principal causes; pollution and hunting appeared significant for some species. The area of built-up land more than doubled between 1960 and 1989, at the expense largely of wetland and other open areas.

A shoreline protection programme was approved in 1990 to help conserve coastal and lakeshore environments, including a ban on the construction of further holiday homes in some areas.

The conservation of natural areas, wild fauna and flora is based on the Nature Conservation Act of 1923 (and subsequent amendments). The Act provides for five categories of protected areas, and by 1991 there were:

- 27 national parks, covering 702 000ha
- 19 strict nature reserves (151 705ha)
- 173 protected bogs (404 060ha).

With other natural protected areas, natural monuments, 12 wilderness areas (1.49m ha in Lapland, designated under the Wilderness Act 1990) and other nature reserves, some form of protection was extended to around 2.8m ha. Under the Ramsar Convention 11 wetland sites (100 343ha) were designated. Responsibility for protected areas was transferred from the Ministry of Agriculture and Forestry to the Ministry of the Environment in 1983, when the latter was established.

ENERGY

Finland is relatively poor in indigenous fuels, and all fossil fuel supplies except peat are imported. Energy consumption per capita is relatively high, on account of the cold climate and energy-intensive industries (wood-processing, metals etc). Primary energy consumption grew to 30.7mtoe in 1990, industry accounting for 43 per cent and domestic use for 25 per cent.

Hydroelectric power is the most important indigenous energy source, generating 10–12TWh annually (around 20 per cent of electricity production). Wood-based energy sources provide about 15 per cent of the total primary energy supply, including 40 per cent of the fuel used by industry. Oil's share fell from 56 per cent in 1973 to 30 per cent in 1990; coal and gas together supplied around 19 per cent. Four nuclear power stations with a capacity of 2300MW supplied 29 per cent of electricity demand in 1990. Parliament voted in 1993 against construction of a fifth plant.

A CO_2/energy tax on fossil fuels was introduced in 1990.

AGRICULTURE

Agriculture occupies about 9 per cent of the land area and is concentrated in the south and south-west. The share of GDP contributed by agricultural production fell from 4.5 per cent in 1980 to 2.8 per cent in 1988. Farm size is relatively small, at an average of 13ha, and holdings are often family owned and run in conjunction with other activities such as forestry, aquaculture or fur-farming. Around one-third of agricultural land is devoted to hay, silage and pasture; barley and oats are the principal cereals grown, largely for animal feed. Intensification has enabled Finland to become more than self-sufficient in most major agricultural products.

Water pollution is probably the most severe environmental impact of agriculture in Finland; arable farming was thought to produce around half the total phosphorus discharged into water in the late 1980s, and taxes on nitrogen and phosphorus fertiliser were introduced in 1991–92. A range of schemes encourage the development of organic agriculture and more extensive production methods, and afforestation is intended to reduce overproduction.

FOREST RESOURCES

Forests have long constituted one of the country's most valuable natural resources and a basis of economic development; forest products account for around 60 per cent of export earnings. More than 26.8m ha of the country is wooded, 75 per cent of which is productive. Scots pine and Norway spruce make up more than 80 per cent of tree cover; birch is the most common broadleaved species (15 per cent). The annual timber cut has been consistently lower than annual growth since the early 1970s, at 55m m^3 and 79m m^3 respectively during 1985–89. The 1991 forest damage survey showed 16 per cent of sampled trees suffering 25 per cent or more defoliation; atmospheric pollution was considered a contributing factor.

The Forest Department is responsible for implementing legislation on state-owned and private forests. The Private Forestry Act (1928) prevents the destruction of forests and remains largely unchanged since its introduction. The Forest Improvements Act (1928) regulates the grants and loans available to private forestry for forest improvement works.

TRANSPORT

As in many other OECD countries, transport volumes grew greatly during the 1970s and 1980s, with a steady transfer from rail to road of both passenger and freight traffic. The number of passenger-km travelled by private car doubled between 1970 and 1990, to 46.8bn; the equivalent figure for rail rose from 2.2bn to 3.3bn.

Economic growth in the 1980s was reflected in increased car ownership; the number of passenger cars in use rose from 1.23m in 1980 to 1.94m in 1990. By then, transport accounted for around 50 per cent of NO_x and hydrocarbon emissions, and 30 per cent of CO_2 emissions.

The rail network contracted during the 1980s, to 5867km in 1990, whilst maintaining passenger and freight volumes. There were more than 77 000km of public roads by 1992. Around 6300km of inland waterways are navigable, with a greater length accessible for floating timber.

France

Area	543 965km²
Population	57.46m
Urban	74%
Rural	26%
Capital	Paris (2.18m; conurbation 9.06m)
City populations	34 > 100 000; 11 > 200 000
Economy	
GNP per capita	US$20 380 (1991)
Climate (Paris)	
Average daily max and min	25/15°C (July)/6/1°C (January)
Annual precipitation	619mm
Land-use cover	
Agriculture	56%
Forest	26%
Other	18%

France is in northwestern Europe, with a long coastline on the Atlantic Ocean, the English Channel and North Sea to the west and north, and the Mediterranean Sea to the south. Two-thirds of the country is low-lying and flat, particularly in the north and west, and dominated by the basins of large rivers; around 7 per cent of the land rises above 1000m, mostly in the south and east. The Pyrenees form the border with Spain to the south-west, and the Alps and Jura span the borders with Switzerland and Italy. Other borders, to the east, are shared with Germany, Luxembourg and Belgium. French territory includes the island of Corsica, in the Mediterranean, and some overseas territories and departments which are not covered here.

INSTITUTIONS AND POLICY

France is a republic headed by an elected President; under the constitution of 1958, parliament consists of an elected National Assembly (577 deputies) and Senate (321 senators). Local government is exercised at five levels, including the 22 regions and 96 departments, which have both locally elected authorities and representatives of central government; local administrative matters are handled by around 36 500 communes. All levels have some environmental responsibilities.

The Ministry of the Environment was first created in 1971; it was restructured in 1992 when its powers were extended. Some of the Ministry's functions are undertaken at regional level through:

- the Regional Directorates for the Environment (DIREN)
- the Regional Directorates for Industry, Research and the Environment (DRIRE) and
- six River Basin Agencies.

The Ministry's work is also supported by a number of other bodies, including:

- the Agency for the Environment and Energy Management (ADEME), formed in 1991 out of three national agencies responsible for waste, air quality and energy management, and
- the French Institute for the Environment (IFEN), which concentrates on monitoring and statistical work.

Environmental permitting is based on the Act on Installations Scheduled for Purposes of Environmental Protection (76/663), which requires class 1 installations to obtain a permit and class 2 (less polluting) installations to report to the authorities and meet operational safety requirements. The system is overseen by the DRIRE and the regional authorities. Applications for permits must be accompanied by an EIA; EIA provisions are contained in Act 76/629 on the Conservation of the Natural Environment and Act 83/630 on Public Enquiries and Environmental Protection. A National Environment Plan was produced by the Ministry of the Environment in 1990.

AIR POLLUTION

Annual emissions of SO_2 have fallen significantly over the past 20 years, from 3.9mt in 1973 to 1.37mt in 1991, reflecting reductions in the sulphur content of fuels and other pollution controls, as well as the expansion of nuclear-generated electricity. However, SO_2 emissions increased during 1989–91, principally because:

- thermal power stations were used more, accounting for 34 per cent of emissions in 1991,
- drought limited the use of hydroelectric stations, and
- output from some nuclear stations was reduced.

Particulate emissions show a comparable trend, falling from 427 000t in 1980 to 288 000t in 1991.

Although emissions of NO_x fell slightly during the early 1980s, from a peak of 1.9mt in 1979, they have since increased again, largely as a result of transport growth. The proportion originating from the transport sector has grown to 76 per cent of the 1.81mt of NO_x emitted in 1991, compared with 56 per cent in 1980; only 8 per cent came from power stations in 1991.

Transport also accounts for an increasing share of emissions of SO_2 and CO_2. Emissions of CO_2 fell from 503mt in 1980 to 389mt in 1991; emissions from transport increased by 38 per cent over this period. Air quality has generally improved with regard to SO_2, annual average concentrations in most major cities having declined during the 1980s. Elevated levels are found around industrial areas and major sources. Five breaches of the EC limit values for SO_2 and smoke were recorded in 1990–91, and improvement plans are intended to reduce levels in ten zones considered to be at risk of exceeding the limit values for SO_2.

Lead levels from vehicles have fallen as a result of the increased market share of unleaded petrol, but in 1991 the EC limit value was breached near a factory in Lille.

High levels of NO_2 are often recorded near main roads in major urban centres, and two breaches of the EC limit value of $200\mu g/m^3$ were recorded in 1991, in Marseille and Lille. Levels have increased recently in many cities.

Concentrations of ozone above $200\mu g/m^3$ were recorded in the summer of 1991, particularly in the south-east of the country.

Emissions from industrial plants are regulated by means of Act 76/663 of 19 July 1976, which established a system of scheduled installations *(installations classées)*. Class 1 plants require authorisation by the prefect, on the advice of the DRIRE; class 2 plants must be notified to the DRIRE or department. The authorisation procedure was laid down in Decree 77/1133 of 21 September 1977, and technical details given through a series of circulars and decrees. A tax on emissions was introduced in 1985, at FF130 per tonne of SO_2 emitted by combustion plants of 50MW or above; in 1990 its scope was broadened to include plants above 20MW and other pollutants (H_2S, NO_X and HCl), and increased to FF150/t. This was expected to increase annual revenue from FF100m to FF190m, to be used for anti-pollution measures. Air quality standards were fixed in accordance with EC Directives by the Decree of 25 October 1991, replacing earlier circulars. By 1991, 28 networks (with more than 1200 samplers) were in use to monitor air quality, measuring concentrations of ten pollu-

WATER RESOURCES AND POLLUTION

tants.

France is generally well-endowed with water resources; precipitation is fairly evenly distributed through the year, although with regional variations. There are five major river basins: the Garonne, Rhône, Rhine, Seine and Loire. Water supply is not usually a problem, although droughts in 1989, 1990 and 1991 led to greater reliance on groundwater. Total abstractions rose from 23.5bn m³ in 1970 to 37.7bn m³ in 1990, including 22.27bn m³ for cooling in energy production. Excluding the latter, virtually all of which comes from surface sources, 40 per cent of abstractions came from groundwater in 1990, including 57 per cent of domestic supplies (6.1bn m³); 4.9bn m³ were abstracted for irrigation and 4.45bn m³ for industrial use.

A national network monitors the quality of surface waters at 900 points, measuring key parameters such as BOD and dissolved oxygen. The results of recent years appear to indicate limited progress in improving water quality; many point sources of pollution have been tackled by installing treatment facilities, but the quality of smaller rivers in particular seems to have declined. In 1990, 38 per cent of samples failed to meet quality objectives, compared with 48 per cent in 1988; quality appeared poorest in the Artois-Picardie basin, where a 20 per cent compliance rate was recorded in 1990. France had identified 1932 seawater bathing areas in 1992 under the EC Directive; 87 per cent of those sampled in accordance with the Directive met the mandatory values for coliforms.

Polluting discharges from industrial sources were reduced significantly between 1978 and 1989, by more than 30 per cent for suspended solids and organic matter, and by 54 per cent for toxics. Overall, facilities for industrial discharges were estimated in 1989 to treat:

- 92 per cent of suspended solids
- 79 per cent of organic matter
- 86 per cent of toxics.

Agriculture and food-processing industries accounted for 40 per cent of organic discharges from industry in 1989, and chemical and metalworks for almost 90 per cent of toxic disharges. Industrial discharges are also concentrated geographically, half originating from plants in just four regions (Haute-Normandie, Nord-Pas-de-Calais, Ile de France and Rhône-Alpes).

The proportion of the total population served by sewage treatment works increased from 19 per cent in 1970 to 68 per cent in 1987; the figure is much lower in some rural areas and higher in urban areas. The proportion of total discharges of organic matter which received treatment in sewage works was raised from 32.5 per cent in 1981 to 43 per cent in 1990; by 1990 there were 9936 treatment plants with a capacity of 68.4m population equivalents. Treatment facilities are inadequate in some coastal cities and in rural areas.

Nitrate pollution of groundwater resources, largely a result of agricultural activities, has become a serious problem in some areas. Elevated nitrate concentrations are associated with:

- intensive livestock farming in Brittany,
- intensive arable production in the Paris basin, and
- irrigation in the south-west.

Levels above 50mg/l in groundwater are not uncommon in the worst-affected areas, and can reach more than 100mg/l. In some cases, drinking water supplies have been affected, and eutrophication has occurred in surface and coastal waters, particularly in Brittany.

Water pollution control is based on Act 64/1245, which together with the law on scheduled installations provides the basis for authorisations for discharges. Six River Basin Agencies are responsible for overseeing water management on the basis of major hydrographic basins; they levy charges on emissions to water and provide financial support for management and treatment facilities. Agreements between water suppliers, users and authorities form an important part in the planning process with regard to water management and treatment. A new Water Act (92/3) is intended to improve the system of water resource management and pollution control. Water management plans are to be drawn up for each river basin, the permitting system for abstractions and discharges will be strengthened and provisions will be made to improve enforcement.

SOLID WASTE

Total waste arisings are estimated at around 573mt annually, including

400mt of agricultural waste and 100mt from extractive industries. Industrial waste generation is currently around 50mt and household waste 20mt annually (compared with 15.6mt in 1980). Virtually the entire population is served by household waste collection services, and 45m people live in areas which offer separate collections for glass. Landfills take around 60 per cent of household waste, the remainder being incinerated (33 per cent) or composted (6 per cent). Arisings of hazardous waste were estimated at 4mt in 1990, over half of which was landfilled.

Waste management policy is based on Act 75/633 on Waste Disposal and Recycling, which was amended by Act 92/646. Landfill sites, treatment and transfer stations, and industrial waste incinerators are subject to controls under Act 76/663 on scheduled installations. The new Act includes the objective that by 1 July 2002 landfills should receive no waste which has not undergone treatment of some kind, ie only residues resulting from incineration, composting etc. Each department is to draw up a management plan for household waste, in consultation with interested parties. In addition, regional and national plans must be made for industrial waste disposal. Detailed obligations concerning plans were set out in Decrees 93/139 and 93/140.

A tax of FF20/t is collected by ADEME to finance research and develop treatment centres, and provisions on liability were introduced into authorisations for new disposal sites.

Legislation on waste shipments was amended by Decree 92/798 to restrict further the import of waste.

A mandatory system for household packaging waste was introduced by Decree 92/377, requiring producers and importers to ensure this waste is taken back and recovered (including incineration with heat recovery). A company (Eco-Emballages) was established in November 1992 to make arrangements with producers and local authorities in accordance with the Decree.

NATURE CONSERVATION

France has a wide range of habitat types, which include extensive areas of forest, mountains, wetlands, and Mediterranean and Atlantic coast. The number of species found includes: 115 mammals, 353 birds and 36 reptiles. There are an estimated 4700 species of vascular plants, and around 40 per cent of European plant species are present in France. Half the mammal and reptile species are thought to be threatened, largely as a result of habitat loss, and 1050 plants are listed in the national Red Data Book.

Nature conservation policy is based on Act 76/629, which provides for species protection as well as the designation of nature reserves. Protected species are listed in decrees which implement the Act. National parks, established under Act 60/708, numbered six by 1992, covering 360 700ha, with a further two planned. In addition, there were 25 regional natural parks extending to over 3.9m ha, and 103 natural reserves (113 000ha).

The Conservancy for the Coastline and Lakeshores was created in 1975 and acquires and protects sensitive areas, eg those under pressure from development; it managed 37 800ha by 1991.

Act 93/24 on the protection and enhancement of the countryside, adopted in January 1993, is intended to provide local authorities with more powers to protect the countryside through land-use planning.

ENERGY

France has relatively small reserves of oil and gas, mainly in the southwest of the country, and of coal, but is dependent on imports for the majority of supplies. Production was 2.9mt of oil in 1992 and 33.7bn m³ of gas in 1989; coal output declined from 20.7mt in 1980 to 10.1mt in 1991. Energy policy has aimed at lowering dependence on imports, primarily by developing domestic production of electricity from hydroelectric and nuclear stations. Primary energy production doubled from 43.2 to 97.3mtoe during 1980–90.

France's nuclear power programme was expanded during the 1980s and by 1992 there were 56 reactors in operation with a capacity of 57 688MW; five more reactors were under construction. Nuclear generation accounted for 73 per cent of electricity produced in 1992 (compared with 8 per cent in 1973), with hydroelectric stations contributing 14 per cent and conventional thermal stations 13 per cent. There are significant reserves of uranium at Crouzville, and the ore is refined for use in power stations. Electricity exports rose from 29bn kWh in 1985 to 59bn kWh as nuclear generating capacity increased; the United Kingdom and Italy are important customers.

AGRICULTURE

France is a major producer of agricultural goods, accounting for 23 per cent of EC production, and the second largest exporter in the world; wheat and wine are important exports. The total area in agricultural use decreased by around 2m ha between 1970 and 1991 to 30.6m ha, comprising 11.4m ha of grassland and 19.2m ha of arable and permanent crop land. The arable area has increased during the past 20 years, at the expense of grassland. More than half of French farm holdings are below 20ha, including 27 per cent under 5ha; the trend is towards consolidation and average farm size grew from 19ha in 1970 to 31ha in 1990.

Irrigation has become more important in recent years, the area irrigated having doubled between 1970 and 1988, and extending into areas north of the Loire. Livestock farming has become more intensive, and pig and poultry numbers increased during the 1970s and 1980s, whilst dairying declined. Pork and poultry production is concentrated in Brittany and the Pays-de-Loire; farms above threshold levels (eg 50 pigs) are covered by the legislation on scheduled installations. The pollution of surface and groundwater by nitrates from livestock waste and artificial fertiliser has become a major concern in some areas. The abandonment of agricultural land, as a result of farmers giving up agriculture, has also attracted attention because of its environmental and social consequences.

The French fishing fleet numbered over 9000 vessels in 1991; the catch totalled 544 000t of marine fish and 277 000t of shellfish (1990).

FOREST RESOURCES

Forest cover extended to 14.4m ha in 1991; the areas with the highest proportion of forest are found in the south and east of the country. Broadleaved species, predominantly oak, account for 63.5 per cent of the forested area. 43.7m m³ of timber was cut in 1989, including 10.4m m³ as fuelwood.

The 1992 forest health survey indicated that 8 per cent of trees suffered notable defoliation (25 per cent or more). Forest fires destroy large areas of forest in some years, including more than 70 000 ha in 1989 and 1990; the drier regions of the Mediterranean are usually worst affected. Drought in recent years has increased susceptibility to fires and to other damage factors.

The National Forestry Office was established in 1964 to manage publicly owned forests and coordinate forest policy. The Office is supervised jointly by the Ministries of Agriculture and of Environment. Clear-cutting in state forests requires Ministry authorisation, and is restricted in privately owned forests, too. Areas may be designated as forests in need of protection by virtue of their role in preventing erosion or other reasons of public interest, including amenity value. Land use changes must not adversely affect forests so designated.

TRANSPORT

France's principal transport routes are focused largely around Paris. The road network covers more than 800 000km and by 1992 included 7500km of motorway. The volume of traffic carried by motorways trebled between 1970 and 1990, and it is planned to extend the motorway system to more than 11 000km by 1997.

The number of motor vehicles in use increased from 17.9m in 1980 to 28.6m in 1991. Over 80 per cent of passenger journeys were made by private car in 1990, compared with 9 per cent on the national rail network.

There were 33 400km of railway in 1991, when 831m passengers were carried. Development of the rail system is concentrated on extending the high-speed train (TGV) network, which runs between Paris and the west, the south-east, and north. The latter route is intended to link with the Channel Tunnel to England, and with lines to Brussels. The TGV network expanded from 2500km in 1988 to around 4700km in 1992.

The amount of inland freight carried by rail fell by 30 per cent and that by inland waterways by 40 per cent during the 1980s; by 1991, 60 per cent of freight movements went by road and 25 per cent by rail (measured in tonne-km).

The energy consumption of the transport sector doubled during the 20 years to 1990, when it accounted for over 25 per cent of total consumption. Emissions from the transport sector constitute a significant and growing proportion of total emissions to air, especially for particulates (43 per cent) and NO_x (76 per cent). Transport also accounted for 33 per cent of CO_2 emissions in 1991.

Germany

Area	356 850km²
Population	79.8m
Urban	80%*
Rural	20%*
Capital	Berlin (3.42m)
City populations	83 > 100 000; 13 > 500 000
Economy	
GNP per capita	US$23 650* (1991)
Climate (Berlin)	
Average daily max and min	24/14°C (July)/2/–3°C (January)
Annual precipitation	603mm
Land-use cover	
Agriculture	52%
Forest	30%
Other	18%

Germany stretches from the North and Baltic Seas, and a border with Denmark, in the north, to the Alps in the south, where it shares borders with Switzerland and Austria. It is bounded by France, Luxembourg, Belgium and the Netherlands to the west, and by Poland and the Czech Republic to the east. The northern half of the country is predominantly low-lying and flat, whilst the hills in central Germany rise to over 1000m and the Alps to 3000m.

INSTITUTIONS AND POLICY

Germany is a federal republic with 16 states *(Länder)* and a federal parliament of two houses; the upper house *(Bundesrat)* consists of representatives of the elected *Land* governments. For most environmental matters, competence is shared between the federal government and the *Länder*, but federal powers are limited to the adoption of framework laws in some areas (eg water, land-use, nature conservation). Each *Land* usually has two or three levels of administration and local government, and local authorities generally have some environmental responsibilities.

The Federal Ministry for Environment, Nature Protection and Nuclear Safety was established in 1986. Its work is supported by the Federal Environment Agency, which undertakes scientific research. Permitting requirements are based on the Federal Emission Control Act (1974) for air, the Waste Act (1972) and the Water Management Act (1957). The Environmental Impact Assessment Act (1990) introduced EIA as an essen-

* Refers to western Germany only

tial part of the statutory approval process for development projects. The Environmental Liability Act (1990) sets out arrangements for liability for environmental damage caused by listed installations and requires the owners of some businesses (eg chemical plants and incinerators) to have insurance cover for environmental liabilities.

The former German Democratic Republic became part of the Federal Republic of Germany in October 1990. Target dates for compliance with key items of federal environmental legislation in the new eastern *Länder* were drawn up, ranging from 31 December 1990 to 2005. A series of environmental programmes was initiated to help address urgent problems. Total investment expenditure required for 'environmental reconstruction' in the eastern *Länder* was estimated at DM83–320bn.

AIR POLLUTION

Total emissions of SO_2 in western Germany decreased significantly during the 1980s, from 3.2mt in 1980 to 0.94mt in 1990, as a result of the installation of flue-gas desulphurisation equipment in fossil fuel power stations and other measures. Annual emissions in eastern Germany, however, continued at more than 5.2mt during the latter half of the 1980s before falling slightly to 2.76mt in 1990. The higher levels recorded for eastern Germany reflect the greater use of lignite and less effective emission control equipment.

NO_x emissions in western Germany increased gradually to 2.98mt in 1986, thereafter declining to 2.6mt in 1990 as catalytic converters in motor vehicles and low-NO_x combustion technology in power plants became more widespread; motor vehicles contributed more than 70 per cent of emissions in 1990. NO_x emissions in eastern Germany remained between around 0.60–0.67mt annually during the 1980s. Emissions of particulates fell from 3.5mt in 1975 to 2.27mt in 1990, as emission abatement equipment was installed in both parts of the country.

Average concentrations of SO_2 and particulates have generally fallen in western Germany in recent years; annual mean values above 40µg/m³ are exceeded only occasionally, in industrial areas. Ambient SO_2 levels in the east, however, often breached quality standards in 1991, affecting some six million people, usually because of the burning of lignite (including for domestic heating) and a lack of modern pollution control technology. The area around Leipzig and Halle has been worst affected.

Elevated levels of NO_2 are more widespread in western than in eastern Germany, exceeding EC standards in some urban areas; levels above 70µg/m³ have been measured close to major roads.

Vehicle emissions contribute to the high ozone concentrations which have been found during some summers, particularly in the western part of the country, exceeding a half-hourly average of 200µg/m³ in some cases.

Air pollution policy is based on the Federal Emission Control Act of 1974, which established a licensing system for industrial plant and contains other provisions on air pollution; for example monitoring, clean-air plans and fuel standards. Detailed requirements are laid down in more than 20 ordinances and regulations. The Technical Instructions on Air Quality Control include:

- emission standards (based on best available technology) for the major industrial sectors,
- air quality standards, and
- a timetable for retrofitting improved abatement equipment to existing industrial plants – by 1994 in western Germany and by 1999 in eastern Germany.

The Ordinance on Large Combustion Plants prescribes emission limits for major pollutants, requiring the retrofitting of flue-gas desulphurisation equipment at many power stations. It is expected to lead to significant reductions in the new *Länder*, too; for example, to around 1mt SO_2 annually after 1996.

The production of CFCs was reduced from 125 000t in 1987 to 65 000t in 1991, and was due to cease by 1995.

Emissions of CO_2 in western Germany fell from 805mt to 725mt, and in eastern Germany from 321mt to 306mt between 1980 and 1990. A national target was adopted in 1990 of reducing CO_2 emissions by 25–30 per cent by 2005, compared with 1987 levels.

WATER RESOURCES AND POLLUTION

Germany is relatively rich in water resources. Most of the country is drained via large rivers (Rhine, Weser, Elbe, Ems) to the North Sea, except in the south, where the Danube basin drains (eventually) into the Black Sea. Run-off from a smaller area flows into the Baltic Sea.

Water abstractions in western Germany rose from 29.5bn m^3 in 1970 to 47.5bn m^3 in 1990, over 85 per cent coming from surface water. Of total abstractions in 1990, 70 per cent was used for cooling in power stations and 11.5 per cent for public water supply; the chemical industry is the largest manufacturing consumer (4bn m^3 in 1987)*. Groundwater sources are of vital importance, providing around 70 per cent of drinking water.

The overall quality of surface waters in western Germany has improved significantly during the past 20 years, although only the upper reaches of the larger rivers are placed in the top two classes (I and I–II) of biological water quality (based on seven classes). Relatively small lengths fall into the poorest two quality classes (III–IV and IV), notably several tributaries of the Rhine, as a result of industrial and urban waste water discharges. Most stretches of the major rivers are of classes II and II–III, with sections of the Weser and Elbe in class III.

Treatment of discharges from industrial plants has been improved in western Germany, as also has treatment in sewage works, helping to reduce emissions of toxics and organic substances; by 1990 the proportion of the population connected to sewage works with biological treatment had reached 90 per cent.

The position in eastern Germany is rather different; surveys after unification found many surface waters seriously contaminated by industrial and sewage discharges. Over 40 per cent of watercourses were unusable as sources of drinking water and only 5 per cent of industrial discharges received adequate treatment; municipal sewage often received primary treatment only and 12 per cent went untreated. The Elbe, Saale and Mulde appear worst affected, although declining industrial activity since 1989 has lessened the pollution load in most rivers.

Groundwater is affected by pollution from industrial sources and from agricultural activities, which in turn affect drinking water supplies in some areas. High levels of nitrogen fertilisation are the principal cause of elevated nitrate levels in groundwater, and some drinking water sources have exceeded the EC limit of 50mg/l in most western *Länder*. In eastern Germany, high nitrate levels are concentrated in southern areas. Levels of pesticides are also found above EC standards, a study in 1987 having indicated that around 10 per cent of groundwater supplies* could be polluted in excess of 0.1μg/l.

Water policy is largely the responsibility of the *Länder,* operating within a framework of federal laws. The Federal Water Management Act of 1957, established a framework requiring authorisation for withdrawals and discharges. Amendments in 1976 introduced minimum discharge and treatment standards, and in 1986 required best available technology to be applied to discharges of hazardous substances (both to water bodies and to sewers). Three types of water protection areas can be established to protect water supplies through restrictions on landuse, covering more than 15 per cent of the land area. Compensation payments are made to farmers in some protection areas. The Water Act also includes provisions on water management and wastewater plans.

Charges on wastewater discharges are levied under the Wastewater Charges Act of 1976, according to the volume and polluting characteristics of discharges. The level of charges is due to increase to DM90 per unit by 1999, in order to discourage harmful emissions.

Standards for drinking water are laid down in the Drinking Water Ordinance, made under the Foodstuffs and Consumer Goods Act.

SOLID WASTE

Waste arisings in 1990, excluding agricultural waste, totalled around 243mt, including:

- 27.96mt of household waste
- 81.9mt of industrial waste
- 29.6mt from energy production
- 19.3mt from mining activities.

This was estimated to include around 6mt of hazardous waste, of which 522 000t was exported. Industrial waste arisings in 1987* included over 1.6mt of waste oils, resins and latex and 0.45mt of organic solvents.

Total annual volumes of waste generated in western Germany did not vary significantly during the 1980s. The majority of municipal waste (over 75 per cent) was disposed to landfill in 1990, including virtually all that arising in eastern Germany; 18 per cent was incinerated and 3 per cent composted. In 1987 there were around 10 400 landfill sites and 160 incinerators. Recycling rates grew during the 1980s to reach 40 per cent for paper and cardboard and 45 per cent for glass in 1990.

The federal Waste Disposal Act was adopted in 1972 and substantially amended by the Waste Avoidance and Management Act of 1986 to place greater emphasis on waste avoidance and recycling, and to implement EC framework directives on waste disposal. Other EC Directives covering specific areas (eg waste oils, transfrontier shipment) have been implemented through ordinances, and technical requirements on waste management laid down in technical instructions.

The Packaging Ordinance (1991) requires manufacturers and distributors of packaging to take it back for reuse or recycling. In response, industrial interests established the *Duales System Deutschland* (DSD) company to collect packaging waste and arrange for recycling on behalf of participating companies (which pay a fee). Other ordinances are expected to cover different sectors, such as vehicles, electronic goods and paper.

Surveys indicated the existence of 50 000 contaminated sites in western Germany (1989) and at least 47 000 in eastern Germany (1991); the total could exceed 200 000. Federal legislation on soil protection and contaminated sites is in preparation.

NATURE CONSERVATION

The country's natural vegetation has been widely affected or displaced by agricultural, forestry, industrial or urban development, although less extensively in upland areas and the south. Many species of wild fauna and flora have declined in recent decades, largely as a result of damage to habitats. The 1988 Red Data Book lists 873 out of 2728 species of vascular plant species and 253 out of 502 animal vertebrate species in western Germany; 75 per cent of reptile species and 70 per cent of freshwater fish species were thought to be threatened.

National policy is based on the Federal Nature Conservation Act, which sets the framework for *Land* legislation and policy. The Act covers species protection as well as establishing six categories of protected area. By 1991 there were ten national parks, covering around 700 000ha, including extensive coastal and marine areas on the Wadden and Baltic Seas. A large number of nature reserves were designated during the 1980s, reaching 5049 (680 000ha) in 1990. Landscape protection areas are less strictly protected and in 1991 numbered around 6200 and covered over 8m ha, often overlapping with 67 nature parks (5.56m ha), which are also intended to provide for recreation and leisure activities. Areas may also be designated as protection forest (0.45m ha) and forest reserves under the Forestry Act. By 1993, 31 Ramsar wetland sites had been designated (672 852ha), and there were 117 Special Protection Areas (291 000ha)* under the EC birds Directive.

ENERGY

Total primary energy supply decreased from 366mtoe in 1988 to 347mtoe in 1991, reflecting decreased industrial activity in eastern Germany. In general, energy demand had increased gradually during the previous 20 years, but more rapidly in eastern Germany. The energy mix in the two parts of Germany was very different.

In western Germany, oil accounted for 40 per cent of primary energy in 1990, coal for 27 per cent, gas 17 per cent and nuclear power 14 per cent.

Gas and nuclear power expanded their share of primary energy supply from 6 per cent to 21 per cent during 1970–90, at the expense of solid fuels and oil.

By contrast, eastern Germany depended on lignite for around 70 per cent of primary energy in 1990, with oil supplying much of the rest (14 per cent). Around half of energy requirements are imported, notably oil and gas; domestic production in 1991 include: 66.5mt of coal, 279mt of lignite, 22mt of coal briquettes and coke, and 17.5bn m³ of gas.

Germany had 21 nuclear reactors in operation in 1992, generating 30 per cent of electricity. The five reactors in eastern Germany were shut down after unification. Spent nuclear fuel is sent to France and the UK for reprocessing; final storage facilities are under construction at two sites (Konrad and Gorleben). District heating, including combined heat and power, has expanded, and provided around 8 per cent of space heating in 1989.

AGRICULTURE

Agricultural uses account for just over half the total land area in Germany, totalling 12.4m ha of arable and permanent cropland and 5.6m ha of permanent grassland in 1990. The area under grass has gradually declined during the past 20 years, particularly during the 1970s, whilst the arable area changed little. Average farm size in 1987* was slightly above the EC average of 13ha, at 17ha; 70 per cent of holdings were below 20ha. Around 30 per cent* of those engaged in agriculture were part time.

Major arable crops include wheat, barley, rape, sugarbeet, potatoes and fodder crops; apples and pears, and vines, are also regionally important.

In general, farming has become more specialised and more intensive; mixed farms have become less widespread and inputs have increased. The consumption of nitrogen fertiliser increased from 1.64mt in 1970 to reach a peak of 2.4mt in 1988; the level of application in 1990 averaged 125kg/ha.* Pesticide use evolved similarly, growing from 25 000t to 36 600t of active ingredient between 1975 and 1988.*

The environmental effects of changes in agriculture include: losses of wildlife habitats and species, pollution from pesticides and nitrogen (notably of groundwater) and damage to soil quality.

Many *Länder* have introduced programmes to support measures for the restoration of biotopes, often destroyed through land consolidation, and for more extensive and traditional forms of agricultural practice, requiring lower inputs.

FOREST RESOURCES

Forest was estimated to cover around 10.39m ha in 1990 (30 per cent of the total land area), figures showing a slight increase during the past 20 years. Coniferous species account for 70 per cent of forest cover, and the timber cut in 1990 was estimated at 75m m³.

Forest damage became an important focus of environmental concern during the early 1980s and encouraged measures to limit emissions of acidic air pollutants. National surveys suggest that forests in parts of central, eastern and southern Germany are worst affected; the 1991 forest survey indicated that the proportion of trees suffering 25 per cent or more defoliation reached 38 per cent in the eastern *Länder*, compared with 11 per cent in the northwest and 25 per cent for the country as a whole. Air pollution is thought to constitute an important factor in forest damage, including 'imports' from neighbouring countries.

Forestry policy is primarily the responsibility of the *Länder*, although the broad framework is formed by the Federal Forestry Act, which came into force in 1975, and is coordinated by the Ministry for Food, Agriculture and Forests. A national 'save the forest' action programme was initiated in 1983, in response to evidence of forest damage.

TRANSPORT

The length of the road network increased from 562 000km in 1970 to 628 000km in 1991, nearly all as a result of roadbuilding in western Germany, where the length of motorway doubled to more than 9000km in this period. Total road traffic in western Germany almost doubled during 1970–90, and private motor vehicles accounted for 82 per cent of passenger transport and 56 per cent of freight transport in 1989 (measured in passenger-km and t-km).

By comparison, transport in the former East Germany was much more geared towards public transport and rail; private motor vehicles accounted for only 60 per cent of passenger transport and rail for over 70 per cent of freight transport (1989).

The rail network in Germany as a whole extended to over 41 000km in 1991, and there were over 6800km of navigable inland waterways, of which the Rhine was the most important.

The continuing shift towards road transport is posing numerous environmental problems, and this trend is expected to continue; by 2010 private car transport is forecast to increase by 29 per cent and road freight by 95 per cent (over 1988 levels). The effects of the EC's single market, the unification of Germany, and more open borders to the east added to other pressures, particularly for freight traffic.

Air emissions from the transport sector increased to over 70 per cent* of NO_X and 50 per cent* of VOCs by 1990; its share of CO_2 emissions reached 23 per cent* in 1990, an increase of almost 70 per cent over 20 years.

Although some emissions from motor vehicles have decreased as a result of greater use of unleaded petrol (80 per cent market share in 1991) and catalytic converters (fitted to 97 per cent of new petrol cars in 1992), a tendency towards heavier, faster and more powerful vehicles is evident. This has offset gains in energy efficiency, and average fuel consumption per km for cars has changed little over 20 years. Energy used for transport in western Germany almost doubled between 1970 and 1990, from 29.0 to 52.7mtoe.

Whilst in some residential areas traffic abatement schemes have been introduced and speed limits reduced to 30km/hr, no general speed limits apply to motorways.

Greece

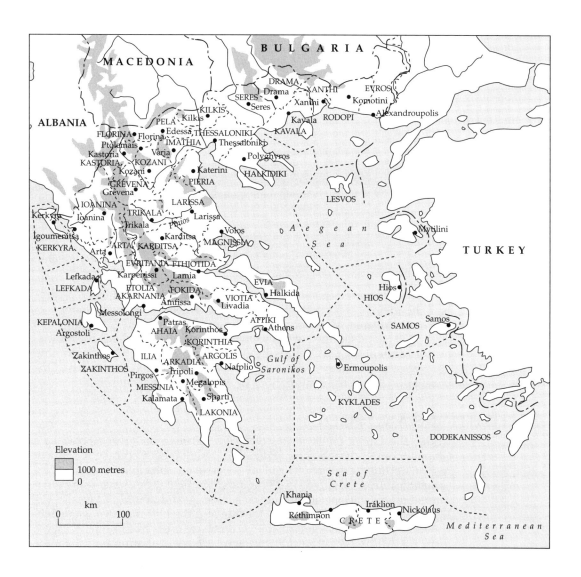

Area	131 957km²
Population	10.26m
Urban	63%
Rural	37%
Capital	Athens (3.1m)
City populations	7 > 200 000
Economy	
GNP per capita	US$6340 (1991)
Climate (Athens)	
Average daily max and min	33/23°C (July)/13/6°C (January)
Annual precipitation	402mm
Land-use cover	
Agriculture	70%
Forest	20%
Other	10%

Greece is located in southeastern Europe, on the Mediterranean Sea. The mainland is predominantly mountainous and has northern borders with Albania, Macedonia, Bulgaria and Turkey. Crete is the largest of over 3000 islands in the surrounding seas, and the mainland coastline is heavily indented. The Pindos mountains cross the peninsula running northwest to southeast, with extensive areas above 2000m. Over half the population live in the conurbations of Athens and Thessaloniki.

INSTITUTIONS AND POLICY

Under the Greek constitution of 1975, 300 members are elected to a Chamber of Deputies by proportional representation. Central government responsibilities are carried out at local level through 54 prefectures (*nomoi*), grouped together in 13 regions. Municipalities have some environmental obligations, including for sewerage and household waste. The Ministry for Physical Planning, Housing and the Environment was established in 1980 and merged in 1985 with the Ministry of Public Works to form the Ministry of the Environment, Physical Planning and Public Works. Each prefecture includes an Environment Quality Control Unit which liaises with the Ministry.

A framework environmental law, Law 1650 on Environmental Protection, was adopted in 1986; it provides for detailed measures to be made through presidential decrees and ministerial decisions, including those required to implement EC directives. Its provisions on EIA were brought into effect in 1990 through two ministerial decisions. Much of Greek environmental policy has developed in response to EC policy.

AIR POLLUTION

Concerns about air pollution in Greece have focused largely on air quality in major cities, notably Athens, which has suffered from smog for the past 20 years. However, other cities such as Thessaloniki, Volos and Kavala also have periodically high concentrations of air pollutants. SO_2 and particulate emissions from lignite-burning power plants are a problem in industrial areas like Megalopolis and Ptolemais. The Athens basin is the location of half the country's industry and the largest conurbation; it is probably the area worst affected by air pollution. The city's car fleet grew from 550 000 to 880 000 during the 1980s, and its geographical situation, surrounded by mountains and the Gulf of Saronikos, tends to discourage the rapid dispersal of pollutants.

Industrial sources accounted for 71 per cent of SO_2 in Athens and virtually all particulates. Vehicles contributed 76 per cent of NO_x emissions and 64 per cent of smoke; oil-fired domestic heating formed the other principal source of air pollutants.

The use of heavy fuel oil for central heating was prohibited in 1977, and limits on the sulphur content of fuel oil subsequently reduced to 0.7 per cent for industrial heavy oil and 0.3 per cent for light oil. A series of emergency restrictions can be introduced when levels of $400\mu g/m^3$ SO_2 or smoke, or $500\mu g/m^3$ NO_2 are reached, including bans on cars and reduced levels of operation for industry. Tax exemptions were introduced in 1991 to encourage the purchase of new cars with catalytic converters when old vehicles were scrapped. Annual average concentrations in Athens in 1991 were $45\mu g/m^3$ SO_2 and $65\mu g/m^3$ NO_2. Total annual emissions have been estimated at 150 000t of NO_x (1990) and 250 000t of SO_2 (1985).

Greek legislation on air pollution control is based on EC directives. The framework environmental protection law, 1650/86, includes provisions for air quality standards, which have been introduced through Acts of the Council of Ministers (No 98 and No 99, 1987, and No 25, 1988). Authorisation and emission limit requirements for industrial plants were introduced by Law 1650/86 and Decree 1180/81.

WATER RESOURCES AND POLLUTION

Greece is relatively well-supplied with water, although rainfall distribution is uneven, being concentrated in the winter and in the mountainous northwest of the country, away from the principal population centres. Around a quarter of surface water flows originate in other countries. Total abstractions are estimated at around 7bn m^3 annually, of which around 70 per cent came from surface water sources. An increasing proportion of consumption is used for irrigation; agriculture accounts for 80 per cent of water use, domestic supplies around 16 per cent. Groundwater makes up 64 per cent of domestic supplies, but some cities, including Athens, depend substantially on surface water.

Water is supplied to smaller islands by tanker, particularly in the summer season when tourists boost demand. Groundwater supplies are affected by increasing salination in some coastal areas, as a result of intensive abstraction. River dam and diversion schemes have been developed to improve supplies, particularly to the drier, eastern half of the country; the Acheloos river diversion project has been a focus of protests over its potentially damaging effects on wetlands at Messolongi.

The majority of the Greek population and economic activities are concentrated close to the coast, and coastal waters receive much of the country's municipal and industrial wastes. Pollution is highest in the gulfs surrounding the larger cities, including Athens, Thessaloniki, Patras and Volos. Polluting discharges into the Gulf of Saronikos (from Athens) were estimated in 1989 at 573,000m^3 daily, including 27t of nitrogen, 12t of oil and grease, and a BOD load of 196t. The proportion of the population served by sewage treatment works has increased greatly in recent decades, but had reached only 10 per cent by 1985 (primary and secondary treatment only). Elevated nitrate, phosphate and ammonium levels have been measured in some rivers, including the Evros, Pinios and Axios, probably from agricultural sources and sewage discharges. The quality of seawater at recognised bathing areas appears satisfactory; 97 per cent of samples in 1992 met the EC Directive's limit value for coliforms.

Water supply and sewerage are the reponsibility primarily of local authorities, as set out in Law 1665/1980. Permits are required for abstractions for industrial use, under Law 1739/1987 on the management of water resources. Ministerial Decision 46399/1352 (1986) was introduced to implement EC directives on water quality; those on discharges of dangerous substances were implemented by Ministerial Council Act 144/1987 and subsequent decisions.

SOLID WASTE

Annual arisings are estimated at around 3.5mt of household waste and 450 000t of hazardous waste. Additional quantities are produced as a result of mining and quarrying activities. Almost all household waste is disposed to landfill, for which there are around 5000 sites; most are not operated in accordance with technical standards needed to ensure safe disposal. Analysis of household waste in Athens indicates a high proportion (57 per cent) of decomposable waste, and a small proportion of the national total is composted, around 179 000t in 1990.

Local authorities are responsible for the collection and disposal of household waste. Producers of hazardous waste are required to collect and store it, and ensure that it receives proper treatment and disposal. Waste management legislation is based on Law 1650/1986 and measures to implement EC directives, including Decisions 49541/1474 (1986), 72751/3054 (1985) on PCBs, and 71560/ 3053 (1985) on toxic waste.

NATURE CONSERVATION

Greece is rich in fauna and flora species and has a wide variety of habitats, including mountains, wetlands, a long coastline, and many islands. The concentration of population and industrial activity in a few areas has helped to conserve areas of biological diversity elsewhere. Existing threats to important habitats include:

- deforestation
- urban and industrial development
- intensive agriculture
- erosion and

- tourism (particularly in coastal areas).

There are around 5500 plant species, of which around 1000 are endemic and concentrated in mountain and island areas; a similar number are thought to be endangered.

The wildlife population includes mammals which are rare in much of Europe, including the brown bear, wolf and jackal. Greek waters and coasts provide important habitats for the few remaining monk seals and loggerhead turtle.

The number of fauna species is estimated at around: 90 mammals, 260 birds, 105 fish, and 67 reptiles and amphibians. Presidential Decree 67 (1981) on the conservation of indigenous species of fauna and flora lists around 800 plant and 200 animal species; the collection, killing, sale or export of these species is prohibited. Ministerial Decision 414985/1985 on the management of wild birds was introduced to implement the EC birds Directive.

Protected areas in Greece include: 10 national parks (95 000ha), 19 aesthetic forests (33 000ha) and 51 natural monuments (16 000ha). In addition, hunting reserves and game refuges cover more than 100 000ha. Law 996/1971 on the management of national parks introduced three principal categories of protected areas, subsequently reclassified under the Environmental Protection Law 1650/1986. Eleven wetland sites (104 400ha) have been designated in accordance with the Ramsar Convention.

ENERGY

Greece relies on imports for over 60 per cent of primary energy supplies, principally oil. Lignite is the main indigenous energy source (49.9mt mined in 1990), although small quantities of oil (0.61mt in 1992) and gas (91m m^3 in 1991) are also produced. Lignite is extracted at open-cast mines near Ptolemais and Megalopolis, and 95 per cent of production is used in electricity power stations. Electricity production is based largely on these 19 plants (73 per cent of generation), the rest made up of oil-fired capacity and hydroelectric stations; 2 per cent of electricity demand in 1991 was supplied by imports. It is planned to decrease dependence on oil by 2000 by:

- building new coal- and gas-fired plant,
- increasing hydroelectric capacity from 2514MW to 3426MW and
- increasing other renewable generation to 64MW.

Greece is well placed to develop renewable sources, particularly wind, solar and geothermal power.

AGRICULTURE

The nature of agricultural activity in Greece reflects the country's predominantly mountainous terrain; almost 60 per cent of agricultural land is used for grazing, mostly sheep and goats. Of the 3.93m ha under cultivation in 1990, 30 per cent was irrigated. Wheat, maize and sugarbeet are the main arable crops; other important agricultural produce includes tobacco, cotton, vine, citrus and other fruits, and vegetables. The trend of the last 20 years of a decrease in the area growing vines and field crops is expected to continue.

Total fertiliser use almost doubled from 321 700t in 1969/70 to 634 200t in 1989/90, reaching an average consumption of 100kg/ha for nitrogen in 1990. Pesticide use increased from 10 250t (active ingredient) in 1980 to 12 975t in 1989.

The pollution of watercourses from agricultural sources is becoming a problem in some areas, and irrigation sometimes leads to salination, thought to affect seriously around 30 000ha. Soil erosion is evident over 30–50 per cent of the land area, and is exacerbated by overgrazing, deforestation and the cultivation of marginal, steep slopes.

FOREST RESOURCES

Forest cover in Greece is estimated at 2.5–2.6m ha; conifers compose 38 per cent of the forest area, predominantly in mountainous areas and the Mediterranean zone; beech is found in mountainous areas, whilst oak is widespread at lower levels; broadleaved evergreens form *maquis* cover in the Mediterranean zone.

Much of the forest area is used for grazing sheep and goats (around 2m ha), which has limited natural regeneration, particularly of fir and oak. Forest fires typically affect 20 000–100 000ha each year, far exceeding the area reafforested (around 4000ha annually). An area totalling 37 000ha has been occupied and deforested illegally.

The annual volume of timber cut each year averaged around 2.8m m^3 between 1970 and 1990, of which 85 per cent was used as fuel and pulp. Imports supply around 45 per cent of wood product consumption. The 1992 forest survey found 18.1 per cent of trees to be notably defoliated (25 per cent or greater).

TRANSPORT

Transport volumes in Greece have grown enormously during the past 20 years, and an increasing proportion of inland freight is moved by road rather than rail. The number of motor vehicles in use increased from 345 000 in 1970 to 2.6m in 1990, and congestion and air pollution can be severe in some urban areas (particularly in Athens as described above). The road network was estimated at 41 000km in 1991, including 116km of motorway. The rail network covers 2500km.

The merchant navy fleet is the largest in the world, with over 50m gross registered tonnes in Greek beneficial ownership (over half under foreign flags of convenience); much of the trade relies on bulk cargoes carried between third countries.

Road, rail and port facilities are being extended and modernised with the help of EC funds.

Hungary

Hungary is a land-locked country, bordered by Austria, Slovakia, Ukraine, Romania, Serbia, Croatia and Slovenia. Most of the terrain is low-lying (73 per cent below 200m) and it is drained by two principal rivers, the Danube and Tisza. Lake Balaton in the west is the largest shallow freshwater lake in Central Europe. Mountains in the north of the country rise to just over 1000m. The climate is continental, with cold winters and hot summers.

INSTITUTIONS AND POLICY

Under a constitution adopted in 1989, Hungary has an elected National Assembly of 386 members. There are 19 counties (*megyei*), plus Budapest, which has equivalent status, and 168 town authorities (*varosi*), which have responsibility for local environmental services and planning under the 1990 Act on Local Government.

Area	90 030km^2
Population	10.3m
Urban	62%
Rural	38%
Capital	Budapest (2m)
City populations	9 > 100 000; 2 > 200 000
Economy	
GNP per capita	US$5740 (1991)
GDP change	−4% (1992)
Climate (Budapest)	
Average daily max and min	28/16°C (July)/1/−4°C (January)
Annual precipitation	614mm
Land-use cover	
Agriculture	70%
Forest	18%
Other	12%

The Ministry of Environment and Regional Policy was formed in 1990, when primary responsibility for water management was moved from the then Ministry of Environmental Protection and Water Management to the Ministry of Transport, Telecommunications and Water Management. The National Agency for Environmental Protection, with 12 Regional Environmental Inspectorates, forms part of the Ministry of Environment and Regional Policy.

The 1976 Law on Protection of the Human Environment set out the basis for environmental policy in Hungary and covered water and air pollution and nature conservation matters and formed the basis for subsequent, more detailed regulations. A new Environmental Protection Act will replace many existing provisions, and provide the framework for a range of measures, including:

- EIA
- permitting
- emission and quality standards
- liability for contaminated land
- environmental fines and charges
- environmental audits for property being privatised.

AIR POLLUTION

Air pollution seriously affects around 11 per cent of the territory, mostly in industrial and urban areas where around 45 per cent of the population lives. Total emissions in 1988 were estimated at: 1.2mt of SO$_2$, 260 000t of NO$_x$ and 420 000t of particulates, principally from industry, thermal power stations, domestic heating and traffic. Borsod, Tatabánya, Budapest, Várpalota, Inota, Pét, Dorog, Miskolc, Pécs and Komló suffered from elevated levels of air pollution.

The high sulphur content of indigenous lignite (3–4 per cent) burned in power stations and heating oil add to emissions from industrial sources such as metalworks, chemical and cement factories. Whilst industrial emissions have generally come under greater control during the past decade, increases in road traffic have exacerbated pollution in urban areas; lead and hydrocarbon levels are a cause of concern in Budapest and elsewhere. High levels of air pollution in urban areas are reflected in the incidence of respiratory diseases.

Transboundary atmospheric pollutants play a significant role: around 50 per cent of acid rain depositions in Hungary originate from beyond its frontiers, and a similar proportion of domestic emissions are 'exported'. Deposition levels are highest in the north and west of the country.

Air quality standards were established for 31 substances in a 1973 Order of the Council of Ministers, and increased to 130 pollutants in 1986. Standards are set at three levels, according to the level of protection deemed appropriate for different types of area (industrial, agricultural, and recreational use). Standards for SO_2 are set at 500, 150 and 100µg/m^3 (24-hour averages), for example. Smog alerts are issued when SO_2 and particulate levels exceed specified limits. Air quality standards are used to calculate emission limits, taking into account the volumes of pollutants, chimney height etc. Air pollution control is the responsibility of the Ministries of the Environment and of Health, with a monitoring network covering 106 towns.

WATER RESOURCES AND POLLUTION

Water resources in Hungary are rather limited, and 94 per cent of the summer flow of surface water originates outside the country. Over 4000km of dykes protect low-lying areas in the Great Plain, in the centre of the country, from flooding. Around 21 per cent of total abstractions, and a much higher proportion of drinking water supplies (80 per cent), come from groundwater sources. Public water supplies are taken mostly from bank-filtered groundwater adjacent to rivers. Water demand doubled to 6m m^3 between 1970 and 1985, and demand in the Tisza basin is putting pressure on supplies there. Industry and irrigation account for over 75 per cent of water demand.

The water quality of Hungary's rivers has continued to decline over the past 20 years, more than 50 per cent of the surveyed lengths showing increases in oxygen demand, and 15 per cent serious deterioration. Industry and sewerage discharges are primarily responsible for this pollution, although agricultural run-off also contributes. Around 75 per cent of discharges come from industrial sources, only one-third of which undergo chemical or biological treatment; 84m m^3 are discharged without treatment. Less than half of the population is connected to the sewerage system, in which around 30 per cent of sewage receives biological treatment. More than 80 per cent of industrial and municipal wastewater discharges receive treatment of some kind.

Surface waters are categorised into three quality classes, according to the limit concentrations of pollutants. Whilst the Danube and Tisza rivers do not fall below water quality classes I or II for their lengths in Hungary, many of their tributaries are of quality class III, notably the Sajo in the northeast. The Sajo valley is one of the country's main industrial centres, and the river receives discharges containing heavy metals, ammonia and petrochemical wastes. Heavy polluting loads originate in other industrial areas, such as Bakony, and Budapest, where only around 20 per cent of the wastewater discharges are treated biologically. Lake Balaton is affected by industrial effluent from Zalaegerszeg and high levels of nutrients from fertiliser and livestock wastes and sewage, which can cause eutrophication.

Groundwater pollution is a serious problem particularly from nitrates in the south and east of the country. Nitrate levels above 200mg/l have been recorded in Szabolcs and Borsod. 75 per cent of water supplies from groundwater require treatment before use as drinking water, and those in shallow aquifers (up to 20m depth) are unfit for use in populated areas. A survey in 1988–89 analysed 100 000 samples and found that 44 per cent failed to meet drinking water standards. Arsenic, mercury, lead, iron and manganese are present locally at elevated levels.

The Water Management Act dates from 1964 and was implemented by the National Water Authority until the creation of the Ministry of the Environment in 1987. Water quality and emissions are now the responsibility of the Ministry of Transport, Telecommunications and Water Management; monitoring and enforcement are undertaken by the regional Environmental Inspectorates. Drinking water standards are similar to WHO standards; 1984 regulations laid down limits for discharges to water for six categories of water, the strictest (category I) for Lake Balaton, then according to intended use, such as:

- drinking water and recreation (II)
- industry (III)
- irrigation (IV)
- Danube and Tisza (V)
- other watercourses (VI).

A series of charges and fines exists for water use and discharges.

SOLID WASTE

Solid waste arisings from industry, agriculture and households were estimated at 100.8mt in 1988. Of this total, 52.4mt were recycled (representing only about 3 per cent by value, however) and 4.95mt classified as hazardous waste, 63 per cent of which was accounted for by 'red mud' from aluminium smelting. Most of the country's waste is deposited in landfills, with the exception of one municipal waste incinerator in Budapest and five hazardous waste incinerators. An estimated 3.2mt of the 4.95mt of hazardous waste produced annually is thought to be stored onsite. Only around 0.5mt receives adequate treatment before disposal.

There are an estimated 2600–3200 landfill sites, but only around 10 per cent appear to be managed effectively and 60 per cent do not meet environmental standards. Leaching from landfills has led to the contamination of soil and water by heavy metals, solvents and pesticides in some areas; a hazardous waste dump at Vác contaminated the city's groundwater supplies in 1981. Pressure on landfill capacity, particularly around Budapest, is a further problem and the construction of more incinerators is planned.

The 1976 Act on the Protection of the Human Environment includes provisions on hazardous waste, and an Order was adopted in 1981 (No 56/1981) and amended in 1992 (No 27/1992). This order lists wastes regarded as hazardous and requires industrial producers to report and keep records of the volumes of hazardous waste generated. Producers and disposers require the consent of the Environment Ministry for handling, storage or disposal. The system of fines for hazardous waste offences was revised by Order No 2/1993.

NATURE CONSERVATION

Wild flora and fauna and their habitats face a range of pressures in Hungary, including those associated with intensive agriculture, flood-prevention construction (embankment and canalisation) and industrial activity. The country includes a wide variety of habitat types, including wetlands, Alpine meadows, and steppe grassland *(puszta)*.

Policy is based on a Bill (No IV) and Order (No 8) from 1982 on nature conservation and the 1961 Nature Conservation Act. It is overseen by the National Agency for Nature Conservation (part of the Environment Ministry). 619 animal species and 415 plant species are listed on schedules for protection, including 46 animal species and 31 plant species which have a greater level of protection. Damage to listed species and breeding sites is illegal. Hungary's Red Data Book of 1990 lists 400 animal and 730 plant species. Protected species include the golden and imperial eagle, great bustard, otter, lynx and beaver. Populations of wolf and brown bear appear to have become reestablished recently.

Also under the 1982 Bill and Order, there are three categories of protected area. Five national parks (159 138ha), 44 landscape protection areas and137 nature conservation areas have been designated, covering a total of 626 000 ha. There are also 877 locally important areas under protection.

ENERGY

Hungary depends on imports for around half its total energy requirements, which doubled during the 1970s and 1980s. Around 20mt of coal are produced annually, lignite and brown coal accounting for 75 per cent of production. There are also oil and gas reserves, mostly in Zala and Szeged; oil production was 1.85mt in 1992 (around 25 per cent of total supplies), gas production around 5000m m³ (1991). The high sulphur content of locally produced lignite and brown coal contributes to elevated SO_2 emissions, although gas is of increasing importance, around 60 per cent of supplies coming from imports.

Industry accounts for around 33 per cent of energy consumption, residential use 30 per cent, and road transport 14 per cent.

Four VVER-440 nuclear reactors at Paks, on the Danube, contribute around 45 per cent of the country's electricity production (29 728m kWh in 1991); an additional 8318m kWh were imported from the CIS. Plans for two further 1000MW reactors have not proceeded. A dry storage facility is planned to take spent nuclear fuel, which was formerly exported to the Soviet Union.

AGRICULTURE

Agriculture and forestry generate around 20 per cent of GDP and employ 18 per cent of the workforce; 70 per cent of the land area is devoted to agricultural production. The country's fertile plains are well suited to growing cereals, fruit and vegetables, and the livestock and dairy sectors are also strong. Agricultural production intensified during the 1960s and '70s and inputs of energy, fertiliser and pesticides grew rapidly to levels comparable with those in Western Europe.

Problems of pollution from agricultural run-off have accompanied the growth in production, however, particularly nitrate pollution of groundwater; limit values have been exceeded in over 1000 waterworks. Nitrate concentrations above 200mg/l have been recorded in drinking water in Borsod, where special water for infants has been supplied in plastic bags. Elevated levels of cadmium have also been detected in some areas, as a result of intensive applications of phosphate fertiliser. Half of all agricultural land is estimated to suffer from erosion, acidification or other degradation.

The large state farms and collectives which dominated Hungarian agriculture since the 1960s are being restructured; private ownership of farm holdings of 30–250ha should become the norm. Gross agricultural production fell by 27 per cent during 1989–92, partly as a result of disruptions and uncertainty in the land reform process, and also because of severe droughts in recent years and the lowering of subsidies. Organic farming has attracted a growing number of producers, with a tenfold increase in the area under organic production in recent years, to 8000ha in 1992. Most organic produce is exported to Germany and the Netherlands.

FOREST RESOURCES

Forests cover an area of 1.7m ha, around 18 per cent of the country. The largest forested area is in the Matra mountains in the north-east; otherwise, most of the forest is found to the west of the Danube. Although the total forested area is increasing slightly, the area of natural forest is decreasing. Conifers account for around 16 per cent of tree cover; oak, beech, ash, hornbeam, lime and poplar constitute the majority of broadleaved cover. The annual forest damage survey in 1992 showed 21.5 per cent of trees suffering 25 per cent or more defoliation.

TRANSPORT

Hungary has a rail network of 7800km, of which almost 30 per cent is electrified; over 40 per cent of freight (in t-km) is accounted for by rail. Over 1600km of inland waterways are navigable, including the Danube. Road length totals almost 30 000km, including 311km of motorway, and the principal routes are served by long-distance coach services.

The number of cars in use has grown greatly in recent years, virtually doubling to 1.95m between 1980 and 1989. Road transport has become a significant cause of air pollution in cities, particularly Budapest, where vehicle emissions increased by 20 per cent between 1989 and 1991 and account for 90 per cent of lead pollution. Vehicle emissions contribute around half of national NO_x emissions. Although modern models are becoming more widespread, much of the Hungarian car fleet consists of old two-stroke vehicles.

Iceland

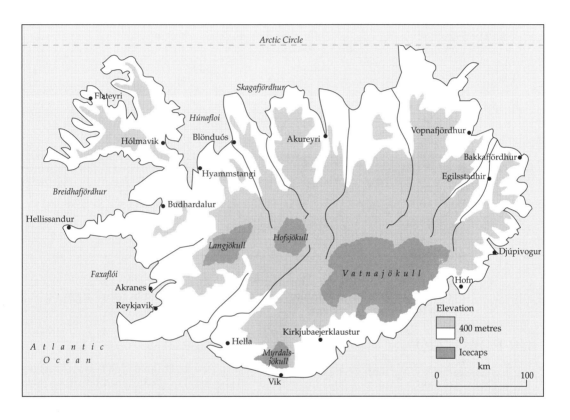

Iceland is a large island in the north Atlantic Ocean, just south of the Arctic Circle. Much of the land consists of a plateau, with only 25 per cent of the landmass below 200m; the population is concentrated around the coast. The central highlands rise to 2119m at their highest point and snow lies throughout the year in higher areas. Most rivers are short and fast-flowing.

INSTITUTIONS AND POLICY

Iceland has a directly elected parliament of 63 members. There are 20 district councils and 201 communes. The Ministry for the Environment was established in 1990, although much environmental legislation was in place earlier. Industrial pollution is controlled through a licensing system; larger and potentially more polluting activities require a licence from the Ministry for the Environment, others from the local authority. There are around 300 companies licensed by the Ministry, of which half are fishmeal

Area	103 000km²
Population	260 000
Urban	90%
Rural	10%
Capital	Reykjavik (99 600)
City populations	4 > 10 000; 1 > 20 000
Economy	
GNP per capita	US$24 066 (1991)
Climate (Reykjavik)	
Average daily max and min	14/9°C (July)/2/–2°C (January)
Annual precipitation	779mm
Land-use cover	
Agriculture	79%
Glaciers	11%
Other	10%

plants, aquaculture developments or waste sites. The National Physical Planning Agency, a Ministry institution, is responsible for bringing EIA into the planning system.

AIR POLLUTION

Man-made emissions in 1990 were estimated at 11 000t of SO_2 and 20 000t of NO_X. Transport and industry were the principal sources, including the fishing fleet, which accounted for 16 per cent and 44 per cent of the respective totals. An aluminium smelter, a ferro-silicon plant, a cement factory and a nitrogen fertiliser plant are the major industrial emitters. Most electricity is produced from renewable sources, so combustion emissions from the energy sector are not large; however, the sulphur emitted from geothermal areas exceeds that originating from fossil fuel use.

Air quality is generally good, with localised exceptions: because of emissions from metal smelters or fishmeal factories, for example, or vehicle emissions in Reykjavik in calm weather. The annual average for particulate concentrations in Reykjavik is 20–35μg/m³; lead in dust levels have fallen from 0.46μg/m³ in 1986 to 0.12μg/m³ in 1989, reflecting the increased use of unleaded petrol (almost 70 per cent of consumption in 1991). Ambient air quality standards are set at 50μg/m³ SO_2, 100μg/m³ NO_2 and particulates (24-hour averages).

Emissions of CO_2 totalled 2.9mt in 1990, almost half from domestic transport and the fishing fleet, and methane 20 000t (50 per cent from landfills, 47 per cent from livestock). CFC consumption in 1990 was 140t.

WATER RESOURCES AND POLLUTION

Freshwater is generally in abundant supply, as a result of high levels of precipitation (2000–4000mm annually in upland areas) and low average population density. Total water abstractions are estimated at 100m m^3 annually, of which 95 per cent comes from groundwater. An additional 60m m^3 of hot water is abstracted from geothermal areas for domestic heating or other energy uses. Water demand from the fisheries sector increased greatly during the 1980s, both for processing and for fish-farming; at least 25t of water is needed for every 1t of frozen fish produced, and water consumption for fish processing is three times the level of household demand in some fishing villages. The most worrying pollution threat to groundwater supplies appear to be the urban developments in and around Reykjavik and tourism developments inland.

The majority of sewage is discharged into the sea without treatment; only 6 per cent of the population is connnected to sewage treatment plants (primary treatment only). Pollution from sewage is evident in some coastal areas, but eutrophication has not been adequately studied.

SOLID WASTE

Total waste arisings are estimated at 236 000t annually, 53 per cent originating from industry and 42 per cent from households. 28 000t are recycled (including some exported for recycling), and most of the remainder is landfilled (67 per cent). Around 21 per cent of waste is burned, mostly in open pits; there are three incinerators, which lack satisfactory pollution abatement equipment. Reykjavik has a modern waste-handling centre where waste is sorted for recycling or baled for landfill disposal. Hazardous waste accounts for only 1.8 per cent of total arisings, and most is exported to Denmark for treatment and disposal; a national collection centre for hazardous waste is planned for Reykjavik.

Waste collection and disposal is the responsibility of local authorities, under the Pollution Control Regulations of 1990. A national waste management strategy, drawn up by the Ministry for the Environment, envisages improvements in the collection and disposal of waste, the minimisation of waste production and the levying of fees on potentially hazardous materials.

NATURE CONSERVATION

Iceland has 483 species of vascular plants, of which 46 are listed in the Red Data Book; 31 species are protected under the Nature Conservation Act 47/1971. Birch is the only native tree which forms woodlands; only 125 000ha of original scrub and woodland remain. Rowan and willow are also found. The Arctic fox is the only native terrestrial mammal; mink, reindeer and woodmice are also common. 73 species of bird are thought to nest regularly in Iceland, of which 42 are totally protected and 26 partially protected (outside the specified hunting season); 20 species are listed in the Red Data Book. Large seabird populations occur on cliffs and islands. Seals are not protected by law and some are hunted. Whales traditionally have been hunted but commercial exploitation is not permitted in Icelandic waters; some small cetaceans (eg porpoises) are caught for local consumption.

Protected areas under the Nature Conservation Act cover 926,400ha, and include:

- 3 national parks
- 29 nature reserves
- 29 natural monuments and
- 9 country parks.

Development is restricted in all four categories. There are two Ramsar wetland sites in Iceland, covering 57,500ha. Nature conservation activities are overseen by the Nature Conservation Council, which comes under the authority of the Ministry for the Environment.

ENERGY

Iceland's indigenous energy supplies, geothermal resources and hydro-electricity, provide almost 70 per cent of primary energy supplies; the remainder is met through imported oil and a small proportion of coal. Geothermal energy, extracted as hot water, now accounts for 85 per cent of domestic heating, having largely replaced oil (45 per cent of space heating in 1973). Hydroelectric stations generated 93.5 per cent of electricity produced in 1990, with a further 6.4 per cent from geothermal resources. The remaining 0.1 per cent came from diesel-powered generators used in remote areas or for emergency back-up supplies. Only around 14 per cent of the country's total hydro-energy resources have been exploited so far.

Although Iceland derives a large proportion of its energy supplies from renewable sources, these are not without environmental impact. They include:

- dams
- reservoir creation and management
- the construction of powerlines and pipelines
- heat and effluent pollution
- H_2O emissions from geothermal developments.

AGRICULTURE

Farming is based on livestock production, principally sheep and dairy cattle. Only 140 000ha (1 per cent of the land area) is cultivated, almost entirely under grass to provide fodder for livestock; horses, pigs and poultry are also raised. Crop production is limited to around 600ha for potatoes and 400ha for grain; turnips and carrots are also grown, and other vegetables and flowers grown under glass (20ha), heated by geothermal energy. Mink- and fox-farming, for fur, have been encouraged.

Fertiliser use on grassland was estimated at 85kg/ha nitrogen in 1990; pesticide use (active ingredients) in 1991 was 32kg/km^2 (on cropland and horticulture).

Pollution from agricultural sources is not considered a major problem, but overgrazing by sheep and horses has caused large-scale vegetation loss and subsequent soil erosion. Extensive areas of wetland have been drained, 1200–1400ha this century, for conversion to grassland.

FISHERIES

Iceland's economy depends heavily on marine produce, which accounted for 71 per cent of exports in 1989. An exclusive economic zone of 200 miles (320km) was declared in 1975. The principal commercially fished species are cod, haddock, redfish, saithe, herring, capelin, halibut and lumpsucker. Lobster, shrimp and scallop are also fished.

Catches are regulated by means of total allowable catches (TACs) set for each of the main species by the Ministry of Fisheries. The total annual catch varies between around 0.8mt and 1.6mt, peaking at 2.05mt in 1986; in 1990 it was 1.5mt, in 1991 1.04mt.

TRANSPORT

Motor vehicles are the main mode of inland transport; 136 874 were registered at the end of 1991. Vehicle emissions account for almost a quarter of NO_x and CO_2 emissions; emissions from international transport and fishing vessels increase transport's overall share further. There were 1000 ocean-going fishing vessels in 1992.

The road network extends to 12 400km, including a 1400km ring road around the island. Over half the country's motor vehicles are found in Reykjavik, but windy and wet weather conditions ensure that high concentrations of pollution are rare.

Increasing numbers of tourists could result in undue pressure on some of Iceland's fragile habitats: for example where all-terrain vehicles are used to take visitors to remote areas in the central highlands.

Irish Republic

Area	68 890km²
Population	3.52m
Urban	57%
Rural	43%
Capital	Dublin (1.02m)
City populations	4 > 50 000
Economy	
GNP per capita	US$11 120 (1991)
Climate (Dublin)	
Average daily max and min	20/11°C (July)/8/1°C (January)
Annual precipitation	762mm
Land-use cover	
Agriculture	82%
Forest	6%
Other	12%

The island of Ireland lies in the Atlantic Ocean to the west of Britain, separated from it by the Irish Sea. The Irish Republic comprises all but the six counties of Northern Ireland, which forms part of the United Kingdom. Central limestone lowlands extend to the coast in some parts of the east and west; elsewhere they are surrounded by numerous upland areas which rise to peaks above 500m.

INSTITUTIONS AND POLICY

Ireland is a republic and under the 1937 constitution 166 members are directly elected to a House of Representatives *(Dáil)*; the Senate *(Seanad)* forms the upper house of the parliament. Local government is exercised through:

- 27 county councils
- 5 county boroughs
- 6 borough corporations
- 49 urban district councils and
- 30 boards of town commissioners.

The counties and county boroughs have extensive environmental responsibilities.

The Department of the Environment was established in 1977, and an Environmental Protection Agency created in 1992 under an Act of the same name. Launched in July 1993, the Agency is intended to:

- take over the licensing from local authorities of major polluting activities, under a new system of integrated pollution control;
- undertake monitoring and research work, and
- advise public authorities.

EC legislation has had a major influence on Irish environmental policy, implemented often by means of regulations made under the European Communities Act of 1972. Most of the requirements of the EC Directive on EIA were introduced through regulations made under this Act and the Local Government (Planning and Development) Acts. A National Environment Programme was published in 1990.

AIR POLLUTION

Total SO_2 emissions were estimated at 171 400t in 1987, of which 55 per cent came from thermal power stations; industrial and domestic sources contributed most of the remainder. Emissions decreased during the early 1980s but have since risen slightly.

NO_x emissions have continued to rise in recent years, from 91 000t in 1985 to 128 000t in 1990; road transport and power stations respectively account for around 42 per cent and 35 per cent of the total. Low NO_x burners are being fitted to help reduce emissions from Moneypoint coal-fired power station on the west coast.

Air quality in Ireland is generally good except in some urban areas. Dublin in particular has suffered from high levels of smoke and SO_2 in winter, primarily as a result of coal burned for domestic heating; other cities such as Cork and Dundalk have also recorded high levels. Air quality standards for smoke were exceeded in Dublin in most winters during the 1980s, before a ban on the marketing of bituminous coal was introduced in 1990. Increasing domestic use of gas has also helped reduce pollution levels.

Legislation is based on the Air Pollution Act 1987, which requires specified categories of industrial plant to obtain a licence from the local authority before commencing operation. The licences may specify limit values and should ensure the use of best practicable means to prevent or limit pollution and compliance with emission and air quality standards. The Air Pollution Act also provides for local authorities to introduce air quality management plans and designate special control areas in order to improve air pollution control. Quality standards have been set by regulations made under the Act.

WATER RESOURCES AND POLLUTION

Ireland is well-endowed with water resources: rivers and lakes are fairly evenly distributed and although precipitation is highest in the west of the country (over 2000mm annually in some areas) and demand is highest in the east, supply has not generally posed major difficulties. The Shannon is the longest river (340km), and the western half of the country has numerous lakes. Water supplies depend largely on surface water sources which account for around 78 per cent of total public supplies. Of total abstractions, 61 per cent are for domestic use, 26 per cent are for industry, and 13 per cent are for agriculture.

Total abstractions were estimated at 790m m³ annually in the early 1980s.

The European Communities (Quality of Water Intended for Human Consumption) Regulations 1988 were introduced to implement the EC drinking water Directive; results of the first year's comprehensive monitoring showed some parameters to be exceeded, particularly for coliforms (19 per cent of samples), fluoride (17 per cent), aluminium (14 per cent) and iron (14 per cent).

Surveys of rivers since 1971 indicate a decline in overall quality. Of the 2900km river length in the baseline survey:

- The proportion classified as unpolluted (class A) decreased from 83 per cent in 1971 to 65 per cent in 1990;
- The lengths considered seriously polluted (class D) also decreased, from 7 per cent to 2 per cent;
- Classes B and C (slightly and moderately polluted) increased their joint share from 10 per cent to 33 per cent over the same period.

Sewage effluent and industrial discharges appear responsible for the majority of cases of serious pollution. Agricultural wastes (usually silage effluent or livestock slurry) were the sources for around a quarter of the Class D cases. Monitoring in 1989/90 of rivers designated under the EC freshwater fish Directive showed numerous exceedances of the parameters set, particularly those for nitrites and dissolved oxygen. Eutrophication affects some lakes and rivers, as a result of excessive nutrient discharges.

The majority of towns are situated around the coast and discharge sewage into the sea, and most have no treatment facilities; around two-thirds of Dublin's sewage receives primary treatment only. An investment programme was announced in 1990, with the objective of providing treatment for discharges from major coastal towns to the sea by 2000 and improving treatment inland. Four of the five sea sampling points for bathing water quality which did not meet EC standards were in the Dublin area.

Water resource management and sewerage, including the preparation of water quality management plans, are the responsibility primarily of local authorities. Licences for the discharge of effluent are required under the Local Government (Water Pollution) Act 1977, which was amended in 1990. EC directives have been implemented through regulations made under this Act and the European Communities Act 1972.

SOLID WASTE

Annual waste arisings in the mid-1980s were estimated at around 28mt, of which 22mt originated from agriculture; estimates for 1991 arisings included 1.22mt of household waste and 0.75mt of commercial waste. Virtually all this waste is disposed to landfill. Over 52 000t of toxic waste was produced in 1984, of which 28 per cent was exported. Sewage sludge is mostly dumped at sea or spread on agricultural land.

Policy on waste has been shaped by EC legislation in recent decades, and regulations have been made under the European Communities Act 1972 to implement EC Directives, including the EC (Waste) Regulations 1979 and the EC (Toxic and Dangerous Waste) Regulations 1982. Other obligations stem from the Public Health (Ireland) Act 1878. Local authorities are responsible for most aspects of waste management, including disposal plans and licensing arrangements. The Environmental Protection Agency Act 1992 envisages some waste disposal operations (eg hazardous and hospital waste incineration) coming within the proposed system of integrated pollution control; hazardous waste planning may also be brought under the Agency's control. A new waste bill was being drafted in 1993.

NATURE CONSERVATION

The range of fauna and flora present in Ireland is generally more limited than in continental Europe. The Red Data Books for Ireland list 6 vascular plant species as endangered and 44 as vulnerable. Species protection is based on the Wildlife Act 1976, under which 14 mammal and 7 other fauna species are protected, and 68 species of flora. Bird species are protected also under regulations made to implement the EC birds Directive.

Wetlands form important habitats for birds and other species, and Ireland has extensive areas of peatland bogs. These have been affected by cutting, drainage or afforestation and over 90 per cent of the area of raised bogs in the Midlands has been lost or modified. Around 500 000ha of land was drained or reclaimed during 1975–91, and the shift away from haymaking to silage production, with other more intensive agricultural practices, has also affected wildlife habitats. Little ancient woodland remains.

Five national parks have been designated under the State Property Act 1954, covering a total of over 26 000ha. Other protected areas are designated under the Wildlife Act, including 71 nature reserves, 68 wildfowl sancuaries and7 refuges for fauna. In accordance with the EC birds Directive, 20 special protection areas (6600ha) have been established, some of which are also amongst Ireland's 21 Ramsar wetland sites (13 035ha). Around 1600 Areas of Scientific Interest (600 000ha on land and water) have been identified, but only around 10 per cent of their area is protected. Nature conservation matters are handled primarily by the National Parks and Wildlife Service of the Office of Public Works.

ENERGY

Ireland depends on imports for much of its energy supplies, particularly oil, which accounts for around half of primary energy. Total primary energy supply increased from 6.3mtoe in 1970 to 10.5mtoe in 1991. Crude oil is imported for refining at Cork. Indigenous supplies include gas, from the Kinsale Head field offshore from Cork, some coal reserves, and extensive use of peat. Exploratory drillings for offshore oil and gas have been conducted since 1970.

Large-scale peat extraction is centred on raised bogs in the Midlands, and a total of 7.99mt was produced for fuel in 1990. Peat is burned in thermal power stations, providing around 14 per cent of electricity, and for domestic heating.

Electricity generating capacity in 1991 was 3932MW, 40 per cent from coal-fired stations and 25 per cent from gas. Hydroelectric schemes have been developed since the 1920s, including on the rivers Shannon, Liffey and Lee, and generate 5 per cent of electricity.

AGRICULTURE

Agriculture remains an important sector, accounting for 13 per cent of employment, 10 per cent of GDP and around 20 per cent of export earnings in 1991. Livestock production dominates, particularly beef cattle and dairying, and composes over 80 per cent of agricultural output by value. Over 90 per cent of farmland is under grass; barley, wheat, oats, potatoes and sugarbeet are the principal arable crops. Over half of all farms are 10–40ha in size, larger farms tending to be found in the south and east.

The use of nitrogen fertiliser increased from 275 000t in 1981/82 to 358 000t in 1991/92, reflecting a shift from traditional haymaking to silage production. A farmyard pollution control scheme was introduced in 1989 to tackle water pollution from silage and livestock wastes by improving storage facilities. Pesticide consumption almost doubled from 1116t of active ingredient in 1970 to 2006t in 1991. Overgrazing and soil erosion affect some upland areas, the number of sheep having increased from 4.4m to 9m between 1985 and 1991.

A pilot scheme of two environmentally sensitive areas, covering 11 500ha, was launched in 1992, and an Organic Unit was established in the Ministry of Agriculture and Food in 1990 to develop organic farming.

Annual landings of sea fish have totalled 220–250,000t in recent years, mackerel being the most important species. Aquaculture has expanded rapidly, mostly on the west coast, producing salmon, trout, mussels and oysters.

FOREST RESOURCES

A policy of afforestation increased forest cover from 1–1.5 per cent at the start of the century to over 6 per cent in 1991. Broadleaves, mostly ash, constitute only around 10 per cent of the 475 000ha of forest, the majority of the cover being spruce and pine. Timber production in 1991 was 1.5m m^3. Continued planting by the public authorities, which own around 80 per cent of the forest area, and incentives for private afforestation, are intended to increase forest cover to 715 000ha by 2000.

EIA is required for new forestry developments over 200ha, and the afforestation of unenclosed land (eg bogs) and without broadleaved species is to be discouraged. Guidelines on forestry practice were produced in 1991. The state-sponsored Irish Forestry Board was established by the Forestry Act 1988.

TRANSPORT

Road transport dominates the transport sector, carrying 90 per cent of inland freight and 96 per cent of passenger traffic; the road network extends to 92 320km. Although overall traffic density is low by Western European standards, the increasing use of motor vehicles has led to congestion and associated pollution in urban areas. The number of road vehicles in use increased from 572 000 in 1975 to 1.04m in 1990, and the transport sector accounted for 46 per cent of NO_x emissions in 1987. The rail network of 2300km is focused largely on Dublin; bus services provide more extensive national coverage.

Internationally, most goods traffic and substantial passenger movements are carried by sea; Dublin, Cork, Rosslare, Waterford and Limerick are the principal seaports, although numerous smaller ports are found around the coast.

The main international airports are at Dublin, Shannon and Cork. Ireland's transport infrastructure is being further developed with the support of EC funds.

Italy

Area	301 302km²
Population	57.8m
Urban	69%
Rural	31%
Capital	Rome (2.79m)
City populations	17 > 200 000; 6 > 700 000
Economy	
GNP per capita	US$18 520 (1991)
Climate (Rome)	
Average daily max and min	30/20°C (July)/11/5°C (January)
Annual precipitation	744mm
Land-use cover	
Agriculture	66%
Forest	29%
Other	5%

Mainland Italy consists of a peninsula which extends southwards from its borders with France, Switzerland, Austria and Slovenia into the Mediterranean Sea, and two large islands, Sicily and Sardinia. The north includes the Italian Alps, which rise to over 3000m, and the north Italian plain, around the Po valley. The interior of the peninsula to the south is mountainous, with the Appennines rising to over 1800m.

INSTITUTIONS AND POLICY

Italy is a democratic republic and under the constitution of 1948 a Chamber of Deputies and a Senate are elected to form the parliament. There are twenty autonomous regions, also with elected councils and governments, 95 provinces and over 8000 communes; the regions have extensive environmental responsibilities, some of which were transferred from central government under Presidential Decree 616/1977.

Further changes in local government took place after a referendum in April 1993 endorsed the removal of responsibility for local environmental monitoring from local authorities. A National Environment Protection Agency is intended to deal with monitoring and inspection and provide advisory services for national and regional governments. The Ministries of Agriculture and Forests and of Tourism were to be abolished and their functions transferred to the regions.

The Ministry of the Environment was created in 1986 and shares some competences for environmental matters with other ministries and regional authorities. Strategic priorities for environmental policy are set out in a three-year environmental plan; the plan for 1989–91 included 11 operative programmes covering different sectors. The plan is implemented by the regions, for which agreements are drawn up with the ministry. Funding of 9.7bn lire was allocated for the 1989–91 plan.

Law 349/1986, which established the ministry, also included provisions for EIA, which have been required for certain projects since the adoption of a series of decrees, from 1988 onwards. An EIA Commission was set up in 1989 to review EIA studies. The development of Italian environment policy has been influenced by EC environmental legislation, especially where little or no domestic legislation predated EC policy. Implementation of EC law has sometimes been slow, particularly before the late 1980s, since when laws have provided for the legal implementation of EC Directives by decree.

AIR POLLUTION

Annual emissions of SO_2 have decreased in recent years, from 2.23mt in 1985 to 1.98mt in 1989; just over half of this total came from thermal power stations. A reduction in the sulphur content of gas oil and increased use of natural gas have contributed to the fall in emissions.

Total emissions of NO_x and particulates have risen steadily, both increasing by 22 per cent between 1985 and 1989, to 1.93mt and 549 000t respectively; a growing proportion originates from the transport sector.

Air quality measurements are taken for eight pollutants; there were 806 monitoring sites in 1986. Despite the overall decrease in SO_2 emissions, concentrations are still above legal standards in some cities. Widespread breaches of the limit values for NO_2 and particulates were recorded during the late 1980s, particularly in major cities such as Turin, Milan, Bologna, Rome and Venice. Much is attributable to vehicle emissions, the effect of which is sometimes aggravated by old, narrow streets which limit dispersion.

Air pollution legislation is based on Law 615/1966 and Presidential Decree 203/1988, which established air quality standards and a permitting system for industrial plants. The decree was made largely to implement EC directives. Emission limits for industrial plants were set by a ministerial decree of 12 July 1990. Much of the authorisation system is handled by the regions, and criteria for regional pollution abatement and air quality plans were laid down in two ministerial decrees of 20 May 1991.

WATER RESOURCES AND POLLUTION

The natural distribution of water resources varies greatly, both geographically and seasonally. Northern Italy receives over 40 per cent of the total estimated volume of precipitation (290bn m^3 annually) and rainfall in the summer months ranges from 50mm in the south to 700mm in areas of the Alps. Allowing for evapotranspiration and run-off, the volume of water resources available is estimated at 110bn m^3 annually. Total water abstractions rose from 41.9bn m^3 in 1970 to 56.2bn m^3 in 1987; around 70 per cent of the total volume is drawn from surface water.

Agriculture accounts for 60 per cent of total water demand, primarily for irrigation, and industry for 25 per cent. Groundwater supplies provide around 90 per cent of the country's drinking water, and are more abundant in the north. Water shortages are particularly evident in southern Italy; only 11 per cent of the population in Calabria and Molise, and 18 per cent in Campania, are supplied with adequate quantities of water. A total of 5.8bn m³ water was delivered through the household supply networks in 1987; around 75 per cent underwent purification treatment.

Groundwater supplies are heavily polluted by industrial discharges and nitrate and pesticide run-off from agriculture in some regions; high concentrations of iron, manganese and ammonium are present in some aquifers. Derogations from the quality parameters of the EC drinking water Directive have been issued in many regions, including Piedmont, Lombardy, Veneto, Emilia Romagna, and Marche.

Surface waters also show signs of pollution from industrial and agricultural sources; sewage discharges increase the oxygen demand and nutrient load downstream of some conurbations. A study of the four principal rivers in the 1980s indicated that:

- the Adige was moderately polluted or less (quality classes 1 and 2) for most of its length.
- the Tiber was heavily polluted in its lower reaches (classes 3 and 4).
- the Arno was heavily polluted downstream of Florence.

Florence lacked any major sewage treatment plants, as, too, did Milan and Palermo. A total of 2568 municipal wastewater treatment plants were built during 1981–86, and 61 per cent of the population were estimated to be served by plants in 1987; many more will have to be built or improved to comply with the EC urban wastewater Directive. The Po is severely affected by pollution downstream of the industrial cities of Turin and Milan, and by nutrient run-off from livestock wastes.

A national survey in 1985 found excessive levels of nutrients in 41 per cent of lakes, 10 per cent of which were regarded as critically eutrophic. Italy has over 8000km of coastline, at 380km of which bathing was prohibited because of pollution in 1991; 92 per cent of seawater sampling points (and 79 per cent of freshwater points) in 1992 complied with the mandatory values for coliforms in the EC bathing water Directive. The Adriatic Sea has become affected periodically by extensive blooms of mucilaginous algae since 1988, appearing in the spring and summer; they are thought to be associated with high levels of nutrients, and have also affected the Tyrrhenian Sea.

Discharges to water and sewers are regulated under Law 319/1976, which also required the regions to draw up water quality improvement plans. EC Directives on discharges of dangerous substances are implemented by Presidential Decree 133/1992, and other EC water directives were also implemented by decrees in January 1992. Emissions and the implementation of national legislation are handled by the regions. Law 183/1989 is aimed at soil conservation, but also provided for the designation of important watersheds, with soil conservation and water management activities coordinated by Watershed Authorities.

SOLID WASTE

Total waste arisings in 1991 were estimated at 97.1mt, including 20.03mt of municipal waste and 34.7mt from industry; 3.25mt was classified as toxic/hazardous. According to statistics for disposal at authorised sites:

- 33.68mt was disposed to landfill,
- 1.91mt incinerated, and
- 6.32mt received other treatment.

Most municipal waste is disposed to landfill – around 90 per cent in 1991: There were 785 category 1 landfill sites in 1991, with a capacity of 17.16mt annually. Additional capacity is provided by 40 incinerators (1.2mt) and 67 other treatment plants (1.95mt). As landfills with an annual capacity of around 2mt were thought to fall below technical standards, 35 per cent of municipal waste appears to go to unsatisfactory disposal. The capacity of plants taking special (non-inert) industrial waste was sufficient to handle around 50 per cent of annual arisings in 1989.

Separate collection has been introduced in some cities to improve recycling rates, not only for glass and paper but also for cans, batteries, plastics and organic waste. Consortia of manufacturers and importers have been established, in accordance with Law 475/1988, to collect and recover key materials in commercial use.

Presidential Decree 915/1982 was introduced to implement the principal EC Directives on waste disposal; the regions are responsible for regulating waste disposal and management, including the issuing of permits. Authorisation is required for all operations involving toxic or hazardous waste. Under Law 475/1988 an inventory of special waste produced must be kept by larger companies.

NATURE CONSERVATION

Italy is a country of diverse habitats and climate, ranging from the Alps, which form the southern limit of some European species, to the Po basin, the Appenines and lower areas of the peninsula, and the islands and extensive Mediterranean coastline. There are around 5820 vascular plant species, of which 463 species were listed in the 1990 Red Data Book. Estimated numbers of animal species include:

- 97 mammals,
- 406 birds,
- 44 reptiles, and
- 32 amphibians.

Species protection policy is the responsibility of the regional authorities, 15 of which had introduced measures by 1990 to protect flora. Hunting is widely practised and is regulated on the basis of fauna maps under Law 157/1992, which also shortened the hunting season. Most mammal and bird species are otherwise protected in principle under Law 968/1977 on hunting and wildlife protection.

By 1992, 11 national parks had been established, covering a total of around 682 000ha (including 65 000ha of water). A new framework law on protected areas, Law 394 of 6 December 1991, is expected to provide the basis for a comprehensive system of protected areas at national, regional and local levels. It is envisaged that the total area under protection will be increased from 1.77 to 2.47m ha, which will include:

- 146 nature reserves,
- 5 marine reserves,
- 18 parks,
- 46 wetlands, and
- 396 regional protected areas.

A national register of protected areas was established by a ministerial decree of May 1991. By 1993, 46 wetland sites were designated under the Ramsar Convention (56 950ha), and 74 areas were identified in 1988 under the EC birds Directive.

ENERGY

Total energy consumption in 1990 was 163.5mtoe, having increased by an average of 2.4 per cent per annum since 1983. Italy relies on imports for over 80 per cent of its energy supplies; energy intensity and per capita consumption is relatively low. The proportion of primary energy consumption met by oil decreased from 75.4 per cent in 1973 to 56.7 per cent in 1990, whilst the share provided by gas grew from 10.2 per cent to 24 per cent over the same period. Domestic production in 1990 included 4.6mt oil and 16.9bn m^3 gas.

Almost half of electricity generation comes from oil-fuelled power stations, the remainder primarily from gas and coal combustion; hydroelectric plants provided 35.1TWh in 1990, 16 per cent of total production. Electricity demand doubled between 1970 and 1990, to 235TWh, and the proportion supplied by imports increased to 34.7TWh in 1990.

Nuclear power production was abandoned following a referendum in 1987, and a National Energy Plan was approved by the government in 1988. The plan identified energy-saving and environmental protection as two of its five principal objectives. Law 10/1991 introduced incentives for CHP plants, district heating and refuse-derived power plants, and promoted technical criteria, grants, consumption-based charging and tax exemptions for energy-saving measures.

AGRICULTURE

The total area of land used for agriculture, the number of farms and agricultural employment have declined steadily over recent decades, to 22.65m ha, 3.04m holdings and 7.9 per cent of employment in 1990/91. The average farm size, 7.7ha, is small compared with most other EC countries. Wheat and maize are the main cereals grown, although the country is a net importer of grains, meat and dairy products. Fruit, vine and olive cultivation are other important sectors. Cattle and pig numbers have fallen over the past 20 years, whilst the numbers of sheep and goats have increased, particularly in the south and the islands.

In contrast to the barren terrain which dominates the uplands, the plain of the river Po is fertile, and is one of the areas which suffers most from agricultural pollution. In 1990, 64 per cent of all cattle and pigs were concentrated in four regions (Lombardy, Emilia Romagna, Veneto and Piedmont) which also had amongst the highest levels of fertiliser use in the country (eg nitrogen 126kg/ha in Lombardy and phosphorus 95kg/ha in Veneto in 1989, compared with a national average of 73kg/ha and

54kg/ha respectively). Intensive livestock production adds to the nutrient load from chemical fertilisers, and pesticide traces are found extensively in water supplies, particularly where used on maize, rice or fruit. Pesticide use in the Po valley was above the national average of 14.9kg/ha, at 28.3kg/ha in Veneto and 25.5kg/ha in Emilia Romagna in 1989.

A total of 330 000ha of arable land was entered into the EC set-aside programme by 1991, over half the area being left fallow, 22 per cent used for extensive grazing, and 24 per cent for legumes.

FOREST RESOURCES

Forest cover in the mid-1980s was estimated at 8.68m ha, almost 29 per cent of the land area. Broadleaved species account for more than 80 per cent of the forested area, including oak, beech, hornbeam and chestnut; conifers are concentrated in the Alpine regions and Calabria. The regions of Liguria, Trentino Alto Adige, Tuscany, Umbria and Sardinia had the highest proportion of forest cover (40 per cent or above).

Fires damage extensive areas of forest every summer and affected 1.1m ha between 1970 and 1990; 98 000ha of forest were burned in 1990 alone. Air pollution, particularly acid deposition and high ozone levels, has added to forest damage caused by drought, pests and grazing. The 1992 forest damage survey found 18.2 per cent of trees to be notably defoliated (25 per cent or above); pine, oak and chestnut were worst affected.

Forest management is primarily the responsibility of the regional authorities, coordinated nationally by the Ministry of Agriculture and Forestry; the State Forestry Agency undertakes research and survey work. A National Forest Plan was drawn up in 1988, with the aim of improving the productivity and management of forests.

TRANSPORT

Transport demand is heaviest in northern Italy, around the country's major urban and industrial centres, and has grown enormously during the past two decades. Inland freight traffic increased by 82 per cent and passenger traffic by 104 per cent between 1970 and 1990, and most of this growth has been concentrated on the road network. The General Transport Plan of 1986 envisaged an increase in transport demand of 45 per cent by 2000, based on annual GDP growth of 2.5–3 per cent. Around 80 per cent of inland freight is carried by road, although over 60 per cent of import/export tonnage goes by sea; there are 47 category 1 ports, and Genoa, Trieste, Taranto and Augusta handled the largest volumes of freight in 1989.

The road network extended to 303 900km including 6193km of motorway in 1989; the motorway network was expanded greatly during the 1970s. The number of road vehicles increased from 11.13m in 1970 to 29.73m in 1990, and congestion is widespread in cities and on some major routes; the motorway between Florence and Bologna carries more than 11 times its designed vehicle capacity, for example.

The rail network has contracted slightly since 1970, to 19 595km (1991). The most important inland waterways are the Po and connecting rivers and canals between Milan, Venice and Trieste; leisure traffic is replacing freight. Air traffic carried 44.75m passengers in 1991, over half via Rome and Milan.

Latvia

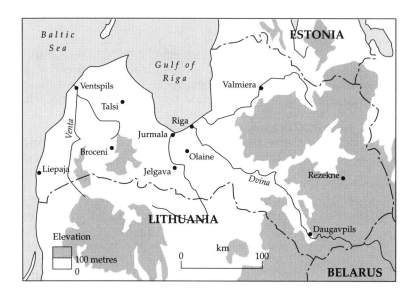

L atvia is situated to the east of the Baltic Sea, south of Estonia and north of Lithuania; it borders Russia to the east and Belarus to the south-east. Much of the country is low-lying, particularly close to the Gulf of Riga and the Baltic; the uplands (26 per cent of the territory) rise to 312m.

INSTITUTIONS AND POLICY

Latvia became an independent republic in 1991. The Environmental Protection Committee was established in June 1990 as the central state body for environmental matters, with nine regional committees, responsible to the Supreme Council. The Law on Environmental Protection (6 August 1991) sets out the basic principles and objectives of environmental policy in Latvia, and the Law on State Environmental Impact Assessments provides for EIA as a prerequisite for new industrial projects. A system of taxes on resource use and polluting activities was introduced in 1991.

AIR POLLUTION

Emissions from stationary sources were estimated at 58 484t of SO_2 in 1991 (71 023t in 1985) and 27 659t of particulates (1991). NO_x emissions totalled 48 480t in 1991, 70 per cent of which originated from road vehicles and

Area	64 589km²
Population	2.66m
Urban	71%
Rural	29%
Capital	Riga (897 000)
City populations	6 > 50 000; 3 > 100 000
Economy	
GNP per capita	US$4690 (1992)
GDP change	–34% (1992)
Climate (Riga)	
Average daily max and min	22/11°C (July)/–4/–10°C (January)
Annual precipitation	567mm
Land-use cover	
Agriculture	39%
Forest	35%
Other	26%

railway locomotives. Industrial production is centred on Riga, and over half the country's domestically generated electricity comes from hydro-electric plants. Air quality is monitored at 19 permanent sites in nine cities. Standards for NO_2 (40μg/m³ 24-hour average and 85μg/m³ peak) were exceeded in all nine cities in 1990 and 1991 and for dust (150μg/m³ and 500μg/m³) in six cities; Riga, Olaine, Jurmala and Valmiera appeared worst affected.

WATER RESOURCES AND POLLUTION

Latvia has 777 rivers longer than 10km, out of a total of 12 000; the largest are the Gauja, Venta and Daugava. There are also more than 3000 lakes. Total water consumption in 1990 was 642m m³, which came:

- 53 per cent from surface waters
- 47 per cent from groundwater.

Consumption (1990) breaks down as follows:

- industry 230m m³
- domestic supplies 191m m³
- agriculture 188m m³.

Wastewater discharges amounted to 569m m³ in 1990, of which 36 per cent was considered 'pure' and 44 per cent went untreated. Wastewater discharges contributed in 1990:

- 51 400t of BOD
- 8.15mt of nitrogen
- 1.04mt of phosphorus
  158 000t of iron,

much of which was ultimately discharged into the Baltic Sea. Virtually all Riga's sewage flowed into the Daugava river without treatment until the first phase of the main sewage works came into operation in 1991. Bathing is restricted along some parts of the Gulf of Riga, because of polluted coastal waters, and 87 per cent of the country's lakes were estimated to suffer from eutrophication. A surface water survey in 1991 found pesticides present in an increasing number of samples.

SOLID WASTE

Waste arisings in 1990 were estimated at:

- 560 000t of municipal waste
- 265 000t of industrial waste
- 386 000t of non-toxic sludge
- 250 000t of hazardous industrial waste and sludge.

17 per cent of hazardous industrial waste contained oil products and 61 per cent was inorganic material. A small quantity of hazardous waste is incinerated (1,330t in 1990); most is landfilled at 504 sites (total area 664.5ha). A composting plant to take organic household waste is planned for Riga.

NATURE CONSERVATION

Latvia has 1609 higher plant species, of which 112 are listed in the national Red Data Book. There are 465 animal vertebrate species, including 60 mammals, and the Red Data Book lists 119 animal species. After adoption of the 1968 law on nature protection, the Gaujas National Park was established (92048ha), and lists of protected natural monuments were approved in 1977 and 1987, covering a total of 441 666ha. Ten nature parks have also been established, and five protected landscape areas.

ENERGY

Latvia does not have significant indigenous reserves of energy and is heavily dependent upon imports of oil, gas and coal (from Russia and Poland). Some peat is extracted and produced as briquettes for fuel; 30 000m^3 were produced in 1991, down from 128 000m^3 in 1980. Around half of electricity supplies is imported, the remainder being generated by thermal power stations and three hydro-electric power stations on the Daugava (capacity 1487MW). The hydro plants supply around 60 per cent of the electricity generated within the country.

AGRICULTURE

Agriculture accounted for around 12 per cent of GNP and 18 per cent of employment in 1989; 2.57m ha of land was used for agriculture. Livestock production, primarily dairy and pork, constituted around two-thirds of agricultural output, which fell by 20 per cent in 1990–91. Pork production has been concentrated at large units (32 units of 10,000–25,000 pigs in 1990) which can be a major source of pollution. Barley, oats, potatoes and sugar-beet are amongst the main arable crops. Pesticide use doubled between 1978 and 1989, by which time chemical fertiliser was applied at an average of 307kg/ha.

Land reform was initiated under the 1990 law on land tenure reform in rural areas, and the number of private farms trebled during 1992 to around 50 000, with an average size of 16ha. Price liberalisation and the severe drought of 1992 added to difficulties in the agricultural sector and output declined further in 1992. The number of head of pigs and cattle fell by 28 per cent and 20 per cent in the 12 months to October 1992.

FOREST RESOURCES

Estimates of forest cover range from 1.66 to 2.26m ha. Pine, birch and spruce are the dominant species. The 1990 forest survey found 43 per cent of conifers and 27 per cent of broadleaved species sampled with moderate or worse defoliation (25 per cent or more). Latvia has extensive areas of swamp forest (ie growing on wetland areas) – approximately 290 000ha. Timber production in 1989 was 2.4m m^3.

TRANSPORT

Latvia's main road network extended to 20 600km, and the number of private cars increased by 23 per cent between 1985 and 1989 to 254 000. 90 per cent of inland freight is carried by road. Riga and Ventspils are the principal ports; the latter handles most of the country's international oil movements. There is 2397km of railway (271km electrified). The transport sector was the source of 70 per cent of NO$_x$ emissions in 1990, and vehicle inspections in recent years have found 30 per cent of cars in breach of emission standards.

Lithuania

Lithuania is the southernmost of the three Baltic states, bordering Latvia to the north, Belarus to the east, and Poland and the Russian region of Kaliningrad to the south. It has a coastline of 94km on the Baltic Sea. Much of the terrain is low-lying, with an average altitude of 100m, although uplands in the east rise to 294m.

INSTITUTIONS AND POLICY

Lithuania became an independent republic in 1991 and a new constitution was approved in 1992. An Environmental Protection Department was established in 1990 as the primary state body with environmental responsibilities, attached to the Supreme Council. A new framework law on environmental protection was adopted in January 1991, and other new legislation is being developed to replace the 1959 law on nature protection. Taxes on natural resource use and pollution were introduced in 1991, revenue accruing to the State Environment Fund.

Area	65 200km²
Population	3.7m
Urban	68%
Rural	32%
Capital	Vilnius (592 500)
City populations	5 > 100 000; 2 > 400 000
Economy	
GNP per capita	US$3710 (1991)
GDP change	–38% (1992)
Climate (Vilnius)	
Average daily temperature	17°C (July)/–5°C (January)
Annual precipitation	540–930mm
Land-use cover	
Agriculture	54%
Forest	28%
Other	18%

AIR POLLUTION

Total emissions in 1990 were estimated at:

- 143 000t of SO_2
- 60 000t of particulates
- 68 000t of NO_X.

The country's main oil-fired power station, located between Kaunas and Vilnius, was responsible for one-third of SO_2 emissions from point sources in 1989 (66 000t). The oil refinery at Mazeikiai, in the northwest, and CHP plants in these three cities and in Klaipeda are other major emitters. Few industrial plants have effective pollution abatement equipment, except for particulates, and amongst other sources the fertiliser plant at Jonava, chemical works at Kedainia and cement factory at Akmene are thought to be responsible for local health problems.

Almost half of NO_X emissions in 1990 came from motor vehicles, along with the majority of carbon monoxide and hydrocarbons. Lower lead-content petrol (0.15 rather than 0.35g/l) began production in 1990. CFC consumption in 1990 consisted primarily of 4110t of CFC-11 and CFC-12.

Air quality is monitored regularly in seven cities; on the basis of an index of the principal pollutants, Siauliai, Kaunas, Klaipeda and Vilnius appear worst affected. Peak values were recorded in 1990 of 0.20mg/m³ NO_2 or above in all four conurbations, 1.5mg/m³ dust in Siauliai, and 0.12mg/m³ SO_2 in Klaipeda.

WATER RESOURCES AND POLLUTION

Lithuania is rich in water resources and has 722 rivers over 10km in length. Most of the country lies in the basin of the Nemunas river, which rises in Belarus and flows through Lithuania into the Baltic, via Kursiu bay. Of the country's 4000 lakes, 25 are greater than 1000ha in surface area. Surface water provided 89 per cent of total supplies in 1990. Consumption in 1990 was:

- energy sector: 79 per cent
- domestic use: 7 per cent
- industry: 4 per cent
- agriculture: 3 per cent.

Most drinking water comes from groundwater, which can contain high levels of iron, often 2–3mg/l, and with pollutants from industry and agricultural sources, 51 per cent of wells were found to produce water below environmental health standards. Surface waters tend to show the effects of polluting discharges downstream from urban areas and industrial plant; 70 per cent of rivers were thought to suffer from pollution by organic pollutants with an oxygen demand of 2–4 mg/l, and 20 per cent at 4–6mg/l.

Wastewater discharges totalled 4.04bn m³ in 1990, 51 per cent of which did not receive adequate treatment. There were 819 wastewater treatment plants in 1990, with a total capacity of 1.37bn m³; over half (by volume) depended on mechanical treatment and less than 60 per cent of them were fully operational. The country's major cities had no sewage works, and Vilnius and Kaunas together accounted for half of all national discharges to water. The construction of sewage works there and in Klaipeda and Siauliai is a priority objective and should help reduce pollution in the receiving waters of Kursius bay and the Baltic Sea.

SOLID WASTE

Annual waste arisings have been estimated at:

- 5mt domestic waste
- 5mt other non-hazardous waste
- 750 000t recyclable waste
- 150 000t hazardous waste.

There are 326 landfill sites (total area 350ha) taking solid domestic waste. Legislation requires companies to store hazardous waste on their own premises or where allocated for temporary storage, to store until satisfactory disposal is possible.

NATURE CONSERVATION

Lithuania has around 1300 recorded species of vascular plants, of which 195 are listed in the national Red Data Book; 97 out of 485 vertebrate animal species are listed, too. A network of protected areas was initiated in 1960 and a new law on protected areas was adopted in 1992; 30 regional parks were added to the 5 national parks (140 983ha) and 4 strict nature reserves (23 548ha) already designated. With 290 nature conservation reserves, protected areas now cover 11.2 per cent of the country.

ENERGY

Lithuania is almost totally dependent on imports for its energy supplies, except for small quantities of peat, firewood and hydrogenerated electricity. The energy sector is a major source of air pollution, partly because oil supplies tend to have a high sulphur content, typically 2.5–4 per cent. Gas consumption has increased steadily, accounting for 32 per cent of primary energy use in 1990.

Lithuania generates twice its own electricity needs, more than 40 per cent of which is consumed by the ten largest industrial users. Two nuclear reactors at Ignalina, on Lake Druksiai in the northeast, produced 60 per cent of national electricity output in 1990; thermal power stations produced nearly all the remainder, with a small proportion from hydroelectric stations.

The Ignalina nuclear plant has two 1500MW reactors of the same design (RBMK) as those at Chernobyl; safety precautions were strengthened after the major accident at the latter in 1986, but concerns remain also over the plant's location on a geological fault line and its effects on the ecology of Lake Druksiai.

A national energy conservation programme drawn up in 1991 envisages improvements in energy efficiency of 20–25 per cent, particularly in industrial and domestic use.

AGRICULTURE

The agricultural sector accounted for almost 30 per cent of net material product and 18 per cent of employment in 1990, and is geared towards livestock production; grassland and pasture occupy 32 per cent of agricultural land, and arable production concentrates on forage plants and animal feed. Wheat, barley, sugarbeet and potatoes are the main arable crops. Waste from intensive pig, poultry and dairy units have been major sources of pollution. Price deregulation, the abolition of farm subsidies, drought and land reform have affected agricultural production recently; grain production fell by 40 per cent in 1992 and the number of head of cattle and pigs had decreased by over 40 per cent compared with 1985 levels. An agreement with Russia was signed in 1992 to supply meat and dairy produce in exchange for oil and gas deliveries.

FOREST RESOURCES

Forest cover extends to 28 per cent of land area and is dominated by conifers; birch, ash and oak are also present. Recent heavy exploitation has involved the felling of 8000ha annually, producing 3.2m m³ of timber. Air pollution has affected forest health, notably around industrial areas, and the 1991 forest survey found 28 per cent of conifers and 15 per cent of broadleaves to be moderately defoliated or worse.

TRANSPORT

The road network extends to 43 100km and there were 474 000 cars in 1990. Vehicle emissions contribute around half the total air pollutants. The transport sector as a whole accounted for 15 per cent of primary energy consumption. There are 2007km of railway track (122km electrified). Klaipeda, on the Baltic coast, is the main port.

Luxembourg

Luxembourg is a small country south-east of Belgium, sharing other borders with France and Germany. The northern third of the territory lies in the Ardennes hills and rises to over 600m. The main centres of population are in the central and southern areas, which are lower-lying.

INSTITUTIONS AND POLICY

The Grand Duchy of Luxembourg is a constitutional monarchy; a Chamber of Deputies is directly elected and shares legislative powers with the Grand Duke. Local government is exercised principally at the level of 118 communes, which have responsibilities for local planning matters and public health and safety. The Ministry of Environment is assisted by two Administrations, for Water and Forests (which handles nature conservation) and for Environment. The Administrations undertake many of the Ministry's executive functions. Environmental

Area	2586km^2
Population	389 800
Urban	57%
Rural	43%
Capital	Luxembourg (75 400)
City populations	1 > 50 000
Economy	
GNP per capita	US$22 856 (1989)
Climate (Luxembourg)	
Average daily max and min	23/13°C (July)/3/–1°C (January)
Annual precipitation	760mm
Land-use cover	
Agriculture	49%
Forest	33%
Other	18%

legislation has been influenced extensively by EC policy, national regulations sometimes reproducing the wording of EC Directives.

The Act on Dangerous or Unhealthy Establishments of 1990 amended the previous licensing system and is based on three classes of trade, industrial and commercial operations. Applications for permits for those in classes 1 and 2 involve a public enquiry, the permit being issued by the Ministries of Labour and of Environment (class 1) or the communes (class 2). Class 3 plants are authorised by the ministries through a simplified procedure. The law also provides for an EIA to be carried out, and requires this for class 1 establishments. The 1982 Law on the Protection of Nature and Natural Resources also includes provisions on EIA and a new regulation is intended to extend the scope of their requirements.

AIR POLLUTION

Total emissions of SO_2 decreased from 24 000t in 1980 to 10 000t in 1990; over 80 per cent of emissions in 1985 came from industrial processes and combustion. Reductions in the maximum levels of sulphur in gas oil and the contraction of the steel industry have helped curb emissions.

Emissions of NO_x totalled 21 930t in 1985, 55 per cent from industrial sources and 39 per cent from vehicle emissions. Despite the introduction of catalytic converters, the overall growth of road traffic is expected to lead to increases in the level of NO_x emissions, to around 22 200t in 2000. Annual emissions of particulates appear to be stable at around 3000t.

Air quality is monitored by networks which measure concentrations of the principal pollutants, including an automatic monitoring network of five stations which began operation in 1988. Average figures for the country indicate a general reduction in concentrations between 1972 and 1990–91; for example (98th percentile annual averages):

- From 113 to 58µg/m^3 for SO$_2$
- From 286 to 58µg/m^3 for NO$_X$.

However, some stations have recorded increases in recent years, and peak values of 205µg/m^3 SO$_2$ (24-hour average) and 280µg/m^3 NO$_2$ (30-minute average) were found in the centre of the city of Luxembourg in 1991.

As a small country situated between two industrial areas, Lorraine in France and the Saar and Ruhr in Germany, Luxembourg is affected significantly by transboundary air pollution. Around 90 per cent of the country's electricity needs are imported, so power stations are not a major contributor to air pollution within Luxembourg, although there are steelworks around Esch-sur-Alzette.

Air pollution legislation is based on the Air Pollution Act of 1976, which laid down the basic provisions for the control of emissions, and the 1990 Act on Dangerous or Unhealthy Establishments, which governs licensing arrangements. EC Directives on air quality have been implemented by means of decrees.

WATER RESOURCES AND POLLUTION

Luxembourg's eastern boundary is formed by the rivers Our, Sûre and Moselle; the Alzette, a tributary of the Sûre, flows north through the southern half of the country. Total abstractions in 1990 were estimated at 59m m^3 (excluding withdrawals for agriculture), 46 per cent of which came from groundwater sources, which are more widespread in the south. A large reservoir at Esch-sur-Sûre is an important contributor to supplies from surface water. Around 95 per cent of abstractions in 1990 fed into the public water supply; most of the remainder was used by industry.

Rising levels of nitrate in groundwater have become a problem in some areas, and are associated with intensive arable cultivation, particularly of maize. Nitrate concentrations in samples from two monitoring points rose from 15 to 60mg/l and 34 to 70mg/l over a period of 15 years.

Regular surveys of the watercourses (covering 692km) indicate that the proportion of river length considered as class 1 (the best quality of five classes) increased from 46 per cent in 1973 to 57 per cent in 1991. The length in classes 3 and 4 together decreased from 16 per cent in 1973 to 11 per cent in 1990, before returning to 16 per cent in 1991. The Alzette and its tributaries in the south appear worst affected. 15 out of 20 bathing areas sampled under the EC bathing water Directive in 1992 complied with the mandatory coliform limits.

Pollution by heavy metals from industrial sources is evident in the south. Although the 19 plants handling heavy metals in 1991 had effluent treatment facilities, breaches of emission limits were recorded for iron, copper, zinc, nickel and silver.

The sewage treatment system was extended to serve over 90 per cent of the population by 1990 (compared to 28 per cent in 1970), providing mostly secondary treatment.

In addition to the 1990 Act on Dangerous or Unhealthy

Establishments, legislation on water pollution control is based largely on the Act on Clearing, Maintaining and Improving Watercourses (1929) and related regulations. Other relevant provisions are included in the 1982 Act on the Protection of Nature and Natural Resources, which requires authorisation before water engineering works are undertaken, and the Fishing Act of 1976.

SOLID WASTE

Total waste arisings in 1990 were estimated to include:

- 170 000t of municipal waste
- 1.3mt of industrial waste
- 5.24mt of demolition waste.

The amount of municipal waste generated annually increased by a third between 1980 and 1990; most is incinerated (70 per cent) at one plant, the remainder going to three main landfills and a small amount to a composting centre (2000t in 1990). As a large proportion of municipal waste consists of organic matter (44 per cent), it is planned to expand the composting system. Many communes also operate landfills intended to take inert waste, eg from excavation or demolition work, but these sites often have little capacity available and a survey in 1988 found that at least 35 out of 123 authorised landfills contained heavy metals.

Industrial waste arisings have continued to increase, whilst treatment and disposal capacity has become more limited; one landfill is designed to take industrial waste but by 1991 was virtually full, and some industrial plants have their own waste facilities (notably at steelworks). Hazardous waste is exported.

The Act on Waste Disposal of 1980 is the principal law on waste, requiring it to be disposed of in a proper manner; collection and disposal of household waste is the responsibility of the communes. EC Directives on waste have been implemented through regulations made under the 1980 Act.

NATURE CONSERVATION

The fauna and flora found in Luxembourg include:

- 1200 vascular plant species
- 62 mammal species
- 7 reptile species and
- 15 amphibian species.

30 per cent of the vascular plant species are thought to be in decline, and all but one reptile and two amphibian species are threatened. A national plan published in 1981 and an accompanying government declaration listed potential sites for protected areas, including 113 nature reserves; the list was revised in 1990, increasing the number of potential nature reserves to 137. By 1991, twelve nature reserves had been established, covering 416ha. A nature park of 36 000ha was created in 1964, spanning the border with Germany at the river Our.

The Law on the Protection of Nature and Natural Resources (1982) provides the legal basis for nature conservation, on which the Environment Ministry is advised by the Higher Council for Nature Conservation.

ENERGY

Total primary energy supply decreased from 4.2 to 2.8mtoe between 1970 and 1983, reflecting the decline of the iron and steel industry and a shift from manufacturing to service industries. Primary energy supply rose to 3.8mtoe in 1991. Luxembourg depends on imports for most of its energy supplies, including all its oil and coal. 90 per cent of electricity is also imported, although 1.39bn kWh were generated within the country in 1991. Oil products accounted for half of final energy consumption that year, compared with 30 per cent in 1980, when coal was the principal fuel. Much of the increased use of oil products can be attributed to the growth of transport, which accounted for one-third of final energy consumption in 1991, up from 15 per cent in 1980.

AGRICULTURE

The area of land used by agriculture in 1990 was estimated at 57 000ha of arable and permanent cropland and 69 000ha of permanent grassland. Average farm size increased to 37ha in 1991.

The annual consumption of nitrogen fertiliser more than doubled during the 1960s, and between 1970 and 1988 the average application increased from 78.5 to 133t/ha; nitrate pollution of groundwater has become a focus of concern, particularly where aquifers are used to supply drinking water.

Increasing intensification and land consolidation are considered the principal causes of the loss of wildlife habitats.

FOREST RESOURCES

Forests covered 87 800ha in 1987, broad-leaved species accounting for over 60 per cent of this area. The northern part of the country is heavily wooded, forming part of the Ardennes hills. Timber production was around 327 000m^3 in 1988. Annual forest surveys indicate a general decline in tree health during the 1980s; the proportion of sample trees suffering defoliation of 25 per cent or above increased from 5 per cent in 1986 to 21 per cent in 1991.

TRANSPORT

Much of the traffic in Luxembourg is in transit between neighbouring countries, and road transport predominates. The road network extended to around 5000km in 1991, including 84km of motorway connecting the capital with France, Belgium and Germany. The number of cars in use increased steadily from 94 000 in 1975 to 190 000 in 1991, by which time 12.5 per cent were fitted with a catalytic converter.

The transport sector has become a major contributor to air pollution, accounting for over 35 per cent of NO_x and VOC emissions (1985), and one-third of final energy consumption (1991).

The railway system covered 270km in 1991.

Malta

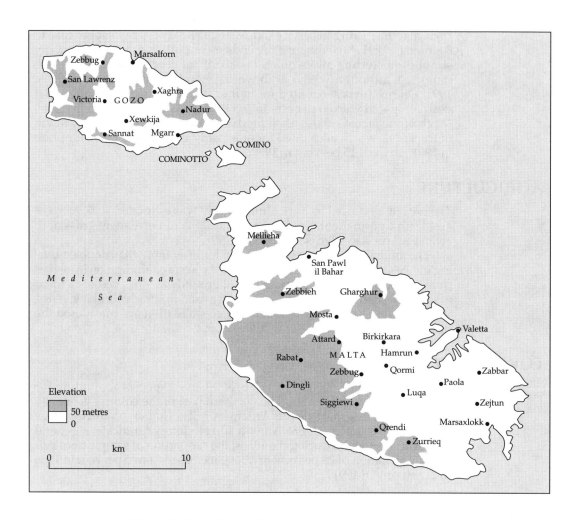

The Maltese Republic consists of three islands, Malta, Gozo and Comino, and some islets, in the Mediterranean Sea, south of Sicily and east of Tunisia. The island of Malta has steep cliffs on the south-west coast, rising to a plateau 230m above sea level. A plain slopes down to the eastern coast, which has a number of large bays. There are no major lakes or rivers and the length of the shoreline totals 190km.

INSTITUTIONS AND POLICY

Malta gained independence in 1964, and under the constitution of that year, a House of Representatives is directly elected by popular vote.

Area	316km^2
Population	361 700
Capital	Valetta (9200; conurbation 101 750)
City populations	3 > 10 000
Economy	
GNP per capita	US$7341 (1991)
Climate (Valetta)	
Average daily max and min	29/22°C (July)/14/10°C (January)
Annual precipitation	519mm
Land-use cover	
Agriculture	40%
Tree/scrub cover	4%
Urban	15%
Other	41%

Environmental responsibilities rest with the Ministry for the Environment, which also handles physical planning, infrastructure development and energy policy. An Environment Protection Act was passed in 1990 as the basis for an extensive new regime of environmental regulations, including EIA and a permitting system for potentially polluting activities.

AIR POLLUTION

Air pollution has not been a significant problem in Malta; in general, pollutants are dispersed rapidly by the strong winds. The two electricity generating stations, which burn coal and oil, are the major point sources. Emissions also come from motor vehicles, industrial plant and domestic fuels. A Clean Air Act was passed in 1967 and an air quality survey was to be undertaken during 1993.

WATER RESOURCES AND POLLUTION

Malta is heavily dependent on groundwater; surface water provides only around 2 per cent of total supplies. Around half of all drinking water comes from desalinated sea water, treated at two reverse osmosis plants and one distillation plant. Total abstractions in 1987 were 39.3m m^3, of which 69 per cent came from groundwater. Some groundwater supplies are polluted by nitrates from fertiliser run-off. Total water production increased from 28.1m m^3 in 1983 to 44.5m m^3 in 1991. Around two-thirds of sewage is discharged to the sea; the remainder is treated and the effluent (12 000m^3 per day) used for irrigation, in order to limit the demand on groundwater.

SOLID WASTE

Arisings of household waste were estimated at 97 000t in 1992, of which 86 per cent was disposed to landfill; the two major sites are located near the coast in order to minimise the danger of leachate contaminating ground-water aquifers. Recommendations have been made to the government to increase the proportion of waste being recycled or composted, and to begin incineration (with heat recovery to generate electricity).

NATURE CONSERVATION

Malta has around 1000 flowering plant species, 21 of which are endemic to the islands; 21 mammal species are present, and in addition to the 13 resident bird species, 50 species overwinter in Malta and 112 visit as migrants. 79 invertebrate species and 1 reptile are endemic. Regulations were made in 1992 and 1993 to protect some species of fauna and flora under the Environment Protection Act of 1990. The shooting and trapping of birds is widespread; there were 13 400 licensed hunters and an estimated 12 000 trappers in 1987.

Very small areas of native forest remain, at four sites; trees and scrub cover amounts to 4 per cent of the surface area. Coastal areas include important sand dune and saline marsh habitats; some of these and other seminatural areas face pressure as a result of tourism, quarrying or other activities. In 1992 there were five nature reserves, including one Ramsar wetland, and a further three were planned.

ENERGY

All the country's energy is imported, including oil and coal supplies for the two thermal power stations. Kerosene and liquid petroleum gas are imported mainly for domestic use, petrol and gas oil for transport and industry. Electricity demand increased steadily during the mid-1980s, necessitating the construction of a second (oil-fired) power station. Total electricity generation was 1278m kWh in 1991, more than double production in 1983. Exploration licences for offshore oil and gas supplies have been awarded since 1990.

AGRICULTURE

Around 13 500ha is used for agriculture, including an area of 1200ha which is irrigated. Although water shortages limit production, a range of crops is cultivated, including vegetables, grapes and cereals; poultry, pork and dairying are also important. The average size of farm holding on Malta is less than 2ha. The fishing industry is small, employing only 235 people full time in 1991 (although over 1000 part time); the total catch was around 800t. A National Aquaculture Centre was established in 1988 to promote fish-farming, which began commercial operation in the following year.

TRANSPORT

The number of motor vehicles increased rapidly from 16 000 in 1957 to around 160 000 in 1990; over the same period, the length of road increased from 893km in 1957 to around 1500km. A total of 2700 ships entered Maltese seaports in 1991.

Transport infrastructure developments are often linked to the tourism industry, which is a major sector of the economy; tourist arrivals increased from 490 800 in 1983 to 895 000 in 1991. A new international airport was opened in 1992, with a capacity of 2.5m passengers per year.

Netherlands

The Netherlands is a small and densely populated country in northern Europe, with a northern and western coastline on the North Sea. It shares land borders with Belgium and Germany. Most of the country is low-lying and a substantial area (27 per cent) is below sea level, and much

Area	41 526km^2
Population	15.13m
Urban	89%
Rural	11%
Capital	Amsterdam (1.08m)
City populations	20 > 100 000; 3 > 250 000
Economy	
GNP per capita	US$18 780 (1991)
Climate (De Bilt, Utrecht)	
Average daily max and min	22/13°C (July)/4/–1°C (January)
Annual precipitation	766mm
Land-use cover	
Agriculture	64%
Forest	8%
Urban	15%
Other	13%

of which has been reclaimed from the sea. The land rises above 300m in part of Limburg, in the south.

INSTITUTIONS AND POLICY

The Netherlands is a constitutional monarchy, with an elected parliament *(Staten-Generaal)* of two chambers. Local government is exercised by the 12 provinces and around 650 municipalities, the provinces in particular having wide-ranging responsibilities for implementing environmental legislation. The Ministry of Housing, Physical Planning and Environment (VROM) handles most environmental matters, although other ministries take the lead for water (Ministry of Transport and Water Management) and nature conservation (Ministry of Agriculture, Nature Management and Fisheries). A number of advisory and research bodies assist the government, including the National Institute for Public Health and Environmental Protection and the Council for the Environment.

A National Environmental Policy Plan (NEPP) was published in 1989, revised the following year and endorsed as government policy. Taking sustainable development as its objective, the plan sets out policy aims for a range of sectors, including pollution reduction targets of 70–90 per cent by 2010. EIA was introduced by means of amendments to the Environmental Protection (General Provisions) Act of 1979, which covers permitting arrangements, and decrees; an EIA Commission was also established. A new Environmental Control Act came into force in March 1993 as the framework legislation on environmental matters. The Act replaces five existing permits with a single environmental permit (but

215

excludes discharges to surface waters), for which all environmental impacts of a proposed activity must be considered.

AIR POLLUTION

Total SO_2 emissions fell from 464 000t in 1980 to 208 000t in 1990, largely as a result of abatement measures in industry and electricity generation. Combustion in furnaces accounted for 65 per cent of emissions in 1990, but the greater use of coal rather than heavy fuel oil helped reduce the level of sulphur emissions. Limits on the sulphur content of fuel oils have been tightened. Oil refineries, which are concentrated round Rotterdam, contribute around one-third of SO_2 emissions, but declining production and stricter emissions limits cut emissions by more than half between 1970 and 1988.

Annual total NO_x emissions remained between 550 000t and 590 000t during the 1980s; half now originates from road traffic, and 36 per cent from combustion plant.

Ambient concentrations of SO_2 and NO_x are generally highest in the south and west of the country, where the larger conurbations and industrial centres are located.

Agriculture is the largest contributor to acidifying emissions, because of ammonia (225 000t in 1990) from livestock manure and fertiliser. The areas most susceptible to acidification are in the south-east.

Requirements for permits for emissions to air were introduced under the Air Pollution Act 1970 for industrial plant and the Nuisance Act 1952 for smaller establishments. Permits are issued by the provincial or municipal executive and were brought into an integrated system under the Environmental Control Act 1992. The Air Pollution Act was amended in 1985 to provide for the establishment of air quality objectives. The act also provides for regulations on the sulphur content of oil and the lead content of petrol.

The NEPP set emission reduction targets by 2000, compared with 1985 levels, for a number of air pollutants, including cuts of:

- 60 per cent for SO_2
- 50 per cent for NO_x
- 67 per cent for ammonia
- 57 per cent for VOCs.

An action programme was drawn up by government and industry in 1990 to reduce the consumption of ozone-depleting substances.

Policy seeks to stabilise emissions of CO_2 at 1990 levels by 1995, followed by a reduction of 3–5 per cent by 2000. CO_2 emissions were estimated at 199.7mt in 1990.

WATER RESOURCES AND POLLUTION

The Netherlands is situated on the North Sea and the deltas of three major rivers, the Rhine, Meuse and Scheldt. Coastal dunes and extensive dykes help prevent large areas of land from being flooded. Freshwater abstractions rose from 13.27m m^3 in 1972 to 14.48m m^3 in 1986, excluding water for agricultural use and most of which is used in industry and cooling power stations. Over 90 per cent of these abstractions came from surface water. Agricultural use is estimated to range between 0.34 and 1.46m m³ annually, for average and very dry years respectively, and draws on groundwater for 40–50 per cent of supply. Groundwater accounted for 70 per cent of the 1.11m m³ abstracted by water companies in 1986, and studies indicate that groundwater levels in woodland areas and nature reserves have fallen by an average of 20cm since 1950, particularly in the east of the country, and by more than 50cm in some areas.

Around 90 per cent of wastewater sources discharge to the sewerage system, and the proportion of domestic wastewater treated in public sewage works increased from 35 per cent to 92 per cent in the 20 years to 1990. Their treatment capacity was raised from 8m to 24m population equivalents (PE) and the capacity of treatment facilities at industrial plants increased more than tenfold to 10m PE over the same period. A growing number of sewage treatment plants have phosphate removal facilities (21 in 1985 and 34 in 1990), reflecting the widespread risk of phosphate pollution to surface waters. Domestic wastewater and the chemical industry accounted for over 75 per cent of phosphate discharges to surface waters in 1986, and 80 per cent of small streams were estimated in 1989 to exceed the 0.15mg/l quality objective for phosphate.

The water quality of the Rhine has generally improved since 1970; oxygen levels have increased and heavy metal and organic halogenated hydrocarbons decreased. Agricultural activities constitute the source of much water pollution, particularly of groundwater, principally from livestock wastes and fertiliser; some abstraction points for drinking water have been closed because of high nitrate levels, with a quarter at risk in coming decades.

Sampling in accordance with the EC bathing water Directive in 1992 found 93 per cent of seawater bathing areas and 89 per cent of freshwater bathing areas in compliance with the mandatory value for faecal coliforms.

Responsibilities for water policy are shared between the Ministry of Transport and Water Management, VROM, the regional water boards and the provinces. The Pollution of Surface Waters Act (1969) requires licences for polluting discharges to surface waters, issued by the Ministry of Transport and Water Management in the case of large surface waters (including the Rhine, Scheldt and Meuse) and otherwise by the provinces or water boards. A system of levies applies and emission limits and quality objectives are established under the act. Under the Water Management Act (1989) national and regional management plans for surface waters are drawn up every four years by the two ministries and the water boards respectively. Provincial water management plans cover groundwater and surface water, and other provisions cover water transfers, abstractions and discharges, for which licences are required above specified volumes; licences for abstractions from groundwater are regulated by the Groundwater Act (1981). Discharges at sea of harmful substances are prohibited under the Seawater Pollution Act (1975), unless granted exemption.

SOLID WASTE

Total arisings are estimated at around 133mt annually, including 65mt of dredging spoil. Of the 5.88mt of household waste generated in 1991:

- 45 per cent was disposed to landfill
- 38 per cent was incinerated
- 12 per cent was removed for composting.

In 1990, 940 000t was classified as chemical waste (ie hazardous); 270 000t was disposed to landfill, 160 000t incinerated and 195 000t exported. Coal-fired power stations produced 1.27mt of fly-ash, slag and gypsum in 1990; 85 per cent was used for construction purposes. Agricultural waste included 17.5mt of 'surplus' manure in 1990; a total of 84mt of manure was produced in 1988. In 1990 there were eight public waste incinerators with an annual capacity of 2.4mt; four installations which did not meet emission standards were closed that year.

Under the Wastes Act (1977), household waste collection and disposal are the responsibility of the municipal authorities; the licensing of waste disposal and storage operations is handled by the provinces. Permits for chemical waste, as defined in the Chemical Waste Act (1976), are granted by VROM. Permits under both Acts are to be integrated under the Environmental Protection Act (1992). Separate collection for all glass, textiles, paper, chemical waste and used batteries is planned by 2000; 50 per cent of organic household waste is to be composted.

NATURE CONSERVATION

The environment in the Netherlands is shaped very largely by human activities, notably agriculture, roadbuilding and urban and industrial development. Many areas of conservation interest are small, fragmented and under pressure from human activities. Nevertheless, important areas of natural and seminatural habitat remain, including extensive wetlands, areas of grassland, and coastal dunes. Many species are in decline, and 542 out of 1448 known vascular plant species are listed in the national Red Data Book; more than 70 have become extinct since 1950. Animal species have also declined in recent decades, particularly reptiles, amphibians and butterflies; 20 out of 66 mammal species, excluding cetaceans, are regarded as vulnerable. The decline in species of flora and fauna has been most marked in the south and east of the country.

Species protection policy is based on the Bird Protection Act (1936)and the Nature Conservation Act (1967), which also provides the legal basis for protected areas in the Netherlands. A list of 21 potential national parks was drawn up in 1975, covering a total of around 83 000ha. By 1992 six national parks had been formally designated (23 900ha) and five more were being prepared for designation. National park status alone does not confer special protection. A total of 236 400ha was protected under the Nature Conservation Act by 1991, on the basis of scientific or scenic features; over 100 000ha country estates had been nominated by landowners for conservation under the Scenic Area Act. 15 Ramsar wetland sites covering 313 000ha had been designated by 1993.

Nature conservation matters are primarily the responsibility of the Ministry of Agriculture, Nature Management and Fisheries, and a Nature Policy Plan was produced in 1990. The plan sets out long-term policy (30 years, subsequently shortened to 25 years) for nature conservation, with the objective of sustainable development and the restoration of ecosystems and landscapes. A national ecological network is envisaged for the conservation of important species and ecosystems, with existing core areas and nature development areas linked by 'ecological corridors' to permit migration.

ENERGY

The Netherlands relies heavily on gas, which supplies almost half of domestic primary energy requirements; production totalled 81.66bn m^3 in 1991, nearly half of which is exported. Relatively small quantities of crude oil are also produced, 3.26mt in 1991, also from fields offshore in the North Sea. Coal was mined until the 1960s.

Total primary energy supply increased from 49.9mtoe in 1970 to 70.0mtoe in 1991, an increasing share being supplied by gas. Industry and transport accounted for over 60 per cent of final consumption in 1990.

Electricity production is also dominated by gas, which accounts for over 55 per cent of generation. Some gas-fired power stations have been converted to burn coal in recent years, to take advantage of low-cost imports, and combined heat and power generation is expected to increase in capacity from around 2000MW in 1987 to 6500MW by 2000.

Two nuclear reactors, with a combined capacity of 504MW, provided 4.9 per cent of domestic electricity generated in 1992.

Renewable energy sources make little contribution to the energy economy of the Netherlands, but the government aims to expand wind turbine capacity to 1000MW by 2000, with the assistance of incentives.

A carbon tax was introduced in February 1990, levied on all fossil fuels.

AGRICULTURE

Dutch agriculture is probably the most intensive in the world, production having trebled since 1950. Mechanisation, drainage, greater use of inputs and specialised breeds have enabled the Netherlands to become a major exporter of agricultural produce, which accounts for 17 per cent of export income.

The number of holdings decreased from 308 000 in 1959 to 123 000 in 1991, but their average area increased from 7.5ha to 19.2ha. More than 60 per cent of the land area is used for agriculture.

Livestock form the largest sector in agriculture, accounting for around 60 per cent of production and concentrated in the south and east. The number of livestock animals has grown rapidly over recent decades, particularly pigs and poultry; in 1992 there were 4.9m cattle, 14.1m pigs and 102m poultry. Many livestock farms are intensive indoor units which rely on imported feed stuffs (eg cassava). They also produce large quantities of manure which can be a major source of pollution, notably nitrogen and phosphates which leach into the soil and water, and ammonia which results in acid emissions to air. Heavy metals from manure spread on land can also become concentrated in soil, including copper. Manure production rose from 67.5mt in 1970 to 89.5mt in 1990; much is spread on agricultural land primarily for disposal rather than for fertilisation. Despite widespread use of manure in some areas, the consumption of chemical fertiliser is high at around 240kg nitrogen per hectare of cultivated land in 1988.

Arable farming is concentrated in the north of the country and the area under cereals has decreased by more than 50 per cent during the past 30 years. Rye and oats in particular have given way to the cultivation of green maize for animal fodder, and potato, sugarbeet and wheat production increased during the 1970s and 1980s.

Horticulture is also important, including the cultivation of vegetables, flowers and bulbs. Energy and pesticide use can be intensive, especially where produce is grown under glass, the area of which increased by 9 per cent between 1979 and 1987. Pesticide use in the Netherlands is the highest, per hectare, in the world (over 9kg of active substance per ha cultivated land in 1987). Arable farming accounts for two-thirds of national consumption, but application rates, at 19kg/ha, are lower than in greenhouse horticulture (106kg/ha) and bulb-growing (120kg/ha). Over 40 per cent of pesticides are used for soil disinfection, particularly where potatoes are grown. Agriculture accounted for 6.5 per cent of national energy consumption in 1987, around 80 per cent being used for cultivation under glass.

As a major source of pollution in the Netherlands, including 80 per cent of nitrogen and 70 per cent of phosphates, the environmental impact of agriculture has attracted great attention in recent years. A decree made under the Soil Protection Act of 1986 restricts the application of manure by quantity and season and some provinces have introduced stricter controls through their groundwater protection plans. A manure bank was established in 1987 with storage facilities intended to assist the redistribution of manure from areas with a surplus to those with farms wishing to use it as fertiliser. Measures introduced under the Fertilisers Act (1986) are intended to reduce the quantities of manure produced by limiting phosphate production on new farms to 125kg/ha and imposing a surplus levy above this level. Capacity for the storage and reprocessing of manure is being expanded, and subsidies are available to assist farmers construct storage facilities, transport manure etc.

Agricultural policy is based on the Agricultural Structure Memorandum published in 1990 and envisages significant reductions in inputs and emissions, including a 50 per cent cut in pesticide use and a reduction of 50–70 per cent in ammonia emissions by 2000. Energy efficiency improvements in greenhouses are intended to reduce consumption per product unit by 50 per cent by 2001.

FOREST RESOURCES

Forest cover in the Netherlands is estimated to have increased from around 260 000 to 330 000ha during the past 30 years. Conifers, principally Scots pine, cover two-thirds of the area, with oak the main broadleaved species. Timber production amounted to 1.26m m^3 of roundwood in 1990, compared with imports of over 18m m^3. The 1991 forest survey found 17.2 per cent of trees to be notably damaged (25 per cent or more defoliation); conifers appeared worse affected than broadleaved species. Acidification and the lowering of the water table in some areas have contributed to a general decline in forest health; forested areas on sandy soils in the east of the country seem to have suffered more than elsewhere.

Forestry policy is based on the Forestry Act of 1961 and seeks to conserve the existing area of forest; felled areas must be notified and replanted. The Long-term Forest Programme sets out objectives to 2000 and beyond. Forestry matters are handled by the Ministry of Agriculture, Nature Management and Fisheries.

TRANSPORT

The Netherlands has a dense road network which expanded from 77 000km in 1970 to 105 000km in 1990 (surfaced roads only) and occupies 3 per cent of the surface area. The number of cars increased more than ten-fold in 30 years, reaching 5.66m in 1992.

Around 30 per cent of sea freight in the EC passes through Dutch ports, mainly Rotterdam, which handled 291mt in 1991; much is container traffic, otherwise transported mainly by road. The Rhine is another impor-tant waterway for freight traffic, and there is an extensive canal network of 3700km.

The rail network covers 2780km and carried 304m passengers and 17.8mt of freight in 1991.

The number of bicycles increased from 7.3m in 1970 to over 12m in 1991; there are 17 100km of cycle paths (1992) and bicycles accounted for 8 per cent of private passenger transport movements (1991, measured by passenger-km).

Road transport volumes were projected in 1988 to increase by 70–80 per cent by 2010, although annual growth during the late 1980s was higher, including 14 per cent for road freight. Congestion and heavy envi-ronmental impacts result, with road traffic accounting for over half of national NO_x emissions and 15 per cent of energy consumption. The road network has been extended by around 1000km annually in recent years.

Whilst technical standards for the control of emissions continue to improve, government policy also aims to limit the projected increase in car use to 35 per cent, rather than the 72 per cent baseline figure for the period 1986–2010. Other measures are planned to encourage modal shifts in favour of public transport and bicycles for passengers and rail and water transport for freight.

Norway

Area	324 219km²
Population	4.27m
Urban	75%
Rural	25%
Capital	Oslo (0.46m)
City populations	17 > 100 000; 4 > 400 000
Economy	
GNP per capita	US$24 220 (1991)
Climate (Oslo)	
Average daily max and min	22/13°C (July)/−2/−7°C (January)
Annual precipitation	730mm
Land-use cover	
Agriculture	3%
Forest	31%
Other	66%

The kingdom of Norway forms the western part of Scandinavia, bordered by Sweden to the east and, in the far north, by Finland and Russia. The long coastline on the North Sea is heavily indented by fjords. The landscape is generally mountainous, with an average height above sea level of 534m; the lowest regions are in the south-east, which is still hilly. The population is concentrated in coastal areas. Norwegian territory includes the archipelago of Svalbard, which lies to the north in the Barents Sea.

INSTITUTIONS AND POLICY

Norway is a constitutional monarchy with an elected parliament *(Storting)* of 165 members. A new section on the environment was added to the constitution in 1992. Local government is exercised at the level of 19 counties (including the urban district of Oslo) and 448 municipalities; both have responsibilities for some aspects of environmental protection, and all county governor's offices have an environment department.

The Ministry of the Environment was created in 1972 and reorganised in 1989 into six principal departments. It oversees a number of other bodies, including the State Pollution Control Authority (SFT), and coordinates efforts to integrate environmental matters into other policy areas. The Pollution Control Act of 1981 (amended in 1989) forms the basis for policy on emissions from stationary sources, including a permitting system. The SFT is the principal authority for emissions from industry; permits for other emissions are granted by the county governors. Provisions on EIA for major development projects are included in the Planning and Building Act of 1985 (amended in 1989).

Norway applied in November 1992 to join the European Community, but a referendum in 1994 rejected accession, echoing the previous referendum of 1972. Norway's relationship with the EC was strengthened when it joined the European Economic Area in May 1992.

AIR POLLUTION

Annual emissions of SO_2 fell significantly during the past two decades, from around 171 000t in 1970 to 46 000t in 1991. Much of this reduction reflects the lowering of the permitted sulphur content of oil, a clean-up programme aimed at older industrial plants and requirements to install pollution abatement equipment. Industrial processes accounted for half of total SO_2 emissions in 1989. Several mild winters, the availability of electricity generated by hydroelectric stations, and increases in tax on sulphur in mineral oil also contributed.

Emissions of particulates declined less rapidly, and increased during the mid-1980s because of the greater use of wood for heating and of private cars. 21 000t of particulates were emitted in 1990.

Emissions of NO_x increased substantially during the 1980s, from 186 000t in 1980 to 230 000t in 1990, mainly as a result of higher traffic volumes. More than 75 per cent of NO_x emissions came from mobile sources in 1989. Norway's large fishing and coastal merchant fleets were thought to produce 30 per cent of the total. Emissions from industrial processes have remained fairly stable during the past 20 years.

Norway is affected significantly by acidic depositions originating in other countries; 85–90 per cent of the sulphur and nitrogen falling as acid rain in the late 1980s was thought to come from foreign sources. Southern parts of the country are worst affected by acidification.

Unleaded petrol was introduced in 1986, helping to reduce lead emissions from around 800t in 1979 to 265t in 1989, when unleaded supplies accounted for 30 per cent of sales. Increased activity in the oil and gas sector since the mid-1970s have led to increases in emissions of VOCs, from almost 140 000t in 1978 to around 210 000t in 1991. Emissions of CO_2 rose slightly during the 1980s, reaching 33.9mt in 1989; mobile and stationary sources each accounted for about 40 per cent of the total, the remaining 20 per cent coming from industrial processes, notably metal manufacturing.

Air quality measurements have been made regularly since 1977, and 24-hour concentrations of the principal pollutants recorded at 37 stations in 29 urban areas since 1990. Average concentrations of SO_2 in larger conurbations show a decreasing trend since the late 1970s, although the 24-hour critical level of $100\mu g/m^3$ was exceeded at seven stations in the winter of 1990/91 (above $150\mu g/m^3$ in one case). Periodically elevated levels are found predominantly in areas close to large industrial emitters. Soot and particulate levels have fallen less markedly, and several breaches of the 24-hour critical level of $100\mu g/m^3$ were recorded in 1990/91, close to heavily trafficked roads. Emissions from motor vehicles are considered the principal reason for the high levels of NO_2 measured in some areas; the 24-hour critical level of $100\mu g/m^3$ was exceeded at 9 out of 13 monitoring stations in 1990/91.

Air pollution control is based on the Pollution Control Act (1981), which covers all types of pollution from stationary sources. Potentially polluting activities must be undertaken in accordance with legal provisions and/or permits, which are issued by the State Pollution Control Authority (SFT), or the local county governor for non-industrial emissions. Large companies granted emission permits by the SFT may carry out control and monitoring work themselves, subject to annual reporting requirements and spot checks by the SFT. Standards for emissions from vehicles and other mobile sources are set through the Product Control Act (1976). Policy goals include the reduction of NO_x emissions by 30 per cent between 1986 and 1998, and the stabilisation of CO_2 emissions by 2000 at the level of 1989.

WATER RESOURCES AND POLLUTION

Norway is rich in water resources, with more than 200 000 lakes covering around 5 per cent of the surface area, and abundant precipitation. Abstractions in 1983 totalled 2.03bn m^3, of which around one-quarter fed into the public water supply. Surface water sources provide around 85 per cent of drinking water supplies.

Population centres, industry, and agriculture are relatively concentrated in particular areas, resulting in some water quality problems. Eutrophication has become a major concern, particularly in the waters of central eastern Norway which are most sensitive to pollution; an estimated 1.5m people live close to eutrophic water sources and a survey in 1988 found 28 per cent of 355 lakes sampled to be heavily or moderately polluted by nutrients.

Total discharges were estimated in 1988 at 5900t of phosphorus and 65 600t of nitrogen; sewage and run-off from agriculture constitute the principal sources.

Sewage treatment works with a capacity to serve 11 per cent of the population were constructed between 1983 and 1990, by which time 43 per cent of domestic sewage was treated. A total of 1387 wastewater treatment plants were registered in 1990, with a capacity of 3.9m population equivalents. 0.45m m^3 of sewage sludge (wet matter) was produced in 1988, 40 per cent of which was disposed to landfill and 55 per cent used in agriculture.

Polluting discharges from industrial sources include heavy metals and organic compounds, often from large point sources such as metallurgical plants, extractive industries, refineries, pulp and paper and chemical works. 13 out of 70 substances classified as micropollutants have been identified as the most serious pollutants which should be eliminated as soon as possible. Oil is discharged from drilling and refining operations (around 1000t annually) and illegally from ships (20 000t annually). Acidification has affected extensive stretches of lakes and rivers, particularly in the southernmost counties of Vest-Agder and Aust-Agder, where damage to fishlife has been severe.

Discharges to water are regulated under the Pollution Control Act, permits being granted by the SFT or the county governor. The counties are responsible for permits for municipal wastewater discharges (except in the case of very small plants, which are handled by the municipalities) and the inspection of sewage treatment plants. Technical guidelines are drawn up by the SFT.

SOLID WASTE

Annual waste arisings in the late 1980s were estimated at:

- 0.8mt of household waste and 12mt of production waste (together including 2mt of municipal waste)
- 200 000t of hazardous waste
- 100 000t of sewage sludge
- 70 000t of scrapped cars and large household appliances.

The majority of waste is disposed to landfill, including over 75 per cent of municipal waste; around 450 000t way incincerated in 1990. A census in 1990 found that 37 per cent of households sorted their waste for separate collection and recycling, although this figure varied widely between regions. Quantities recycled in 1989 include 160 000t of paper and card-board, 32 000t of oils, 10 000t of plastics, and 6000t of glass bottles.

Of the 200 000t of hazardous waste generated each year, more than 60 per cent is oily waste (including waste from oil-drilling). Around 90 000t of hazardous waste is treated and/or disposed of by the companies pro-ducing it, the remainder being delivered to approved waste reception facilities or treatment plants. In 1988 a company called NORSAS was established jointly by the state, industry and municipalities to coordinate plans for hazardous waste disposal, including a central treatment plant. A national register of waste disposal and other sites contaminated with haz-ardous waste was initiated in 1987, and by 1991 listed 2452 sites, of which 108 fell into the two most urgent of five categories. The Ministry of Environment aims to clean up the worst contaminated sites by 2000.

The Pollution Control Act provides the legal framework for the man-agement and disposal of hazardous waste. The SFT licenses waste incineration and the collection and treatment of hazardous wastes. Licensing for municipal waste disposal and coordinating work on waste plans between municipalities are the responsibility of the county governors. The collection of household waste is handled by the municipalities.

NATURE CONSERVATION

The territory of Norway includes extensive areas of coniferous forest and mountainous uplands, temperate deciduous forest in the south, wetlands, a mainland coastline of more than 20 000km with many islands and fjords, and Arctic ecosystems on Svalbard. Species of fauna present include:

- 54 terrestrial mammals
- 249 birds
- 5 reptiles and
- 5 amphibians.

A number of mammals are rare elsewhere in Europe, including bear, wolf, wolverine and lynx. A 1988 report identified 79 species of vertebrate ani-mals (excluding fish) considered to be rare or endangered, including 14 mammal and 61 bird species. 1310 indigenous species of vascular plants are found in Norway.

Species protection for wild terrestrial mammals, birds, amphibians and reptiles is based on the Wildlife Act 1981. No species may be caught, hunted, killed or injured unless explicitly provided for. Hunting was permitted for 55 species in 1991 and commercial whaling resumed in 1993. Protection for species of flora is more limited, under the Nature Conservation Act 1970, and depends significantly on protected habitats. The same act governs protected areas, establishing four categories. By 1992 there were:

- 18 national parks covering 1.35m ha,
- 74 landscape protected areas (464 800ha),
- 951 nature reserves (147 400ha) and
- 280 natural monuments.

This represented around 6 per cent of the land area. 14 sites were designated under the Ramsar wetland convention (16 256ha). Some protection is extended to coastal areas under the Planning and Building Act 1965, amended in 1985 to allow also for the designation of conservation areas in local municipal plans.

ENERGY

Norway has become one of Europe's major energy producers, as a result of exploiting offshore reserves of oil and gas and developing hydropower for electricity generation. The first exploratory wells were drilled in 1966 and by 1989 oil production had risen to almost seven times the domestic consumption, coming largely from four principal fields. Oil production rose to 106.3mt in 1992, accounting for 14 per cent of GDP and 30 per cent of export earnings. Virtually all gas production is exported, and supplies are projected to increase greatly during the rest of the 1990s (from 27.28bn m^3 in 1991).

Over 99 per cent of Norway's electricity is produced by hydroelectric power stations. Average potential capacity in 1992 stood at 108 400m kWh (at normal levels of precipitation). Electricity is exported to neighbouring countries. Some areas are protected from hydropower development for conservation reasons. Total primary energy supply has remained stable over recent years, at 21–22mtoe.

Taxes on CO_2 and energy were introduced in 1991 with the objective of limiting CO_2 emissions.

AGRICULTURE

The area of agricultural land is Norway is low relative to the population and the total area of land. There were 864 000ha of arable and permanent cropland and 112 000ha of permanent grassland in 1990. Climatic conditions limit the cultivation of many types of crops, although the influence of the Gulf Stream allows some farming even in the northernmost regions. Grain production (mostly barley, oats and wheat) is concentrated in the south and east of the country.

Agriculture accounted for 5.4 per cent of employment and 1.8 per cent of GDP in 1990, and the country is almost self-sufficient in meat and dairy produce and animal feed. Livestock production contributed over 65 per cent of gross agricultural revenue in 1987. Fox and mink are raised for fur.

Less than 15 per cent of farms have more than 20ha of arable land, and 70 per cent combine farming and forestry. Owner-occupation of farms and part-time farming are widespread; in 1986, 54 per cent of all farm households earned more than half their income from off-farm employment. Norwegian policy has sought to maintain agricultural activity in marginal areas and prevent the depopulation of rural areas, particularly in the north, where alternatives to agriculture are very limited. State subsidies are relatively high and include direct income aids and assistance to offset high transport costs.

Emissions from agriculture account for around 27 per cent of nitrogen and 16 per cent of phosphorus discharges, and measures have been introduced to curb excessive fertiliser use and nutrient run-off, as well as to prevent soil erosion and reduce the environmental impact of pesticides. Annual consumption of nitrogen fertiliser has remained at around 110 000t in recent years, whilst annual pesticide consumption fell by more than 20 per cent between 1985 and 1990 (measured by active ingredients).

FISHING

The fishing industry has always been of enormous importance to the coastal settlements of Norway, which lie on some of the world's most productive seas. A 200-mile (320km) exclusive fishing zone was established in 1977. Cod, capelin, saithe and herring are the most important species fished, but overfishing in the 1960s and 1970s led to huge reductions in stocks. Government regulations have sought subsequently to manage stocks more sustainably. The number of fishermen has more than halved since 1970, to around 20 000 in 1992; most vessels are relatively small (under 12m). Commercial whaling was banned in 1983 by the International Whaling Commission, but resumed by Norway in 1993.

The total fish catch reached 1.9mt in 1991, with an additional 0.2mt of crustaceans, molluscs and seaweed. 90 per cent of the catch is exported. Fjords and inlets provide ideal conditions for fish-farming, which has increased greatly since the 1970s. Production concentrates on trout and salmon, and made up 30 per cent of export earnings from fish products in 1990. More intensive fish-farming has resulted in increases in chemical inputs; 26 798kg of antibiotics were used in 1991, compared with 3640kg in 1981.

FOREST RESOURCES

Norway has an estimated 9.57m ha of woodland, including 7.04m ha of productive forest. Around 80 per cent of forest cover consists of coniferous species; deciduous species, such as birch, are concentrated in western parts of the country.

A survey conducted in 1981–87 estimated the annual growth in productive forest at 15.5m m^3 (excluding bark). The annual cut increased slightly during the late 1980s to 11.0m m^3 of roundwood in 1989/90, with a further 0.7m m^3 cut for fuel or use on owners' property.

The forest survey of 1992 found 26 per cent of trees suffering 25 per cent or worse defoliation, appearing to confirm a trend of deterioration in recent years.

TRANSPORT

The road network extended to 89 135km at the end of 1991. The number of passenger cars in use increased by 70 per cent between 1975 and 1991, to over 1.6m.

The rail network covered 4027km, of which 60 per cent was electrified. In 1991 it carried 33.4m passengers and 2170.6m passenger-km. State Railways carried 21.5mt of freight in 1990.

Oslo has 98km of underground trains and 54km of tram/light rail; a road-charging scheme was introduced in 1990, requiring vehicles to pay on entering the city by road.

Shipping carries a large proportion of the country's trade, and Norway's merchant fleet is one of the largest in the world, with a gross tonnage of 21mt dead weight in 1991.

Poland

Poland is situated to the east of Germany, with a northern coastline on the Baltic Sea; Lithuania, Belarus and Ukraine lie to the east. Much of the country is lowlying, 92 per cent below 300m. In the south the Sudeten and Carpathian mountains rise to over 1600m and 2400m respectively and form the border with the Czech Republic and Slovakia. Virtually all the territory drains north to the Baltic, primarily via the Oder and Vistula rivers. A band of shallow lakes is found in the north, before the land descends to the coastal lowland area.

Area	312 683km²
Population	38.5m
Urban	62%
Rural	38%
Capital	Warsaw (1.65m)
City populations	25 > 150 000; 5 > 500 000
Economy	
GNP per capita	US$4880 (1992)
GDP change	2% (1992)
Climate (Warsaw)	
Average daily max and min	24/15°C (July)/0/–6°C (January)
Annual precipitation	555mm
Land-use cover	
Agriculture	62%
Forest	29%
Other	9%

INSTITUTIONS AND POLICY

Under Poland's 1952 constitution, amended in 1992, a parliament *(Sejm)* of 460 members is directly elected by popular vote; the Senate of 100 members forms the upper house. Local government is exercised through 49 voivodships and over 2000 communes *(gmina)*, both of which have some environmental competences.

The Ministry of Environmental Protection, Natural Resources and Forestry is assisted by the State Inspectorate of Environmental Protection, which undertakes monitoring and enforcement work. The State Sanitary Inspectorate has similar responsibilities for public health matters. The Law on Protection and Development of the Environment (31 January 1980) is the main environmental framework law and includes basic aims and principles for environmental protection, the legal basis for air pollution, waste and noise regulation. It also established the National Fund for Environmental and Water Management, into which charges for air and water pollution, water abstraction, waste disposal and tree removal are paid, along with penalties for infringements. Charges in Katowice, and for air emissions in Krakow, are generally twice the level elsewhere, reflecting their higher levels of pollution. EIA was provided for in the 1980 law but not widely implemented until amendments and regulations were made in 1989 and 1990. A National Environmental Policy was prepared and endorsed by parliament in 1991.

AIR POLLUTION

Air pollutants in Poland originate primarily from the energy sector, which is dependent on coal and lignite, and from heavy industry. Total emissions have declined in recent years, partly reflecting a downturn in industrial activity. Emissions in 1991 totalled:

- 2.99mt of SO_2, down from 4.18mt in 1988, half from energy plants.
- 1.2mt of NO_x, down from 1.55mt in 1988, one-third each from energy plant and from transport.
- 1.6mt of particulates, 28 per cent from energy plant and 41 per cent from other industrial sources, down from 2.65mt in 1988.

Although most combustion plants have particulate filters, in 1992 no power or heating plants had pollution control technology fitted to deal with SO_2 or NO_x emissions.

A large proportion of emissions originate from a relatively small number of major industrial sources. A survey in 1989 showed that 14 plants emitted over 200 000t of SO_2 each, accounting for 37 per cent of emissions in that year; 10 were power plants, and 3 iron and steel plants. Upper Silesia, in the south-west, accounts for 20–25 per cent of total national emissions to air. Centred on Katowice, this region has a high concentration of industrial plants built to process the locally mined bituminous coal, lead and zinc ore. Kracow and other urban/industrial centres also suffer from high levels of air pollution, and air quality standards are often exceeded. Coal-fired heating boilers and inefficient domestic stoves (of which there were around 10m in use in 1991) add significantly to emissions from industry and vehicles.

Air quality standards for 44 pollutants are laid down in a regulation of February 1990, with maximum concentrations for 30-minute and 24-hour periods and annual averages. Stricter limits apply to specially protected areas, such as national parks and health resorts. Emission permits are determined and issued by the voivodships, and charges paid by polluters on the basis of the quantities emitted. In addition, the regulation fixes deposition limits for cadmium, lead and particulates, and emission limits for SO_2, NO_x and particulates from combustion plant above 200kW.

WATER RESOURCES AND POLLUTION

Virtually all the country's territory (99.7 per cent) lies within the catchment area of the Baltic Sea, into which the country's four largest rivers flow; the Vistula, Oder, Warta and Bug have a total length of 3184km within Poland. There are 9300 lakes with an area greater than 1ha, concentrated in the north.

Total water abstractions increased from 10.11 bn m^3 in 1970 to 15.45 bn m^3 in 1985. Of the 13.27 bn m^3 abstraced in 1991, over 80 per cent came from surface water sources; almost half of public supplies came from groundwater. Of water consumption in 1991:

- industry accounted for 70 per cent,
- agriculture for 11.5 per cent and
- domestic supplies for 22 per cent.

Drinking water is in short supply in some areas (eg Silesia, Lodz, Lublin, Kielce and Radom), principally because of limited local reserves and storage capacity.

Much of Poland's water resources are seriously polluted, largely as a result of industrial and municipal wastewater discharges. Around 40 per cent of surface waters were evaluated as highly polluted in 1987. Total effluent discharges to water increased from 8.49 bn m^3 in 1970 to 12.9 bn m^3 in 1985. Of the total discharged in 1991 (10.58 bn m^3), around 80 per cent came from industrial sources, including 6.83 bn m^3 of cooling water. 3.75 bn m^3 were considered to require treatment, but 30 per cent received none and 35 per cent mechanical treatment only. 251 out of the 729 towns with sewerage systems had no treatment plant in 1991.

Water quality surveys indicate a significant decline in the health of Polish rivers:

- The lengths surveyed qualifying as class 1 (potable) fell from 25 per cent in 1968–70 to just 2.3 per cent in 1991, according to physicochemical criteria.
- The lengths classified as poorer than class 3 (unfit for industrial or agricultural use) increased from 23 per cent to 35 per cent over the same period.

When assessed by biological criteria, the position appears worse, with 78 per cent of river length poorer than class 3 in 1991. The water of only four out of 161 lakes surveyed in 1984–88 was of class 1 quality.

Saline discharges from coalmines pose a problem in Upper Silesia, where the upper reaches of the Vistula and Oder receive around 9000t of salts daily. In agricultural areas, run-off from fertiliser and manure from large livestock farms add to pollution from industrial sources. Polish sources are major contributors to pollution in the Baltic Sea, including around 38 per cent of its phosphorus and nitrogen load.

Water policy is based on the Water Law of 1974, under which permits are issued by, and charges payable to, the voivodships for abstractions and discharges. An Ordinance of December 1987 (amended in 1990) provided for the classification by the Environment Ministry of inland surface waters into three quality classes, with parameters for more than 40 substances; discharges should not lead to these standards being exceeded. It also fixed maximum concentrations for pollutants in wastewater discharged to sewerage systems.

A new Water Law will bring more water management functions under the seven Regional Water Management Authorities created in 1991. Under Poland's National Environmental Policy, approved in 1991, the water pollution load from industry and municipalities is to be reduced by half and the proportion of wastewaters receiving biological and chemical treatment increased from 48 per cent to 70 per cent by 2000. Water protection and management are expected to account for half of all environmental investments.

SOLID WASTE

Waste arisings from industry increased from 136.2mt in 1975 to 170.9mt in 1989; industrial decline and restructuring contributed to a subsequent decrease to 128.3mt in 1991. Mining waste accounted for around 45 per cent of these totals, and around half of all industrial waste is further 'used' in some way, eg in the construction industry, road-building and filling redundant mineworkings. Large quantities have been accumulated in dumps – over 1.7bn t by 1991, and as high as 4bn t by some estimates. Hazardous waste arisings were estimated at 1.98mt in 1989.

Municipal waste generation almost doubled over 12 years to reach 46m m³ in 1989, and is disposed to around 700 municipal landfills covering a total area of 2500ha. Most lack advanced compacting or other technical equipment and over 10 000 unauthorised waste dumps are thought to exist. Some waste in Warsaw and Katowice is composted. Remaining landfill capacity is low in many urban areas, and domestic waste arisings are predicted to rise to 70m m³ by 2000.

The 1980 Law on the Protection and Development of the Environment requires anyone undertaking business activities to deal with waste in accordance with their local urban plan and so as to ensure that the environment is protected. Imports of waste are prohibited. Waste producers, under a Regulation on environmental protection against waste (September 1980), must apply for a permit covering storage and other conditions. Four levels of disposal fees are levied, according to the toxicity of the waste concerned. A new waste law is under discussion, with the intention of improving the existing system of regulation.

NATURE CONSERVATION

Despite having some of the most heavily polluted areas in Europe, Poland also has many valuable areas of natural habitat, including lowland peatbogs and ancient forest in the east, dunes bordering the Baltic, and the Carpathian mountains in the south. The country's climate reflects both oceanic and continental influences and many species are found towards the edges of their natural ranges. Poland has around 30 per cent of mammals, 40 per cent of higher plants and 16 per cent of bird species found in Europe; 25 per cent of high plant species and 28 per cent of vertebrate species are threatened.

Under the 1949 Law on Nature Conservation and subsequent regulations, 471 species of fauna and 212 species of flora and their habitats are protected, including 97 and 72 species respectively which are strictly protected. The same law established four categories of protected area, supplemented by protected landscape areas provided for under the 1980 law on protection and development of the environment. A new Nature Conservation Act came into force in December 1991. Poland has 17 national parks (total area 177 797ha) and with over 1000 nature reserves and 68 landscape parks, the total protected area extends to around 5.5m ha, around 18 per cent of the total land area. The total area under protection increased fivefold during the 1980s.

ENERGY

Poland is one of the world's largest producers and exporters of hard coal, and also has considerable reserves of brown coal. Hard coal production fell from 193mt in 1988 to 140mt in 1991; 69.4mt of lignite were mined in 1991. Coal accounts for over 90 per cent of the country's energy production, supplemented by around one-third of national gas consumption and small quantities of oil: gas and oil are imported, in the past mostly from the former Soviet Union. 70 per cent of electricity supplies are generated by coal-fired power stations, and coal is also the dominant fuel for domestic heating.

Most forms of energy, particularly electricity, have been low-priced; the reduction in subsidies in recent years has led to large increases in energy prices. They rose, for example, 22-fold for electricity and 47-fold for gas for household supplies between 1989 and 1991.

A small proportion of electricity is produced from hydroelectric stations (113 plants with a combined capacity of 677MW). Poland's nuclear power programme was halted in 1990 by a ten-year moratorium, leaving its plant at Zarnowiec unfinished; another, larger power station (4000MW) had been planned for Pila.

The country is likely to continue to depend on coal for much of its energy supplies, but plans to improve energy efficiency and reduce pollution from the energy sector by:

- washing hard coal (to reduce the sulphur content),
- installing desulphurisation equipment, and
- increasing the use of imported gas, particularly for domestic heating.

AGRICULTURE

Poland has 18.8m ha of agricultural land, 77 per cent of which is arable. Over 70 per cent of the land is privately owned, and small farms predominate; over half were under 5ha in size in 1990. The principal arable crops include wheat, rye, sugarbeet, oilseeds and potatoes. The livestock sector is significant, particularly pork and poultry.

Agricultural production fell by 21 per cent in 1990–92, reflecting depressed domestic demand, lower farm incomes, and severe drought in 1992.

Overall fertiliser use has decreased in recent years. Much of the soil is light and sandy, which exacerbates problems of run-off from fertilisers and livestock wastes; agriculture is estimated to contribute 62 per cent of the Poland's nitrogen load to the Baltic Sea. Water from local wells is contaminated by pesticides and nitrates in some rural areas.

Of agricultural land, 35 per cent is of poor quality, and 700 000–800 000ha could probably be used more profitably for forestry; 10 per cent is severely affected by industrial pollution.

A new programme for rural areas and agriculture was presented in September 1992, with the intention of improving agricultural productivity. The programme included the privatisation of all state-owned farms, measures to modernise foodprocessing and marketing, and a project to promote more environmentally sustainable agriculture. Organic agriculture appears to be increasing rapidly.

FOREST RESOURCES

Forests cover 8.7m ha, most of which consists of conifers, particularly pine; broadleaved species include oak, birch and beech. Timber production in 1990 was 18.7m m^3.

Poland's forests have been severely affected by acid rain, particularly in the south of the country, where 13 000ha have been completely deforested and 85 pe r cent moderately or severely damaged. Only 1.8 per cent of the forest area in the Sudeten mountains remains healthy. The 1991 forest survey found 45 per cent of trees sampled to be moderately damaged or worse. The total forest area considered to suffer from damaging levels of industrial pollution increased from 239 000ha in 1971 to 983 000ha in 1989.

TRANSPORT

Poland's transport network includes 226 000km of roads and 25 800km of railways (45 per cent electrified). The share of freight carried by road rather than rail has grown in recent years, and the Ministry of Transport envisages the construction of 1960km of major roads by 2010, under a US$3bn programme. This would complete three cross-country motorway routes, one running south from Gdansk to the Czech Republic, and crossed by two east–west routes at Lodz and Katowice, aimed at improving road links with neighbouring countries.

The numbers of road vehicles in use has increased greatly in recent years; the private car fleet more than doubled between 1982 and 1991 to 6.1m vehicles. Traffic contributes around 31 per cent of NO_x and 35 per cent of lead emissions, and constitutes a major factor in urban pollution.

Poland has three major ports on the Baltic (Gdynia, Gdansk and Szczecin) and 4000km of navigable inland waterways.

Portugal

Portugal is located in the west of the Iberian peninsula, on the Atlantic seaboard. The islands of Madeira to south and Azores in the mid-Atlantic also form part of Portugal. The Tagus river divides the northern half of the country from the southern half. The north is mountainous and heavily forested, with high rainfall; the south is characterised by rolling plains and a more arid climate. Both population and industry are heavily concentrated along the coastal strip between Setubal and Braga.

Area	91 985km²
Population	9.86m
Urban	34%
Rural	66%
Capital	Lisbon (0.83m)
City populations	8 > 50 000; 2 > 300 000
Economy	
GNP per capita	US$5930 (1991)
Climate (Lisbon)	
Average daily max and min	28/17°C (July)/14/8°C (January)
Annual precipitation	708mm
Land-use cover	
Agriculture	44%
Forest	35%
Other	21%

INSTITUTIONS AND POLICY

Portugal is a unitary republic and under the constitution of 1976 a National Assembly of 230 members is elected by universal suffrage. Local government is exercised primarily at the level of the 305 elected councils. Apart from the Autonomous Regions of Madeira and Azores, there are no regional elected governments, but for administrative purposes the country is divided into 22 districts. Regional Coordination Commissions (CCR) oversee some functions of central government at regional level.

The Basic Environmental Law (11/87) of 1987 forms the principal framework for legislation on the environment. The Ministry of the Environment and Natural Resources (MARN) was established in 1990, taking over environmental matters from the Ministry for Territorial Planning and Administration (MPAT). Nature conservation is the responsibility of the Nature Conservation Institute (ICN). Other relevant bodies include the National Environment Institute (INAMB), established in 1987 by the Basic Environmental Law, which concentrates on environmental education and informing the public, and the National Meteorological and Geophysical Institute. All three report to the Ministry of the Environment, which is also advised by the Consultative Committee on the Environment.

Portugal became a member of the European Community in January 1986, and EC directives and regulations have influenced significantly the development of Portuguese environmental policy. Criteria for projects requiring EIAs in accordance with the EC directive were established by Regulation 38/90 of November 1990.

AIR POLLUTION

Total SO_2 emissions in 1990 were estimated at 211 000t, produced mainly by industry (42 per cent) and power stations (38 per cent). NO_X emissions totalled 142 000t, over 60 per cent of which came from the transport sector. Emissions of VOCs rose steadily during the 1980s, reaching 156 000t in 1988. Between 1985 and 1987, annual emissions of SO_2 increased by 10 per cent and of NO_X by 20 per cent, although remaining below the peak levels of 1983. Road transport and industrial combustion accounted for most of these increases. Further increases in emissions are expected during the next 20 years; growth in SO_2 emissions should be limited as power stations meet stricter standards, but NO_X emissions are projected to rise by over 50 per cent.

Air pollution control is based largely on Law 352/90 and reflects the requirements of EC Directives on emission standards, permitting and air quality standards. Air Management Commissions (CGAs) have been established to monitor and improve air quality in priority zones with particular air pollution problems, such as Lisbon, Porto, Sines and Barreiro/Seixal.

WATER RESOURCES AND POLLUTION

The main rivers in Portugal are the Tagus, Douro, Guadiana and Minho, all of which rise in Spain. Seen as a whole, Portugal is well supplied with water, particularly in the centre and north. However, serious droughts have affected dryland farming in the southern half of the country (Alentejo) in recent years.

Agriculture accounts for the majority of water consumption (60 per cent), followed by energy production (22 per cent), industry (13 per cent) and domestic use (5 per cent).

Groundwater provides 80 per cent of public water supplies, and 42 per cent of total abstractions (of 7.3bn m³ in 1989).

In general, the quality of surface waters is reasonable. The most polluted rivers are the Ave, Leco, Vouga, Lis and various tributaries of the Tagus. Notable sources of surface water pollution include the paper-pulp and wine industries and urban wastewater. The Aveiro estuary is heavily polluted with organic matter from paper-pulp plants, distilleries and slaughter-houses. Groundwater pollution is a problem in specific areas, such as:

- The Ave basin and in industrial zones around Aveiro.
- Under chalky soils north of Lisbon where there are urban concentrations and intensive pig farms.
- On the Algarve coast where seawater has intruded as a result of excessive abstraction from aquifers.

Implementation of the EC urban waste water Directive in Portugal requires a major investment programme in new sewage systems and treatment plants, as around 60 per cent of wastewater (by volume) goes untreated. The total cost of this programme, including staff training, has been estimated at 1.4bn ECU. Almost half the population lives in towns of fewer than 2000 inhabitants, of which only 30 per cent have a sewerage system and 13.5 per cent have wastewater treatment. 60 per cent of towns of over 10 000 (ie 40 per cent of the population) have treatment facilities.

The management of water resources is governed by Decree-Law 70/90 of March 1990 and is the responsibility of the Directorate General for Natural Resources within MARN. Discharges to water and standards for drinking water quality are governed by Decree-Law 74/90 of March 1990, which set emission limits for the first time in Portuguese law.

Water quality is the responsibility of the Directorate General for Environmental Quality within MARN, which authorises discharges to watercourses.

SOLID WASTE

Total arisings of municipal waste were estimated at 2.54mt in 1990; around 1.8mt of urban waste is disposed of adequately, either to landfills (28 per cent) or by composting (10 per cent). The destination of the remainder is not recorded, but most probably goes to uncontrolled landfill. Urban waste in Portugal is characterised by a high proportion of organic matter.

In 1987 1.05mt of hazardous industrial waste were generated. The main areas of output are near Setubal, where there is a concentration of chemical industries and power stations, Castelo Branco, where many mines and quarries are situated, and Aveiro, due to the large number of chemical and paper-pulp plants.

The disposal of hospital wastes (around 50 000t arising annually) is unsatisfactory, particularly in Lisbon and Porto; incinerators are being built, with EC support, to tackle this problem.

A national programme for recycling liquid containers was launched in 1990, and for battery recycling in 1992, on the basis of EC Directives. The amount of glass recycled increased from 1460t in 1985 to 9766t in 1990. In 1991, the recovery rate for paper and cardboard was 39 per cent and for glass 30 per cent. There is also a programme for the disposal of tyres, 15 000t of which are incinerated annually for energy recovery.

Under Decree 768/88, local councils are required to record the quantity and nature of urban wastes and the methods of disposal used. The use and storage of PCBs is controlled by Decree-Law 221/88. Over 510 000kg of PCBs were in use in 1990/91; a further 134 000kg were no longer used and almost 60 000kg disposed of.

NATURE CONSERVATION

Despite its relatively small size, Portugal is an important country for nature conservation. Steppeland habitats in the south are of great importance for birds such as the bustard. The interior of the north and centre include extensive mountain ranges which represent some of the few remaining refuges in western Europe for rare mammals such as lynx and wolf, as well as for a variety of raptors. Portugal also has a number of coastal wetlands of international importance as feeding areas for wintering and migrating birds. There are 3150 known species of vascular plants.

Most protected areas are designated on the basis of Law 9/70 or Decree 613/76, providing for five categories. The national parks, natural parks and nature reserves of continental Portugal cover just over

501 000ha. All these protected areas are in mountainous regions or along the coast and river estuaries. By 1992, 34 Special Protection Areas had been designated under the EC birds Directive, covering around 320 000ha, and further areas were planned. Two Ramsar wetland sites were designated, covering 30 563ha.

The National Ecological Reserve (REN) is a classification system for coastal and riverine zones and areas highly prone to erosion. Candidate areas are put forward by the regional authorities (CCR) for joint approval by the Ministries of Agriculture, Planning, Public Works, Commerce and Tourism and Environment. If an REN is approved, developments within its area will have to be approved by the CCR, which may impose environmental conditions. Exemptions apply to projects for which there is deemed to be no economic alternative and to forestry projects approved by the Forest Service.

ENERGY

Total primary energy supply doubled between 1975 and 1990, to 16.4mtoe. Of final energy consumption in 1990:

- industry accounted for 46 per cent,
- transport for 27 per cent and
- domestic use for 19 per cent.

Consumption is expected to continue to rise, by 50 per cent between 1990 and 2010.

Imported oil is the principal fuel, although the National Energy Plan for 1985–2010 seeks to reduce dependence on oil by increasing the use of coal and gas. In particular, the use of natural gas is to be promoted in industry, energy generation and households. Renewable energy sources are expected to contribute up to 6 per cent of energy needs in future. Hydroelectric stations produced almost a quarter of the 25.8m kWh of electricity generated in 1989.

AGRICULTURE

Agriculture in Portugal is amongst the least developed in Europe. Most farms are small and of low productivity, and large areas are farmed using relatively traditional methods, especially away from the coasts and in the mountainous regions, which often are of high environmental value. Production is higher in the coastal plain, river estuaries and the Tagus valley. The country is a net importer of foodstuffs, with imports almost three times greater than exports. Agriculture provides just under 20 per cent of employment and is the mainstay of social and economic life in rural areas.

In the more densely populated north and centre, farms tend to be extremely small and fragmented (averaging 4ha but with many less than 1ha). Irrigated crops predominate, mainly maize, potatoes and vegetables, using traditional surface-water irrigation channels. Non-irrigated crops (rye, forage and pasture) and livestock tend to take a secondary role. Vines are also widely cultivated, often along the boundaries between holdings, as well as over larger areas, such as the Upper Douro. Fruit trees and grazed woodlands add to a very diverse countryside.

In the sparsely populated Alentejo south of the Tagus, farms tend to be larger than in the north (average size over 30ha). Production concentrates on wheat, with barley, oats, chickpeas and sunflowers as secondary crops. Other economically significant products are olive oil and cork. A typical land use in this region is the *montado*, combining open tree cover of cork and holm oaks with extensive grazing and some cultivation.

The combination of infrequent but heavy rainfall and thin soils in the Alentejo makes large areas prone to soil erosion, a situation exacerbated by cultivation and the removal of tree cover. Erosion is also reported to be a severe problem on the island of Madeira, due to overgrazing. In some coastal areas of the Alentejo, intensive, irrigated production of high-value vegetables for export to northern Europe is developing.

Taking the country as a whole, agriculture is generally much less intensive than elsewhere in western Europe. Portugal has not suffered from such wide-ranging problems of agricultural pollution and habitat loss, and consequently retains a rich diversity of flora and fauna. However, localised environmental problems arise, mostly from intensive cultivation in areas with better soils and irrigation, or from intensive livestock units and foodprocessing factories:

- In Lourinha, the Algarve coast and Aveiro, a combination of intensive agriculture and inadequate sewage treatment, in a densely populated area, produces serious problems of nitrate pollution in ground and surface waters.
- Heavy herbicide applications in areas of intensive rice cultivation causes water pollution in the Tagus and Sado estuaries.
- In the Algarve, high levels of chemical inputs in greenhouses lead to groundwater contamination, as well as salinisation caused by irrigation.
- Zinc and copper have leached into groundwater in the vineyard region of the Upper Douro.

A major EC-funded programme for the development of Portuguese agriculture (PEDAP) began in 1986. It is intended primarily to modernise and intensify agriculture, involving drainage, irrigation and the grubbing up of old olive groves. In addition, agricultural land is in the process of being classified as National Agriculture Reserve (RAN), to identify the areas of greatest agricultural potential and to preserve them for agriculture. Further urban encroachment and fragmentation are to be avoided in RAN areas, and greater modernisation and rationalisation encouraged.

FOREST RESOURCES

Portugal has one of the highest proportions of afforested land in the EC, with considerable areas of natural forest and woodland. Maritime pine and broad-leaved species such as oak and chestnut dominate in the north; woodlands of a more Mediterranean type are found in the south and interior, where the principal native species are cork and holm oaks, wild olives and stone pine.

However, much of the forest resource consists of plantations (often eucalyptus or maritime pine) less than 100 years old, forestry having replaced farming in some central areas. The social and environmental impacts of afforestation have become a major issue; particularly in the case of eucalyptus, plantations are extremely low in biological diversity, consume large quantities of water, and are highly vulnerable to fire.

Forest products make an important contribution to the Portuguese economy, primarily through exports of paper-pulp and cork.

A forestry action programme forms part of the EC-funded agriculture development programme; projects during 1987–89 involved improvement work over 100 000ha of woodland and the planting of 40 000ha. The average area of forest lost to fire annually, at over 50 000ha, is greater than the average area planted. This means not only an overall decline in the area of productive forest, but also an increase in soil erosion, air pollution and in the destruction of seminatural habitats. In 1990, 130 000ha of forest, scrub and grazing were destroyed by fire. The forest health survey of 1992 found 22.5 per cent of trees sampled suffering 25 per cent or more defoliation.

TRANSPORT

When Portugal joined the EC in 1986, the road network was very underdeveloped. With help from the EC Structural Funds, an extensive programme of motorway construction was initiated, key sections including Lisbon–Porto (completed), Lisbon–Algarve and the Portuguese section of the Lisbon–Madrid motorway. Between 1986 and 1991, the total road length was expanded from 57 000 to 85 000km, and motorway length from 183 to 453km.

The number of passenger cars in use doubled during the 1980s, to reach 1.8m in 1991. Road traffic produced over 60 per cent of NO_x emissions in 1989.

The rail network extended to 3,120km in 1990.

Romania

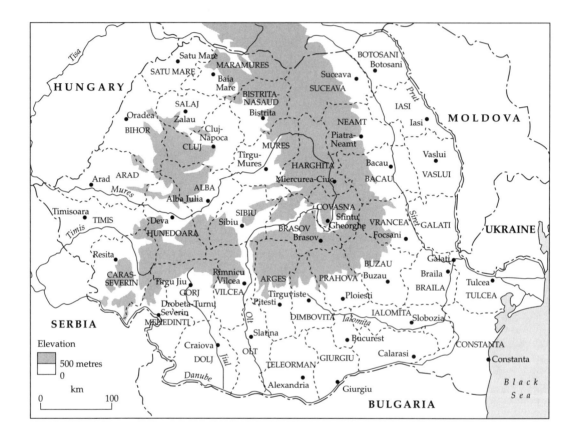

Romania is in south-east Europe and shares borders with Bulgaria, Serbia, Hungary, Moldova and Ukraine. It has an eastern coastline of 245km on the Black Sea and its land area consists in almost equal proportions of mountainous areas, hills and plateaux, and plains. The Carpathian mountains run through the centre and west of the country, rising to over 2000m in the Transylvanian Alps. The river Danube marks much of Romania's southern border until it turns north and enters the Black Sea at the delta bordering with Ukraine. The plains of Transylvania form a plateau in the north-west, whilst fertile lowlands of Wallachia and Moldavia are situated along the Danube in the east and the rivers Siret and Prut in the south.

Area	237 500km²
Population	22.7m
Urban	54%
Rural	46%
Capital	Bucharest (2.3m)
City populations	26 > 100 000; 8 > 300 000
Economy	
GNP per capita	US$2750 (1992)
GDP change	−14% (1992)
Climate (Bucharest)	
Average daily max and min	30/16°C (July)/1/−7°C (January)
Annual precipitation	592mm
Land-use cover	
Agriculture	64%
Forest	27%
Other	9%

INSTITUTIONS AND POLICY

Romania is a unitary state with 41 counties *(judet)*. A new constitution was adopted in 1991, under which an Assembly of Deputies and a Senate are directly elected by popular vote.

A framework Environmental Law was passed in 1973 (Law 9/1973), and a series of measures was drawn up, including quality standards for:

- surface water (STAS 4706/88)
- drinking water (STAS 1342/84)
- mineral water (STAS 4450/76)
- irrigation water (STAS 9450/88)
- air (STAS 12574/87).

Other laws cover:

- waste disposal and recovery (1975; amended 1988)
- the transport of hazardous substances (1972)
- the control of chemical substances (1972).

Until 1989, environmental matters were handled by the National Council for Environment Protection, but the Ministry of the Environment was established in 1991 (Decision 264/1991). The ministry works with local environment protection agencies in each of the 41 counties. A new general environment law was prepared for presentation to parliament in 1993. A 1991 report by the Ministry of the Environment set out general provisions on environmental management.

AIR POLLUTION

Air pollution is a severe problem in urban and industrialised areas. Emissions in 1990 included:

- 1.5mt of SO_2
- 700 000t of NO_x
- 600 000t of particulates.

The principal sources of emissions to air consist of power stations, other industrial plants (notably metalworks and petrochemical installations), motor vehicles and domestic heating. Some large power stations are located away from conurbations, but many industrial plants are situated in urban areas and so impact directly on the local population. District and domestic heating often depend on high-sulphur gas oil or low quality coal. Motor vehicles use petrol with a high lead content or diesel with a high sulphur content and, although small, the vehicle fleet is old and poorly maintained.

The metalworks at Copsa Mica, Baia Mare and Zlatna, which produce lead, zinc, copper and other non-ferrous metals, are responsible for very high levels of pollution of these metals, arsenic, cadmium, selenium and other heavy metals. High concentrations of SO_2, NO_2 and particulates are often found, too. 24-hour average concentrations at Copsa Mica have been recorded above $60\mu g/m^3$ for lead and $7000\mu g/m^3$ for SO_2, although annual average concentrations fell during 1989/90 because of a decrease in production. Aluminium works at Slatina, Tulcea and Oradea give rise to less acute pollution. Other major sources of air pollution include petrochemical plants, pulp-paper mills, fertiliser factories, coke and iron/steelworks, and coal-fired power stations.

Air pollution in Bucharest is compounded by emissions from industrial plants (notably ceramics, glass, chemicals and engineering) and power stations, as well as from domestic heating and motor vehicles. Concentrations can reach $200–300\mu g/m^3$ NO_2 and $2–3.5\mu g/m^3$ lead; phenols, fluorine and HCl can also be present at high levels.

Acid rain has become a significant problem in Romania, caused by SO_2 and NO_x emissions emitted primarily from power stations and industrial plants which have little or no emission reduction equipment. Acidic pH values of 4–5.6 are often detected, and although long-range transport may account for some acid deposition, many of the areas worst affected are found close to industrial emitters. Alkaline pH values of up to 8.8 have also been found in some areas, attributable at least in part to industrial emissions from cementworks.

WATER RESOURCES AND POLLUTION

The length of rivers in Romania totals around 70 000km, with the majority of watercourses ultimately flowing into the Danube, which forms a delta before entering the Black Sea. Average annual flows are estimated at 170bn m^3 for the Danube, 40bn m^3 for other surface watercourses and 9bn m^3 groundwater.

Abstractions for drinking water in 1989 were estimated at 3.39m m^3, of which 10–20 per cent was lost in the distribution system. Industrial abstractions in 1989 were estimated at 7.87bn m^3, of which thermal power stations and the chemical industry used 75 per cent. Abstractions for agriculture accounted for a further 6.88bn m³, principally for irrigation, in addition to 2.2bn m³ for fish-farming. Most water is abstracted from surface water (89 per cent), with groundwater sources providing only around 11 per cent of total abstractions of 19.7bn m³ in 1988.

More than 6.1mt of pollutants was discharged to rivers in 1989, including chlorine, ammonia, nitrates, phosphates and hydrogen sulphide. Around 85 per cent of Romania's main rivers are estimated to provide water which is unfit for drinking. Around 19 000km river length was surveyed in 1990, of which around 41 per cent fell into the highest water quality category 1; 21 per cent were found to be of poorer quality than category 3. The river lengths falling into each category have not changed significantly during recent years, and in 1991 over 30 per cent of the length of the Somes, Tisa, Mures, Olt, Jiu, Prut and Ialomita rivers were below class 3 quality. Figures for the water quality of lakes in 1990 show 45 per cent of the 47 lakes sampled for pollution met category 1 standards.

Groundwater pollution is extensive, resulting primarily from agricultural sources in rural areas (eg ammonia, nitrites, nitrates, livestock wastes) and industrial discharges (eg phenols, zinc, lead, cadmium, iron, manganese). Microbiological pollution is a further problem in some areas, probably caused by municipal wastewater and livestock waste. Surveys have found 90 per cent of wells to contain levels of bacteria in excess of permissible limits, and 70 per cent of wells in some agricultural areas with nitrate levels over 100mg/l. Nitrate pollution is a particular problem in the south of the country, where irrigation is extensive.

In addition to discharges from agriculture and from industry (principally chemical, petrochemical, fertiliser, pulp and paper and metallurgical plants), municipal wastewater is a major contributor to water pollution in Romania. Bucharest, for example, had no wastewater treatment plant in 1991, and those in other large towns, such as Iasi, Timisoara, Cluj and Brasov, appeared not to operate satisfactorily. In 1989, 204 towns were connected to wastewater treatment plants; there were 1460 plants with advanced treatment technology, including 546 with mechano-chemical-biological treatment. Only around 10 per cent of total volume of discharges to water, estimated at 8.96bn m³ in 1988 was 'sufficiently treated' in 1989. The chemical industry accounted for 45 per cent of the inorganic pollutant load in 1989, whilst most of the organic load resulted from domestic sewage (39 per cent) and agriculture (29 per cent).

The levels of metals in industrial wastewaters and sludge is indicated by calculations that 32t of copper, 23t of zinc, 8t of cadmium, 8t of nickel and 50t of chromium could be recovered annually from industrial discharges in Bucharest.

SOLID WASTE

Information on waste arisings in Romania is scarce. The total is estimated at 77.9mt, including 35.6mt from mines and quarries and 13.3mt of ash and slag from coal-fired power stations. Arisings of municipal waste in 1991 were 5.6mt, and of industrial waste 17.3mt. Most waste is disposed to landfill, although only around 9 per cent of 1900 known waste sites have permits. Municipal waste sites are thought to receive a wide variety of types of waste, including industrial waste and sludge. The leaching of heavy metals and other toxics from industrial waste sites and tailings from mineworkings is a problem in some areas.

NATURE CONSERVATION

Little natural or seminatural habitat remains in Romania's lowlands, which are dominated by agriculture. However, the country's mountainous areas and Danube delta retain important populations of flora and fauna which have significantly decreased or disappeared in other parts of Europe. These include numbers, estimated in 1989, of:

- 1150 lynx
- 8900 wild goats
- 2000 great bustards
- 7800 bears and
- 1m hares.

Romania has around 3700 plant species, 40 per cent of Europe's total; 23 plant species are protected.

A series of protected areas has been designated, from 1932 onwards, as natural monuments, national parks, nature reserves and forest reserves. 13 future national parks, totalling 492 057ha, were identified in 1990, and by 1993 Romania had a total of 586 protected areas of different categories, a figure which includes around 400 scientific reserves and monuments of nature.

Romania is a party to the Ramsar Convention on wetlands, under which the Danube delta (647 000ha) is listed as of international importance. Three further areas have been identified as Biosphere Reserves under UNESCO's MAB programme.

ENERGY

Romania has significant oil reserves and produced nearly 15mt of crude oil in 1976, by which time it had become a net oil exporter. Production fell to around 6.6mt in 1992, although refining capacity was expanded and came to depend on imports for supplies. Coal and lignite production increased during the 1980s, as Romania followed a policy aimed at increasing self-sufficiency; around 80 per cent of production is used in thermal plant to generate electricity and heat. Gas has also made a major contribution to Romania's indigenous energy supplies, accounting for over half the country's domestic energy supplies in 1990.

Electricity generation is dependent on fossil fuels, with a small proportion produced by hydroelectric plants at the Iron Gates complex on the Danube border with Serbia.

A nuclear power station has been under construction at Cernvoda since 1981; of Canadian Candu design, it is planned to consist of five 685MW units and to generate around one-third of the country's electricity. The first reactor is expected to come into operation in 1995 and will be supplied from indigenous uranium reserves.

Energy shortages became extreme during the winter of 1984–85, when gas, electricity and communal heating supplies were drastically restricted or turned off completely, whilst temperatures fell as low as –25°C. The energy sector is a major contributor to air pollution, power generation alone accounting for around 65 per cent of emissions. Coalmining, and oil-drilling and refining are responsible for some discharges to watercourses, too.

AGRICULTURE

Agriculture accounted for 20 per cent of GDP in 1990 and the country was an important food exporter before 1945. Around 15m ha of Romania's land area is devoted to agriculture, with 10m under arable crops. 3.4m ha had been developed for irrigation by 1989, although power shortages and technical difficulties meant that only 2.5m ha received irrigation water, mostly in the Danube basin.

Wheat and maize are the main cereals grown; sugarbeet, potatoes and sunflower seeds form other important crops. Livestock farming generated 45 per cent of agricultural production in 1989, much of which came from large-scale complexes producing pork or beef; livestock wastes are a major source of water pollution in some areas.

4225kg/ha of organic fertiliser was applied in 1989, compared with 118kg/ha for mineral fertiliser.

In 1992 agricultural price subsidies represented 3 per cent of GDP, the most highly subsidised sector after energy, and are being reduced. A process of land privatisation and reform has been allocating collective farms to private ownership, following adoption of a land law in February 1991, involving more than 8m ha of land and 5.1m new land-owners. Such changes, coupled with severe drought in 1992 and lower inputs, have reduced agricultural production in recent years. Overall agricultural production fell by around 20 per cent between 1988 and 1992, and cereal production fell by 36 per cent in 1991–92. As a result, the export of some basic commodities was banned or restricted in 1992.

Soil erosion is thought to affect more than 4m ha of agricultural land, with around 1m ha suffering severe losses of 10–15t of soil annually.

FOREST RESOURCES

Forests cover around 6.2m ha, predominantly in mountainous areas like the Carpathians. Sixty-nine per cent of forest cover is deciduous, mostly beech and oak, and 31 per cent coniferous. Romania participated in the European forest damage survey for the first time in 1991, when 9.7 per cent of sampled trees had defoliation of 25 per cent or above; the 1992 survey increased this figure to 16.7 per cent. Drought and other climatic stress factors are thought to be major causes of forest damage, along with acid rain in some areas. Damage is acute downwind of major industrial plants at Copsa Mica, Baia Mare and Zlatna. Total forest cover has decreased by almost 30 per cent during the past 100 years, and timber extraction appears to have exceeded regeneration and afforestation for much of the 1970s and '80s. Clear-cutting has led to soil erosion problems, particularly in the Buzau basin and Vrancea.

TRANSPORT

Romania's transport system is underdeveloped by comparison with western European standards. By the end of 1991, there were 1.43m passenger cars and 94,172km of roads, including 113km of motorway. 85 per cent of goods traffic (by tonnage) was transported by road in 1989, and the road development plan for 1991–95 envisaged the construction of more than 3000km of motorway.

The railway network extended to 11 365km in 1991 and carried around 75 per cent of Romania's international freight. Bucharest is served by an underground railway and a tram/light rail system.

Constanta is the country's principal port on the Black Sea, which is connected to the Danube by a canal opened in 1984. Galati and Braila are the main ports on the Danube. Sea and inland waterway transport carried 2.6 per cent of Romania's freight in 1989.

Slovakia

Slovakia is bordered to the north by Poland and to the south by Hungary; its eastern border adjoins Ukraine, the western border Austria and the Czech Republic. Much of the country is mountainous, the High Tatras in the north rising to over 2500m, the Low Tatras dominating eastern and central areas. Low land is situated along the plains of the Danube, which forms part of the border with Hungary, and the river Uh in the east. The climate is more extreme than in the Czech Republic.

INSTITUTIONS AND POLICY

Slovakia became an independent republic on 1 January 1993, with a new constitution adopted in 1992. A National Council of 150 members is elected by popular vote and in turn elects a President. Local government operates at the level of 38 districts (each with an environment office) and 121 subdistricts. The constitution includes references to environmental rights and obligations (Article 6).

The Slovak Commission for the Environment was established in 1990 and became the Ministry of the Environment in 1992. An Environment Inspectorate undertakes water, air and waste management monitoring work, and an Environment Agency operates with six regional offices, also as part of the ministry. A State Fund for the Environment receives fees for air and water discharges, and water abstractions, and fines for infringe-

Area	49 035km²
Population	5.26m
Urban	64%
Rural	36%
Capital	Bratislava (440 420)
City populations	7 > 70 000; 2 > 200 000
Economy	
GNP per capita	US$5620 (1992)
GDP change	–7% (1992)
Climate (Kosice)	
Average daily max and min	26/13°C (July)/0/–7°C (January)
Annual precipitation	605mm
Land-use cover	
Agriculture	50%
Forest	40%
Other	10%

ments; the money is spent on environmental improvement work.

A number of important environmental provisions remain in force from the body of law of the Czech and Slovak Federal Republic, as well as from the federated Slovak Republic. These include the Act on the Environment 17/1992, which sets out the principles for environmental protection and environmental impact assessment. New Slovak laws are intended to replace existing measures on water, air, waste and nature conservation.

AIR POLLUTION

Slovakia has less acute air pollution problems than the neighbouring Czech Republic; emissions in 1989 totalled:

- 565 000t of SO_2
- 203 000t of NO_x
- 317 000t of particulate matter.

SO_2 emissions declined from 621 000t in 1985, whilst NO_x emissions increased slightly over the same period. The most heavily polluted areas tend to be found in the valley areas close to industrial sources, such as the Novaky thermal power station near Nitra, and major conurbations of Bratislava and Kosice. Hydrocarbons, heavy metals and other toxic pollutants originate at the chemical industry and municipal waste incinerators around Bratislava and the aluminium plant at Ziar nad Hronom. Transboundary pollution from Hungary and Poland contributes to sulphur and NO levels and deposition.

Air pollution policy is based on the CSFR Clean Air Act 309/1991, with pollution sources listed and emission limits laid down in Regulation 407/1992. The responsibilities of the authorities are set out in Act 134/1992 and a system of penalties in Act 311/1992.

WATER RESOURCES AND POLLUTION

Slovakia has a river network with a total length of around 45 000km, and 64 reservoirs with a total volume of 1.66bn m³. Two-thirds of annual water abstractions of 2.1bn m³ come from surface waters, 75 per cent for industrial and energy use and 17 per cent for agriculture. Of the 0.7bn m³ of groundwater abstracted each year, 79 per cent is used for drinking water supplies.

1.6bn m³ of wastewaters were discharged in 1988, less than 40 per cent of which received adequate treatment. Emissions to water in 1987 were estimated to contain:

- 305 300t organic matter
- 145 500t heavy metals
- 145 500t BOD.

The number of reported accidents involving discharges to water increased from 112 in 1985 to 200 in 1988. Many towns have no or little sewage treatment facilities, and those in Bratislava are inadequate to deal with the volume produced, as in other urban areas.

Water Act 138/1973 and Law 135/1974 provide the basis for policy on the exploitation and protection of water resources, with permissible levels of pollutants set in Decree 30/1975. A new Water Act is in preparation.

SOLID WASTE

A total of 35.4mt of waste was produced in 1987, including mining and industrial waste. Detailed information on waste arisings is patchy, but waste management and disposal appear little regulated and most waste is stored, dumped or disposed to landfill. There are incinerators with heat-recovery facilities in Bratislava and Kosice.

Under the Waste Act 238/1991, all producers of waste are required to monitor and dispose safely of their waste; waste management operations must be approved by the Ministry of the Environment. The Federal Committee for the Environment issued a Decree (69/1991) on the categorisation of waste. Other measures include Act 494/1991 on state administration in waste management, Act 309/1992 on fees for waste storage, Regulation 76/1992 on waste management programmes, and Order 606/1992 on waste treatment.

NATURE CONSERVATION

Much of Slovakia is mountainous and/or forested, with the Carpathian massif extending across the country. Human impacts from land-use changes and pollution are generally localised but can be severe; species and habitats are threatened by more intensive recreational use in some mountain areas.

Of around 2500 higher plant species, 50.5 per cent were estimated to be threatened or requiring attention in 1979; a similar proportion of the 449 known animal vertebrates surveyed were placed in the same categories. Fauna and flora species are protected on the basis of the Nature Conservation Act 1/1955 and subsequent decrees listing protected species (211/1958 and 125/1965). A new Nature Protection Act is in preparation.

An extensive system of protected areas includes:

- 5 national parks
- 16 protected landscape areas and
- 369 state nature and other reserves.

The total area under protection of some kind extends to 9281km², around 19 per cent of the territory. Slovakia has designated four Ramsar wetland sites with a total area of 1855ha.

ENERGY

Slovakia has some reserves of gas, oil and brown coal, but is largely dependent on imports to meet its energy requirements, primarily from the Czech Republic and the former Soviet Union. Domestic oil production runs at around 110 000t annually and is used in the chemical and pharmaceutical industry. A series of hydroelectric power stations on the Vah, Orava, Slana and Hornad rivers contribute to the country's electricity production, almost half of which is produced by the nuclear power station at Bohunice, near Trnava, which has four reactors with a capacity of 1632MW. A similar station is under construction at Mochovce. Thermal power stations at Novaky (570MW) and Vajany (1200MW) burn brown coal.

AGRICULTURE

With forestry and the water industry, agriculture accounted for over 14 per cent of employment in 1990 and was practised on half the land area. 1.78m ha was arable land, and around 817 000ha meadows and pastures. Wheat, barley, oats, rye, maize, sugarbeet and potatoes constitute the main arable crops. As in the livestock sector, output has fallen in recent years; gross agricultural production fell by around 17 per cent* in 1990–92. Agricultural land is being returned to private ownership or leasehold, but most farms seem likely to continue operating as cooperatives.

Water and soil pollution from fertiliser and pesticide run-off and livestock wastes add to pollution from non-agricultural sources, the latter affecting around 200 000ha*. Fertiliser use declined slightly during the 1980s to 240kg/ha in 1987/88. Around 17 per cent* of agricultural land is severely affected by erosion.

FOREST RESOURCES

Slovakia is well endowed with forests, which cover 40 per cent of the land area (1.92m ha). Although the amount of clear-cutting and coniferous plantations increased in recent decades, over half of forest cover in 1989 was accounted for by deciduous species, 29 per cent by beech and 11.5 per cent by oak. Overall timber production rose 35 per cent during 1950–1980, reaching 5.7m m^3 in 1985. The effects of air pollution on forest health are generally less extensive than in the Czech Republic, although the area damaged increased from 8.5 per cent in 1975 to 30.4 per cent in 1988. Around 30 000ha have been severely affected, notably around Ziar nad Hronom and in the Bedisky mountains, bordering Moravia. The 1992 forest survey recorded 36 per cent of trees moderately defoliated (25 per cent) or worse.

TRANSPORT

The former Czechoslovakia had one of the highest levels of car ownership in CEE, 45 per cent of households having a car (3.12m* cars in 1989). The road network of Czechoslovakia covered 73 640km*, the rail network 13 100km*. Around 80 per cent of freight (by weight) was carried by road. Slovakia's rail system was said to be on the verge of collapse in 1991, lacking investment for modernisation. Vehicle emissions contribute up to 60 per cent of the total air pollution in the larger conurbations, and a survey in the late 1970s showed that noise limits were exceeded in 43 towns in Slovakia. A motorway connects Bratislava to Brno in the Czech Republic (and continues to Prague). Bratislava and Komarno are the principal ports on the Danube.

---

* Refers to former Czech and Slovak Federal Republic

Spain

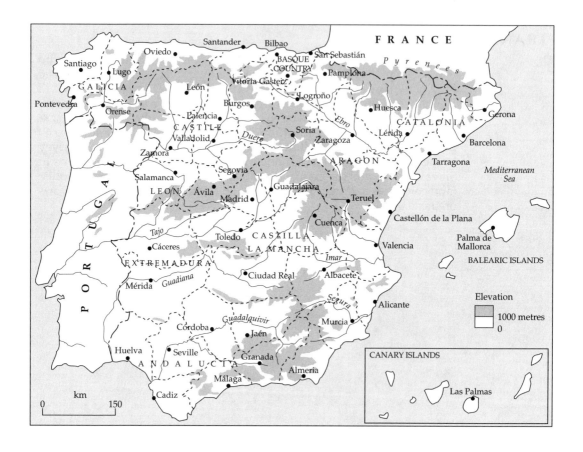

Spain lies south of the Pyrenean mountains in the Iberian peninsula, which it shares with Portugal. The Balearic Islands (in the Mediterranean) and Canary Islands (off the north-west African coast) also form part of Spain. The climate and natural conditions are predominantly Mediterranean, except in the Atlantic region of the north and northwest. The country is notable for its mountainous terrain, divided by extensive plains and plateaux, and for its many rivers and artificial lakes.

INSTITUTIONS AND POLICY

Spain is a constitutional monarchy with a bicameral parliament (*Cortes*). Under the constitution of 1978, many powers are devolved to the 17 regions or autonomous communities, each of which has its own parliament and administration. Some of the autonomous communities (eg

Area	504 750km²
Population	38.9m
Urban	79%
Rural	21%
Capital	Madrid (2.9m)
City populations	20 > 200 000; 6 > 500 000
Economy	
GNP per capita	US$12 450 (1991)
Climate (Madrid)	
Average daily max and min	31/17°C (July)/9/2°C (January)
Annual precipitation	444mm
Land-use cover	
Agriculture	61%
Forest	31%
Other	8%

Catalonia, the Basque Country, Canary Islands) have a greater degree of self-government than others. Framework legislation is developed at national level and then applied by the autonomous communities, some of which have competence to adopt further legislation of their own. All the regions have the power to assume competence for environmental management, land-use planning and forestry. Each regional administration includes an environment department, either as part of a Council for Public Works or as an agency in its own right. Local authorities (municipalities) also have some environmental responsibilities.

In central government, responsibility for environmental matters lies primarily with the Ministry for Public Works, Transport and the Environment (MOPTMA). The new post of Secretary of State for Water and Environmental Policy was established in 1991, and expanded in 1993 to include housing. Nature conservation is the responsibility of ICONA, the National Institute for Nature Conservation, which comes under the Ministry of Agriculture, Fisheries and Food. Other national bodies with environmental interests include the Ministry for Health and Consumers:

- the Centre for Energy, Environment and Technology Research (CIEMAT) under the Ministry for Industry, Commerce and Tourism, and
- the Higher Council for Scientific Research (CSIC) under the Ministry for Education and Science.

Spain joined the European Community on 1 January 1986, and EC legislation has exerted a considerable influence on the development of Spanish environmental legislation. The EIA directive (85/337) was implemented by Royal Decree 1131/1988; some autonomous communities have produced EIA legislation of their own.

AIR POLLUTION

SO_2 emissions in 1990 totalled 2.32mt, down from 3.32mt in 1980; over 70 per cent resulted from electricity generation and the oil and coal industries. Power stations burning coal with a high sulphur content are the principal source of SO_2, contributing 1.4mt in 1987.

NO_X emissions from power stations were estimated at 250,000t in 1987, slightly lower than the annual average of the previous seven years. Emissions from vehicles reached 577 000t of NO_X in 1988, up from 406 000t in 1980.

Industry accounts for the majority of particulate emissions, notably cement, electricity and steel production. Particulate emissions from vehicles rose considerably during the 1980s, from 19 000t in 1980 to 31 000t in 1988.

CO_2 emissions in 1990 were estimated at 262mt; around 30 per cent of the total was produced by transport, and 20 per cent by the energy sector.

Air pollution control is the responsibility of MOPTMA, the Ministry of Health and Welfare, the Ministry for Industry and Energy and the autonomous communities. Air quality monitoring is undertaken by the autonomous communities and coordinated by the Directorate-General for Environmental Policy (DGPA) of MOPTMA. The municipalities also are involved in monitoring and in implementing measures for reducing pollution when statutory limits are breached. Air pollution problems in Spain are exacerbated by meteorological conditions, typically involving long periods of high pressure in the winter and dry spells in the summer.

The basic national law for the prevention and control of air pollution is Law 38/1972, which is implemented by Decree 833/1975. These have been supplemented by further regulations (Royal Decrees 1613/86 and 177/87) to implement EC Directives on air quality.

Government objectives in the 1991–2000 National Energy Plan include:

- The reduction of SO_2 emissions from large combustion plants by 42 per cent by the year 2000 as compared with 1980, which should result in an overall reduction in SO_2 emissions of 30 per cent.
- NO_X emissions from large combustion plants are to be reduced by 21 per cent by 1998 compared with 1980 and to a total of 263 000t by 2000.

CO_2 emissions are projected to increase by around 25 per cent between 1990 and 2000.

WATER RESOURCES AND POLLUTION

There are ten major river catchment areas in peninsular Spain: North Spain, Duero, Tajo, Guadiana, Guadalquivir, South Spain, Segura, Jucar, Ebro and the Eastern Pyrenees. The total length of rivers is around 173 000km and their total annual flow estimated at just over 100bn m^3. The Duero and Ebro have the largest flows. Despite the large number of rivers, surface water is generally scarce, due to the lack of rainfall, high evaporation rates and irregularity of natural flows; many smaller rivers run dry during the summer. The exception is the high-rainfall region of the north, where there is no shortage of water. There are few natural lakes, but around 700 reservoirs have been created by damming rivers to supply water to towns and irrigate agricultural land. Many reservoirs suffer from eutrophication.

The total volume of natural water resources in Spain (surface and groundwater) is estimated at just under 113bn m^3 annually, of which around 46bn m^3 is made available for consumption. By the year 2010, demand is expected to reach 50bn m^3, 70 per cent for irrigation.

Most of the principal rivers suffer from high levels of pollution, particularly in the Mediterranean regions, where river flows are reduced greatly in the summer. For example, the Guadarrama exceeds the levels allowed under EC legislation for ammonia, phenols, oil and grease. The quality of water in rivers flowing into the Atlantic is mostly adequate. Groundwater pollution is a serious problem in certain areas as a result of high fertiliser and pesticide usage in intensive, irrigated agriculture. In many Mediterranean coastal areas, the excessive abstraction of groundwater for irrigation and domestic consumption has led to intrusions of seawater. The dumping of municipal and industrial wastes has also caused serious cases of local pollution, although figures are lacking for the national situation.

At the end of the 1970s, less than 10 per cent of municipal wastewater was treated, but by 1990 half of the population was served by treatment facilities, although in many cases only primary treatment is undertaken. Compliance with EC Directive 91/271 on wastewater treatment requires considerable further progress in this area.

Including the island regions, Spain has a coastline of over 6000km. This coastline has provided the basis for the Spanish tourist industry, which is extremely important in national economic terms. At the same time, tourism has had a massive environmental impact on many coasts, as a result of rapid and poorly controlled developments, and inadequate waste treatment facilities. 93 per cent of sea bathing waters sampled in 1992 in accordance with the EC Directive complied with its coliform standards.

The management of water resources is the responsibility of 12 water boards. Four of these come under autonomous communities (Balearic and Canary Islands, Catalonia and Andalucia) and the remainder are independent bodies answerable to the central administration. A National Hydrological Plan has the primary objective of redistributing water from catchment areas with surplus water to those with insufficient resources to meet current and future demands.

A new Water Law (29/1985) was introduced in 1985 as the legal basis for meeting EC obligations. It includes a number of measures designed to protect groundwater and control its abstraction. Water quality standards were established by Royal Decree 927/1988, based on the EC drinking water Directive. A significant change introduced by the 1985 Water Law was that groundwater ceased to be regarded as private property and became a public resource (like surface water). Private owners of boreholes are now required to register with the authorities and to obtain permission for extracting groundwater. There are estimated to be 546 000 boreholes, of which only 164 000 were registered in 1991.

SOLID WASTE

Solid waste arisings are estimated at 272.6mt per year. as follows:

- almost 34 per cent from the livestock sector
- 26 per cent from mining and quarrying
- 16 per cent from urban waste
- 13 per cent from agriculture
- 5 per cent from industry.

Municipal waste amounts to 12.8mt per year, almost half of which is produced in the three regions of Catalonia, Madrid and Andalucia. This is disposed of as follows:

- 30 per cent through uncontrolled dumping,
- 49 per cent to controlled landfills,
- 15 per cent composted and
- 5 per cent incinerated.

A total of 1.8mt of toxic waste is produced annually, mostly by the chemicals industry, paper and pulp factories, and 23 per cent by metalworks. Attempts to improve the regulation of this sector were introduced with Law 20/1986 and Royal Decree 833/1988. A National Plan for Toxic Wastes aims to ensure the treatment of 785 000t annually, to be implemented by the State company EMGRISA.

NATURE CONSERVATION

The Iberian peninsula is an area of high diversity of flora and fauna, landforms and environmental conditions. Large areas of wilderness survive, where human impacts have been limited. Furthermore, the continuation of relatively traditional and non-intensive forms of agriculture over extensive tracts of land has helped maintain a rich heritage of seminatural habitats. Notable examples include steppelands, wooded pastures (*dehesas*) and mountain pastures.

Of the 884 species of vertebrate animal present on the European continent, 657 are found in Spain; 56 are endemic to the country. Thirty-six animal species are considered threatened with extinction, including the brown bear, spotted lynx, black stork, imperial eagle and giant hieroo lizard. A large number of birds pass through on migration, and Spain has the largest area of Special Protection Areas under the EC wild birds Directive. There are estimated to be over 8000 vascular plant species in peninsular Spain and the Balearic Islands and 2000 in the Canaries, many of which are endemic to the islands. Around 200 plant species are considered endangered, including 177 endemic species.

A particular nature conservation challenge in Spain concerns the survival of the many extensive seminatural habitats currently maintained by farming. A combination of influences, including competition in the EC, the EC's common agricultural policy, and changing social expectations in rural areas, seem to point towards increasing abandonment of land in some areas and intensification of farming practices in others. Such changes often affect nature conservation adversely.

Law 4/1989 for the Conservation of Natural Areas and Flora and Fauna forms the main national framework for legislation on nature conservation. Protected area designations can take various forms, including national park, natural park, nature reserve, natural monument and protected landscape. In total, there are 354 protected areas in Spain covering over 2.2m ha. ICONA is the competent authority for national parks, the autonomous communities being responsible for other protected areas.

ENERGY

Total primary energy supply increased from 68.7mtoe in 1980 to 91.9mtoe in 1991. Oil amounts for over half of total energy requirements and is mostly imported; domestic reserves produced 1.1mt in 1992. There are considerable deposits of coal and lignite with a high sulphur content (3.5–7 per cent). Coal meets around 20 per cent of energy needs, a proportion which is declining steadily; 8.6mt of hard coal and 19.6mt of lignite were mined in 1991. Hydroelectric power stations produced 17 per cent of electricity generated in 1991 and ten nuclear power stations 35 per cent. Most of the remainder was generated by thermal plant.

A new National Energy Plan was launched in 1991 and runs to the year 2000. The plan includes specific objectives for reducing emissions, to be achieved through a combination of improved energy efficiency and conversion to cleaner energy sources. Final energy consumption by the year 2000 is to be cut by 7.6 per cent, compared with 'business as usual' growth projections. The plan includes a programme of conversion to natural gas, which provided less than 6 per cent of energy consumed in 1990. Most gas is imported by pipeline through neighbouring countries; domestic production totalled 1.3m m^3 in 1990. The plan maintains the moratorium on new nuclear installations introduced by the previous plan in 1983. A Renewable Energy Plan seeks to increase the contribution of renewable energy to the total primary supply from 1500 to 5700GWh. The main sources being developed are solar panels, windfarms, small hydroelectric plants and energy recovery from the incineration of agricultural and urban wastes.

AGRICULTURE

In 1990 there were an estimated 20.54m ha of arable and permanent cropland and 10.12m ha of grassland. In addition, there are some 5m ha of scrub and scrub woodland, some of which is browsed and grazed by livestock; Spain is the second-largest producer of sheep meat in the EC.

Arable land covers the largest area, amounting to 15.34m ha in 1990; over 4m ha is left fallow each year. The main cereals grown are barley, wheat and maize; sunflowers, sugarbeet, fruit and vegetables, cotton and tobacco are also important crops. Olives cover over 2m ha and dominate the landscape in certain regions of the south, particularly Jaen (Andalucia). Other fruit trees, such as almonds, citrus fruits, peaches and carobs, cover a further 1.3m ha, and vineyards almost 1.5m ha throughout Mediterranean Spain.

A land use typical of Spain and Portugal is wooded pasture or parkland, often combined with some cultivation in an integrated agri-silvo-pastoral system. In Spain this is known as *dehesa* and, in its various forms, covers some 4.6m ha; it is of high nature conservation value.

Farming and the rural environment have undergone dramatic changes since the early 1960s, with widespread modernisation of agriculture (mechanisation and the introduction of chemical inputs) and a large-scale decline in rural populations, including the total abandonment of villages and land in some regions. Accession to the EC provided an apparent boost to many sectors of farming through higher prices and support measures. However, greater competition has resulted in considerable economic pressures to raise productivity.

The total irrigated area has increased by 1.4m ha (65 per cent) since the early 1960s and many wetlands have been destroyed through the lowering of water tables and drainage. Large areas of *dehesa* have been cleared for arable cultivation; the total area of wooded pasture fell by almost 1m ha between 1973 and 1989. The area of permanent pasture and dry grassland declined by 0.8m ha over the same period, whilst the area of scrub increased by over 1m ha, due largely to the concentration of livestock on better grazing land.

Other environmental problems associated with agriculture in Spain include water pollution from the run-off of pesticides, fertiliser and slurry, saltwater intrusions into overexploited aquifers, river pollution from olive-processing plants and the accumulation of plastic waste associated with intensive horticulture in some coastal areas, such as Almeria. Horticulture under plastic covers over 50 000ha.

Overall consumption of non-organic fertilisers is low by European standards. In 1988, 976 023t of nitrogen were used on a 'fertilisable area' of 17.5m ha. Fertiliser (and pesticide) usage tends to be concentrated in areas of irrigated agriculture and horticulture.

Farm size averages 15.2ha, although the majority of farms consist of less than 5ha. However, farms over 50ha make up 55 per cent of the area farmed. Farm holdings tend to be extremely fragmented in some regions, and consolidation has been encouraged. Consolidation projects affected 5.2m ha during 1953–81.

Spain has the largest fishing fleet in Western Europe, based mainly in Galicia. Landings have declined in recent years (to 842 077t in 1991). The North and South Atlantic are fished, as well as EC waters.

FOREST RESOURCES

High forest covers 7.2m ha, scrub and scrub-woodland 5m ha and open *dehesa* woodland 4.6m ha. There are extensive areas of natural forest as well as new plantations. Fine examples of beech forest are formed in the north, with a variety of other broadleaved and native coniferous species; Mediterranean forests are typified by evergreen oak species in combination with a wide range of shrubs. The most important area of production in economic terms is livestock grazing and foraging, in both upland forests and *dehesa* woodlands. The latter also produce cork. Timber and pulp are important products of high forests, particularly in northern and upland areas.

Afforestation programmes have been undertaken since the 1941 Law on the State Forest Heritage, involving over 3m ha. Most of these schemes have created single-species plantations, mainly of pines and other fast-growing species, such as eucalyptus and poplar, to boost timber production.

Erosion control has also been a major objective in Mediterranean regions, although soil erosion may be encouraged where mechanical scrub clearance and terracing are used. Soil erosion affects 22.1m ha and reaches severe levels on 9.16m ha, mostly in the southern half of the country. A national plan for watershed-forestry restoration and erosion control involves afforestation and projects to improve the control of storm waters.

Forest fires affected an average of almost 240 000ha annually between 1980 and 1987; pine plantations are especially vulnerable. The forest condition survey of 1992 found 12.3 per cent of sample trees suffering from moderate or worse defoliation (25 per cent or above).

At national level, forestry is the responsibility of ICONA. Each autonomous community has its own forestry service which manages forests on public land, including those owned by the municipalities.

Road transport predominates in Spain, carrying over 90 per cent of inland

TRANSPORT

freight (in t-km). A major construction programme was launched in 1983 under the General Plan for Roads, which included the objective of building 5000km of motorway. By 1991 there were 162 000km of road, including 2700km of motorway.

The rail network extends to 13,060km and is generally underdeveloped, but a modernisation plan was endorsed in 1987. The first part of a high-speed train system linking Madrid and Seville began operation in 1992; the next stage will connect with the French TGV network via Barcelona.

The majority of international trade is carried by sea (92 per cent of imports and 83 per cent of exports). There are over 200 seaports, but in some cases, major investments in port infrastructure since the 1960s appear excessive in the light of current usage.

The construction of major new transport infrastructure, such as roads and high-speed railways, may have a considerable impact on wildlife species such as lynx and bear which require large and uninterrupted habitats.

The transport sector produced 67mt of CO_2 (31 per cent of the total) in 1990, projected to rise to just under 87mt by 2000. SO_2 emissions from transport are expected to rise from 131 000t to 160 000t over the same period.

Sweden

Area	449 964km²
Population	8.7m
Urban	86%
Rural	14%
Capital	Stockholm (680 000; conurbation 1.6m)
City populations	11 > 100 000; 4 > 150 000
Economy	
GNP per capita	US$25 110 (1991)
Climate (Stockholm)	
Average daily max and min	22/14°C (July)/−1/−5°C (January)
Annual precipitation	554mm
Land-use cover	
Agriculture	8%
Forest	68%
Other	24%

Sweden is in northwestern Europe, at the centre of the Scandinavian peninsula. It borders Norway to the west, Finland to the north-east, and has a long coastline on the Baltic Sea and the Kattegat. Much of the land is low-lying, but mountains in the north-west rise to 2000m; numerous lakes and marshes cover around 20 per cent of the territory. The population is concentrated in the southern half of the country.

INSTITUTIONS AND POLICY

Sweden is a constitutional monarchy with a unicameral parliament (*Riksdag*) of 349 elected members.

The 24 counties are headed by governors appointed by central government and have some environmental responsibilities, including monitoring, nature conservation, water supply and sewerage.

The 286 elected municipalities have extensive competences for environmental protection, including emission permits and waste management.

At national level, the Ministry of the Environment is assisted by an Environmental Advisory Council. The National Environmental Protection Agency (SNV), established in 1967, is the central administrative body responsible for nature conservancy and environmental protection. The National Franchise Board for Environment Protection is responsible for examining permit applications for larger and more hazardous activities, under the provisions of the Environment Protection Act (1969), the principal item of legislation on environmental permitting. The Environmental Damage Act (1986) regulates civil liability for environmental damage and requires holders of permits to contribute to a fund used to pay compensation where responsible parties cannot be identified or are unable to pay.

Sweden became a member of the European Community on 1 January 1995.

AIR POLLUTION

Air pollution has caused considerable problems through the acidification of land and water, particularly in central and southern Sweden.

Reductions in the sulphur content of oil, the expansion of district heating schemes and the installation of abatement equipment at major combustion plants have helped curb sulphur emissions. SO_2 was reduced greatly from a peak of 930 000t in 1970 to 106 000t in 1991. However, only 12 per cent of depositions result from domestic emissions and levels of sulphur deposition have not decreased as rapidly. Indeed the majority of emissions from sources within Sweden are transported abroad.

Annual emissions of NO_X remained above 400 000t during the 1980s, largely as a consequence of increasing traffic volumes, before declining slightly. 80 per cent of the 389 000t emitted in 1991 came from mobile sources.

Agriculture and forestry contribute about 40 per cent of total nitrogen emissions, mostly as ammonia from manure and fertiliser. However, over 75 per cent of nitrogen depositions originate outside Sweden.

'Imported' air pollution appears to come predominantly from western Europe in the case of nitrogen, corresponding to high levels of traffic there. Sulphur tends to be associated more with emissions in CEE.

Transport accounts for over 50 per cent of VOCs. However, controls in vehicles and at petrol stations are expected to reduce emissions from 200 000t in 1988 to 70 000t in 2000. Emissions from industrial sources are expected to decline during the 1990s as a result of stricter limits. Heavy metal emissions have been reduced significantly during the past 20 years, for example:

- Annual emissions of mercury (mainly from incineration and iron and steelworks) fell from 6t in the early 1970s to 3.1t in 1991.
- Annual emissions of cadmium fell from 25t to 2.5t (1988).
- The widespread use of unleaded petrol helped reduce lead emissions from 2200t to 720t by 1988.

Ambient concentrations of SO_2 generally decreased during the past decade, and the mean winter value for SO_2 in Stockholm is around one-third of that in 1970. Target values ($200\mu g/m^3$ hourly and $100\mu g/m^3$ 24-hour average) are sometimes exceeded in southern Sweden. The air quality target values for NO_2 ($110\mu g/m^3$ hourly and $75\mu g/m^3$ 24-hour average) and CO ($6mg/m^3$) are breached more frequently in urban areas, principally where road traffic is heaviest. It is expected that the target values will be met by 2000 in all cities except Stockholm, Gothenberg and Malmö. Ozone levels above $200\mu g/m^3$ have been recorded in southern Sweden in the summer months.

The Act and Ordinance on the Sulphur Content of Fuel Oil (1976) limits the level of sulphur in oil, eg to a maximum of 0.8 per cent for heating oil. Limits on vehicle emissions are fixed by the Automobile Act (1986). Licensing arrangements are governed by the Environment Protection Act

(1969) and emission limits imposed through licences are amongst the strictest in Europe. Swedish policy targets include the reduction of sulphur emissions by 80 per cent by 2000 and of NO_X by 30 per cent by 1995 (compared with 1980 levels). A range of environmental taxes has been introduced on some polluting substances in fuels and on emissions, including sulphur, NO_X, hydrocarbons and CO_2.

WATER RESOURCES AND POLLUTION

Sweden has 100 000 lakes, which cover around 9 per cent of the territory, and around 60 000km of rivers. The country is relatively rich in water resources, although localised shortages have arisen in some former wetland areas drained for agricultural use. Total abstractions in 1990 were 2.93bn m^3, 80 per cent of which came from surface water. This was consumed:

- 70 per cent by industry
- 15 per cent by households
- 5 per cent by agriculture.

Acidification from air pollutants affects many water bodies, particularly in southern and south-western areas. A survey in 1990 found that over 45 per cent of lakes had a pH value below 6 in winter, and in 7 per cent the pH was below 5, threatening the survival of fish fry. Smaller lakes tend to be affected worse than larger lakes, and severe acidification has removed or damaged sensitive species in around 16 000 lakes. An extensive liming programme was introduced in the 1970s to combat acidification and appears to have halted deterioration in the 6000 lakes treated. Acidification may have exacerbated pollution by heavy metals by increasing their solubility in affected waters; 10 000 lakes are thought to contain pike with more than 1mg of mercury per kg of muscle tissue.

An increasing proportion of sewage has received tertiary treatment, serving 84 per cent of the population by 1990; 10 per cent received secondary treatment. However, high levels of nutrients have caused some watercourses to become deoxygenated and encouraged algal blooms. Extensive areas of the seas around the coast of Sweden have been affected, although nitrogen and phosphorus levels stabilised during the 1980s, except in the Kattegat and the Gulf of Riga. Nitrogen emissions from agriculture and from vehicle emissions add to those from sewage and have polluted groundwater as well as surface water. Over 100 000 people receive water supplies with nitrate above recommended levels.

The Natural Resources Act (1987) includes general provisions on the use of resources, including water. More detailed measures concerning water protection are based on the Water Act (1983), and discharges to water are covered by the Environment Protection Act (1969).

SOLID WASTE

Total waste arisings in 1987 were estimated at 52.4mt, including 28mt from mining activities and 8mt from forestry. Municipal waste generation was estimated at 3.2mt in 1990, having increased from 2.5mt in 1980. Most household waste is incinerated at 20 plants or sent to landfill (5000 sites). A small proportion is composted, around 100 000t in 1990, and an increasing proportion recycled (400 000t in 1990); recycling rates reached 43 per cent for paper and cardboard and 44 per cent for glass in 1990.

Hazardous waste arisings are estimated at around 0.5mt annually, half of which consists of oily or metal waste. One central plant for the disposal of hazardous waste deals with 40 000t per year and is due to be expanded.

The Cleansing Act (1979) is based on a rule of prudence requiring waste to be managed so that it does not create a public health or environmental hazard. Amendments to this act in 1990 seek to reduce the quantity of waste through increased recycling and anti-pollution controls. Municipalities have responsibility for handling waste and for drawing up waste management plans.

The Natural Resources Act (1987) provides for land suitable for waste treatment facilities to be protected from actions which might obstruct such uses, and waste disposal facilities require a permit under the Environment Protection Act. A national Waste Management Programme was adopted in 1990 with the aim of restricting the volume and contents of hazardous substances in waste, increasing recycling and improving waste disposal techniques. Municipalities can require waste to be separated at source, to facilitate recycling.

NATURE CONSERVATION

As one of the major land uses, forestry has had a significant impact on wildlife and habitats. Around 3m ha of wetlands in southern and central Sweden have been drained over the past 190 years. Sweden has around 2000 species of vascular plants, 20 per cent of which are considered to be threatened or in decline. Fauna species include 63 mammals and 242 birds; 14 of 19 reptile and amphibian species are threatened or decreasing.

The Nature Conservation Act of 1964 (amended in 1991) forms the legal basis for both species protection and protected areas. By 1991 there were:

- 22 national parks (626 640ha),
- 88 nature conservation areas (180 740ha),
- More than 1300 nature reserves (1.9m ha),
- 853 wildlife sanctuaries and
- 1425 natural landmarks.

This made a total of 2.66m ha under some form of protection. Proposals were made in 1989 for 20 further national parks. By 1992, 30 Ramsar wetland sites had been designated, covering 382 750ha. Hunting is regulated through the Hunting Act of 1987, which protects some game species and allows hunting under particular conditions.

ENERGY

Sweden is highly dependent on imports of fuel supplies, which account for almost 70 per cent of its energy needs. Total final energy consumption has not changed greatly during the past 20 years (32.7mtoe in 1990) but the share of energy provided by hydroelectric and nuclear power stations has increased at the expense of oil. Oil provided 43 per cent of national energy supplies in 1990, compared with 70 per cent in 1970. Industrial and domestic use each accounted for approximately 40 per cent of energy consumption in 1990.

Sweden is self-sufficient in electricity, and generation more than doubled in 20 years to reach 146TWh in 1990; most is produced by hydro-electric (71TWh in 1990) and nuclear power stations (65TWh). Nine rivers in the northern half of the country provide the source of most of the hydropower; four rivers have been given legal proctection from further hydropower development. The twelve nuclear reactors at four sites in southern Sweden have a total capacity of 9970MW and use imported uranium fuel (although there are some indigenous deposits). A deep-level repository is intended to ensure the safe disposal of radioactive waste, funded through a levy on nuclear-generated electricity. Following a referendum in 1980, parliament voted to phase out nuclear power by 2010, although the phase-out was subsequently made conditional on the development of environmentally acceptable methods of electricity generation and successful efforts to improve energy efficiency.

An energy-saving programme began in 1975 and was expanded to encourage the use of indigenous energy sources rather than oil, introduce stricter insulation requirements and provide subsidies for energy conservation measures. In 1990–91 environmental charges were introduced on electricity and fossil fuels, according to sulphur and carbon dioxide output, and value added tax imposed on energy, at the rate of 25 per cent.

AGRICULTURE

There were around 2.8m ha of arable land and 0.33m ha of pasture in 1991. The pattern of agriculture reflects the differences in climate found in the north and south of the country. Farmers in the south can grow a variety of crops including wheat, sugarbeet, potatoes, oilseed and peas, whilst production in the north is geared more heavily towards livestock, including grains for feed. Barley, oats and wheat are the principal cereal crops. Around 4500 holdings in the south specialise in horticulture. Average farm size increased from 12ha of arable land in 1951 to 28ha in 1990; farms in the north of the country tend to be smaller. A growing proportion of farmers derive part of their income outside farming, and 75 per cent of farms include forest on their land. Agriculture accounted for 3 per cent of employment and 1.2 per cent of GDP in 1990; three-quarters of agricultural earnings came from livestock production.

Swedish agricultural policy underwent major reforms in 1990–91, involving a reorientation to market conditions in order to reduce surpluses of some products. The new policy includes the objective of preserving a rich and varied agricultural landscape and minimising the impact of farming on the environment. Subsidies for conversion to organic farming were introduced in 1989, and other programmes have reduced input levels. Pesticide use was halved between 1985 and 1990, and is to be halved again by 1996. Fertiliser applications also fell, to an average of 70kg of nitrogen, 10kg of phosphorus and 20kg of potassium per hectare in 1990; nutrient leaching was projected to fall by 50 per cent between 1985 and 1995.

FOREST RESOURCES

Woodland covered around 28m ha in 1990, of which 23m was productive forest. Almost 85 per cent of the growing stock consists of Norway spruce and Scots pine, and 11 per cent are birch; aspen, oak, beech, alder and other deciduous species make up the remainder. Forestry and related industries are of great economic and social importance in Sweden. The forest stock has increased since the beginning of this century, and annual fellings and losses through natural mortality amounted to 65m m^3 in recent years, compared with annual growth of around 95m m^3 (including bark). Around 195 000ha are clearcut each year, with a further 30 per cent of the timber harvest coming from thinning. Clear-cutting must be notified to the forestry authorities in advance, and clearcut areas replanted or regenerated within three years; other requirements cover thinning rates and permit felling only after a specified level of maturity. Fertiliser application (usually from aircraft) is also regulated. The 1992 forest survey found 16.5 per cent of trees sampled suffering from 25 per cent or more defoliation.

TRANSPORT

During the five years to 1990, road transport grew more rapidly than ever before. The number of passenger cars in use in Sweden increased from 2.29m in 1970 to 3.6m in 1990. By 1992 there were over 415 000km of roads (two-thirds of which were private), including 999km of motorway. The rail network extended to 10 970km.

Investment in infrastructure projects in cities is set to double during the 1990s, and is likely to include measures to improve public transport. Greater restrictions on vehicles and fuels and the implementation of traffic planning measures which take environmental effects into consideration are also envisaged.

Significant expansions of the railway system have been initiated with the aim of reducing the environmental impact of road transport, and since 1989 all new car models have been required to have catalytic converters.

Fuel prices were increased by around 35 per cent in 1990, helping to reduce annual CO_2 emissions from the transport sector for the first time in ten years.

Switzerland

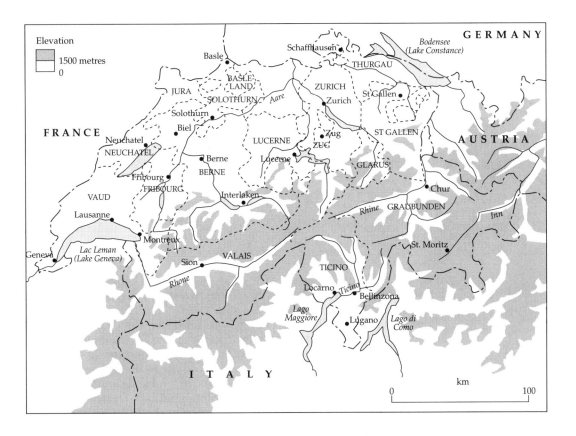

Switzerland is a landlocked country bordered by France, Germany, Austria and Italy. Much of the country is mountainous, notably the Jura and the Alps, whose peaks rise above 4000m. Two-thirds of the population live in the central plateau which extends from Lake Geneva in the south-west to Lake Constance in the north-east. The climate can vary significantly in different parts of the country, according to influences from the Atlantic, eastern Europe, and, in the south, the Mediterranean.

INSTITUTIONS AND POLICY

Switzerland is a federal republic of 26 cantons and demicantons. A National Council of 200 members is directly elected, and the cantons are represented through the Council of States. The canton authorities are autonomous to the extent that their powers are not limited by the constitution, and they have extensive competences in the field of environmental

Area	41 293km²
Population	6.87m
Urban	60%
Rural	40%
Capital	Berne (135 000; conurbation 299 000)
City populations	5 > 100 000; 1 > 300 000
Economy	
GNP per capita	US$33 610 (1991)
Climate (Zurich)	
Average daily max and min	25/14°C (July)/2/–3°C (January)
Annual precipitation	1089mm
Land-use cover	
Agriculture	45.5%
Forest	29%
Other	25.5%

protection, as do the communes for some matters. The Federal Office for Environment, Forests and Landscape forms part of the Department of the Interior.

The Federal Environmental Protection Act (1983) came into force on 1 January 1985 as the principal framework law on the environment. It sets out the basic provisions on air pollution, noise, dangerous substances, waste, soil pollution, and EIA. The act also defines the different (and sometimes overlapping) responsibilities of the federal and canton authorities, the latter often dealing with implementation. Details of EIA requirements and procedures were laid down in the EIA Ordinance of 1988.

Switzerland applied in May 1992 to join the European Community, but in December 1992 a referendum rejected membership of the European Economic Area, the first step towards joining the EC.

AIR POLLUTION

Total emissions of many air pollutants show a decreasing trend in recent years. Emissions of SO_2 were more than halved between 1980 and 1991, from 126 000t to 63 000t. Two-thirds originated from fuel combustion in industry and households (excluding power stations), and the lowering of limits on the sulphur content of heating oil and stricter emission standards for plants burning heavy oil have helped reduce emissions.

Particulate emissions also fell during the past decade, from 28 000t in 1980 to 20 000t in 1990. Annual emissions of NO_x reached a peak of 214 000t in 1984, since when they have been reduced gradually, to 175 000t in 1991. Vehicle emissions constitute the major source of NO_x, accounting for over 65 per cent of the total in 1991.

Ambient air concentrations of SO_2 have generally fallen during the past decade; levels recorded at the eight monitoring stations in 1987–89 met the annual average standard of $30\mu g/m^3$, except at Lugano. Short-term limits for SO_2 ($100\mu g/m^3$ 24-hour average and 95th percentile of annual 30-minute averages) were exceeded in relatively few cases.

The $30\mu g/m^3$ annual average standard for NO_x was exceeded widely at sites in urban areas and near heavily-trafficked roads; the impact of vehicle emissions was evident when a motorway was opened in 1988 and the annual average recorded at a rural monitoring site nearby increased from around 30 to over $50\mu g/m^3$. The annual averages in Zurich approached $60\mu g/m^3$ during the 1980s.

Elevated levels of ozone were also recorded, particularly during the summer months, sometimes above the hourly average standard of $120\mu g/m^3$.

Air pollution control is based on the Federal Environmental Protection Act and the Clean Air Ordinance, which came into force on 1 March 1986. The latter fixes emission and air quality limits, but implementation is largely the responsibility of the cantons.

Targets for national emissions of the major air pollutants were set in 1986 in the Clean Air Concept, including the reduction of emissions of SO_2 to 1950 levels by 1990 and of NO_x and hydrocarbons to 1960 levels by 1995. Vehicle emission standards have generally been tighter than EC norms, regulations having required catalytic converters since 1987, for example. Speed limits on roads have also been reduced, for environmental protection purposes.

WATER RESOURCES AND POLLUTION

Switzerland is rich in water resources and its territory drains from the Alpine massif into four main water basins: via the Rhine into the North Sea, the Rhône into the Mediterranean, the Inn into the Danube and thence the Black Sea, and the Ticino into the Po and the Adriatic Sea. Within the country there are 42 000km of rivers and 1600 lakes. Glaciers cover more than 3000km² and constitute large reserves of water; higher average temperatures in recent years have forced most glaciers into retreat. Annual precipitation varies widely according to situation; for example, below 600mm in Sion but 2480mm in Santis in the Alps.

Total annual abstractions have remained at 11.0–11.6bn m³ during the past 20 years; the country is highly dependent on groundwater supplies, which provide over 80 per cent of the total. Almost 60 per cent of the 11.66bn m³ abstracted in 1989 was used for public water supplies.

Springs provide 40 per cent of drinking water, groundwater 44 per cent and lakes 16 per cent; most of the spring and groundwater requires no treatment but undergoes disinfection as a precaution. In some areas, groundwater is polluted by nitrate and pesticides, as a result of leaching from agriculture and, in the case of some herbicides, from applications used to keep certain areas (such as railway lines) clear of plant growth. Nitrate levels in groundwater and springs in the central plateau display a rising trend during the past 35 years, more than doubling to an average of around 20mg/l by the mid-1980s.

Health Ministry figures from 1989 indicated that 40 per cent of surveyed drinking water supplies included pesticide concentrations above the 0.1µg/l standard, although this study partly targeted supplies at risk.

Pollution by chlorinated hydrocarbons, used as solvents, also pose problems in some groundwater supplies, at levels of 50–200g/l in affected areas. Around 3500 groundwater protection zones help to minimise pollution risks to half the important supply aquifers.

The construction and improvement of sewage treatment plants in recent decades meant that by 1990 connections using secondary treatment served around 90 per cent of the population (compared with 55 per cent in 1975). However, in 1991 it was estimated that 35 per cent of treatment plants required improvements or increased capacity. A ban on phosphates in household detergents was introduced in 1986 to reduce the phosphate discharge to surface waters.

Water policy is based on the Water Protection Act of 1971, amended in 1990. The Ordinance on Wastewater Discharges (1975) set over 50 parameters for water quality and discharges; regulations on discharges of dangerous substances were made in 1981.

SOLID WASTE

Waste arisings in 1988 were estimated to include around 3mt of construction waste and 3.7mt of municipal waste. Incineration was the principal means of disposal for municipal waste (2.3mt), with 0.85mt collected separately for recycling. Around 0.25mt was composted in 1990. Most of the 4mt of waste disposed to landfill was construction waste.

Many waste disposal facilities are overstretched, both in terms of technical equipment and capacity. A programme of retro-fitting incinerators is intended to reduce emissions to air, and some existing landfill sites require improvements to tackle leachate problems.

Hazardous waste generation was estimated at 520 000t in 1990, of which almost one-quarter (121 000t) was exported.

Recycling rates are relatively high, reaching 49 per cent for paper and cardboard and 65 per cent for glass in 1990.

General requirements on waste management are set out in the Environmental Protection Act, which includes provisions on licensing (by the cantons) of the construction and operation of waste disposal facilities. The Technical Regulations on Waste were adopted in 1990 and require the cantons to assess their waste management needs and ensure that sufficient disposal capacity is available; other regulations cover special waste. The Ordinance on Beverage Packaging is intended to promote reusable containers and the recovery of other packaging materials. In general, Swiss policy envisages increased levels of recycling and incineration (of both special and household waste) and a reduction in volumes disposed to landfill.

NATURE CONSERVATION

Switzerland has an estimated 2696 species of vascular plants, 579 of which are considered threatened. Species of fauna include 22 mammals, 204 birds, 11 reptiles and 20 amphibians; over 70 per cent of species in the latter two categories are threatened.

There is one national park, at Engadin (16 900ha). Other areas are given protection as nature reserves or landscape protected areas under the 1966 Law on the Protection of Nature and National Heritage. This law forms the basis of federal legislation on nature conservation.

Ordinances established national inventories of important landscapes and natural monuments, bogs, mires and wetlands. Federal hunting reserves are designated under the Hunting Law (1986) and related Ordinance (1981). Eight Ramsar wetland sites (7049ha) were designated by 1993.

The Federal Office for Environment, Forests and Landscape is advised on nature conservation matters by the Federal Commission for the Protection of Nature and National Heritage, although much of the responsibility for nature conservation rests with the cantons.

ENERGY

Switzerland is not rich in indigenous supplies of mineral fuels, but has developed hydroelectric and nuclear power to help meet rising demand and lessen reliance on imports.

Total primary energy supply rose from 18.0mtoe in 1975 to 25.2mtoe in 1991, just over half of the 1991 total being met by oil. The transport sector has become a major energy user, doubling its share of consumption since 1950 to account for 30 per cent of the total in 1988.

Thermal power stations produce only a small proportion of the country's electricity. Hydroelectric generation, from over 450 stations, accounted for over 55 per cent of production in 1990. Around 40 per cent came from five nuclear power reactors; plans for a sixth plant were shelved in 1988 and a referendum in 1990 approved a ten-year moratorium on the construction of new nuclear stations.

AGRICULTURE

The area of land used by agriculture in 1990 amounted to 0.49m ha of arable and permanent cropland and 1.26m ha of permanent grassland. 130 000ha of agricultural land was used for building and infrastructure development between 1952 and 1990.

Arable cultivation is concentrated on the central plateau and the principal crops are wheat, barley, maize, potatoes, sugarbeet and orchard fruit. Dairying accounted for around onethird of agricultural earnings in the late 1980s, with other livestock production contributing 42 per cent.

Agricultural production has intensified during the past 30–40 years; the number of people employed in agriculture has decreased by 65 per cent since 1945 and output doubled. Nitrogen fertiliser use almost doubled between 1970 and 1987 to 73 000t, and insecticide consumption increased by 30 per cent between 1975 and 1989.

Farms are often small (21 per cent under 1ha in 1991) and run part time (40 per cent). Farmers have benefited from very high production subsidies and import restrictions, although a reform programme is intended to promote larger farms, reduce surplus production and lessen the environmental damage of agriculture. Payments are being introduced to encourage farmers to return arable land to pasture, reduce chemical inputs and switch to free-range methods for livestock.

FOREST RESOURCES

Forests covered around 1.2m ha in 1990, the forest area having expanded gradually in recent decades as a result primarily of the natural afforestation of upland areas no longer used for agriculture. Conifers make up 70 per cent of the cover; beech is the most common broadleaved species. Around 12 per cent of the forested area is used for grazing livestock.

Forest damage attributed to air pollution became increasingly evident during the late 1970s, particularly in the mountains, where trees appear to suffer around twice the level of damage elsewhere. Surveys indicated that the proportion of trees with 25 per cent or more defoliation increased from 13 per cent in 1986 to 19 per cent in 1991, coniferous species being worst affected.

TRANSPORT

The road network in 1990 extended to 71 000km, including 1500km of motorway. The number of motor vehicles in use more than doubled in 20 years, from 1.5m in 1970 to 3.38m in 1991. Total transport volumes have increased threefold since 1960, largely as a consequence of the growth in road traffic. Between 1960 and 1987, the proportion of passenger travel made in private motor vehicles increased from 64 to 82 per cent, and the share of freight carried by road from 26 to 54 per cent, largely at the expense of rail. The coverage of the rail network has hardly changed since 1930, whereas the road network has been greatly extended in recent decades.

Turkey

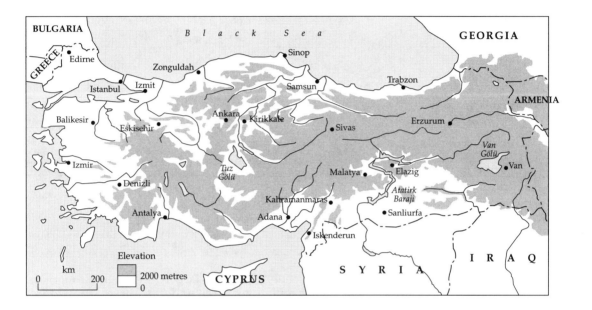

Turkey is a large country at the south-eastern edge of Europe; it shares land borders with Greece and Bulgaria to the northwest and Syria, Iraq, Iran, Armenia and Georgia to the south and east. The coastline extends for more than 8300km along the Black Sea and the Mediterranean and Aegean Seas. Inland from the coastal plains, much of the territory is mountainous; only 10 per cent lies below 250m, and the eastern part of the Anatolian plateau is surrounded by mountain ranges which rise above 4000m. Over 60 per cent of the country has an incline of more than 15 per cent. The climate varies significantly between regions.

INSTITUTIONS AND POLICY

Turkey is a republic and under the 1982 constitution a Grand National Assembly of 450 members is elected. There are 73 provinces, with governors appointed by central government; below this level, local government rests mainly with the municipalities. The constitution refers to environmental entitlements and duties. The Prime Ministry Undersecretariat for the Environment became the Ministry of Environment in 1991. Other ministries are involved in some environmental matters, including the Ministry of Public Works and Settlement, the Ministry of Agriculture, Forestry and Rural Affairs, and the Ministry of Energy and Natural

Area	777 971km²
Population	59.87m
Urban	63%
Rural	37%
Capital	Ankara (2.54m; conurbation 3.02m)
City populations	21 > 200 000; 3 > 2m
Economy	
GNP per capita	US$1780 (1991)
Climate (Ankara)	
Average daily max and min	31/15°C (July)/4/–4°C (January)
Annual precipitation	346mm
Land-use cover	
Agriculture	54%
Forest	26%
Other	20%

Resources. Environmental policy is based largely on the Environment Law (No 2872, 1983) and regulations made under it. Turkey applied in 1987 to join the European Community.

AIR POLLUTION

Air pollution has become severe in urban areas as a result of their rapid growth and industrialisation. Total emissions were estimated at 1.6mt of SO_2 and 175 000t of NO_X in 1989. Power stations (many burning lignite) contribute around 55 per cent of SO_2 emissions and up to 30 per cent of particulate matter; industrial plant and domestic heating are other major sources. Around half of NO_X emissions are produced by motor vehicles, and in coastal cities shipping can contribute significantly to local air pollution.

High levels of SO_2 and particulates have been recorded in many cities, especially during the winter months. During the winter of 1989–90, the SO_2 limit value of 250µg/m³ (six-month average) was exceeded in 11 cities and 24-hour limits for SO_2 and particulates were breached widely for extended periods. The use of imported coal and lignite, with a lower sulphur content than domestically produced lignite, is encouraged for use in severely polluted areas; gas is replacing coal for domestic heating in some cities. Many power stations have no effective equipment to limit particulate emissions, although flue-gas desulphurisation equipment has been installed at some. Dust-control measures appear lacking in some industrial plant.

Air pollution control is centred on the Environment Law (No 2872) and the Air Quality Control Regulation of 1986, which set limit values for air quality and require emission licences for specified industrial facilities. By

WATER RESOURCES AND POLLUTION

1991 air quality monitoring was being undertaken in more than 130 areas. Turkey is fairly well endowed with water resources, although annual precipitation varies widely between 250mm and 3000mm, being generally higher in the east and along the Black Sea coast than elsewhere. 200 natural lakes and 75 reservoirs make up most of the 650 000ha covered by inland water bodies, and river length totals 175 715km. Surface run-off is estimated at 186bn m³ annually. There are 26 major river basins in Turkey, but the nine largest cover around half the territory. The Euphrates, Kizilirmak, Sakarya and Tigris drain the largest areas.

Total abstractions were estimated at 30.6bn m³ in 1990, around 70 per cent coming from surface water. Irrigation accounts for the single largest share of consumption, at around 70 per cent of the total. 17 per cent of abstractions in 1990 went into the public water supply; 70 per cent of the population was considered to have access to an adequate water supply (60 per cent in rural areas). Annual water withdrawals are expected to continue to increase significantly to meet growing urban, industrial and irrigation demand; most of the additional consumption will be supplied from surface water sources. The huge South-east Anatolian Project is intended to exploit the water resources of the Euphrates and Tigris basins more fully, involving a series of dams, hydroelectric stations and irrigation schemes. Its centrepiece is the Atatürk dam, which has created a reservoir with a storage capacity of 48bn m³.

Detailed information on the level of pollution of watercourses appears scarce, but the relatively low level of treatment of domestic and industrial waste waters suggests that water quality is adversely affected in some areas. Around one-quarter of the population is served by sewerage collection systems, mostly in urban centres, but only around 6 per cent of this number are connected to sewage treatment plants. It was estimated in 1991 that 98 per cent of industrial works had no wastewater treatment facilities. The total organic wastewater load was estimated at around 85m PE (excluding agricultural wastes), 70 per cent of which comes from domestic sewage; the daily BOD load discharged to surface water was thought to total 3000–5000t.

Many industrial plants have developed along the coast of the Mediterranean and Aegean Seas, and around Istanbul, and discharge into their waters. Major industrial activities which cause pollution include textile manufacturing, leather working, foodprocessing, chemical and petrochemical works, fertiliser factories, iron and steel works, and pulp and paper production. The BOD load from some coastal areas has also increased as a result of the expansion of the tourist industry.

Permits are required for discharges to water under the Water Pollution Control Regulation of 1988, which lists standards for wastewater according to different industrial sectors. By 1989 the water quality monitoring network extended to 679 sampling stations.

SOLID WASTE

Municipal waste arisings were estimated at 19.5mt in 1990, on a per capita level comparable with western Europe (at least in urban areas). Ash (from domestic heating) and organic matter accounted for three-quarters or more of the total in some cities. Some cities have composting plants (eg Izmir) and some waste is recycled; however, most is dumped (eg in quarries) or landfilled, including solid waste from industrial sources. The generation of both municipal and industrial waste has increased with urban and industrial growth.

The Solid Waste Control Regulation of 1991, made under the Environment Law, is the main item of legislation governing waste management. The Environment Law prohibits the storage, transport and disposal of waste in ways which damage the environment. Industries are required to use methods which minimise waste production and should avoid generating solid wastes which contain hazardous substances. The dumping of waste on the seashore is forbidden under the Coast Law of 1990.

NATURE CONSERVATION

Situated at the conjunction of three continents, Turkey is recognised as an important area of plant diversity, with around 3000 endemic species. There are thought to be 8575 species of vascular plants, almost 500 of which are threatened. Numerous animal species are present, too, including 120 mammals, 426 birds and 100 reptiles.

The country has many important, large wetlands, which form valuable habitats for birds, including the many migratory species whose routes cross Turkey. Its 16 prime sites cover more than 350 000ha, and the area of wetlands of international significance totals more than 1.32m ha.

The Forest Law No 6831 (1956) and the National Parks Law No 2873 (1983) provide for the designation of protected areas. By 1990 there were 21 national parks covering 301 584ha, the largest five having an area of more than 216 000ha. In addition, three nature parks and 12 specially protected areas were designated in 1988; the latter are concentrated on sites on the coasts of the Mediterranean and Aegean Seas, including nesting beaches used by loggerhead and green turtles. Turkey's coastal areas are under particular pressure because of the concentration of urban, industrial, agricultural and tourism developments in the coastal provinces.

Nature conservation matters are handled principally by the Ministry of Agriculture, Forestry and Rural Affairs.

ENERGY

Turkey relies on imports for over half its energy supplies (54 per cent in 1990). The total primary energy supply more than doubled from 26.8mtoe in 1975 to 54.0mtoe in 1991.

Oil accounted for 45 per cent of energy needs in 1990, mostly from imports; domestic production reached 4.3mt in 1992, nearly all from south-east Anatolia, where gas is also found. There are significant reserves of lignite in Thrace and Anatolia, and 46.9mt was mined in 1990. Lignite and hard coal with a lower sulphur content is imported to reduce pollution in some cities, and the use of gas for domestic heating is becoming more widespread.

Wood, manure and plant wastes are important fuels in rural areas (15 per cent of energy supplies in 1990), solar energy is used to heat water along the Mediterranean and Aegean coasts, and geothermal resources are being developed for electricity production.

Hydroelectric stations accounted for 40 per cent of electricity generated in 1990; capacity will increase (from 7114MW in 1991) as a result of
stations constructed as part of the South-east Anatolian Project.

AGRICULTURE

Turkey has become a major agricultural producer, with 27.7m ha of land
under cultivation in 1990. Agriculture accoun-ted for just under half of
civilian employment in 1990, and around 18 per cent of GDP. Agricultural
production grew by more than 40 per cent between 1975 and 1990, as more
intensive methods of farming were adopted.

Cereal production is concentrated on the central Anatolian plain and
in the northeast. Other crops, including nuts, citrus fruit, vegetables, cotton and tobacco, predominate on the coastal plains; olives, sugarbeet and
oilseeds are also grown. The Cukurova plain around Adana is one of the
most intensively developed agricultural areas, with large-scale farms
which produce partly for export.

The area of irrigated land increased from 1.98m ha in 1975 to 2.37m ha
in 1990, mostly for fruit, vegetables, rice and cotton, and is set to increase
by 1.7m ha as the South-east Anatolian Project develops.

Livestock are raised in upland areas, particularly in the east.
Overgrazing has become a problem as grassland has been brought into
cultivation whilst animal numbers grew and the grazing season was
extended. The area of pasture available decreased from 37.8m ha in the
1950s to 21.7m ha in the 1980s.

The fisheries catch included 290 000t of seafish in 1991. Fish stocks in
the Black Sea appear to have declined significantly in recent years.

FOREST RESOURCES

Forests cover around 20.2m ha, of which broadleaved species cover just
over half. Over 567 000ha are not available for commercial forestry as they
lie within national parks or are categorised as conservation forests (to
combat erosion, flooding etc). The wood harvest amounted to 17.12bn
m³ in 1990. Large areas are burned in forest fires in some years (260 00ha in
1985).

TRANSPORT

Road infrastructure has been developed greatly in recent decades; by 1991
there were over 59 000km of state highways and provincial roads. The
Anatolian Highway is intended to improve road transport from Bulgaria
and Greece, via Istanbul and Ankara, to Iran and Syria. The number of
cars in use almost doubled between 1984 and 1991, from 0.92m to 1.83m.
Seaports handled 76.9mt of imports in 1991. The rail network extended to
8430km in 1991.

United Kingdom

WESTERN
ISLES

Moray Firth

HIGHLAND

GRAMPIAN

TAYSIDE

*North
Sea*

CENTRAL   FIFE

LOTHIAN

STRATHCLYDE

BORDERS

NORTHUMBERLAND

DUMFRIES AND GALLOWAY

NORTHERN
IRELAND

TYNE AND WEAR

CUMBRIA   DURHAM   CLEVELAND

ISLE OF
MAN

NORTH YORKSHIRE

LANCASHIRE   HUMBERSIDE

*Irish
Sea*

W YORKS

MERSEYSIDE   GR MAN   S YORKS

IRISH
REPUBLIC

CHESHIRE   NOTTS   LINCOLNSHIRE

CLWYD   DERBYSHIRE

GWYNEDD   STAFFS

SHROPSHIRE   LEICS   NORFOLK

W MIDLANDS WAR   CAMB

NORTHANTS   SUFFOLK

POWYS   HEREFORD &
WORCESTER   BEDS

DYFED   BUCKS   HERTS

GLOS   ESSEX

WEST GL   GWENT
MID GL   OX   GR LONDON

AVON   BERKS

SOUTH GL   SURREY   KENT

WILTSHIRE

SOMERSET   HANTS   W   E
SUSSEX   SUSSEX

DEVON   DORSET

St. George's Channel

CORNWALL

English Channel

Isles of
Scilly

FRANCE

Strait of Dover

ORKNEY   SHETLAND

Abbreviations

BEDS	BEDFORDSHIRE
BERKS	BERKSHIRE
BUCKS	BUCKINGHAMSHIRE
CAMB	CAMBRIDGESHIRE
E	EAST
GL	GLAMORGAN
GLO	GLOUCESTERSHIRE
HANTS	HAMPSHIRE
HERTS	HERTFORDSHIRE
LEICS	LEICESTERSHIRE
NORTHANTS	NORTHAMPTONSHIRE
NOTTS	NOTTINGHAMSHIRE
STAFFS	STAFFORDSHIRE
YORKS	YORKSHIRE
W	WEST

Elevation

500 metres

0

km

0   100

CHANNEL ISLANDS

Guernsey

Jersey

Area	244 429km^2
Population	57.6m
Urban	89%
Rural	11%
Capital	London (6.8m)
City populations	16 > 300 000; 5> 500 000
Economy	
GNP per capita	US$16 550 (1991)
Climate (London)	
Average daily max and min	22/14°C (July)/6/2°C (January)
Annual precipitation	593mm
Land-use cover	
Agriculture	72%
Forest	10%
Other	18%

The United Kingdom (UK) consists of the island of Great Britain (England, Scotland and Wales), to the north-west of the European mainland, and Northern Ireland. Great Britain is bounded by the North Sea, English Channel and Irish Sea. The south and east of Britain are predominantly low-lying with some hills; extensive areas of Wales, Scotland and northern England are mountainous. Numerous islands are found along the diverse coastline.

INSTITUTIONS AND POLICY

The United Kingdom is a parliamentary monarchy with an elected House of Commons (651 members); peers, created by the sovereign, and bishops of the established church form the House of Lords. The UK is a unitary state but some institutional arrangements differ in England, Scotland, Wales and Northern Ireland, including for local authorities.

England and Wales are divided into 47 counties and Scotland into nine regions; below this level are 333 districts and 53 districts respectively. All have elected councils. The functions of both levels are combined in single-tier authorities in some major conurbations in England and island areas in Scotland. Further single-tier authorities were created in 1995. The responsibilities of local authorities include environmental health, waste regulation, air pollution control and planning. There are 26 districts only in Northern Ireland, where some matters are handled centrally by the Northern Ireland Office.

At national level, the Department of the Environment was established in 1970 and is responsible for planning, local government, energy efficiency and housing, in addition to environment policy. The Scottish,

Welsh and Northern Ireland Offices each have an environment department covering their own territory, and legal structures in Scotland and Northern Ireland differ from those in England and Wales.

Much recent environmental legislation is based on the Environmental Protection Act 1990, the provisions of which partly replace those of the Control of Pollution Act 1974. The Environmental Protection Act introduced a system of integrated pollution control, which requires specified processes to obtain a single 'integrated' authorisation covering emissions to air and water, and of waste, on the basis that processes use the best available techniques not entailing excessive cost to control emissions. Authorisations are granted by Her Majesty's Inspectorate of Pollution (HMIP) in England and Wales and Her Majesty's Industrial Pollution Inspectorate (HMIPI) in Scotland. Other emissions to air, and waste disposal, are regulated by local authorities.

The National Rivers Authority (NRA) in England and Wales and the River Purification Boards in Scotland are responsible for water quality and pollution control.

The Northern Ireland Office is the competent authority for most matters not covered by the districts there.

Provisions on EIA, implementing the EC Directive, were incorporated into the existing planning system, which falls primarily within the competence of local authorities.

A White Paper on the Environment was published in 1990, followed by annual reviews and a strategy for sustainable development. Structures for environmental regulation were likely to change following plans announced in 1991 for the creation of new Environment Agencies for England and Wales and for Scotland.

The UK became a member of the European Community in 1973, since when EC policy has increasingly influenced UK environmental legislation.

AIR POLLUTION

Annual emissions of SO_2 declined steadily from 6.42mt in 1970 to 3.56mt in 1991, as a result of greater use of low-sulphur fuels and falling energy demand from industry. Power stations contributed 71 per cent of total emissions in 1991, and emissions from other industrial sources fell by 35 per cent during the 1980s. The majority of SO_2 originates from coal combustion (78 per cent in 1991). Emissions of black smoke also fell significantly during the past two decades, from 1.03mt in 1970 to 0.49mt in 1991. Much of this reduction is attributable to households switching away from coal for domestic heating; however, smoke emissions from road transport (mainly diesel vehicles) doubled during this period and accounted for 42 per cent of the total in 1991.

Emissions of NO_x rose from 2.29mt in 1970 to 2.75mt in 1991. Lower industrial emissions were more than offset by emissions from road transport, which increased by 800 000t. They accounted for 51 per cent of the total in 1991, and power stations for 26 per cent.

Ambient concentrations of SO_2 and smoke, associated with coal combustion, have generally decreased. 29 areas were granted derogations from meeting EC standards until 1993, subsequently reduced to 22; seven breached the EC limit values in 1983–84, but only two in 1991–92.

A survey in 1991 indicated that average levels of NO_2 had increased by around 35 per cent since 1986, reflecting the growth in emissions from road traffic; levels above EC guide values (hourly means of $50\mu g/m^3$, 50th percentile; $135\mu g/m^3$, 98th percentile) were recorded in many urban areas.

Concentrations of lead fell significantly after reductions in the lead content of petrol, although limited by increased traffic volumes.

Elevated concentrations of ozone (above 100ppb) have been measured during recent summers, notably in southern England.

Acidification most affects upland areas of Wales, Scotland and northern England, where depositions exceed critical loads.

Until German reunification, the UK was the largest emitter of SO_2 in the EC, but some coal-fired power stations are being fitted with flue-gas desulphurisation equipment and/or low-NO_X burners. The introduction of catalytic converters is expected to help reduce emissions of NO_X from vehicles. A national programme on CO_2 emissions was published as a discussion document in 1992; government policy aims to return emissions to 1990 levels (160mt) by 2000.

WATER RESOURCES AND POLLUTION

The UK is generally rich in water resources, particularly in the north and west, where precipitation is highest. Abstractions totalled 15.5bn m^3 in 1990 (in Great Britain), of which around 80 per cent came from surface waters. Groundwater sources are most important in southern and eastern England, where surface water is less readily available. Around half of the total abstracted is fed into the mains water supply; 36 per cent was used in power stations in 1990.

Water shortages occur rarely, although projected increases in demand into the next century may put pressure on supplies particularly in the south and east. High volumes of water abstraction appear to have caused some rivers to dry up or have lowered flows.

The quality of drinking water is generally satisfactory, although limited supplies in some areas have not met EC standards (eg for nitrate, nitrite, pesticides and lead) in recent years.

Survey results indicate a minor overall deterioration in the quality of rivers and canals in England and Wales during the 1980s. Of the 42 380km surveyed in 1990, 29 per cent was classed as 1A (the best of five quality classes), and 11 per cent as class 3 or 4 ('poor' or 'bad'). The equivalent figures (1990) for Scotland were 50 963km surveyed, 97 per cent as class 1 (of four quality classes) and 0.6 per cent as class 3 or 4. The worst polluted stretches of river are often in major industrial areas, such as the West Midlands and South and West Yorkshire, and along the rivers Tees, Mersey, Forth and Clyde. 27 636 water pollution incidents were reported and substantiated in 1991.

Emissions from agricultural activities and sewage have a significant impact in some areas, contributing to algal blooms and other symptoms of eutrophication. Sewerage systems serve 96 per cent of the population; treatment removes around 95 per cent of the resulting polluting load discharged to inland rivers, but only 50 per cent of that discharged to estuaries and the sea. A major investment programme is intended to improve sewage treatment to comply with the EC Directive on urban wastewater.

The marine environment around the UK also receives pollutants from other sources, and British rivers contribute around 20 per cent of pollutants entering the North Sea by river. Around 9.3mt of sewage sludge (wet weight), and 5.1mt of industrial waste were dumped at sea in 1990, but sea disposal is being phased out. The number of reported oil spill incidents increased to 800 in 1990, 45 per cent involving offshore operations in the North Sea. Coastal clean-up work was undertaken in the case of 136 spills, the majority in the south Wales/Bristol Channel area and in Scotland. In 1992, 358 out of 455 bathing waters met the mandatory standards of the EC Directive.

Policy and structures concerning water resources and pollution underwent major changes in England and Wales as a result of the Water Act of 1989 (subsequently consolidated with other legislation into the Water Resources Act and four other Acts in 1991). It provided for statutory water quality objectives, drinking water standards and binding improvement plans, and established ten private water service companies responsible for water supply and sewerage in England and Wales, regulated by the NRA. Discharges require authorisation from HMIP or HMIPI, or from:

- The NRA in England and Wales.
- The seven River Purification Boards (RPBs) and three islands councils in Scotland.
- The Department of the Environment in Northern Ireland.

Many provisions of the Control of Pollution Act 1974 continue to apply in Scotland.

The Drinking Water Inspectorate (for England and Wales) was established in 1990.

Waste disposal at sea is controlled through licences issued by the Ministry of Agriculture, Fisheries and Food.

SOLID WASTE

Annual waste arisings were estimated in 1992 at 402mt. This figure included:

- 80mt from livestock
- 108mt from mining and quarrying
- 20mt of household waste.

In addition, more than 3000mt of waste from mines and quarries had accumulated on spoil tips. Arisings of special waste (considered dangerous to the environment) rose from 1.6mt in 1986/87 to 2.9mt in 1991/92.

Landfill is the principal disposal route, accounting for 85 per cent of household, industrial and commercial waste and 70 per cent of special waste; 4–5 per cent is incinerated. In 1992 there were 4196 landfill sites and 212 incinerators licensed. Leachate from landfill sites has contaminated surface and groundwater in some cases, and methane from landfills is thought to account for a quarter of total emissions.

Imports of hazardous waste increased from 40 450t in 1988/89 to 48 460t in 1991/92, 50 per cent of this coming from Switzerland and Belgium. Around half underwent physico-chemical treatment and a quarter was incinerated.

Recovery and recycling of many materials increased during the 1980s, whilst remaining at a lower level than in many EC countries. Recycling rates reached 31 per cent for paper and cardboard and 21 per cent for glass in 1990; rates were higher for ferrous (46 per cent) and some non-ferrous metals. The government set a target in 1990 of recycling 50 per cent of recyclable household waste by 2000, considered to mean increasing the proportion of household waste being recycled from 5 to 50 per cent. A number of pilot recycling projects for household waste have been established, involving composting, separated collection and recycling banks. Industry and commerce are being encouraged to develop systems to recover and reuse waste materials in key sectors, eg vehicles, electronic equipment and packaging.

The waste licensing requirements of the Control of Pollution Act 1974 have been replaced and extended by those in the Environmental Protection Act 1990. A 'duty of care' applies to anyone who handles controlled waste (most household, industrial and commercial wastes), and operations including disposal, treatment or deposit require a licence from the relevant local authority. Waste recycling and disposal plans must be drawn up by local authorities, which are also responsible for arranging for collection and disposal. Some waste operations (eg incineration and recovery processes) fall within the system of integrated pollution control and so are regulated by HMIP/HMIPI. Measures to require local authorities to draw up registers of potentially contaminated land were postponed in 1992.

NATURE CONSERVATION

Virtually all the UK's natural environment has been shaped extensively by human activities. Upland areas form the largest areas of natural and semi-natural habitat of value for nature conservation, including hill pasture, moorland, peat bogs and high mountains. Coastal areas, meadows and ancient woodlands also represent key habitats. Native species present in the UK include 44 land-breeding mammals, 520 birds and 12 reptile and amphibian species, and 1400 vascular plant species.

Changes in agricultural practice and land-use are the cause of much habitat loss and declines in wildlife populations. Hedgerows, woodlands and heath have been cleared for agricultural production, and wetlands drained; the more intensive use of agrochemicals and the effects of pollution have also had an effect.

Nature conservation policy is based largely on the Wildlife and Countryside Act 1981, which covers species and habitat protection. By 1992 it covered 93 animal species and 165 plants. Over 5600 sites of special scientific interest (SSSIs) had been designated, covering 1.7m ha, and 286 national nature reserves (172 500ha). Other protected areas include:

- ten national Parks (1.4m ha) in England and Wales, designated under the National Parks and Access to the Countryside Act 1949,
- 48 areas of outstanding natural beauty (AONBs), and
- 40 national scenic areas in Scotland.

Together these covered almost 20 per cent of the land area.

Institutional arrangements for nature conservation were reorganised in 1990–91. The principal agencies involved are:

- Scottish Natural Heritage,
- the Countryside Council for Wales,
- English Nature, and
- the Department of Environment (Northern Ireland).

The Countryside Commission is responsible for countryside amenity and recreation in England, including the designation of national parks and AONBs. The government is advised on matters of national and international importance by the Joint Nature Conservation Committee.

ENERGY

Primary energy consumption in 1991 totalled 207.7mtoe, an increase of more than 30 per cent over consumption in 1960. The fuel mix changed considerably over this period, as the proportion of energy supplied by gas and oil grew respectively to 33 and 42 per cent of final consumption, whilst the share provided by coal and other solid fuels fell from 62 to 9 per cent. Power stations accounted for 78 per cent of coal consumption in 1991.

Coal production has fallen by more than 50 per cent since 1960, and is set to decline further following a review of the industry undertaken in 1992/93. Production of oil and gas, principally from fields offshore in the North Sea, expanded rapidly during the 1980s, enabling the UK to become a net oil exporter. Production in 1991 totalled 91.3mt of oil and 55bn m^3 of natural gas.

Nuclear power stations supplied 23 per cent of electricity generated in 1992, from 37 reactors; a review of the prospects for nuclear power was due to begin in late 1993. Fuel is reprocessed at British Nuclear Fuel's Sellafield plant in Cumbria, where a deep-level repository for nuclear waste is planned.

The government's target is for the UK to have 1500MW of new renewable electricity generating capacity by 2000; obligations on electricity supply companies to purchase from renewable sources, and premium rates available to generators, have encouraged schemes such as of windfarms and generation from waste incineration.

The Department of Energy was abolished in 1992, when the Energy Efficiency Office became part of the Department of the Environment; its other responsibilities were taken over by the Department of Trade and Industry. An Energy Saving Trust was established jointly with energy companies to encourage energy efficiency measures.

AGRICULTURE

Agriculture is the dominant land-use in most of the UK, occupying over 70 per cent of the surface area. The total area of land in agricultural use fell by 0.5m ha during the 1980s, to 18.54m in 1990. Farms are generally larger than elsewhere in the EC, averaging 107ha in 1989. Just over 5m ha were used for crops, of which wheat, barley, oilseed rape, sugarbeet and potatoes are amongst the most important.

In the livestock sector, concentrated in the west of the country, the size of the dairy herd has decreased during the past decade, as has the number of pigs, whilst the number of sheep rose by 39 per cent to 44m and the beef cattle herd increased by 8 per cent. These changes partly reflect the availability of allowances payable for sheep and cattle raised in upland areas, and have led to overgrazing in some areas.

Farming accounted for 26 per cent of the major water pollution incidents recorded by the NRA in England and Wales in 1991. A series of Codes of Practice for farmers have been drawn up to help curb pollution from agriculture. The main areas of concern include eutrophication and the contamination of drinking water supplies by nitrates and pesticides.

The consumption of pesticides in England and Wales fell by 20 per cent between 1980 and 1990 (in terms of tonnes of active ingredient), whilst the area treated increased by 9 per cent.

Southern and eastern England are the regions most affected by nitrates in groundwater, originating mainly from nitrogen fertiliser; the total used was 46 per cent higher in 1990 than in 1975. A scheme of nitrate sensitive areas was introduced by the Ministry of Agriculture in 1989/90, to encourage farmers to modify certain practices in the catchments of vulnerable aquifers, in return for compensation payments.

Agreements are also signed with farmers in environmentally sensitive areas, in accordance with EC policy, for less intensive forms of agriculture and for countryside management.

FOREST RESOURCES

Forest and woodland cover increased from 1.4m ha in 1947 to more than 2.3m ha in 1991, largely as a result of the afforestation of marginal agricultural land in upland areas. Most of this planting involved coniferous species, which now account for 70 per cent of forest cover. An estimated 316 600ha of ancient seminatural woodland remain in Britain. Timber removals amounted to 6.8bn m^3 in 1990, compared to annual growth of around 15bn m^3.

Forest health surveys in recent years have recorded an increasing number of trees suffering defoliation; in 1992, 58 per cent of trees sampled suffered from 25 per cent or more defoliation.

The Forestry Commission is the primary state body concerned with forestry policy and management; it advises government, undertakes research, oversees grant payments and controls felling, as well as owning and managing almost 40 per cent of forests and woodland in Britain. Most forestry activity is regulated on the basis of the Forestry Act 1967.

TRANSPORT

Road traffic dominates the transport sector in the UK, and has grown greatly in recent decades. Road vehicles carried 93 per cent of passenger traffic and 90 per cent of overland goods traffic in 1991, compared with 72 per cent and 46 per cent respectively in 1952. Freight movements increased by 22 per cent (in t-km) between 1980 and 1991, to 212.3bn t-km; the proportion taken by road increased by 15 per cent, to 61 per cent, at the expense of rail and water transport. The number of cars in use increased from 14.66m in 1980 to 19.74m in 1990; there are over 13m bicycles. The road network in Britain extended to 358 000km in 1990, including 3000km of motorway.

The growth in road traffic means that road transport has become a significant contributor to air pollution, in 1991 accounting for:

- 52 per cent of NO_x
- 42 per cent of black smoke
- 46 per cent of VOCs
- 19 per cent of CO_2.

A major roads programme was announced in 1989, following forecasts in road traffic growth of 83–142 per cent by 2010. Some road construction projects subsequently became a focus of environmental protests, particularly where important habitats were threatened. Private toll roads and road-pricing schemes in cities are under consideration.

As an island, the UK depends more heavily on sea and air transport than many European countries; it has at least 18 airports with regular international flights. The Channel Tunnel to France, opened in 1994, provides the first fixed transport link with the Continent.

Appendix I
Country groupings

Baltic republics
Estonia
Latvia
Lithuania

CEE
Albania
Bulgaria
Czech Republic
Slovakia
Hungary
Poland
Romania
Former Yugoslavia
Slovenia

CIS
Belarus
Ukraine
Moldova
Georgia
Armenia
Azerbaijan
Russian Federation
Kazakhstan
Kirghizia
Tajikistan
Turkmenia
Uzbekistan

EU
Austria
Belgium
Denmark
Finland
France
Germany
Greece

Irish Republic
Italy
Luxembourg
The Netherlands
Portugal
Spain
Sweden
United Kingdom

EAA
Belgium
Denmark
France
Germany
Greece
Irish Republic
Italy
Luxembourg
The Netherlands
Portugal
Spain
United Kingdom
Austria
Finland
Iceland
Norway
Sweden

EFTA
Iceland
Liechtenstein
Norway
Switzerland

European CIS
The Russian Federation
excluding the five
Central Asian Republics
of:
Kazakhstan
Kirghizia
Tajikistan
Turkmenia
Uzbekistan

OECD
Australia
Austria
Belgium
Canada
Denmark
Finland
France
Germany
Greece
Iceland
Irish Republic
Italy
Japan
Luxembourg
The Netherlands
New Zealand
Norway
Portugal
Spain
Sweden
Switzerland
Turkey
United Kingdom
USA

Appendix II
Environment Ministries and Agencies

This appendix lists the principal ministries and agencies responsible for environmental affairs at national level.

Albania
Committee for Environmental
  Preservation and Protection
  (CEPP)
rue Deshmozet e Kombit
Tirana
Fax: + 355 42 286 96

Austria
Federal Ministry for Environ-
  ment, Youth and Family
Section II and V
Untere Donaustrasse 11
A-1020 Vienna
Tel: + 43 1 711 580
Fax: + 43 1 711 584 221

Belgium
Ministry for Public Health and
  the Environment
rue de la Loi 66
B-1040 Brussels
Tel: + 32 2 238 28 11
Fax: + 32 2 230 38 62

Flanders
Administration for Environment,
  Nature and Rural
Development
  (AMINAL)
rue Belliard 14–18
B-1040 Brussels
Tel: + 32 2 507 31 11
Fax: + 32 2 507 67 05

Wallonia
Directorate for Natural Resources
  and the Environment
Avenue Prince de Liège 15
B-5100 Jambes
Tel: + 32 81 32 12 11
Fax: + 32 81 32 57 75

Brussels
Institute for the Management of
  the Environment
Gulledelle 100
B-1200 Brussels
Tel: + 32 2 775 75 11
Fax: + 32 2 775 76 11

Bulgaria
Ministry of the Environment
67 William Gladstone Str
1000 Sofia
Tel: + 359 2 87 47 77
Fax: + 359 2 52 16 34

Cyprus
Ministry of Agriculture and
  Natural Resources
Loukis Akritas Ave
Nicosia
Tel: + 357 2 302 171
Fax: + 357 2 445 156

Czech Republic
Ministry of the Environment
Vrsovicka 65
10010 Prague 10
Tel: + 42 2 673 10311
Fax: + 42 2 673 10973

Denmark
Ministry of the Environment
Slotsholmsgade 12
DK-1216 Copenhagen K
Tel: + 45 33 92 3388
Fax: + 45 33 32 2227

Environmental Protection Agency
Strandgade 29
DK-1401 Copenhagen K
Tel: + 45 32 66 01 00
Fax: + 45 32 66 04 79

Estonia
Ministry of the Environment
Toompuiestee 24
Tallin 200110
Tel: + 714 452 963
Fax: + 714 453 310

Finland
Ministry of the Environment
PO Box 399
FIN-00121 Helsinki
Tel: + 358 019 911
Fax: + 358 019 91499

France
Ministry of the Environment
Blvd du Général le Clerc 14
F-92523 Neuilly sur Seine Cedex
Tel: + 33 1 40 81 21 22
Fax: + 33 1 40 81 18 18

Agency for the Environment and
  Energy Management
  (ADEME)
27 rue Louis Vicat
F-75015 Paris
Tel: + 33 1 47 65 24 96

Germany
Federal Ministry for the Environ-
  ment, Nature Protection and
  Nuclear Safety
Kennedyallee 5
D-53048 Bonn
Tel: + 49 228 3050
Fax: + 49 228 305 3225

Federal Environment Agency
Bismarck Platts 1
D-10044 Berlin
Tel: + 49 30 89 03
Fax: + 49 30 89 03 2285

Greece
Ministry of the Environment,
  Physical Planning and
  Public Works
17 Amaliados St
GR-11523 Athens
Tel: + 30 1 64 461/462–469
Fax: + 30 1 64 47 608

Hungary
Ministry of Environment and
  Regional Policy
Fö utca 44-50
PO Box 351
H-1394 Budapest
Tel: + 36 1 201 4572/201 3843
Fax: + 36 1 201 2846

Iceland
Ministry for the Environment
Sölvholsgötu 4
ISL-150 Rekjavik
Tel: + 354 1609 600
Fax: + 354 1624 566

Irish Republic
Department of the Environment
Custom House
IRL-Dublin 1
Tel: + 353 1 679 33 77
Fax: + 353 1 676 11 70/674 27 10

Environmental Protection
  Agency
Floor 5
St Stephens Green House
Earlsfield Terrace
Dublin-2
Tel: + 353 1 678 5933
Fax: + 353 1 676 1170

Italy
Ministry of the Environment
Piazza Venezia 11
I-00187 Rome
Tel: + 39 6 703 61
Fax: + 39 6 675 93297

Latvia
Environmental Protection
  Committee
25 Peldu Street
LV-1492 Riga
Fax: + 371 222 8159

Lithuania
Environmental Protection
  Department
A Juozapaviciaus 9
2600 Vilnius
Fax: + 370 235 80 20

Luxembourg
Ministry of Environment
18 Montee de la Petrusse
L-2918
Luxembourg
Tel: + 352 4781
Fax: + 352 400 410

Malta
Ministry for the Environment
Floriana
Tel: + 356 222 378
Fax: + 356 231 293

The Netherlands
Ministry of Housing, Physical
  Planning and Environment
  (VROM)
Van Alkemadelaan 85
PO 20951
NL-2500 EZ The Hague
Tel: + 31 70 339 39 39
Fax: + 31 70 317 42 05

Ministry of Agriculture, Nature
  Management and Fisheries
PO 20401
NL-2500 EK The Hague
Tel: + 31 70 339 39 39

Norway
Ministry of the Environment
Myntgaten 2
PO Box 8013 DEP
N-0030 Oslo
Tel: + 47 2 34 57 15
Fax: + 47 2 34 95 62

State Pollution Control Authority
  (SFT)
Stromsvn 96
PO Box 8100
N-0032 Oslo
Fax: + 47 2 267 67 06

Poland
Ministry of Environmental
  Protection, Natural Resources
  and Forestry
52/54 Wawelska Street
POL-00-922 Warsaw
Tel: + 48 22 00 01
Fax: + 48 22 25 39 72

State Inspectorate of
  Environmental Protection
ul Plwa 36/39
POL-Gdansk

Portugal
Ministry of the Environment and
  Natural Resources (MARN)
Rua do Século 51
1200 Lisboa
Tel: + 35 1 13 46 27 51
Fax: + 35 1 13 46 84 69

National Environment Institute
  (INAMB)
Rua Filipe Folque No 46-1
1000 Lisboa
Tel: + 35 1 13 52 30 18
Fax: + 35 1 15 74 771

Romania
Ministry of the Environment
Blvd Libertatii 12
70005 Bucharest
Tel: + 40 1 781 63 94
Fax: + 40 1 312 04 03

Slovakia
Ministry of the Environment
Hlboka 2
81235 Bratislava
Tel: + 42 7 311 003
Fax: + 42 7 311 384

Environment Agency
Lazovna 10
97401 Banska Bystrica

Spain
Ministry for Public Works,
  Transport and the
  Environment
  (MOPTMA)
Dirección General de Medio
Ambiente
Paseo de la Calellana 67
28071 Madrid
Tel: + 34 1 597 50 00

Ministry of Agriculture,
Fisheries
   and Food
Paseo de la Infanta Isabel, 1
28071 Madrid
Tel: + 34 1 347 50 00

Sweden
Ministry of the Environment and
   Natural Resources
Tegelbacken 2
10333 Stockholm
Tel: + 46 8 763 1000
Fax: + 46 8 24 1629

Environmental Protection
   Agency
Smidesvägen 5
S-171 85 Solna
Tel: + 46 8 799 1000
Fax: + 46 8 292 382

Switzerland
Federal Office for Environment,
   Forests and Landscape
Hallwylstrasse 4
3003 Berne
Tel: + 41 31 61 93 11
Fax: + 41 31 61 99 81

Turkey
Ministry of the Environment
Istanbul Caddesi 88
Iskitler 06060
Ankara
Fax: + 90 43 411 356

United Kingdom
Department of the Environment
2 Marsham Street
London SW1P 3EB
Tel: + 44 71 276 3000
Fax: + 44 71 276 0818

Her Majesty's Inspectorate of
   Pollution (HMIP)
Romney House
43 Marsham Street
London SW1P 3PY
Tel: + 44 71 276 8061
Fax: + 44 71 276 8605/8800

EC
Directorate General for
   Environment (DG XI)
European Commission
200, Rue de la Loi
B-1049 Brussels
Belgium
Tel: + 32 2 235 1111

Sources of Information

OVERVIEW/GENERAL

Anderson, K and Blackhurst, R (1992) *The Greening of World Trade Issues*, Harvester Wheatsheaf, Hemel Hempstead.

anon (1993) *Administrative Structures for Environmental Management in the European Community*, Office for Official Publications of the European Communities, Luxembourg.

anon (1993) *Agricultural Policies, Markets and Trade in the Central and Eastern European Countries, the New Independent States and China*, Organisation for Economic Cooperation and Development, Paris.

anon (1993) *Annual Economic Review 1992*, European Bank for Reconstruction and Development, London.

anon (1992) *The Environment in Europe and North America, Annotated Statistics 1992*, United Nations, New York.

anon (1993) *Environmental Action Programme for Central and Eastern Europe*, World Bank, Washington.

anon (1992) *The Future Development of the Common Transport Policy*, COM(92)494, European Commission, Brussels.

anon (1992) *Green Paper on the Impact of Transport on the Environment* COM(92)46, European Commission, Brussels.

anon (1993) *Investing for a better environment*, European Bank for Reconstruction and Development, London.

anon (1991) *Nature Conservation in Austria, Finland, Norway, Sweden, Switzerland, Bulgaria, Czechoslovakia, Hungary, Poland, Romania, Yugoslavia and the Soviet Union*, European Parliament, Luxembourg.

anon (1993) *Nuclear Power Reactors in the World*, International Atomic Energy Agency, Vienna.

anon (1986) *OECD and the Environment*, Organisation for Economic Coooperation and Development, Paris.

anon (1993) *OECD Environmental Data Compendium 1993*, Organisation for Economic Cooperation and Development, Paris.

anon (1992) *Protected Areas of the World, Volume 2: Palaearctic*, International Union for the Conservation of Nature, Gland, Switzerland/Cambridge.

anon (1993) *Quality of Bathing Water 1992*, European Commission, Brussels.

anon (1993) *Report from the Commission of the Implementation of Directive 85/337/EEC on the assessment of the effects of certain public and private projects on the environment* COM(93)28, European Commission, Brussels.

anon (1992) *Report of the Commission of the European Communities to the United Nations Conference on Environment and Development*, Office for Official Publications of the European Communities, Luxembourg.

anon (1992) *Saving Our Planet, Challenges and Hopes*, United Nations Environment Programme, Nairobi.

anon (1991) *The State of the Environment*, Organisation for Economic Cooperation and Development, Paris.

anon (1993) *The State of the Environment in Europe: The Scientists Take Stock of the Situation*, Council of Europe/Cariplo Foundation for Scientific Research, Strasburg/Milan.

anon (1992) *The State of the Environment in the European Community*, COM(92)23 Vol III, European Commission, Brussels.

anon (1992) *Towards Sustainability, A European Community Programme of Policy and Action in Relation to the Environment and Sustainable Development*, COM(92)23, European Commission, Brussels.

anon (1990) *Transport Policy and the Environment*, ECMT Ministerial Session, European Conference of

Ministers of Transport ECMT, Paris.

anon (1991) *Transport Statistics for Europe*, United Nations, New York.

anon (1989) *Water and Sanitation in Europe*, World Health Organisation, Copenhagen.

anon (1992) *World Development Report 1992, Development and the Environment*, Oxford University Press, Oxford.

anon (1993) *World Development Report 1993, Investing in Health*, Oxford University Press, Oxford.

anon (1990) *'1992' The Environmental Dimension*, Economica Verlag, Bonn.

Arden-Clarke, C (1991) *The General Agreement on Tariffs and Trade, Environmental Protection and Sustainable Development*, WWF International, Gland.

Baldock, D, Beaufoy, G, Haigh, N, Hewett, J, Wilkinson, D and Wenning, M (1992) *The Integration of Environmental Protection Requirements into the Definition and Inplementation of Other EC Policies*, Institute for European Environmental Policy, London.

Bennett, G (ed) (1991) *Air Pollution Control in the European Community*, Graham and Trotman, London.

Bergesen, H and Parmann, G (1993) *Green Globe Yearbook 1993*, Oxford University Press, Oxford.

Bernes, C (ed) (1993) *The Nordic Environment – Present State, Trends and Threats*, Nordic Council, Copenhagen/Stockholm.

Brealey, M (ed) (1993) *Environmental Liabilities and Regulation in Europe*, International Business Publishing Limited, The Hague.

Carter, F and Turnock, D (ed) (1993) *Environmental Problems in Eastern Europe*, Routledge, London.

Cutrera, A (ed) (1991) *European Environmental Yearbook*, DocTer International, Milan/London.

Ekins, P (1993) *Trading off the Future*, New Economics Foundation, London.

Enyedi, G, Gijswijt, A and Rhode, B (eds) *Environmental Policies in East and West*, Taylor Graham, London.

Fisher, D (1992) *Paradise Deferred: Environmental Policymaking in Central and Eastern Europe*, Royal Institute of International Affairs, London.

French, H (1993) *Costly Tradeoffs, Reconciling Trade and the Environment*, Worldwatch Paper 113, Washington.

Gillespie, B and Zamparutti, A (1993/94) 'A Framework for the Environment in Eastern Europe' *OECD Observer*, December/January.

Gourlay, K (1992) *World of Waste*, Zed Books, London.

Haigh, N (1992) *Manual of Environmental Policy: The EC and Britain*, Longman, Harlow.

Hammond, A (1992) *World Resources 1992–93*, Oxford University Press, Oxford.

Hunter, B (1993) *The Statesman's Year-Book 1993–94*, Macmillan, London.

Jenkins, T (ed) (1992) *West Goes East: National Reports on Technology Transfer to Central and Eastern Europe*, Friends of the Earth International, Brussels.

Jones, T (ed) (1993) *Repertoire des zones humides d'importance internationale, troisieme partie: Europe*, Bureau de la Convention de Ramsar, Gland.

Juhasz, F and Ragno, A (1993) 'The Environment in Eastern Europe: From Red to Green?' *OECD Observer* April/May.

Kageson, P (1993) *Economic Instruments in European Environmental Policy*, European Environmental Bureau, Brussels.

Lang, T and Hines, C (1993) *The New Protectionism*, Earthscan, London.

Mnatsakanian, R (1992) *Environmental Legacy of the Former Soviet Republics*, Centre for Human Ecology, Edinburgh.

Pracht, L (1992) *Europe in Figures*, Office for Official Publications of the European Communities, Luxembourg.

Ribeiro, T (ed) (1993) *The European Common Garden*, Group of Sesimbra/GLOBE, Brussels.

Russell, J (1990) *Environmental Issues in Eastern Europe: Setting an Agenda*, Royal Institute of International Affairs, London.

Schreiber, H and Huchthausen, R (1991) *Europäischer Umweltplan – Europäischer Plan für den ökologischer Aufbau in Mittel – und Osteuropa*, Institute for European Environmental Policy, Bonn.

Tolba, M and El-Kholy, O (1992) *The World Environment 1972–1992*, Chapman and Hall, London.

International Cooperation and the Environment

American Chamber of Commerce (1995) *The EU Environment Guide 1995* Earthscan Publications, London

Sands, Philippe (ed) (1993) *Greening International Law* Earthscan Publications, London
Figure on page 10: Childers, Erskine (1994) *Challenges to the United Nations* CIIR, London

The European Union

Amercian Chamber of Commerce (1995) *The EU Environment Guide 1995* Earthscan Publications, London
Figure on page 25: The European Environment Agency (1994) *Putting Information to Work* EEA, Copenhagen
Figure on page 26: information from the Institute for European Environmental Policy

Central and Eastern Europe

Manser, R (1993) *The Squandered Dividend: The Free Market and the Environment in Eastern Europe* Earthscan Publications, London
Table on page 32: United Nations (1992) *The Environment in Europe and North America, Annotated Statistics 1992* United Nations, New York
Table on page 36: information from the World Bank, European Commission, OECD

Trade

Lang, T and Hines, C (1993) *The New Protectionism: Protecting the Future Against Free Trade* Earthscan Publications, London
Folke, C et al (1995) *Trading with the Environment* Earthscan Publications, London
Figure on page 37: Worldwatch Institute (1995) *Vital Signs 1995–6: The Trends that are Shaping our Future* Earthscan Publications, London
Figure on page 38: UNCTAD (1987 and 1990) *Handbook of International Trade and Development Statistics* UNCTAD, New York
Figure on page 44: Information from Eurostat COMEXT

Energy

Commission communication to the European Parliament and the Council (1994) 'Community Guidelines on Trans-European Energy Networks', 19 January, Brussels.
European Commission (1993) 'Energy in Europe: Annual Review of Energy', April, Brussels.
European Commission (1993) 'The European Energy Charter: Fresh Impetus from the Commission', 4 November, Brussels.
European Commission (1994) 'The European Renewable Energy Study', Brussels.
European Commission (1993) 'The Market for Solid Fuels in the Community in 1993 and the Outlook for 1994', 29 November, Brussels.
Hill, R, Snape, C and O'Keefe, P (1995) *The Future of Energy Use* Earthscan Publications, London
Figure on page 45: Smalley, M (1991) *Energy in Europe* Wayland Publications Ltd, Hove
Figure on page 46: European Environment Agency (1995) *Europe's Environment: The Dobris Assessment* HMSO/Earthscan Publications, London

Transport

Hughes, Peter (1993) *Personal Transport and the Greenhouse Effect* Earthscan Publications, London
Blowers, A (ed) (1993) *Planning for a Sustainable Environment* Earthscan Publications, London
Figure on page 60 (top): Department of Transport (1992) *Transport Statistics: Great Britain* HMSO, London
Figure on page 60 (bottom): Smalley, M (1991) *Transport in Europe* Wayland Publications Ltd, Hove
Table on page 61: European Commission (1992) *The Impact of Transport on the Environment* CEC, Luxembourg
Table on page 65: *Polish Statistical Yearbooks, 1991* and *1992* using figures from the Annual Bulletin of Transport Statistics for Europe, UN

Waste

Figure on page 68: The European Environment Agency (1995) *Europe's Environment: The Dobris Assessment* HMSO/Earthscan Publications, London
Figure on page 69: Adapted from The European Environment Agency (1995) *Europe's Environment: The Dobris Assessment* HMSO/Earthscan Publications, London

Agriculture and Forestry

Baldock, D, *Forests in Trouble: A Review of the Status of Temperate Forests Worldwide*, WWF International, Gland, Switzerland.
Nature Conservation and New Directions in the EC Common Agricultural Policy, Institute for European Environmental Policy, London.
Figure on page 79: Flint, D (1991) *Farming in Europe* Wayland Publications, Hove
Table on page 87: Agren, C 'Forest decline continues' *Acid News* December 1990
Table on page 92: Information from WCMC, 1992; Council of Europe, 1993, European Environment Agency, 1993

COUNTRY PROFILES

Albania

anon (1992) 'Albania' *Mining Journal*, Vol 318, No 8172.
anon (1993) 'Parliament Approves Framework Law to Protect Environment, Curb Pollution' *International Environment Reporter*, 10 February.
Atkinson, R (ed) (1990), 'Environmental Status Report 1990, Albania' in Karpowicz, Z (ed) (1991) *Environmental Status Reports: 1990, Volume 2: Albania, Bulgaria, Romania, Yugoslavia*, International Union for the Conservation of Nature, Cambridge.
Committee of Environmental Preservation and Protection (1993) *Albania – the Environmental Situation and Problems*, Tirana
Cullaj, A (1992) *Environmental Situation in Albania*, Organisation Protection and Preservation of Natural Environment in Albania, Tirana.
Hope, K (1993) 'Reform changes the face of Albania's farming sector' *Financial Times*, 15 June 1993.
Hope, K (1993) 'Albania offers onshore exploration blocks' *Financial Times*, 30 April 1993.
Kollodge, R (ed) (1993) 'Albania Revives Rural Areas Neglected for Decades' *World Bank News*, Vol XII, No 8.
Kosmo, M (1993) 'Two-part Strategy Designed to Aid Albania's Environmental Problems' *World Bank Environment Bulletin*, Vol 5, No 2.
Ministry of Health and Environmental Protection (1992) *Albania – Presentation by the Committee for Environmental Preservation and Protection to the G-24 Working Group on the Environment*, Brussels.

Austria

anon (1992) *Austria – Facts and Figures* Federal Press Service, Vienna.
anon (1992) *Austria in Figures* Federal Press Service, Vienna.
anon (1992) *Bundes-Abfallwirtschaftsplan* Ministry for Environment, Youth and Family Affairs, Vienna.
Academy for Environment and Energy (1992) *Recommendations of the Austrian CO2 Commission for a Programme of Activities in order to Achieve the Toronto-Recommendations* and *Annual Report 1991*, Federal Ministry for Environment, Youth and Family Affairs, Vienna.
Austrian Institute of International Politics (ed) (1992) *Austria: National Report to UNCED 1992*, Austrian Federal Government, Vienna.
Federal Ministry for Environment, Youth and Family Affairs (1992) *Europa und Unsere Umwelt*, Federal Ministry for Environment, Youth and Family Affairs, Vienna.

Lukschanderl, L (1992) *Environmental Protection in Austria* Federal Press Service, Vienna.
Schwank, F and Mitchell, W (1992) 'Environmental Legislation' *European Environmental Law Review*, July 1992.
Umweltbundesamt (1991) *Zweiter Umweltkontrollbericht*, Federal Ministry for Environment, Youth and Family Affairs, Vienna.

Belgium

anon (1992) *Rapport de la Belgique à la Conference des Nations Unies sur l'Environnement et le Développement*, Ministry of Foreign Affairs, External Trade and Development Cooperation and Ministry of Public Health and the Environment.
Belgian Institute for Information and Documentation (1990) *Geography of Belgium*, Ministry of Foreign Affairs, External Trade and Cooperation for Development, Brussels.
Berghe, van den Mieke (1991) *Belgique – Un SurVol Statistique*, Belgian Institute for Information and Documentation, Brussels.

Bulgaria

anon (1992) *Environment and Development of Republic Bulgaria*, Ministry of Environment, Sofia.
Marsh, V (1992) 'Bulgarian farming's post-communist crisis' *Financial Times*, 19 November
Mileva, M (1992) 'Bulgaria' *IUCN East European Programme Newsletter* No 3.
Tassev, C and Mileva, L (ed) (1989) 'Environmental Status Report 1990, Bulgaria' in Karpowicz, Z (ed) (1991) *Environmental Status Reports: 1990, Volume 2: Albania, Bulgaria, Romania, Yugoslavia*, International Union for the Conservation of Nature, Cambridge.
Toshev L (1993) *Report on the State of the Environment and the role of the Non-Governmental Organizations for the Protection of the Environment in Bulgaria*, Ecoglasnost, Sofia.

Cyprus

anon (1992) *Cyprus*, Press and Information Office, Republic of Cyprus, Nicosia.
anon (1991) *Cyprus Industry and the European Community*, Press and Information Office, Republic of Cyprus, Nicosia.
anon (1991) *The European Community and the Agriculture of Cyprus*, Press and Information Office, Republic of Cyprus, Nicosia.
anon (1991) *National Report of Cyprus*, Republic of Cyprus, Nicosia.
European Commission (1993) *Commission Opinion on the Application by the Republic of Cyprus for Membership*, COM(93)313, Brussels.

Czech Republic and Slovakia

anon (1993) *Enviro Guide Slovakia 1993*, Ministry of the Environment of the Slovak Republic, Bratislava.
anon (1991) *Environmental Year-Book of Czech Republic*, Ministry of the Environment of the Czech Republic, Prague.
Cerovsky, J (ed) (1989) 'Environmental Status Report 1988/89, Czechoslovakia' in Goriup, P (ed) *Environmental Status Reports: 1988/89, Volume 1: Czechoslovakia, Hungary, Poland*, International Union for the Conservation of Nature, Cambridge.
Hrasky, A and Hrasky, M (1992) 'Czech and Slovak Federal Republic' country reports *European Environmental Law Review*, July, August/September, October, December.
Hrasky, A and M (1993) 'Czech Republic' country report *European Environmental Law Review*, February.
Mininberg and Associates (1992) *Environmental Handbook for Industry*, Czech and Slovak Federal Committee for the Environment, Prague.
Moldan, B (ed) (1992) *National Report of the Czech and Slovak Federal Republic*, Czechoslovak Academy of Sciences and the Federal Committee for the Environment, Prague.
Urban, F (1993) 'Czech Republic' *IUCN East European Programme Newsletter* No 6.

Vacek, V (ed) (1993) *Environmental Laws of the Czech Republic Vol 1*, Ministry of the Environment of the Czech Republic in cooperation with The National Information Center of the Czech Republic, Prague.

Denmark

Akerman, E and Hasselager, A (eds) (1992) *Environmental Protection in Denmark*, Royal Danish Ministry of Foreign Affairs and Danish Ministry of the Environment, Copenhagen.
anon (1992) *Action Plan for Waste and Recycling 1993–97*, Danish Ministry of the Environment, Copenhagen.
anon (1991) *Denmark – National Report to UNCED – 1992*, Danish Ministry of the Environment, Copenhagen.
anon (1993) *Energy Trends*, Energy and Environmental Data, Aalborg.
anon (1992) *Environmental Indicators 1992*, Danish Ministry of the Environment, Copenhagen.
anon (1992) *Environmental Initiatives in the 1990s*, Danish Ministry of the Environment, Copenhagen.
anon (1991) *Environmental Protection Act*, Danish Ministry of the Environment, Copenhagen.
anon (1991) *The State of the Environment in Denmark*, Danish Ministry of the Environment, Copenhagen.
Carnegy, H (1993) 'Roads over northern waters' *Financial Times*, 29 November.

Estonia

Aher, G (1992) 'Estonia' *IUCN East European Programme Newsletter* No 5.
Kallaste, T, Roots, O, Saar, J and Saare, L (1992) *Air Pollution in Estonia 1985–90*, Environmental Data Centre, National Board of Waters and the Environment, Helsinki.
Lahtmets, M (ed) (1992) *National Report of Estonia to UNCED 1992*, Ministry of Environment of Estonia, Tallinn.
Ministry of the Environment of Estonia (1991) *Estonian Environment 1991*, Environmental Data Centre, National Board of Waters and the Environment, Helsinki.
Ministry of the Environment of Estonia (1993) *Estonian Environment 1992*, Environment Data Centre, National Board of Waters and the Environment, Helsinki.

Finland

anon (1993) 'Are the Finnish Shores up for Sale?' WWF *Baltic Bulletin* No 2.
anon (1991) *Finland – National Report to UNCED 1992*, Ministry for Foreign Affairs and Ministry of the Environment, Helsinki.
European Commission (1992) *Finland's application for membership*, SEC(92)2048, Brussels.
Wahlstrom, E, Hallanaro, E and Reinikainen, T (eds) (1993) *The State of the Finnish Environment*, Environment Data Centre and the Ministry of the Environment, Helsinki.

France

anon (1991) *Environnement et Développement: l'Experience et l'Approche Francaises*, Ministere de l'Environnement, Paris.
anon (1991) *Etat de l'Environnement 1990*, Ministere de l'Environnement, Paris.
anon (1993) *Etat de L'Environnement 1991–1992*, Ministere de l'Environnement, Paris.
Chabason, L and Theys, J (eds) (1990) *Plan National pour l'Environnement*, Secretaire d'Etat a l'Environnement, Paris.
Juin, D with Comolet, A, Fernandez, V, Gras, F and Lavoux, T (1992) *L'Application de la Legislation Communautaire Environnement en France*, Institut pour une Politique Europeene de l'Environnement, Paris.

Germany

anon (1993) *Environmental Performance Review: Germany*, Organisation for Economic Cooperation and Development, Paris.

Federal Ministry for the Environment (1992) *Environmental Protection in Germany*, Economica Verlag, Bonn.

Hermann, H (1992) *Functions and Organization of Environmental Protection in the Federal Republic of Germany*, Umweltbundesamt, Berlin.

Umweltbundesamt (1992) *Daten zur Umwelt*, Erich Schmidt Verlag, Berlin.

Greece

anon (1983) *Environmental Policies in Greece*, OECD, Paris.

anon (1991) *National Report of Greece*, Ministry of the Environment, Physical Planning and Public Works, Athens.

Brown, P (1993) 'Greek dam project drains EC's funds leaving poor high and dry' *The Guardian*, 26 June.

Hope, K (1993) 'A Greek tragedy in the making' *Financial Times*, 5 May.

Scoullos, M and Kaberi, H (1989) *The Implementation of the EEC Environmental Legislation in Greece*, Elliniki Etairia and Institute for European Environmental Policy, Athens.

Tsipas, S 'Country Profile: Greece' *European Environment* Vol 2, No 4.

Hungary

anon (1991) *Hungary's National Report to UNCED 1992*, The Government of the Hungarian Republic, Budapest.

anon (1992) *Review Environment, Nature Conservation, Building and Regional Policy in Hungary, 1992/2*, Ministry for Environment and Regional Policy, Budapest.

anon (1993) *Review Environment, Nature Conservation, Building and Regional Policy in Hungary, 1993/1*, Ministry for Environment and Regional Policy, Budapest.

anon (1992) *State of the Environment in Hungary*, Ministry for Environment and Regional Policy, Budapest.

Juhasz, I and Szaszne, I (1992) *Our Environment in Facts*, Ministry for Environment and Regional Policy, Budapest.

Lakos, L (1993) 'Ministry for Environment and Regional Policy' *IUCN East European Programme Newsletter* No 7.

Ormai, G and Kovari, I (1993) 'Hungary – General' *European Environmental Law Review*, March.

Ormai, G and Kovari, I (1992) 'Hungary – Waste' *European Environmental Law Review*, October.

Szilassy, Z (ed) (1989) 'Environmental Status Report 1988/89, Hungary', Budapest in Goriup, P (ed) *Environmental Status Reports: 1988/89, Volume 1: Czechoslovakia, Hungary, Poland*, International Union for the Conservation of Nature, Cambridge.

Iceland

anon (1993) *Environmental Performance Review: Iceland*, Organisation for Economic Cooperation and Development, Paris.

anon (1992) *Iceland: National Report to UNCED*, Ministry for the Environment, Reykjavik.

Irish Republic

anon (1990) *An Environment Action Programme*, Department of the Environment, Dublin.

anon (1991) *An Environment Action Programme – First Progress Report*, Department of the Environment, Dublin.

anon (1992) *Environment Bulletin*, Department of the Environment, Dublin.

anon (1990) *Environmental Legislation*, Fact sheet 12, ENFO, Dublin.

anon (1992) *Ireland – An outline geography*, Department of Foreign Affairs, Dublin.

anon (1992) *Towards a Recycling Strategy for Ireland*, Department of the Environment, Dublin.

Cabot, D (1987) *EEC Environmental Legislation*, An Foras Forbartha, Dublin.

Green 2000 Advisory Group (1993) *Report presented to the Taoiseach*, Dublin.

Greenwood, G (1992) 'The State of the Environment in Ireland', *European Environment*, Vol 2, No 1.

Scannell, Y (1992) 'Ireland – The Environmental Protection Agency', *European Environmental Law Review*, October.

Italy

anon (1993) 'Italian government establishes national environmental protection agency', *International Environment Reporter*, 11 August.
anon (1991) *The Italian Government Report for UNCED 1992*, Ministry of the Environment, Rome.
anon (1993) *Report on the State of the Environment in Italy*, Ministry of the Environment, Rome.
Capria, A (1992) *Direttive Ambientali CEE e Stato di Attuazione in Italia*, Giuffre Editore, Milan.
Guttieres, M and Sikabonyi, M (1992) 'Italy', *European Environmental Law Review*, October.
Liberatore, A (1992) 'National Environmental Policies and the European Community', *European Environment*, Vol 2, No. 4
Liberatore, A and Lewanski, R (1990) 'The Evolution of Italian Environmental Policy', *Environment*, June.
Melandri, G and Conte, G (eds) (1992) *Ambiente Italia 1992*, Vallecchi Editore, Florence.
Tudini, A (1992) 'Environmental Policy in Italy', *UK CEED Bulletin*, July/August.

Latvia

anon (1993) *Ambient Air Pollution in Latvia*, Environment Protection Committee, Riga.
Kraukulis, A (1992) 'Landscapes and nature conservation in Latvia' *Naturopa Newsletter* No 92/2.
Krikis, A (ed) (1992), *National Report of Latvia to UNCED 1992*, Environment Protection Committee, Riga.
Prieditis, N (1993) 'Swamp forests – Latvia's riches' *WWF Baltic Bulletin* No 2.

Lithuania

Andrikis R (1992) *Lithuania – National Report to UNCED 1992*, Environmental Protection Department, Vilnius.
anon (1992) 'Environmental Protection Department of the Republic of Lithuania' *IUCN East European Programme Newsletter* No 6.
Vaiciunaite, R (1993) 'New provisions for land use in Lithuania', *WWF Baltic Bulletin* No 1.

Luxembourg

anon (1992) *Rapport National Pour la Conférence des Nations Unies sur l'Environnement et le Développement*, Grand Duchy of Luxembourg, Luxembourg.

Malta

anon (1992) *Malta's National Report to UNCED*, Office of the Parliamentary Secretary for the Environment, Valletta.
anon (1993) *The Maltese Economy in Figures*, Ministry of Finance, Valletta.

The Netherlands

anon (1991) *Environmental Policy in the Netherlands*, Ministry of Housing, Physical Planning and the Environment, The Hague.
anon (1993) *Environmental Statistics of the Netherlands 1993*, Central Bureau of Statistics, Voorburg/Heerlen.
anon (1989) *National Environmental Policy Plan – to Choose or to Lose*, Ministry of Housing, Physical Planning and the Environment, The Hague.
anon (1991) *Netherlands National Report to UNCED 1992*, Ministry of Housing, Physical Planning and the Environment, The Hague.
Kroes, H (1991) *Essential Environmental Information, The Netherlands*, Ministry of Housing, Physical Planning and the Environment, The Hague.

Norway

BrunVoll, F (1992) *Natural Resources and the Environment 1991*, Central Bureau of Statistics, Oslo.
anon (1992) *Norway – The National Report to UNCED*, Ministry of the Environment, Oslo.
Sivertsen, S and Lundgaard, H (eds) (1990) *The Future is Now!*, State Pollution Control Authority, Oslo.

Poland

anon (1991) *National Environmental Policy of Poland*, Ministry of Environmental Protection, Warsaw.
anon (1991) *Polish National Report for the UN Conference* 'Environment and Development', Ministry of Environmental Protection, Warsaw.
anon (1992) *The State of the Environment in Poland*, Ministry of Environmental Protection, Warsaw.
anon (1992) *A Strategy for the Protection of Living Resources in Poland*, Ministry of Environmental Protection, Warsaw.
Grzesiak, M (1992) *Ochrona Srodowiska 1992*, Glowny Urzad Statystyczny, Warsaw.
Klimek, K (1989) 'Environmental Status Report 1988/89, Poland' in in Goriup, P (ed) *Environmental Status Reports: 1988/89, Volume 1: Czechoslovakia, Hungary, Poland*, International Union for the Conservation of Nature, Cambridge.
Orszag-Land, T (1992) 'Energy and the environment: Poland seeks help to build a North Sea gas pipeline' *New European*, Vol, 5 No 6.
Rykowski, K (1991) *The State of Forests in Poland*, Ministry of Environmental Protection, Warsaw.
Sommer, J (1993) 'Polish Environmental Law Developments from an EC Perspective' *RECIEL*, Vol, 2 No 1.
Zurek J and Mikuszewski, J (1992) *Environment in Poland*, Ministry of Environmental Protection, Warsaw.

Portugal

anon (1992) *Qualidade do Ambiente 1990/1991*, Direccao-Geral da Qualidade do Ambiente, Lisbon.
anon (1991) *UNCED Brasil 92, Portuguese Report*, Ministry for the Environment, Lisbon.
Santos, F (1991) *Livro Blanco sobre o Estado do Ambiente em Portugal*, Ministerio do Ambiente e Recursos Naturais, Lisbon.

Romania

anon (1991) *National Report for UNCED*, Ministry of the Environment, Bucharest.
anon (1993) 'Protected territories of Romania since 1935' *Carpathi*, 3/93.
anon (1993) *The State of the Environment in Romania*, Ministry of the Environment, Bucharest.
Marsh, V (1992) 'Romanian farmers wait to see how the land lies' *Financial Times*, 10 July.
Vadineanu, A (ed) (1989) 'Environmental Status Report 1990: Romania' in Karpowicz, Z (ed) (1991) *Environmental Status Reports: 1990, Volume 2: Albania, Bulgaria, Romania, Yugoslavia*, International Union for the Conservation of Nature, Cambridge.
Zarafescu, C (1992) 'The state of the environment in Romania' *European Environment* Vol 2 No 2.

Spain

anon (1992) *Conferencia Medio Ambiente y Deserrollo UNCED – España*, Ministerio de Obras Publicas y Transportes, Madrid.
anon (1992) *Medio Ambiente en España '91*, Ministerio de Obras Publicas y Transportes, Madrid.

Sweden

anon (1991/1992/1993) *Fact Sheets on Sweden*, Swedish Institute, Stockholm.
anon (1991) *Sweden: National Report to UNCED*, Ministry of the Environment, Stockholm.
Danell, S (1991) *The Swedish Environment*, Statistics Sweden, Stockholm.
Jernelov, A (1992) *The Swedish Environmental Debt*, Environmental Advisory Council, Stockholm.

Lonnroth, M (1992) *Sweden and the European Environment*, Swedish Institute, Stockholm.
Mansson, T (1992) *Ecocycles*, Ministry of the Environment, Stockholm.
Modig, S (1991) *Waste Management in Sweden*, Swedish Institute, Stockholm.

Switzerland

anon (1987) *Switzerland – Variety and Unity*, Pro Helvetia, Zurich.
anon (1992) *UNCED 1992 – The Swiss Report*, Federal Office of Environment, Forests and the Landscape, Berne.
Bueller, V (1991) *Zur Lage der Umwelt in der Schweiz*, Bundesamt fur Umwelt, Wald und Landschaft, Berne.
Koeppel, H (1991) *Landschaft unter Druck*, Bundesamt fur Raumplanung/Bundesamt fur Umwelt, Wald und Landschaft, Berne.
Muller, J (1990) *Environment Protection: Could Switzerland be a model pupil?*, Swiss National Tourist Office, Zurich.
Muller, J (1990) *Switzerland, Europe's source of water*, Swiss National Tourist Office, Zurich.

Turkey

anon (1992) *Environmental Policies in Turkey*, Organisation for Economic Cooperation and Development, Paris.
anon (1991) *Turkey: National Report to UNCED*, Ministry of Environment, Ankara.
Juhasz, F (1992) 'Environmental policies in Turkey', *OECD Observer*, August/September.
Murray Brown, J (1993) 'Turkish agriculture approaches watershed' *Financial Times*, 14 April.

United Kingdom

anon (1992) *Environmental Digest for Wales*, Welsh Office, Cardiff.
anon (1992) *The Scottish Environment*, Scottish Office, Edinburgh.
anon (1990) *This Common Inheritance*, Her Majesty's Stationery Office, London.
Brown, A (ed) (1992) *The UK Environment*, Her Majesty's Stationery Office, London.
Martin, J (ed) (1993) *Digest of Environmental Protection and Water Statistics*, Her Majesty's Stationery Office, London.